THE NATURE OF
SCOTLAND

THE NATURE OF
SCOTLAND

Landscape, Wildlife and People

Edited by
MAGNUS MAGNUSSON
and
GRAHAM WHITE

CANONGATE BOOKS

•

THE POST OFFICE

First published in Great Britain in 1991 by Canongate Press.
Revised edition published in 1997 by Canongate Books Ltd,
14 High Street, Edinburgh EH1 1TE.

The editors and publishers gratefully acknowledge the contribution of the Scottish Post Office Board in the initiation of the first edition and in the development of both the first and revised editions. It was they who recognised the need for a wide ranging book on Scotland's environment and the publishers recognise that it would not be possible to keep *The Nature of Scotland* in print without their continuing enthusiasm and support.

The publishers acknowledge copyright permission granted from the following sources for the right to reproduce photographs in *The Nature of Scotland*:

Angel, Heather/Bio-photos 65 top; Balharry, Dick 62, 68, 140 foot; Banks, P.J. 64 middle; Baxter, Colin 215; Buckingham, John 58 foot; Campbell Laurie 44, 52 foot, 57 right, 59 top, 59 foot, 65 foot, 66, 69, 70, 76 right, 78, 79, 140 top, 161, 184, 185 top, 189 top and foot, 190 top, 191, 192, 195, 207 foot, 222, 223; Charity, John 131 (lower 3); Charles Tait Photographic 101; Coates, Dr. Michael 23 left, 26; CSWT 139; Dalton, Stephen 197; Daniel, William/National Library of Scotland 151; Dennis, Roy 199; Edinburgh Butterfly World 97; Edinburgh Film Workshop 38, 119, 121 top; George Washington Wilson Collection (Aberdeen University Library) 37 top; Gill, Lorne 142, 213, 217 top and foot, 221; Gillespie, Alex 37 foot, 39, 42, 172 left, 173; Glasgow Museums & Art Galleries 24, 152; Gowans, Dave 67, 82 top, 84, 85, 214; Guthrie Photography 209; Hill, David Octavius/Glasgow Museum & Art Galleries 148; Hinson, Peter 174; Historic Scotland 108; Holt Atherton Institute and The Muir Hanna Family Trust 6; Kay, Paul 71; King, Angus 41; Kitchener, Andrew 63, 77 foot; MacPherson, John 1, 10, 14, 18, 19, 20, 32, 45, 48, 52 top, 55, 58 top, 98, 116, 117, 120, 121 foot, 122, 124 right, 132, 134 foot, 137 top, 137 foot, 145 top, 146 foot, 156, 157, 158, 159, 160 top, 164, 165, 166, 168, 169, 182, 186, 210, 216 top and foot, 220, 225, 226, 231, 236, 237, 239, 241, 242; Maitland, Peter 162, 163 top and foot; Maynard, Sam 61, 124 left, 125, 126, 127, 135 top; Morrison, Paul/Natural Selection 53; Mowle, Alan 136; National Galleries of Scotland 20, 27, 30, 90, 145 foot, 172 right, 177, 179, 204, 206, 27; National Remote Sensing Centre 185 foot; National Trust for Scotland 234; New Lanark Trust 171 top; NHPA 207 top; Oxford Scientific Films 35; Paterson, David 138 top; Paton, W.S./Natural Selection 74; Paton, W.S./RSPB 80, 82 foot; Paul, John H. 131 top; Prentice, Tom 232; Ritchie, Graham 100 foot; Robinson, J. 69 foot; Rodway, Gerald 92 left, 96; Royal Botanic Garden 201; RSPB 76 left, 77 top, 81 top, 81 right, 83; Scott, Mike 50, 51; Scott, Sue 34 (all); Scottish Development Department 146 top; Scottish Mountaineering Club 230; Scottish Nuclear Ltd 181; Sharp, Mick 99, 100 top, 102 left, 102 right, 103 right, 105 top, 105 foot, 107, 109, 123; Sheldon, Tim 19 top; Satterly, Glyn 27, 155 top and foot; Still Moving Pictures 128, 147; Stirling and Trossachs Tourist Board 144; Stronach, Douglas 194; Sutcliffe, Richard 91 left; Tait, T. Norman 91 right, 92 right, 93, 94, 95; Tulloch, Bobby 36, 103 top; Twidell, John 176; Tydeman, Chris/Natural Selection 219; Wade Cooper Associates 180; White, Graham 2, 21 foot, 25, 31 foot, 47, 56, 57 top, 64 foot, 110, 111, 113 top, 113 foot, 114 top, 115 top, 135 foot, 171 foot, 189 top, 189 foot, 193, 196, 198, 204, 205, 208, 235, 240.

British Library Cataloguing in Publication Data:
A catalogue entry for this volume is available
on request from the British Library.

ISBN 0 86241 674 4

Printed in Spain by Artes Gráficas ELKAR S. Coop., 48012 Bilbao.

Contents

John Muir aged 30.

Dedication to John Muir
(1838–1914)

In the growth of environmental awareness one man stands out as the herald and prophet of the international conservation movement: the Scots-born naturalist John Muir. Born in Dunbar on 21 April 1838, he spent his childhood exploring the pristine beaches of East Lothian and the secluded valleys of the Lammermuir Hills. In 1849 he emigrated with his parents to America, where he later won fame as the country's premier conservationist. In his unfinished autobiography, The Story of my Boyhood and Youth, Muir recalled his dawning awareness of nature:

> When I was a boy in Scotland I was fond of everything that was wild, and all my life I've been growing fonder and fonder of wild places and wild creatures. Fortunately, around my native town of Dunbar, by the stormy North Sea, there was no lack of wildness . . . with red-blooded playmates, wild as myself, I loved to wander in the fields to hear the birds sing, and along the seashore to gaze and wonder at the shells and seaweeds, eels and crabs, in the pools among the rocks when the tide was low.

On arrival in Wisconsin aged eleven he faced ten years hard labour as his father's unpaid 'well-digger, ploughboy and lumberjack', carving a farm from virgin forest. It was not until the age of 22 that he escaped to Wisconsin University, where he studied chemistry, botany and geology; but the Civil War cut short his education.

He avoided the draft in Canada for two years and, being mechanically gifted, he became foreman-engineer at an Indianapolis carriage factory. But in 1867 he was blinded in an industrial accident and on recovering his sight devoted the rest of his life to natural history and preaching the newly written gospel of conservation.

Muir's epic adventures as an explorer, mountaineer and botanist are described in My First Summer in the Sierra and The Mountains of California. He was first to discover living glaciers in the High Sierras and to realise that they had gouged-out the great mountain canyons (see Chapter 1) – a theory ridiculed by academic geologists at the time but later proven to be true. As a botanist he led Sir Joseph Hooker of Kew and Asa Gray of Harvard on expeditions of discovery and they named several plant species in his honour.

But it is as a seminal figure in the conservation movement, the first person to call clearly for the conservation and protection of wilderness and wildlife, that we remember John Muir. By the time of his death in 1914 he had become an almost mythic figure in America's environmental pantheon, where today he ranks alongside Emerson, Thoreau and Audubon as 'Father of the National Parks'.

In the 1880s Muir became deeply concerned about the threats facing Yosemite Valley, which designation as a California state park had failed to protect. Sheep had destroyed virtually all the alpine meadows and seedling trees while loggers were stripping the redwoods and sugar pines from the watersheds, triggering flash-floods and consequent droughts. The tourist trade was filling the valley with hotels, coach-roads and people, defiling what Muir regarded as the greatest natural temple in the world.

With the help of Robert Underwood Johnson, editor of Century Magazine, Muir campaigned to halt the desecration of the valley; he achieved apparent success, when in 1890, Congress approved the Yosemite Recession Bill, returning the valley to the protection of the federal government. But it took a further decade of arduous campaigning, before 1500 square miles of Yosemite were designated as America's second National Park in 1905.

In 1892 Muir helped found the Sierra Club as a spearhead for the national conservation movement; today it remains one of the world's most powerful environmental groups with over 600,000 members. Muir strongly influenced President Theodore Roosevelt, whose presidency (1901-12) saw the designation of thirty-three National Parks and 230,000 square miles of American National Forest, as well as twenty-three National Monuments such as the Grand Canyon.

Americans have named over 200 sites in Muir's honour, including: Muir Glacier, and Mount Muir in Alaska, Muir Woods and Muir Beach near San Francisco, and the John Muir Wilderness and John Muir Trail in the High Sierra. In 1964, his Martinez home was designated The John Muir National Historic Site by Congress, in recognition of his historic role in conserving the natural heritage of the United States.

In 1983 Muir's life inspired the creation of the John Muir Trust in Scotland, established to conserve and protect wild land for future generations. To date the Trust has bought four areas of wild land in Scotland, totalling 34,000 acres: Li and Coire Dhorrcail in Knoydart (1988), Torrin on the Isle of Skye (1991), Sandwood Bay, Sutherland (1992), Strathaird and Bla Bheinn in the Skye Cuillin (1994).

The Trust aims to demonstrate exemplary management of these areas, sharing responsibility with local communities for the sustainable use of the landscape, wildlife and natural resources.

John Muir's cosmic and holistic vision of Nature continues to inspire generations of nature-lovers all over the world:

When one contemplates the whole globe as one great dewdrop, striped and dotted with continents and islands, flying through space with all the other stars, all singing and shining together as one, the whole universe appears as an infinite storm of beauty… this grand show is eternal. It is always sunrise somewhere; the dew is never all dried at once; a shower is forever falling; vapour is forever rising. Eternal sunrise, eternal sunset, eternal dawn and gloaming, on sea and continents and islands, each in its turn as the round earth rolls.

Muir believed that communion with Nature was not an optional luxury but a vital necessity and that without the healing balm of such contact, people sickened like 'clocks full of dust', worn out by the cares and anxieties of materialism and money-getting. His antidote was simple:

Go climb the mountains and get their good tidings. Nature's peace will flow into you as the sunshine flows into trees. The winds will blow their freshness into you and the storms their energy, while cares will drop off like autumn leaves.

John Muir has not yet been accorded the place in the Scottish Hall of Heroes at the Wallace Monument which he undoubtedly deserves, but 1997 has seen him elevated to the Scottish National Portrait Gallery. Muir is Scotland's greatest contribution to the global environmental movement, and as we approach the Millennium, his ideas and conservation ethos are being reclaimed and re-assessed in the land of his birth. This book is dedicated to his memory, his achievements and his continuing influence for conservation of the world's wild places.

THE POST OFFICE

FOREWORD

The first edition of this book was initiated by The Post Office and published just before the Earth Summit at Rio in 1992. This Foreword is written at the time of the second Summit in New York in 1997. The connection is both fortuitous and significant.

Scotland can seem a long way removed from Agenda 21 with its global blueprint for achieving sustainable development. With much of the science equivocal, there is still a lot to debate about global warming, biodiversity, sustainable development, the often conflicting priorities of the wealthy nations of the north and the poor of the south – not to mention the huge costs of implementing Agenda 21, and perhaps even larger long term costs of ignoring it. What is beyond dispute is that the preciousness and fragility of our natural heritage, even here in rugged and well endowed Scotland, is a matter of increasing awareness and concern.

I would like to think that the first edition of this book has fostered some of that growing awareness and concern about the very essence of Scotland: its land and water and the way we humans act and interact with our environment and with the flora and fauna, often rare and under pressure, which share it.

Six years on from that book and now just three years off a new millennium, enough has changed in that complex human and natural world equation in Scotland to make this revised edition not just sensible but essential. Magnus Magnusson, Graham White, the team of expert contributors and Canongate have again achieved that difficult balance between scholarly authority and popular accessibility. The paperback format of the book will reach, we hope, an even wider readership.

My predecessor Kenneth Graham saw the link between The Post Office and concern for Scotland's environment as stemming naturally from the way in which post offices, Postbuses, letter and parcel deliveries and collections permeate social and business life, especially in rural and island communities, in quite unique ways despite the challenges of the digital revolution.

I would endorse this completely. I would also like to draw attention to the efforts The Post Office itself is making to minimise its environmental impact. All major building projects, for example, now undergo an environmental impact analysis; and, with a UK fleet of 28,000 vehicles travelling some 442 million miles a year and using 120 million litres of fuel, trials are under way with much cleaner compressed natural gas and liquefied petroleum gas fuels.

Ultimately, Scotland and this planet's environmental future is down to us, the people. Knowledge is the prelude to the best choices; and this book will provide that with pleasure a-plenty.

JOHN WARD, CBE
Chairman, Scottish Post Office Board

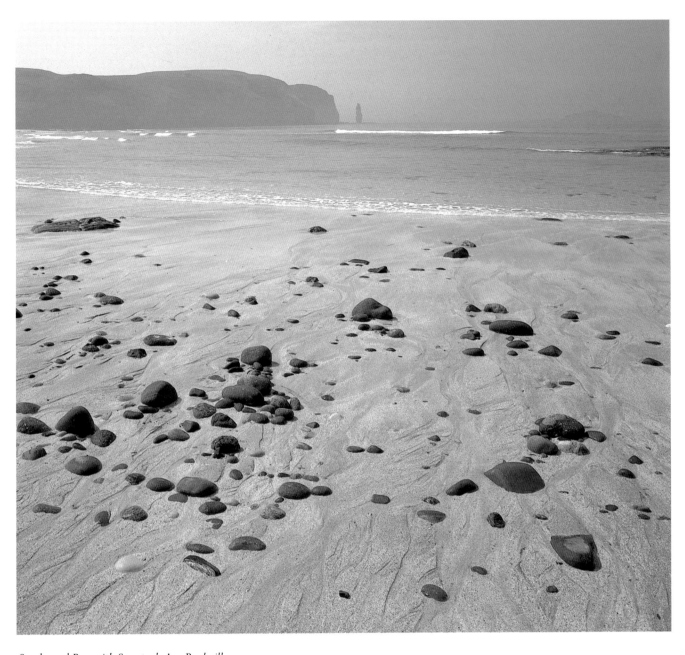

Sandwood Bay with Sea stack Am-Buchaille,
Sutherland; owned and protected by the
John Muir Trust since 1993.

Introduction
Magnus Magnusson

Scotland small? Our multiform, our infinite Scotland *small*?
Only as a patch of hillside may be a cliché corner
To a fool who cries 'Nothing but heather!' where in September another
Sitting there and resting and gazing around
Sees not only the heather but blaeberries
With bright green leaves and leaves already turned scarlet,
Hiding ripe blue berries; and amongst the sage-green leaves
Of the bog-myrtle the golden flowers of tormentil shining;
And on the small bare places, where the little Blackface sheep
Found grazing, milkworts blue as summer skies;
And down in neglected peat-hags, not worked
Within living memory, sphagnum moss in pastel shades
Of yellow, green and pink; sundew and butterwort
Waiting with wide-open sticky leaves for their tiny winged prey;
And nodding harebells vying in their colour
With the blue butterflies that poise themselves delicately upon them,
And stunted rowan with harsh dry leaves of glorious colour.
'Nothing but heather!' – How marvellously descriptive! And incomplete!

More than fifty years ago, Hugh MacDiarmid, that giant of modern Scottish poetry, brilliantly expressed in his autobiography, *Lucky Poet* (1943), the universality to be found in every Scottish microcosm of nature.

This book, by many distinguished hands, is a celebration of the Nature of Scotland: a celebration of Scotland's natural heritage on many levels. But the Nature of Scotland is not just nature in the sense of wildlife and countryside; it is also the quintessential nature of the country Scotland has become as expressed in its people and their history. This book is about the Nature of Scotland in the broadest sense, and seeks to illuminate its natural history in the context of its history proper.

That history is a long process of change which has given us the diversity of river, mountain, field, forest and ocean as well as the special beauty of individual animals and flowers. It is a heritage in a constant state of change. The seasonal cycle brings about migrations of birds, the emergence of insects and changes in vegetation. The dynamics of birth, reproduction and death promote a succession of change in animal and plant communities. On a much longer time-scale, the physical processes of erosion and sedimentation are slowly remoulding the landscape.

The consequences of all these changes have been the formation and survival of a natural heritage which bears the imprint of the past activities of natural processes and, later, of the people who have lived with them: a landscape which can only be fully understood in the light of the history and culture of our people, both individually and together.

To an enormous extent, people have been the key factor in the environment we have inherited; today their power to influence change in the heritage we bequeath to succeeding generations is greater than ever. The way in which people have gone about their livelihoods throughout history is a management, or a mismanagement, of land, water and air. The bleak grandeur of so many of our landscapes hides a perilous biological impoverishment; hillsides once clothed in Caledonian forest are now scoured by erosion; straths and valleys once verdant are now bitten to the quick by man's beasts – not only sheep but also the rabbits he introduced in Norman times and the red deer he has allowed to multiply far beyond the carrying capacity of their natural habitats. Nevertheless in Scotland we are still blessed with a natural heritage of rare quality.

I am thinking of the distinctive landscapes of firth and island which are as rare in Europe as they are beautiful. I am thinking of majestic flocks of migrating geese seeking winter sanctuary here from Greenland, and from Norway; of enchanting little animals like the red squirrel, now finding its last stronghold in Britain in our native pinewoods; of birds like the Scottish crossbill and the capercaillie and the corncrake with its evocative croaking, which all add such distinctiveness to the Scottish scene; of the snub-nosed, inquisitive otter which finds safe harbour and haven in the north-western bastions of the land; of the breathtaking underwater living seascapes of our sheltered sea lochs; of the power and majesty of our dynamic river systems; of the drama of salmon leaping and of red deer at the height of the rut.

We find, still, western oakwoods dripping with lichens, and gorges festooned with ferns – scenery which has probably changed little over the last 10,000 years. Arctic communities persist on the high hills and northern coasts, remnants of those landscapes which once dominated Scotland at the last retreat of the ice-sheets. Much of our inheritance of raised bogs and blanket peatlands still survives. And the farmlands and forests of Scotland are still rich with natural life, modified by man's activities, of course, but adding to the diversity of interest in a land already richly blessed with the kind of infinite variety hymned by Hugh MacDiarmid.

For me personally the task of editing this book, in collaboration with Graham White, was both a great privilege and an opportunity to set out the environmental issues facing Scotland as the millenium approaches. For its role in enabling us to undertake this agenda-setting project, I would like to thank the Scottish Post Office Board whose financial assistance towards both editions of this book reflects its imaginative and positive interest in the health of the Scottish environment.

Much has changed since this book first appeared in 1991. Environmentalism is now something very different, something very much more important. We have had the Earth Summit at Rio de Janeiro in 1992, which gave potency to concepts like 'sustainability' and 'biodiversity'.

Here in Scotland we have seen the establishment of Scottish Natural Heritage, in 1992, a government agency charged with the responsibility of conserving and enhancing Scotland's natural heritage for the benefit of all.

And this book has changed, too, to keep up with changing circumstance. Individual chapters have been revised and up-dated; some have been completely rewritten. But the essence of the book has not changed – a collection of informed essays to provide an integrated picture of the way Scotland's natural heritage is today, the way it came about, and the ways in which we ought to address the pressures and problems facing it.

In order to give shape and purpose to the book, the structure is roughly tripartite in form: the past, the present and the future. And within each individual chapter the many aspects of Scotland's natural history have been given the same type of historical perspective: yesterday, today and tomorrow.

The opening chapter, *The Laying of the Foundations* by George Farrow and Ian Rolfe, forms the bedrock of the book and gives the underlying geological story of Scotland's landscape and environment. It describes how Scotland was formed and assembled from separate parts of the earth's crust like a huge three-dimensional jigsaw puzzle which has been gradually drifting into place for hundreds of millions of years. The 'Scotland' we know today, seemingly anchored since the beginning of time in the northern hemisphere, started out in the southern hemisphere: Edinburgh's friendly neighbourhood volcano, Arthur's Seat, erupted from tropical seas when 'Scotland' was on the equator of the planet, some 400 million years ago.

There is an obvious and striking correlation between geology and the rich variety of Scotland's scenery. But there is much more to it than that. The rocks which are the very foundations of the land not only influence the flora and fauna we find in different parts of the countryside, but also shape and frame the lives of the human communities which live there. The underlying geology of Scotland has determined our agricultural present, but the rocks and minerals also shaped our industrial past: it was the abundance of coal and shale-oil deposits below the Central Belt which literally fuelled the Industrial Revolution in Scotland, with all the environmental consequences we see to this day.

The opening chapter, conceived as a series of snapshots in geological time, peels away the layers of landscape beneath our feet to reveal the story of Scotland's evolution which lies hidden in the rocks.

From there it is a natural step to the next chapter, *The Seas of Plenty* by John Hambrey. Scotland's coastal waters are among the richest in the world; yet our marine environment is relatively uncharted, and the problem of how best to conserve it is still unresolved. For too long we have taken the sea for granted, treating it as a bountiful cornucopia which could never run dry. But modern times, modern demands and vastly improved fishing technologies have put our traditional marine resources under increasing pressure. The world beneath the sea is now as threatened as is the natural heritage of the land.

Scotland can boast a wonderful variety of spectacular and attractive plants, especially in the arctic-alpine species of the mountainous areas. Some of them are extremely rare – and all the more precious for that; but many of them

are under severe threat from human activities and from climatic change. In *The Flowering of Scotland*, Michael Scott gives a historical overview of what happened in Scotland as the last Ice Age receded, 12,000 years ago; what kind of plants and ground cover the new human colonists found waiting for them; what effects the development of settled farming communities and climatic change have brought; and what the picture is today.

Scotland is also renowned for its rich and varied wildlife, and for the great diversity and beauty of its wildlife habitats. Today Scotland is a vital staging post, or an important last refuge, for many species which were once common throughout Europe. Among the more famous and important of its current inhabitants are the wildcat, the red squirrel, the pine marten and the otter, as well as magnificent birds of prey such as the golden eagle, the osprey and the peregrine falcon.

But birds and animals do not occur by chance. They do not exist in splendid isolation. They are found in particular habitats which they share with a whole community of other living things, including human beings. We cannot consider an animal or plant outside the context of the habitat which supports it.

In *The World of the Mammals*, Andrew Kitchener shows how changing habitats have gone hand in hand with changing wildlife, so that today's animals and plants are altogether different from those which our ancestors knew.

On land, for instance, we have lost animals such as the giant deer, the wild horse, the reindeer, the lynx, the moose (elk), the beaver, the wild ox, the brown bear, the wild boar, the wolf, the polecat – and, most recently, the St Kilda house mouse. All down the ages there have been comings and goings of mammal species in Scotland. Some have failed to adapt to a changing climate, some have been hunted to extinction; others have arrived as stowaways or colonisers, or have been deliberately introduced or re-introduced by humans for their own purposes.

Scotland's natural heritage is not 'natural' at all, for however 'wild' or scenic the countryside, it has largely been shaped and contoured by human exploitation. Today, Scotland's wildlife is still being affected by land-use and other environmental changes; so it is vital that we accept full responsibility for the wildlife habitats and the creatures which live in them, for the enrichment of Scotland's countryside heritage and for the future benefit of all.

In *The Birds and their Habitats*, David Minns gives an overview of the special nature of four groups of internationally important birds for which Scotland is justly celebrated as a special place: seabirds, waders and wildfowl, birds of prey and pinewood birds. Some birds, such as starlings, chaffinches, blackbirds, pigeons and gulls, are very catholic in their choice of habitats; others are much more selective, and if their chosen habitat is altered or destroyed, then their very survival is endangered.

Insects are not normally given much prominence in general nature books. Yet butterflies are perhaps the most enchanting creatures you can see on a summer's day, dancing on iridescent wings from flower to flower, little miracles of fragility. 'To break a butterfly upon a wheel', in Alexander Pope's memorable phrase, has become synonymous with the destruction of beauty by brute force. How such creatures manage to survive at all in our rough world is itself little short of miraculous. But survive they do, if only just. Butterflies are very sensitive indicators of the general health of our ecology: when the harsh winds of environmental change begin to rise, they are the first to be blown out of existence. In *The Beauty of Butterflies*, Richard Sutcliffe shows how their presence and/or disappearance are often prime indicators of the loss of habitats and the presence of other factors, such as pesticides, which are adversely affecting the environment.

The Coming of Man, by Anna and Graham Ritchie, heralds the arrival of the creature who would have the most dramatic impact on

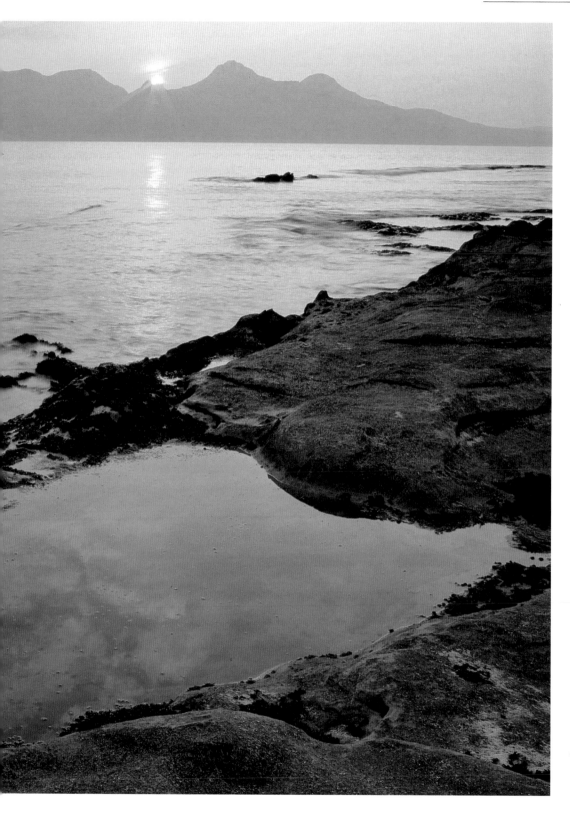

*Sunset over Isle of Rum,
from Cleadale,
Isle of Eigg.*

Scotland's environment, and signals the start of the social history section of the book. In geological terms man has only lived in Scotland for the blink of an eye; but ever since the first human hunting groups began to move into Scotland towards the end of the last Ice Age, man has had an increasingly marked effect. The Ritchies trace the story of the waves of incomers who followed, from the first settled farmers to the Celts, the Romans, the Britons, the Picts, the Angles, the Scots, the Vikings and the Normans.

Man's later impact has been even more profound. In *The Farming of the Land*, Alexander Fenton charts and analyses the immense changes in the forms of land-use which Scotland has seen over the last 300 years up to the Second World War, first in the Lowland farming areas and subsequently, in modified form, in the Highlands and Islands. The powerful environmental forces which have radically altered the landscape and the environment of farming in Scotland, and the local communities dependent upon it, are still operating. They inform and illuminate Scotland's recent social history – nowhere more so than in the so-called Crofting Areas of the Highlands and Islands, where (as Frank Rennie points out in *The Way of Crofting*) the Clearances gave rise to a way of life which is now enjoying a great resurgence in places like Assynt.

In *The Managing of the Land*, Alan Mowle takes up the post-war story of the two major uses to which the land is put – farming and forestry – and likens Scotland's countryside to a garden which has to be managed and tended if we are to halt the inexorable decline of the countryside and sustain the wildlife heritage, the beauty of the landscape and the productive capacity of the land.

The development of transport and communications has also had a major effect on the nature of Scotland, both directly and indirectly. It is not merely a matter of visual impact: with every advance in sophisticated community living, man's ingenuity and aspirations for a more comfortable and prosperous way of life have involved ever greater demands on the natural resources of the environment. In *The Paths of Progress*, John Hume shows how improved methods of transport have changed the face of Scotland and provided the means of changing the physical patterns of life: transport not only met people's existing needs, but created new ones.

Transport by river and canal was a major factor in this revolution; and the lochs and rivers of Scotland are given separate treatment in *The Streams of Life* by Peter Maitland. Scotland is fortunate in having vast amounts of high quality water; yet although we value and constantly celebrate Scotland's fresh waters for their beauty, we often undervalue them as a key national resource.

Water is only one of the energy resources in Scotland. In *The Power of Scotland*, John Butt and John Twidell survey the story of the discovery and exploitation of these resources and their environmental consequences: the application of sun, wind, water and tide for example; the exploitation of the ancient fossil fuels of coal, shale-oil, oil and natural gas; the use of the biological energy sources of peat and timber, now augmented by the potential of domestic waste for fuel and of gas derived from landfills; the splitting of the atom and the creation of nuclear power.

The third section of the book is devoted more specifically to the problems and challenges of nature conservation: how we can safeguard and enhance the diversity and balance of nature in the face of ever-increasing pressures from economic exploitation and environmental pollution. In *The Conservation of Nature*, Alastair Sommerville looks at current conservation issues and suggests practical ways in which we can all become involved in conserving and protecting Scotland's natural heritage.

The remote uplands may be the most fragile parts of our ecological heritage; but to four-fifths of the population, it is the nature within and around towns which is experienced for most of their lives. In *The Greening of the Cities*, Graham White argues that we must look again at our stereotypes of 'nature', 'town' and 'countryside' and realise that nature does not begin somewhere out beyond the green belt but right here in our streets, parks and gardens. We must promote environmental education where nature begins, from the heart of the inner cities outwards. In this chapter he suggests that only by adopting a more holistic environmental ethic, in which we look at the quality of environment of Scotland's towns as well as our wildlife habitats, can a truly broadly based environmental movement be created in Scotland.

The penultimate chapter, *The Protection of the Land*, by John Arnott, considers the many ways in which significant parts of Scotland are protected. Most of the countryside is in private hands and all of it is used in one way or another, whether it be for farming and hill-sheep grazing, forestry, sporting activities, water catchment, amenity or recreation.

In the final chapter of the book, *The Playground of the Future*, Roger Smith tells the story of the manifold development of recreation in Scotland – shooting, mountaineering, rambling, skiing, tourism, 'leisure' resorts and sports. He highlights the conflicting demands which need to be resolved if the nature of Scotland is not to be irrevocably damaged in the coming years.

So there, in summary, is the outline of this book. In addition, in special boxes throughout the text, we have focused on the great Scottish pioneers in various fields who have inspired the way in which we think about the environment: men like James Hutton, the 'father of modern geology'; Hugh Miller, the great populariser of geology; Sir Charles Lyell, the prophet of the theory of 'continental drift'; Sir Frank Fraser Darling, one of the pioneers of the ecological and environmental movement in Scotland; and above all the man to whose memory this book is dedicated, John Muir, the Scots-born American explorer and naturalist who is increasingly regarded as the prophet of the international conservation movement. His is a story of genius; and genius is needed today as never before. I have always had a fondness for the old Welsh Triads which are the foundation of Celtic literature and, therefore, culture. The third of the Triads outlines the three Requisites of Genius: 'an Eye which can see Nature; a Heart which can feel Nature; and a Boldness which does follow it'.

It makes a magnificent slogan for all those who cherish the nature of Scotland and endeavour to nurture it as best they can. Hugh MacDiarmid, I am sure, would have approved.

MAGNUS MAGNUSSON KBE
Chairman, Scottish Natural Heritage
March 1997

Buchaille Etive Mor and
the river Coupall,
Glencoe.

CHAPTER ONE

Laying the Foundations
George Farrow and Ian Rolfe

Dr George E. Farrow has done extensive fieldwork both in Scotland and abroad, especially on shell-sands. He lectured at Glasgow University for thirteen years and has worked for Britoil and the Royal Museum of Scotland in Edinburgh. He is now senior geologist with Croft Exploration in Glasgow. Dr W.D. Ian Rolfe is the Keeper of Geology at the Royal Museum of Scotland and is an authority on fossil arthropods.

Most people have probably never met a geologist and may have little idea of just what they do, but geologists are in a unique position to throw light on the nature of Scotland and its origins in the distant past. It is easy to look at the mountains, valleys and plains of the Scottish landscape today and think that it has always looked like this; but geologists see the present landscape as merely the latest evidence of a series of massive and unending series of transformations of the Scottish scene. They can help people to understand these barely imaginable changes by revealing the story of Scotland's evolution which lies buried in the rocks. We are going to try to describe these changes for you in a rather unusual way.

We have put the story of Scotland's origins together as a series of 'snapshots' in geological time, like a family album, depicting the stages of the land's evolution. Starting with today's landscape, which everyone thinks of as 'the real Scotland', we shall peel away the layers of rock beneath our feet, going further and further back in time with each layer, to reveal the ancient, buried landscapes of Scotland's distant past.

In order to do this we have to set our geological clock to record the passage of 800 million years during a single twenty-four hours; on this scale, one hour represents 33 million years, a minute would be 550,000 years and a mere second would last almost 10,000 years. If we take the present moment to be midnight on our twenty-four-hour clock, then the story of Scotland's origins begins at the previous midnight, twenty-four geological hours and 800 million years ago.

THE BIRTH OF LOCH LOMOND, 10,000 YEARS AGO: 23:59.59 HOURS

Loch Lomond is the largest freshwater lake in Britain and, although it may seem to be 'as old as the hills', in fact on the timescale of our geological clock it was created barely a second ago.

Loch Lomond appeared on the scene just 10,000 years ago, at the very end of the last Ice Age. As the last of the melting glaciers retreated, they dumped vast quantities of rock which had been embedded in the ice, leaving behind piles of rubble which clearly mark the farthest point to which the glaciers advanced. These piles of glacial rubble show us that the last spreading of the ice, termed by geologists the 'Lomond Readvance', finally stopped just short of Dunblane. To the south, beyond the edge of this great ice cap the land was barren, permanently frozen tundra.

The area around Loch Lomond, with its recently acquired covering of thin soils and trees, thus gives us a glimpse of what a late-glacial landscape looked like. When you next drive past it, remember that you are looking at the most recent effects of a glacier (see Chapter 12, Box 1).

Loch Lomond is the largest body of freshwater in Great Britain.

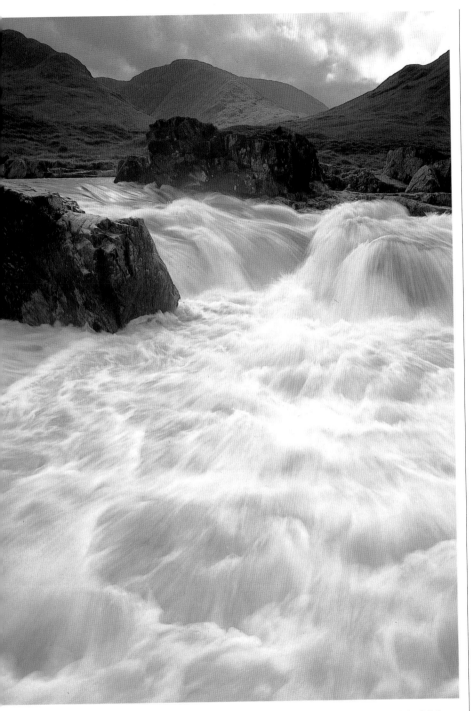

Ancient rivers which once flowed eastwards were diverted to the west by the last advance of the glaciers.

1. SIR CHARLES LYELL (1797–1875)

Sir Charles Lyell, the prophet of the theory of 'continental drift', was born in Kinnordy, the son of an eminent mycologist (a specialist in fungi) who was also a Dante scholar. He was brought up in England and studied law at Oxford, but his career changed dramatically when he attended some lectures in 1819 by William Buckland, who was then the Reader in mineralogy there.

Lyell promptly dropped law, switched to geology, toured and studied in Europe, and during 1830–33 published his *Principles of Geology*, which had a profound impact on scientific thought in the nineteenth century.

His thesis was that the greatest geological changes had been produced by natural forces that were still at work; and he went on in *The Geological Evidence of the Antiquity of Man* (1863) to relate the evolution of the planet to Darwin's theory of evolution (*The Origin of Species by Means of Natural Selection*, 1859).

Lyell was particularly struck by the evidence of massive changes in climate which the rock records reveal. He was a century ahead of his time in acknowledging large-scale movements of the earth's surface and thus anticipating the modern theory of 'plate tectonics', the now-accepted fact that the continents are continually moving around the surface of the planet on the rocky 'plates' which make up the earth's land surface and the ocean floors. In 1875, the year of his death, he made this stunningly prophetic statement:

Continents, therefore, although permanent for whole geological epochs, shift their positions entirely in the course of ages.

It would be almost a hundred years before modern geologists found the conclusive evidence for the new science of plate tectonics which Lyell's mind had envisaged.

RIVERS CHANGE DIRECTION, 50,000 YEARS AGO: 23:59.55 HOURS

At the height of the last Ice Age, glacial erosion removed vast amounts of rock from the landscape, carving out the great valleys, leaving the planed and smoothed mountain tops standing proud above them. These glaciers also caused some intriguing changes in our river systems; the direction in which some rivers flow is certainly very odd in parts of Scotland, particularly around the Campsie Fells, towards Drymen.

Back in the middle of the last Ice Age, about 50,000 years ago, a colossal sheet of ice ground its way relentlessly south, past Ben Lomond, moving at a rate of between 9 and 180 metres a year and gouging out the rocky trench of Loch Lomond to a depth of 200 metres below sea level. As it moved southwards this ice-sheet cut across a series of rivers which had previously run eastwards to the Forth estuary. When they were dammed by the ice, these rivers were diverted and eventually burst out to flow westwards into the Clyde as the result of the gigantic forces of nature's ice-engineering.

THE 'OLD COURSE' LAID DOWN,
500,000 YEARS AGO: 23:59.05 HOURS

It is hard to find any aspect of the Scottish scene that has not been created or shaped by the last Ice Age. This even includes the eighteenth green at St Andrews, the celebrated 'Old Course', which in common with many of our golf links is located on a 'raised beach'. But how did the Ice Age help create the Old Course?

Some 500,000 years ago, Scotland was like a laden cargo ship carrying an incredibly heavy

sheet of ice, over one kilometre thick, on her decks. Under this crushing burden Scotland actually sank into the deep plasticky subsurface of the planet by a depth of several metres; as the ice melted, the weight was removed from the 'ship' and Scotland rose again. We see the evidence of this in 'raised beaches' around our coasts, which are several metres above current sea levels.

In contrast, the south-east of England was never covered by ice; the land was never crushed under the weight of the glaciers and we see no raised beaches there. In fact the south-east coast of England is actually sinking slowly, as opposed to Scotland, which is still rising. Given the current concerns over the 'greenhouse

The Old Course at St Andrews is laid out on an ancient raised beach.

The basalt columns of Staffa and Fingal's Cave were formed by intense volcanic activity in the region of Mull over sixty million years ago.

21

effect' and rising sea levels, it would seem that a Scottish golf course could well be the safest place to be!

WESTERN SCOTLAND OVERRUN BY LAVA, 60 MILLION YEARS AGO: 22:12 HOURS

Our first three geological 'time snapshots' showed Scotland buried under a kilometre-thick shroud of ice, and in fact there were at least five Ice Ages during the last three million years. But Scotland was not always a land of cold and ice. If we dig further down through the rock record to 60 million years ago, we find Bunessan, on the island of Mull, basking in tropical sunshine.

The fossils we find in the rocks of this period tell us that Mull would have looked something like today's Florida. Close relatives of the Californian giant redwoods grew alongside trees similar to those found in the Far East, which now need the heat of Glasgow's Kibble Palace to keep them alive. Beautiful lotus flowers floated in warm lakes on the lava rock surface, and magnolias, the most primitive of flowering plants, lent a splash of vivid colour. It really is a shame that we are 60 million years too late to enjoy it all, since this is only a fossil snapshot, alas!

The landscape of Mull was made up of beds of lava rock, 1800 metres thick, which had poured from giant volcanoes over the previous three million years. This intense volcanic activity happened because the North Atlantic was opening up, as North America slowly split away from Scotland. Volcanoes rose along the line of the north-east/south-west split and their outpourings of lava forced the two rocky plates apart, creating the Atlantic Ocean. The volcanic islands of Iceland and the Azores show the line of the split. The Atlantic is still widening, at the same rate as your finger nails are growing; if your nails grew for 60 million years they would reach from Glasgow to New York!

There are only two possible solutions to the puzzle of Mull's tropical fossils: either the whole world was much warmer at that time, or Scotland must have been located much further south on the planet (Box 1) – or perhaps both were true; we shall discover the answer later on.

HELMSDALE: EARTHQUAKES AND TIDAL WAVES, 120 MILLION YEARS AGO: 20:20 HOURS

If we go even further back in time and look at the east coast of Scotland 120 million years ago, life was very different from the tropical paradise of Mull described above. The northern coast of the Moray Firth, near Helmsdale, had a submarine equivalent of the San Andreas Fault in California. The Helmsdale Fault was an underwater earthquake zone which produced terrific shocks, bringing down boulders the size of houses. Tidal waves created by the quakes broke huge heads off the coral which grew in the seas and swept them into deep water, along with mature trees from the land, forming fossils on the sea bed. The fossilised corals give us another clue that the climate was warmer than it is today, since they are of a type now found no further north than Bermuda. We also find fossils of more than sixty species of sub-tropical plants in the area, which also point to the area's tropical climate.

SCOTLAND IS A DESERT, 260 MILLION YEARS AGO: 16:10 HOURS

The Burrell Collection in Pollok Park, Glasgow, is filled with precious historical objects and paintings of world importance. But it is also a work of art itself in which the combination of fine sandstones, glass, light and space has produced a gallery of international repute. As you enter the Burrell you are surrounded by stone blocks cut from the New Red Sandstone beds of Scotland, which were formed from the sand dunes of a 260-million-year-old desert (Box 2).

At the time when the New Red Sandstone was formed, great geological fault lines were very active in Scotland. Vast geological troughs like the North Minch and the Sea of the

Hebrides were let down like 100-mile-long trapdoors in the rocks along the Minch Fault. At that time, 260 million years ago, there was no sea to fill these troughs and, as they collapsed below sea level, they formed sand deserts with their own drainage basins like Death Valley in California today. Cut off from moisture-bearing winds they would have had rare rainfalls and flash floods, as Death Valley occasionally has.

If Scotland had such great deserts, we can deduce that the country must have been located much further south than it is today; in fact, it probably lay about 15°N of the equator, in line perhaps with today's Khartoum in the Sudan or Madras in India. Scotland was far from green at that time! Scotland's deserts of this period were slowly acquiring the distinctive red sands which we now see compressed and shaped into the

2. NEW RED SANDSTONE QUARRY (CORNCOCKLE MUIR)

Quarries producing New Red Sandstone in the Dumfries area have been worked for more than a hundred years. Corncockle Muir quarry produced the superb fossilised reptile tracks which are now displayed in the Royal Museum of Scotland in Edinburgh. Another at Locharbriggs is still working the stone today; much of the New Red Sandstone used in Glasgow's buildings came from a deep quarry at Mauchline in Ayrshire (now closed, alas). If you are walking in Glasgow you may notice that buildings of New Red Sandstone tend to be later in date than those made of the honey-coloured carboniferous sandstone: 'New Red' buildings became more common after 1900.

Icthyosaurs and nautilus witnessed the submarine earthquakes and tidal waves which devastated Helmsdale.

stones of the Burrell Collection, as red iron oxide began to cement together the perfectly round, wind-blasted sand grains of our desert past.

TROPICAL SWAMPS COVER THE CENTRAL BELT, 300 MILLION YEARS AGO: 15:00 HOURS

If we dig even further, another 40 million years deeper into the rock layers, we find evidence that Scotland was actually on the equator (Box 3). Instead of the hot deserts of the New Red Sandstone era we find Scotland covered in

23

Deserts like those of California's Death Valley once covered much of Scotland.

Artist's diorama of the Fossil Grove which was unearthed in Glasgow's Victoria Park.

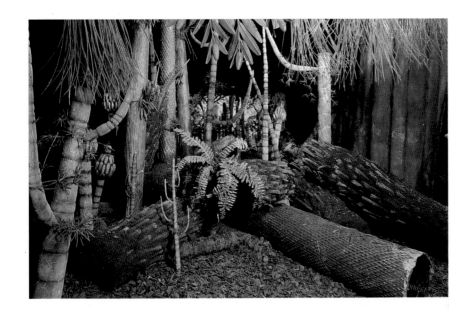

3. QUARRYMEN REVEAL THE FOUNDATIONS

The first tarmacadam road surface was laid in 1845 and since then the demand for good roadstone has never ceased. More than a hundred years ago, quarrymen working in the outskirts of Glasgow accidentally uncovered the famous 'Fossil Grove' of stone trees in what is now Victoria Park. Although they did not realise it at the time, they were revealing a fundamental chapter in Scotland's geological and climatic story. Geologists now reckon that these fossil trees are more than 300 million years old.

Although it is hard for us to accept, these fossils prove that, at that time, Scotland was not actually located where she is today; she stood on the equator, in the tropical rain forest belt. Scotland was then covered in dense rain forest and was far greener than she is today.

equatorial rain forest, with 100 (250 cm) inches of rain a year and a steamy humidity.

These rain forests girdled the planet from mid-America to Russia, via what is now Cowdenbeath! Central Scotland marks the southern edge of a long-vanished super-continent called 'Laurentia', which covered all of what is now the Atlantic Ocean with dry land.

Occasionally the ancient southern ocean invaded the swamps of Laurentia's river deltas, depositing a blanket of sea muds that hardened over millennia and creating the fossils which we now find at Cowdenbeath, Bearsden and Bathgate. These river deltas on the ocean edge must have been very flat, and the animals and plants which lived there must have been very much like those of today's Florida Everglades. However, two-metre-long millipede fossils show us that these creatures were far larger than their modern equivalents.

But surely we're imagining things to picture Cowdenbeath on the equator with a tropical rain forest climate similar to today's Florida? It seems impossible; but don't forget that we are allowing over 300 million years to shift Scotland from the equator to her current position at 56°N, a distance of at least 3,500 miles (5,600 km). It hardly seems possible that forces exist which can move an entire country with all its mountains and rocks for such a distance. But they do, and they did!

The power that moves continents around and builds mountains is driven by the huge volcanic forces operating deep within the earth. The rocky plates which make up the surface of the planet are really just a thin crust, floating on a semi-molten sea of lava or magma. People may find it hard to imagine just how great an impact volcanoes have had on Scotland's past. If we go back another 30 million years deeper into the rock record, beyond the Amazon swamps of Scotland, we find that the sites of modern Glasgow and Edinburgh were deluged by vast lava flows.

These rivers of lava didn't just come from conical volcanoes like Arthur's Seat (Box 4); they also seeped from cracks and fissures,

4. EDINBURGH'S VOLCANO

Arthur's Seat, Scotland's most famous volcano, dominates the landscape of central Edinburgh. It erupted 340 million years ago – but not where Edinburgh stands today. The volcano actually rose from the tropical seas of the equator, and the red-hot lava flows were quenched by tropical thunderstorms. Since that time the whole continental plate on which Scotland sits has drifted north, carrying Arthur's Seat along with it.

We can trace at least thirteen lava flows on the southern slopes of Arthur's Seat. However, the cliffs of Salisbury Crags on the north-facing slopes are not a lava flow from the volcano at all, although they might appear to be so; they are in fact a solidified slab of magma, formed deep in the earth millions of years after the volcano had ceased erupting.

Salisbury Crags were actually buried beneath a kilometre-thick layer of other rocks but most of these have been removed by erosion since the ground was tilted and broken by large-scale earth movements. During the last Ice Age about 150 metres of rock were stripped off by the glacier ice as it ground across the volcano towards the east. However, far more rock was gouged out from the softer rocks on either side of the hard volcanic core. This glacial erosion also affected the rocks of Edinburgh Castle as the glaciers carved out the troughs of the Grassmarket and Princes Street Gardens on either side of the Castle rock; this can be seen distinctly along the line of the fault which lies below the main platform of Waverley station.

creating flat lava beds and plateaux such as those we find in Iceland today. Over 1,000 volcanic vents from the carboniferous era have

Artist's impression of the sharks which once swam in the seas of Bearsden.

been mapped in what is now Scotland's Central Belt in addition to more typical volcanic remnants such as Arthur's Seat and the Bass Rock.

Things were also still bubbling away below the surface of the rocks, even when no actual lavas were being erupted. We know that there was a lava plateau on the site of today's Bathgate in West Lothian, which had hot springs feeding a shallow warm-water lake. The ancient creatures that lived near these lakes have been preserved as fossils which have recently become the centre of world attention, as a result of the pioneering excavations of professional fossil-hunter Stan Wood (Box 5). These fossils include metre-long land scorpions; the ancestors of today's frogs; the world's earliest known reptile and a newly discovered fossil tree that has been given the scientific name of Stanwoodia.

This landscape of lava beds and tropical hot springs eventually sank beneath a shallow tropical sea which covered central Scotland, and the waters of Bearsden were invaded by strange and bizarre sharks whose fossils have been found locally.

SCOTLAND SOUTH OF THE EQUATOR, 400 MILLION YEARS AGO: 12:00 NOON

Beneath the lavas described earlier we find a second layer of red sandstone rocks, similar to the New Red Sandstones of the Burrell Collection; however, these lower layers are much older and consequently are called the 'Old Red Sandstone', a title immortalised in the writings of the Scottish author and amateur geologist, Hugh Miller (Box 6). Whereas the New Red Sandstone was formed north of the

5. STAN WOOD (1940–)

More than 200 years after James Hutton (Box 7) made Scotland the birthplace of the science of modern geology, a former merchant seaman and insurance salesman has thrust Scotland into the limelight of international geology once again.

Stanley Purdie Wood was born and brought up in Edinburgh. He is essentially a self-made and self-taught man (he took an Open University degree in 1986). He first developed an interest in fossils when he saw fossil tree stumps in a coal merchant's yard in 1965; and six years later, in 1971, he found his first fossil fish.

After that there was no stopping him. He became a full-time fossil hunter, opening up quarries, diverting streams, and hiring mechanical diggers and JCBs. Over the next few years he discovered some of the best-preserved fossil sharks in the world, on the foreshore at Granton in Edinburgh and at Bearsden in Glasgow. He also unearthed the oldest fossil reptile found anywhere in the world, at Bathgate.

In 1983, after training with Glasgow University's Business Enterprise programme, he established his own small business collecting and preparing rare fossils for sale to museums all over the world. Stan Wood has revolutionised our knowledge of the evolution of Scotland's natural heritage. Without his discoveries, our ideas about the evolution of reptiles would, quite simply, be wrong by a factor of over 38 million years!

equator, we know that the Old Red was formed some way south of the equator. This period was also highly volcanic, and evidence of this can be found in the Ochil Hills, where the lavas contain some of the finest agates in the world.

It appears that at this time Scotland was once again a dry desert conspicuously lacking rain forests and tropical swamps. This geological period is very early in the story of life on the land; as such we find only a few fossils of primitive plants and spiders which were carrying out a patchy colonisation of the land from the seas. Most of the land suffered from a semi-arid climate and the sandy deserts provided little encouragement for pioneering land plants and animals. However, we know that there was some water about during this period of sandstone formation, since these sandstones of the 'Old Red' period were laid down in river beds, as opposed to the younger 'New Red' Sandstones, which were created from wind-blown sand dunes.

The animals in the lakes of this period were preyed upon by fearsome armoured fish, whose fossils we find preserved in the sandy flagstone rocks of Orkney and Caithness.

SCOTLAND AND ENGLAND SEPARATE, OVER 400 MILLION YEARS AGO NEARLY 12:00 NOON

During our travel down through the rocks, 400 million years backwards in time towards noon on our geological clock, it has not been too difficult to find the evidence for Scotland's northward drift from south of the equator to her present position in the far north. However, even further back in time, beneath the Old Red Sandstone, lies a jumbled stack of highly eroded and contorted layers of rock. These layers were laid down as the bed of an ancient ocean which geologists call 'Iapetus'.

This ocean covered southern Scotland and separated it from England, which lay 1000 miles to the south. James Hutton (Box 7) was the first geologist to realise what these jumbled-up rock layers represented, when he observed them at Jedburgh and at Siccar Point on the

Stan Wood pictured in his workshop.

Berwickshire coast. Spectacular evidence of the existence of the Iapetus ocean comes from rocks on the Ayrshire coast around Girvan and Ballantrae. The green 'pillow lavas' which we find there are only formed when hot lava is extruded into water; these rounded 'pillows' prove that submarine volcanoes were erupting on the floor of an ancient ocean. These eruptions confirm the role volcanoes have played in forming Scotland's landscape down the ages, as we have seen in the Inner Hebrides, Edinburgh, Glasgow, the Ochils and now Ayrshire.

The fossilised remains of the animals that once lived on the Scottish shores of the Iapetus Ocean provide evidence of how wide it must have been at one stage in its past. These fossils are more similar to those found in rocks in North America than they are to those found in the English Lake District. The geological union of England and Scotland only took place much later, when Scotland and Northern Ireland closed on to England, Wales and southern Ireland in a pincer-like movement, which squeezed the Iapetus Ocean out of existence.

SCOTTISH ASSEMBLY II, 450 MILLION YEARS AGO: 10:30 HOURS

It has often been remarked that Scotland has more varieties of rock within its boundaries than many larger countries do. This geological

6. HUGH MILLER (1802–56)

One of the first geological best-sellers was a collection of articles written by an extraordinary Scotsman and entitled *The Old Red Sandstone*. First published in 1841, it ran to no fewer than twenty-six editions and placed Scotland's superb fossil heritage at the centre of the world stage.

Hugh Miller was a remarkable man in every way: stonemason, journalist, churchman, social philanthropist, author and amateur geologist. Born in Cromarty in the north of Scotland, his father was lost at sea when Hugh was only five years old. After a rebellious school career in various academies he was apprenticed as a stonemason at the age of sixteen, but he retained a burning desire to become a man of letters. He devoted his winter months to reading, writing and the study of natural history; and in 1829 he published *Poems written in the Leisure Hours of a Journeyman Stonemason*, followed by *Scenes and Legends of the North of Scotland* in 1835.

Working as a craftsman with stone for seventeen years had aroused in him a passionate interest in fossils; and for the church periodical, *The Witness*, he wrote a series of geological articles which formed the basis of *The Old Red Sandstone*. He pioneered popular science books, but was acutely aware of the irreconcilable conflict between the biblical account of the creation of the earth and the geological evidence for an immeasurably greater timescale indicated by the fossils he found in the rocks. In particular, he disputed the Darwinian evolutionary theory with his book *Footsteps of the Creator* (1850). *The Testimony of the Rocks* (1857) and *Sketchbook of Popular Geology* (1859) were both published posthumously.

Tragically he shot himself in the chest on Christmas Eve, 1856; four doctors concluded 'from the diseased appearances found in the brain . . . that the act was suicidal under the impulse of insanity'.

The thatched cottage in Cromarty in which he was born is now preserved by the National Trust for Scotland.

richness occurred because large geological slices of the planet, each with its own different rocks, gradually converged, ground into one another and fused into one rocky plate along the fault lines we can still see today in Scotland. Geologists call these huge sheets of rock 'terranes'; the blocks which make up the Grampian mountains and the northern Highlands are distinct geological terranes which slid in along lines of weakness like the Great Glen Fault, colliding and fusing together more than 400 million years ago. These fault lines are still active in Scotland and are quite capable of causing earthquakes as the huge sheets of rock grind past each other; the Solway earthquake on Boxing Day, 1979, shows us that Scotland is still an earthquake zone.

SCOTTISH ASSEMBLY I, 700 MILLION YEARS AGO: 03:00 HOURS

If we go back even further in time, deeper through the rock layers, beyond the bed of the Iapetus Ocean, we discover a very bleak picture of Scotland. This layer of rocks was formed long before plants and animals invaded the land, when the only green things visible on the land surface would have been moist patches of blue-green algae and microbial sludge. The older rocks of Islay, Jura, Scarba and the Garvellachs reveal an even bleaker picture. They show us that about 700 million years ago, Scotland suffered no fewer than seventeen successive Ice Ages! Although Scotland was then far down in the southern hemisphere, these Ice Ages do not imply that it was in the Antarctic. Rather, it seems that these periods of glaciation were world-wide, with ice covering much of the planet. It also seems that these Ice Ages were separated by sixteen periods of global warming: an extraordinary scenario of rapid climatic change and temperature reversals at a time before land plants had yet evolved.

GLACIERS EXHUME A BILLION-YEAR LANDSCAPE: 00:00.01 HOURS

On the Isle of Lewis we find one of the oldest and toughest rocks existing anywhere on earth; it is known as Lewisian Gneiss (pronounced 'nice'). It is little wonder that it is a hard rock, because it was formed 2,500 million years ago, under incredible pressure, at a depth of 12 miles (19 km) beneath the crust of the earth. The staggering truth is that up in the north-west of Scotland we can actually stand on a piece of the earth's lower crust, the very foundation of all the rocks, which has been pushed upwards to the surface through a distance that is twice the height of Mount Everest.

We know that these rocks broke through to the surface at least 1,000 million years ago, because the pink sandstones of the Torridon region were deposited on top of this Lewisian rock by ancient rivers flowing across the landscape at that time. Within the last 25,000 years, huge glaciers carved valleys through these Torridonian sandstone beds, grinding down through thousands of feet of rock to reveal the Lewisian Gneiss beneath.

These recent glaciers carved out the valleys between the great mountains of Suilven and Canisp, leaving these eroded sentinels to watch over an exhumed, billion-year-old landscape which was once entirely devoid of plants and animals. It would be a very, very long time before Scotland became as green as she is today.

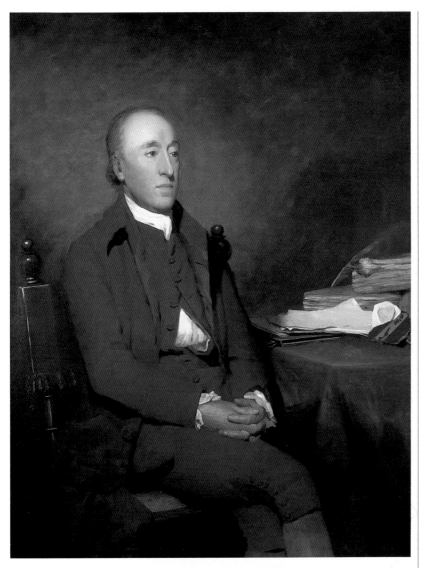

James Hutton (1726–97), the father of modern Geology.

7. JAMES HUTTON (1726–97)

Edinburgh-born James Hutton is now universally recognised as the 'father of modern geology'. He not only accumulated scientific facts through observation and research but also recognised the connections between different aspects of the natural world and showed how they are bound together in cycles of destruction and renewal.

He was the first person ever to grasp the nature of the immense age of geological time. After studying rock formations at Siccar Point on the Berwickshire coast, he had a dramatic and intuitive insight into the nature of the forces which had formed them and the incredible passage of time which must have been necessary. He wrote: 'My mind seemed to grow giddy by looking so far back into the abyss of time'.

It should be remembered that the dominant Bible-based viewpoint of the society in which Hutton lived held that the Book of Genesis was literally true and that the earth was only a few thousand years old.

Hutton first qualified as a doctor, but never practised medicine. Instead he spent some time in Norfolk learning about new agricultural methods there before settling on a small farm in Berwickshire. His interest in geology had begun during his early years as a farmer when he made the first of many journeys on horseback through England, Wales and Scotland. He observed that many rocks are made up of the debris of other rocks and he suggested that sediments derived from rocks on the surface of the earth are compacted and consolidated on the ocean floor and then raised up as dry land by heat from within the earth. From these insights he made the huge imaginative leap which tied together the erosion of mountains and the formation of sedimentary rocks. Hutton recognised that the process was a cyclical one in which the surface of the earth was continually being created and destroyed.

His theory of the igneous origin of many rocks was first expounded to the newly-formed Royal Society of Edinburgh in 1758 and expanded into book form in 1795 as *Theory of the Earth.* This book ranks alongside Darwin's *The Origin of Species*, which was published much later, as one of the greatest scientific contributions of all time.

But he was more than just the world pioneer of geology. He was also a prophet of the unborn science of ecology. He was concerned with the physiology of plants and animals as well as the broad sweep of the earth's history. In his view the cyclical process of earth formation had a clear purpose: it was, he said, 'contrived in consummate wisdom by a Supreme Being...a world beautifully calculated for the growth of plants and the nourishment of men and animals'.

He also wrote:

Man has the disposal of nature so much at his will ...he must, by studying nature, learn what will most conduce to the success of his design. No part [of the surface of the earth] is indifferent to man.

It could almost have been a modern environmentalist speaking.

Fossil of armoured fish from the rocks of Caithness.

Liathach, Beinn Alligin and Beinn Eighe were gouged from the sandstone plateau of Torridon by glaciers only 25,000 years ago.

31

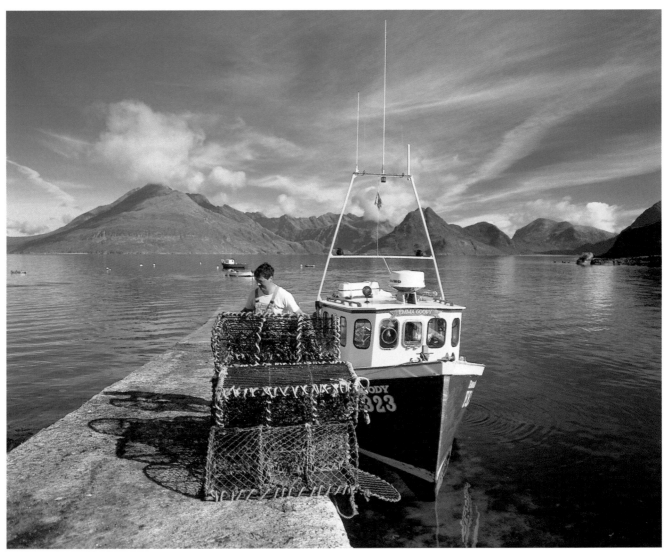

Loading lobster creels, Elgol,
Loch Scavaig, Isle of Skye.

CHAPTER TWO

The Seas of Plenty

John Hambrey

Dr John Hambrey is an ecologist and resource economist who has specialised in rural development, fisheries and fish farming in Scotland and throughout the world; he is currently working in the Agricultural and Aquatic Systems Program at the Asian Institute of Technology in Thailand.

Scotland's coastal waters are among the richest in the world. From them we harvest half a million metric tonnes (t) of wild fish each year. Into them we dump a staggering volume of sewage and industrial effluent. We use these waters for sailing, canoeing, swimming and diving, and our children play on the beaches. We pour in food, chemicals and drugs to raise 64,000t (1994) of farmed salmon; we risk releasing massive quantities of oil, nuclear waste and toxic chemicals from accidental spills. So far the sea has been remarkably forgiving, and we have been very lucky.

An intricate coastline more than 10,000 km in length; the ebb and flow of powerful tides; a great upwelling and mixing of ocean currents on the continental shelf to the west of the Outer Hebrides; shallow sand banks fertilised by the dead bodies of falling plankton: these are the factors that create the wealth of Scotland's marine environment.

Where the North Atlantic Drift swells up over the continental shelf around Rockall and St Kilda there is an explosion of marine life. It is here that the warm surface waters – depleted of nutrients as marine life dies and falls into the ocean depths – become mixed and enriched with cold, nutrient-rich waters from below. This influx of nutrients provides ideal conditions for the growth of the microscopic plants and animals of the plankton. Several other ocean currents replenish the waters around Scotland by bringing a constant supply of nutrients. They also have a major effect on our climate, and sometimes carry exotic creatures from distant lands.

Twice daily a great tidal wave sweeps clockwise around the Scottish coast carrying the enriched water into the sea lochs of the west coast, and across the shallow banks of the North Sea. As the tide passes, the water is washed to and fro, and where it meets obstructions, powerful tidal streams are created. In places these streams become rapids, pouring and breaking over sand and rocks at speeds of up to eight knots per hour, churning the broth of plankton and nutrients, sending them flooding around the islands and into the sea lochs, where they provide the basic food for all the creatures of the sea.

Thus, the ocean currents bring nutrients, clean water, and exotic creatures from the tropics; the tides keep the solution well mixed; and the summer sun powers the production of millions of tonnes of sea life in our coastal waters.

THE PLANKTON

When we gaze down into the clear waters of a sandy bay on the west coast of Scotland the sea seems transparent and empty of life. But in reality this crystal clear water is a thin soup of microscopic creatures. They are called 'plankton', a Greek word meaning 'that which is made to wander or drift', since they are at the mercy of ocean currents and tidal streams. They serve as the grasslands and forests of the sea, since these tiny plants and animals low in the food chain are food for all the fish and mammals which we harvest. It is on the plankton that the fish, the mammals, the birds

*Jewel anemones blossom
in the crystal waters
of St Kilda.*

Scottish sunstar.

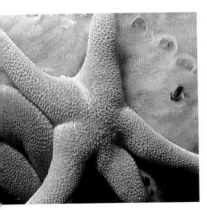

*Starfish on sponge, Berneray
Sound, Western Isles.*

1. The world of a Scottish scuba diver

Sinking slowly to the seabed 100ft below our survey vessel, there is the usual sense of anticipation: probably no human eyes have looked here before – what will we find this time? We land gently on a sandy seabed, and start to explore. Smooth rocks loom ahead of us like sleeping Leviathans in this mysterious, twilight world. Our torch beams transform the grey rocks, illuminating a crust of purple-pink studded with a million cup corals, each one less than three centimetres across. Their delicate green and orange tentacles are expanded over a hard white skeleton to catch even smaller creatures in the water currents. Although cup corals are true corals, we are not on a tropical reef, but in the cold Atlantic waters which bathe the west coast of Scotland.

On the crest of the rocks, are more stunningly coloured creatures. Featherstars perch with ten arms held upwards, the tip of each arm slightly rolled under like a newly-expanding fern. Some are a rich, dark red; others orange banded with white. Our torchlight makes their arms curl in discomfort, and we move on. A tall white anemone tops the next boulder with a powder-puff head of tiny tentacles – pretty, but deadly to small crustaceans. Beneath the boulder a dark blue lobster sits at the entrance to his burrow, tasting the water constantly with two long red antennae. One antenna touches my hand, and he comes towards me with claws outstretched. He is only partly bluffing and I keep my fingers out of range. Beside him an orange cushion starfish edges slowly towards yellow and white soft corals, ready for his next meal of their fluffy white tentacles. Soft corals, like tiny cup corals, are abundant in Scottish waters especially in strong currents. Cuckoo wrasse, lovely, colourful inquisitive fish with their own territories on boulder slopes, come to check out these noisy, lumbering visitors, and peer at us through our masks. Shoals of silvery fish flit past, coming close as we hold our breath but scattering as our exhaled bubbles disturb their peace. We cannot stay too long in their deep-water environment, because our bodies will absorb too much nitrogen as we breathe under the great pressure of the water above. We move upwards into a sand-filled gully.

Some very strange creatures live in sand. My diving buddy points at something, and my eyes take a little while to spot the flatfish, his banjo-shaped outline well disguised by an elaborate lobed edge, like the frilled trim on a Victorian lampshade. He has a curious little fishing rod on top of his head, with a flap of skin on the end for a lure. This he waves in the water attracting smaller fish within range of his huge mouth. He is of course, an angler fish. We have disturbed him, and he swims off lazily to settle invisibly on new ground. My other companion has found another attraction, a little octopus which prickles indignantly and eyes him warily, shuffling across the sand with its coiled, suckered arms. He changes colour from red-brown to white and back again, eventually losing his nerve and jetting off backwards at great speed. We look for him, but without success because he is a master of disguise and has probably changed colour again to match his background.

Now we are in shallow water, and shafts of sunlight filter down through an eerie underwater forest, turning the water beyond into a beautiful greenish-blue. The woodland 'trees' are kelp, a giant brown seaweed which forms dense forest in shallow water all around Scotland. Its thick stalks are covered with red seaweeds, fluffy white corals and oragne featherstars, and are topped with a palm-like frond. On the rocks below the kelp, urchins graze the seaweeds and multicoloured anemones line rock crevices. Eventually, we reach the surface after forty minutes of total absorption, delighted with the underwater creatures and scenery. How on earth can we share this with people who have never been diving? I have described only a single site, and only a small sample of its diverse inhabitants. Scotland's long and complex coast has many different habitats, all with their own characteristic marine communities. The sea lochs of the west and north coats, in particular, are a Scottish speciality. Essentially 'fiords', with deep, sheltered basins, they harbour communities of plants and animals not found elsewhere in diveable depths in Britain.

Microscopic foraminiferans use the equivalent of hooks and lines to ensnare their prey among the plankton.

and the fishermen of Scotland ultimately depend.

To enter and understand the world of the plankton requires a shift in perspective and scale. If we could make ourselves very small and enter the sea we would experience a very different world, half dream, half nightmare. At first sight everything would appear slow and benign, with strange animals and plants drifting gently. Occasionally we might see a flash of light, or a rapid contraction of tentacles; a struggling fish, a strange mass of sounds from near and far.

We would see creatures resembling green and amber crystal caskets turning and tumbling until they stop, caught in a web of glistening protoplasm cast around their delicate silica sphere. There would be creatures with long spines and red eyes, with intricate shells carved by the genius of evolution; or shrimp-like creatures, whose legs bear little beacons of light, scurrying through a dim world, black below, brilliant above. We would feel the vibrations as we struggled through a fluid far thicker and more viscous than the water we remember. A sudden flash and our shrimp-creature is gripped in the fangs of a slender transparent arrow. We could drift on, past snails with delicate wings flying slowly through the dim light, while others parachute through the water beneath sheets of silver mucus. A huge object with transparent bells ejecting jets of water, and rose-coloured petals trailing behind, suddenly envelops us…

But this is no dream. All these creatures exist. Indeed most of them could be found in a bucketful of ordinary Scottish sea water. A single bucket might hold as many as four million tiny plants, animals and bacteria. These would be of immense variety, drawn from every major group or phylum, including several which are not represented on the seabed or on the land.

The 'phytoplankton' is made up of single-celled and small multi-celled plants which use the sun's energy to create food, just as plants on the land do. In a sense they represent the 'pastures of the sea' and they are grazed upon by a great variety of 'zooplankton', the tiny

Danish trawlers take almost a million tonnes of sandeel from the North sea each year.

animals which eat both the phytoplankton and each other.

Amongst the zooplankton there are some tiny creatures that the Greeks named the 'copepods' or 'oar-footed ones', which are vital to the larger animals in the marine food chain. These crustaceans, ranging from pinhead to match-head in size, make up as much as 90 per cent of the zooplankton; they are the staple food of other marine creatures, and may be the most abundant of all multi-cellular animals living on earth. In recent years some larger species known collectively as the Antarctic 'krill', have been harvested by Japanese and Russian factory ships for use as human food.

Plankton are also eaten by fish such as the sand eel and the herring, which are in turn food for salmon, cod, puffins, cormorants, seals, and ultimately man. So the smallest creatures in the sea, the plankton, are the basis for all other life forms, just as the plants on the land sustain all the other creatures of the earth.

SAND EELS

In recent years people have been made aware of the sand eel's immense importance to the ecology of our waters. Everyone has seen pictures of puffins with rows of sand eels stacked in their beaks, and anyone living by the coast will almost certainly have seen these little fish, especially in sheltered bays where huge shoals sometimes gather. Occasionally, if mackerel are hunting them, the sand eels leap from the water in great silver showers.

If the water is clear one can look down and see thousands of the sand eels flashing as they twist and strike at tiny plankton. These fish are food for almost everything in the sea that is bigger than themselves, including herring, salmon, seals, seabirds and increasingly for man. Thus, they are a critical link in the food chain between the tiny plankton and the larger creatures of the sea. It is only since 1974 that significant quantities of these fish have been harvested from Scottish waters, but by 1982 some 63,000t were being landed at Scottish ports. Some experts have cited the disastrous breeding failure of seabirds in Orkney and Shetland in the late 1980s (see Chapter 5) as evidence of overfishing of the sand eel, which is the principal food of many seabirds there. Other scientists have suggested that the sand eel has simply changed its behaviour, is swimming deeper and is thus harder to catch. There is no agreement and little hard evidence, although urgent research and survey is now under way; but it seems self-evident that the sudden competition from humans for a major food item must have had some ecological consequences. It is merely the scale of the effect which is in doubt.

'THE SILVER DARLINGS'

Of all the fish taken from Scottish waters, the best known are the herring, the 'silver darlings', which have had a great influence on the evolution of Scotland's fisheries, economy and culture. Vast shoals of these fish migrate around our coasts every year feeding for most of the time on plankton, especially a shrimp-like crustacean called *Calanus*, which is the most common copepod in Scottish waters. The herring's gills are especially adapted with 'rakers' to comb the tiny plankton from the water, although they also take larger food such as sand eels which make up almost half the diet of adult herring.

There is evidence of a commercial fishery for herring off East Anglia as early as the sixth century AD. The growth of the Hanseatic towns of the Baltic in the twelfth century was founded on a major herring fishery using seine and drift nets. As has happened repeatedly in the history of herring fisheries, the shoals dwindled in the sixteenth century and fishing effort moved to the northern North Sea. By the seventeenth century the Dutch were working a large distant-water herring fishery, centred on Orkney and Shetland; they had about 2,000 boats or 'busses' of around 80t each, each with a crew of fifteen or so men. Each boat could bring home 70t of fish, since herring were barrelled and cured on board. It is reported that in the year 1614 a total of 150,000t of herring was exported from Holland, and by 1669 some 450,000 people – a fifth of the entire Dutch population – were employed in the herring fishery and associated businesses. The herring economy was thus crucial to the development of Dutch sea power. It has been said that Amsterdam was built on a foundation of herring bones; we might add that they were Scottish herring bones.

The Dutch fishery declined during the Napoleonic wars, which enabled Scots fishermen to exploit their home market. They

Herring boats at Fraserburgh.

Herring landed at Mallaig, West of Scotland.

37

were also helped by the increasing demand for fish in the industrial boom towns of Britain, whose markets were made more accessible through the rapid development of railways (see Chapter 11). The government saw an opportunity for economic expansion and, from the late eighteenth century, support grants were offered for boat construction, in addition to subsidies for the number of barrels of herring cured.

Scotland was slow to realise the massive potential of her waters, although there had been a small commercial herring fishery in East Fife from as early as the twelfth century, which culminated in the 'Lammas Drave' (Box 2). There were similar herring fisheries in the Clyde and in Loch Fyne. However, it was not until the late eighteenth century that the 'Great Summer Fishing' of the east coast began to develop. At first this was based along the shores of Caithness, but it became centred on Wick in the early nineteenth century and reached its high point in the early 1880s around Peterhead,

Fraserburgh and Aberdeen.

The 'Great Summer Fisheries' began as local enterprises and were purely seasonal. In the winter crofters did a little line-fishing for haddock or ling, or worked the land. But the money to be made in the short herring season encouraged investment in bigger boats and more nets. Rather than leave these capital assets to lie idle for most of the year, the fishermen began to follow the shoals to more distant fishing grounds, seeking new stocks to exploit, thus maximising their return on investment. They sailed to Lewis and Barra in May, to Shetland in June, to the Scottish east coast in late summer, and down the English coast to East Anglia for the late autumn. A whole troupe of camp followers went with them including the gutters or 'fishwives', the curers, agents and dealers. When the fleet landed a good catch the activity was frantic, for herring 'go off' rapidly and speed was at a premium.

It was perhaps inevitable that this great fishery should founder in a crisis of over-

By the 1950s, Forth fishermen could no longer fish for herring.

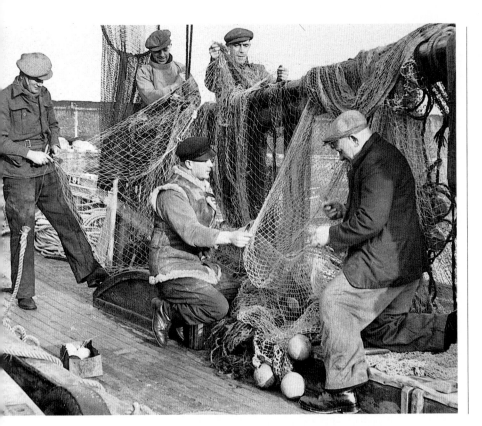

2. The Lammas Drave

'Lammas' is a Celtic festival beginning on the first day of August, associated with the Feast of St Peter ad Vincula. The name was given to an impressive summer fishery, or 'Drave', which took place close to the Fife coast, in the mouth of the Forth estuary. An important fishery for herring existed here as early as the twelfth century, and by the seventeenth century around 20,000 people (including many foreigners) gathered for the season. We can only guess at how much herring they caught but it must have been a huge amount to sustain such a number of people.

The fishery reached its modern peak in 1860 when around 300 boats fishing a relatively small area centred off Pittenweem and Anstruther landed 14,000 tonnes; and on the remarkable night of 21 August 1860, 140 small boats averaged 11 tonnes of fish each. Sadly, this fishery declined rapidly in succeeding years, either because of damage caused to the stocks or spawning grounds, or simply because the herring chose to go elsewhere.

production and slumping prices. By the late 1880s there was widespread unemployment and poverty in all the fishing communities. In the early part of this century, the sailing drifters were replaced by the steam drifters and the North Sea herring fishery catch settled at around 650,000t annually, with a relatively stable market. Ironically, the use of modern technology led to greater instability in the fishery. In 1963 the Icelanders and the Norwegians began to use vast purse-seine nets, measuring around 60 metres deep by 600 metres long, which were adopted by the Scots in 1965.

As a result, over the next few years the North Sea herring catch jumped to a staggering 1.3 milliont, the market was flooded with herring, and fish stocks were rapidly depleted. International attempts to agree on catch restrictions failed; politics and short-term economics dominated decisions, and quotas were adopted which were consistently higher than those recommended by scientists. In the mid 1970s the stocks of herring collapsed; the fishery was partially closed from 1976 and completely closed between 1978 and 1980 as a drastic conservation measure. Everyone suffered, as unemployment hit entire communities and boats were sold off. Modern technology had finally conquered the silver darlings, and although there was some improvement in the early 1990s, stocks are now once more seriously depleted.

THE WHITE FISH

Cod, haddock, ling and related species are known as 'white fish' because of the colour of their flesh. They are very different from the herring since they are exclusively carnivorous, feed in deeper water (often on the bottom) and they do not shoal, except at certain times of year. White fish seem to have been hunted by humans at an earlier stage than herring; perhaps the hook was invented before the net.

The bones of cod, ling, saithe, turbot, and even a 40lb halibut have been found at ancient sites in Orkney, suggesting that hook and line fishing from skin-covered boats was going on as

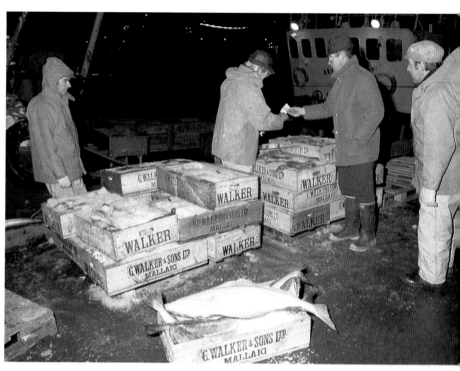

early as 5,000 years ago. The large middens of limpet shells at these sites imply that limpets were probably used as bait for fishing rather than as human food. With so much fine fish available it seems unlikely that these early hunter-gatherers would have eaten limpets, which have tough, unpalatable flesh and little food value. Unfortunately no early hooks, boats, nets or fish traps have survived, and we can only assume that these were swept away or have decayed. Perhaps they will turn up one day preserved in the muds of the sea bed.

There have been commercial line fisheries for white fish in the distant waters of the Arctic and the Grand Banks of Newfoundland since the sixteenth century, but fishing for white fish remained a subsistence affair round Scottish coasts until the close of the last century. At that time trawling, which had been used by the Dutch since the seventeenth century and by the English since the eighteenth century, became far more efficient because of technological developments. Larger steel boats radically improved catching efficiency along with the introduction of steam power, steel cables and power winches. By 1982 a modern fleet, equipped with powerful diesel engines,

Halibut landed at Mallaig, West of Scotland.

lightweight nylon nets and electronic fish finders, was landing 55,000t of cod and 113,000t of haddock at Scottish ports.

As with the herring fishery it seems that such catches simply cannot be sustained. The stocks are now in very poor shape, especially the cod, and there is even talk of cod becoming an endangered species. Although it is difficult to believe that fishing alone could ever directly cause the extinction of a small fish species, fishing pressure may tip an ecological balance between species, causing a rapid change in ecosystem structure with the loss of some species. The recent disastrous decline in cod on the Grand Banks of Newfoundland may be an example of this; however, recruitment to North Sea cod stocks last year was much improved and, dependent upon better management, the stocks appear to have the ability to recover; but this will not be easy.

Although fishermen themselves agree that the situation is serious, many are still prepared to fish illegally because they feel they have no choice. With half a million or more invested in a vessel and its gear, and with high interest on loans, they simply have to fish to the limit; if this means they have to break the rules, some will undoubtedly do so, since the alternative is often bankruptcy.

One of the modern controls on fishing is particularly perverse. The most obvious way to manage the fishery is to use nets with larger mesh sizes, so that only bigger fish are caught and the young ones escape to breed and be caught later. Unfortunately much of North Sea white fishing is a 'mixed fishery', with several different sized species being hunted at the same time. Fish such as whiting are smaller than haddock and the mesh size of the net is therefore designed to catch the smaller whiting, causing undersized haddock to be taken accidentally.

In order to preserve stocks it was, until recently, illegal to land haddock which are below a certain size. However, instead of preventing the capture of small fish, the size regulations meant that vast numbers of undersized haddock were netted along with the whiting and then thrown dead into the sea. This was conservation madness and since the discarded haddock were not recorded, it made a mockery of the scientists' attempts to make predictions about the fishery. Thankfully this policy is now being reviewed and discards may soon become illegal.

THE SALMON

When Pliny the Elder, the first-century Roman natural historian, named the salmon 'salmo' in his *Historia Naturalis*, he did not intend it as an obscure scientific name. To a Latin reader, the name simply meant 'the leaper', and Pliny used it to describe a common but beautiful fish.

The Atlantic salmon, *Salmo salar*, has such a powerful homing instinct that it migrates 1,000 miles (1,600 km) from Greenland waters to the Scottish rivers of its birth. It can survive the transition from a saltwater to a freshwater environment in a matter of days, which few species have managed in millions of years of evolution. Once home, it will swim and leap 60 miles (96 km) or more from the sea to the small burns and headwaters of our rivers to spawn – and then die.

The salmon faces many dangers on its journey. In the open sea it is hunted by men in trawlers, as well as by seals and dolphins. Offshore it runs the gauntlet of invisible nylon drift nets; off rocky headlands, along loch shores, and in river estuaries it must thread its way among a maze of stake nets and traps. As it struggles upstream it must ignore the tempting fly of the angler during the day, and evade the blazing lights, gaffs and spears of the poacher at night. But it is probable that none of these factors is the main cause for the decline of the salmon; their enormous reproductive power means that only a few adults need to survive and spawn in order to maintain the fish stocks.

Salmon were once abundant throughout Europe and the North Atlantic as far south as the Iberian peninsula. However, in the last two centuries they have almost vanished from Portugal, Belgium, the Netherlands, Germany, Switzerland, and Czechoslovakia, while they have been severely depleted in Spain, France, Denmark, the United States and Poland. In England they were once plentiful but are now restricted to just a few rivers. Ranulf Higden, a monk of St Werburg's monastery in Chester in the fourteenth century, noted in his *Polychronicon* that salmon were so cheap that they were fed to pigs. In Scotland they were even more plentiful, and were exported to England and the continent by the thirteenth century. Richard Franck, a soldier in Cromwell's army, wrote at Stirling that 'the river Forth relieves the country with her great quantity of salmon' and noted that the Burgomasters are 'compelled to reinforce an ancient statute that commands all masters not to compel any servant or apprentice to feed upon salmon more than thrice a week'.

The value of salmon was recognised from the beginning, and laws to conserve stocks go back a very long way. As early as 1030 Malcolm II of Scotland introduced a close-season on fishing, from Assumption Day (at the end of August) to Martinmas (11 November); there have been laws governing the taking of salmon ever since.

It seems likely that overfishing had partially depleted the stocks of salmon by the beginning of the nineteenth century. However, stocks were still large: over 100,000 salmon and grilse (a young salmon on its first return to fresh water) were being caught on the River Tweed each year, and the River Tay produced only a few less. By the end of the century, however, the output from Scottish waters was a mere fraction of what it had been, and salmon had disappeared entirely from many rivers. In England the situation was even worse.

The causes of the decline were pollution, dams, and canalisation. Dams meant that fish could not ascend the rivers and spawning beds were buried in silt; pollution reduced survival and breeding success to critically low levels. All the major rivers were seriously polluted by the middle of the last century. Organic wastes from whisky stills poured into the River Spey, textile dyes were dumped into the Tweed, coal washings into the Nith, ammonia into the Don, bleach into the Tay, and great quantities of raw

sewage from the expanding towns flooded most rivers. The salmon was quietly and insidiously poisoned. But increasing scarcity had its benefits, especially to those holding rights to exploit the remaining fish stocks. The economic value of salmon for food and sport soared as

the food of servants became a dish fit only for lords, and this price rise triggered the dramatic development of salmon farming in recent years.

Farmed salmon being harvested, West coast sea loch.

FISH FARMING

Over the last decade a remarkable change has taken place in some of the most isolated parts of Scotland. New life has been brought to declining communities, and for the first time in decades three generations of people may be found living together beside our wildest sea lochs; people are returning to the Highland coasts. The cause of this return has been the dramatic growth of salmon farming. For more than a century, salmon smolts had been reared in hatcheries for the restocking of Scottish and English rivers. But it was not until the early 1970s that serious attempts were made by both government (the White Fish Authority) and industry (the Unilever subsidiary, Marine Harvest) to rear salmon to maturity in the sea. The industry got off to a slow start, following an impressive Norwegian lead, but it was helped by grants from the Highlands and Islands Development Board with research and training being offered by universities and government institutes.

During the 1980s and early 1990s, the expansion was remarkable. By 1990 Scotland's salmon industry was producing around 30,000 t of fish and employing around 2,000 people directly, with 10,000 more in processing and distribution. However, the rearing of salmon in floating cages among sheltered sea lochs, and the rapid expansion of the industry has created conflicts of interest and environmental problems. The first concern that arose related to the quantity of organic fish wastes being dropped from cages in the pristine sea lochs. Most animals are only 10–20 per cent efficient in converting food into body weight; 5–10 kg of food produce only 1 kg of flesh. Salmon are no exception, and most of the fish pellets fed to them are voided into the water as fish wastes. The quantities involved are considerable: a fish farm producing 100t of fish each year releases into the surrounding waters around 10t of nitrogen and 3t of phosphorus, and around 80t (dry weight) of solid wastes, much of which will settle around and beneath the cages. It should be remembered that the lochs in which the cages are sited represent the cleanest and most unspoiled marine habitats which we have in Britain, which is reflected in the richness of the wildlife found there.

The ecological impact of such discharges will depend on the rate of water exchange or tidal flushing in the loch, but in most cases severe effects of solid wastes are relatively local, mainly within 50 metres of the cage. It has proved impossible to evaluate the effect of dissolved phosphorus and nitrogen on the surrounding water and plankton since our understanding of the underlying processes is too limited. It has been suggested, however, that blooms of poisonous algae are related to nutrient levels in the water, and there have been serious algal blooms in recent years in areas with high fish farming activity. The causal link cannot be proven however, and our ignorance of planktonic systems is such that it may take a catastrophe to demonstrate one.

Fish farms also create pollution through the use of antibiotics and chemical pesticides. Dichlorvos or 'Nuvan' is an organo-phosphorus nerve poison currently used to kill parasitic sea lice, which farmed salmon are particularly vulnerable to. A chemical which kills sea lice will clearly kill other crustaceans and small creatures in the plankton. The extent of these effects in the surrounding water is currently

Floating salmon cages on Loch Leven.

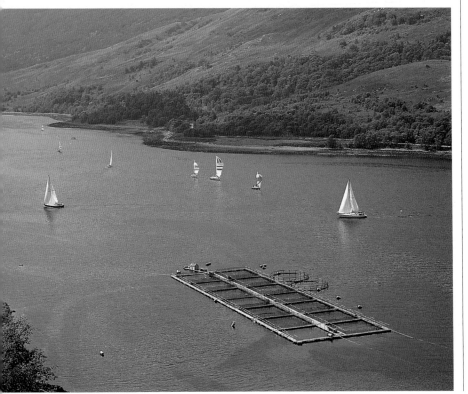

being researched and is the subject of fierce debate. Early results from research by the Department of Agriculture and Fisheries for Scotland (DAFS) suggests that there is indeed an effect, but that it is rapidly diluted and neutralised in the surrounding water.

Clearly, however, the use of large quantities of these chemicals on big farms must affect nearby plankton, which may include the larvae of crabs, lobsters, shrimps and shellfish. Research is currently going on (supported by the salmon farmers themselves) to develop biological control of sea lice using cleaner-wrasse, fish which feed on the sea lice. Early results are encouraging and, if successful, salmon farmers may be able to dispense with Dichlorvos altogether.

The killing of wild creatures which eat salmon has also raised concern. Not surprisingly, seals, otters, cormorants, herons and many other fish-eating animals are attracted by cages full of salmon. Shooting does take place, sometimes illegally, but DAFS may also issue licences to salmon farmers in severe cases. Shooting is often ineffective, and the use of predator nets around the cages has become almost standard practice.

There are also fears about the effects of escaped or released salmon on the wild genetic stock. For although farmed salmon are less fitted to the natural environment than wild fish, they may be released in such numbers that they successfully compete for food and are able to mate with the wild stock. Such competition could endanger the survival of wild salmon and introduce alien and ill-adapted genes to the local population. This is the subject of much debate, but given the poor state of our native salmon and their unique adaptations to different river systems, the dangers must be taken seriously. In recent years there have been massive releases of fish, from both sea cages and freshwater hatcheries, and the threat should not be treated lightly, as it tends to be by some fish farmers. There are also complaints about fish farms from fishermen, yachtsmen, tourists, and professional conservationists, who in their different ways fear salmon farms may

damage their recreation as well as destroying the scenic beauty of some of Britain's wildest areas.

The rate of expansion of salmon farming has now slowed as a result of market pressures and there is less danger of an imminent environmental disaster. But such concerns are valid, and demonstrate a clear need for informed and impartial planning and control if the industry is to prosper in harmony with environmental and other interests. Fish farmers themselves are taking a positive attitude, and have drawn up codes of practice after consultations with other interests.

There are many other kinds of fish and shellfish farming. Not all are as controversial as salmon farming: shellfish for example require no artificial food, on balance produce less waste; and if undertaken in suitable locations may represent an activity which is both economically and ecologically sound. The best salmon feed is a pellet whose major ingredient is fish meal, usually made from sand eel, herring, Norway pout, or capelin. Given the inefficiency of food conversion every kilogram of farmed salmon produced requires the processing into fish meal of several kilograms of wild fish. This is why farmed salmon can only be produced at considerable cost.

In many ways salmon farming is a technical and economic triumph, and has brought great economic and social benefits to some of the most isolated parts of Scotland. But it is also a supreme example of our short-sighted approach to natural resources. If we had managed the wild salmon fishery sensibly and kept our rivers clean, we would still have cheap wild salmon and unspoiled sea lochs. We would need only a net and local fishermen to bring home the salmon. By contrast, industrialised salmon farming is ecologically inefficient and capital intensive. It needs high technology hatcheries, storm-resistant cages, helicopter transport of young smolts and the pouring into the sea of massive quantities of food, of which a large proportion is wasted.

Perhaps the most painful irony of all is that it was pollution that finally destroyed the

43

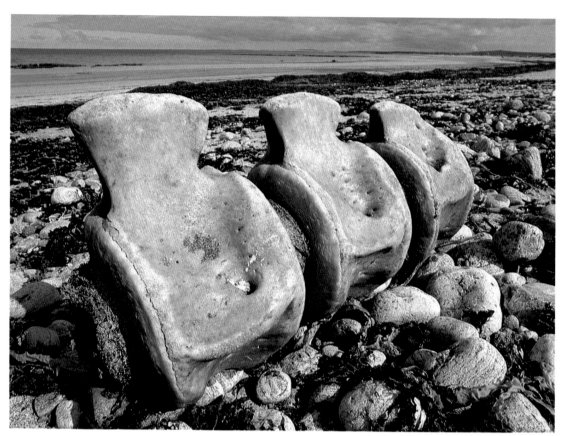

Sperm Whale vertebrae on the beach at South Uist.

salmon in many of our rivers; and now industrialised salmon farming is bringing pollution to our last unspoiled sea lochs. It is essential that we learn from the past, and minimise environmental impact at the same time as we rejuvenate communities in the Highlands and Islands.

THE HUNTING OF THE WHALES

People do not generally think of Scotland as a whaling nation, yet whale and walrus bones have been found at the earliest archeological sites in Scotland, where they were used to make tools and other artifacts. We do not know whether these bones come from whales that were stranded naturally, or driven ashore by hunters, as pilot whales were until recently in Shetland and the Outer Hebrides, and as they are to this day in the Faroe Islands.

Apart from the possibility of deliberate hunting, the accidental stranding of a large whale would have been a valuable windfall for early communities, and we have records of this from historic times. In the sixteenth century the Swedish historian Olaus Magnus recorded in his *Historia de Gentibus Septentrionalibus* (1555) the stranding of a whale; it yielded over 300 wagon loads of meat, blubber and bones for fuel and building, as well as enough hide and skin to make forty sets of clothes. For a small community in Scotland such a stranding represented a massive injection of wealth.

Between 1913 and 1926 an average of more than thirty whales per year were stranded on British coasts, and we can assume that before whale hunting reduced the stocks there would have been many more. The River Forth and other estuaries acted as natural traps for whales; they became confused among sand banks or were stranded by rapid changes in tidal levels. The bones of many great whales have been uncovered in the silted deposits of the Stirling Carse, well up the Forth estuary, showing that such accidents were indeed frequent.

Commercial whaling on a significant scale was first developed by the Basques in medieval times. At first they hunted along their own coasts in the Bay of Gascony, and later off Newfoundland where they also developed the white fishery. Apart from the driving of pilot whales in Shetland and the Hebrides, the Scots did not really join in until the opening up of the Arctic whale fishery of the seventeenth and eighteenth centuries, but they developed a major whaling industry in later times.

It was in 1758 that the first steam-powered whaling ship left Dundee for Arctic waters; it was steam (and later diesel-powered) ships, using explosive harpoons, which hunted many whale species to the verge of extinction. Scotland had its own whale fishery around the Outer Hebrides and Shetland until the 1950s. In the years 1903–29, a total of 5,848 fin whales, 395 blue whales, 100 right whales, 95 sperm whales, 70 humpbacks, and 26 northern bottle-nose whales were taken in Scottish waters; this was before the serious decline of the whale stocks began.

However, from the beginning, there was little attempt at stock conservation in the whaling industry. The Newfoundland whale fishery of the Basques was ruined by the end of the seventeenth century, and Spitsbergen was finished by 1720. As the century wore on, the

Seal at Sangobeg beach, Durness, Sutherland.

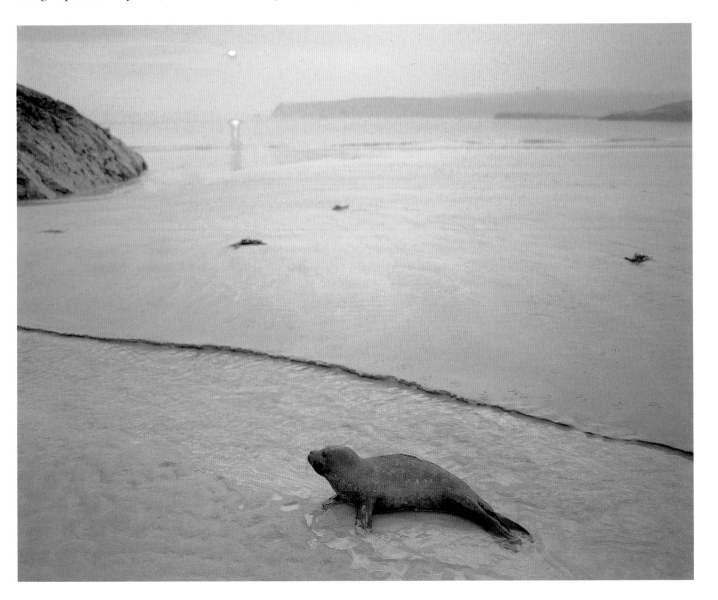

whalers ventured into more distant Arctic waters as more accessible stocks declined. By the middle of the nineteenth century the industry would have collapsed due to the depletion of the stocks had it not been for the new technology which allowed them to catch the faster, heavier 'rorqual' species, such as the blue whale. Soon these too had become scarce, and in 1892 four Scottish whalers headed south seeking new whaling grounds in the Antarctic to continue the plunder. These southern waters were hunted until the near extinction of many species in the 1950s and 1960s. Now, at last, some of the whale stocks are recovering, although it will be many years before they regain even a fraction of their former numbers.

MANAGING OUR MARINE RESOURCES

The story of fishing in Scotland has a thread running through it which begins with abundance and ends in scarcity. For, whether we look at the herring, the salmon, the cod, haddock or the great whales, the story is the same. We have taken and taken, with short-term profit always uppermost in mind, until there was nothing left to take. As highly efficient hunters, we are not unique. Indeed, humans are mere beginners when compared with even the most humble creatures in the sea, the plankton. The drift net, for example, was developed hundreds of millions of years ago by tiny planktonic *Foraminiferans*. The equivalent of long-lines with hooks can be found among *Siphonophores*, close relatives of the jellyfish. But, as deadly and calculating hunters, it is the squid and octopus, the cephalopods, who truly excel; in speed, disguise and ingenuity they make a mockery of man's blunderings and splashings after his prey.

In the natural world each evolution of the hunter has been matched by defensive adaptation by the prey, or the balance has been redressed by the emergence of a new predator to eat the hunter in turn. The result has been a natural balance between prey and predator. The technology of human hunting, however, has developed so rapidly that we have over-exploited the fish stocks, sometimes causing significant ecological shifts, and in some cases crashes. And we have almost exterminated some whale species.

Ironically it was the shoaling behaviour of the herring, helping them to avoid predators, that made them vulnerable to human hunters with nets. The herring's habit of following the zooplankton to the surface waters at night also made them easy prey for fishermen. The great size of the whale, which made it invulnerable to sharks, made it an easy target for the whalers. And the salmon, returning to fresh waters and migrating up the rivers *en masse* were so easy to trap that even medieval kings saw the need to protect them. Fortunately our seas are so productive, and the fish are so fertile and resilient, that although fishing may decimate stocks they will usually recover; the greatest losers in the overfishing game are always fishermen themselves. Man the industrial hunter-fisherman has become lethally efficient, but has still not learned to control his power for his own benefit. History teaches us two important lessons for fisheries management. Firstly, open access to fisheries encourages heavy capital investment in larger boats. This allows vessels to exploit many different fish stocks in widely spaced locations; this trend began as long ago as the seventeenth century when fishermen began to follow the herring. Secondly, heavy capital investment in boats and gear encourages overfishing. Various forms of restricted access, and a greater degree of local control over management offer the greatest hope in terms of encouraging smaller boats, increased ownership and responsibility on the part of fishermen, and more widely distributed benefits to coastal communities.

But there is some hope. The whalers did not quite exterminate the great whales, and these – the most vulnerable of creatures – are making a slow recovery. The herring, given their stunning fecundity, could recover fully in a few years if given the chance. The dangers to fish stocks from the human predator, although sometimes spectacular, are generally temporary; and although there are immense difficulties, there are at least some mechanisms for controlling and managing our fisheries. And the problems are clearly visible.

However, the microscopic world of the plankton, and the entire pyramid of life that depends upon it, is much more vulnerable to invisible chemical and nuclear pollution. We have already lost the dragonflies and salmon from many of our rivers through pollution by sewage, pesticides and industrial effluents. Much of this pollution eventually enters the sea, where it accumulates in sediments and becomes more concentrated as it passes up the food chains. Man, as the top predator, is likely to absorb the final cumulative dose of pesticides, chemicals or radioactivity.

We have little idea of the likely environmental impacts of all these substances, but they will generally affect the plankton in the first place. And although we understand virtually nothing about the processes governing the populations of these microscopic creatures, we do know that they are the basis for all the other life in the sea. They even play a vital part in controlling levels of atmospheric carbon dioxide, thereby regulating the so-called 'greenhouse effect'.

The sea is not an endless sink for all our wastes; it is a world of great beauty and complexity, made up of thousands of ecosystems which provide us with food, drinking water, aesthetic inspiration, and simple recreational pleasure. It has a profound influence on our climate and even helps control the temperature of our planet.
We abuse it at our peril.

Fishing Boat, Plockton.

Nymphaea Alba, white water-lily,
Glen Affric, West of Scotland

CHAPTER THREE

The Flowering of Scotland
Michael Scott

Michael Scott is a natural history writer and co-editor of SCENES *(Scottish Environment News). He is Scottish Officer of Plantlife, the wild plant charity, and serves on Scottish Natural Heritage's North Areas Board.*

When the glaciers retreated at the end of the last Ice Age, about 12,000 years ago, they left behind a slate wiped clean of plants and animals. At its peak the ice was up to 8,000 ft (2,400 m) thick, almost twice the height of Ben Nevis; so it is highly unlikely that any islands of rock projected above the ice to provide a refuge for any flowers, or even the most resilient of lichens.

As the climate warmed and the glaciers retreated, they left a landscape stripped of soil and covered in a debris of rocks ground by the ice into gravel or boulder clay. This material was rich in minerals, but lacked the humus essential for plant growth. Today these so-called 'primitive soils' are found only in the Arctic, although in Scotland some of the highest mountains and most windswept hills have small areas of similar material.

Throughout the height of the Ice Age the south of England had remained glacier-free and the plants that survived there were now poised to extend their range, following the glaciers as they retreated. Mosses, liverworts and lichens were the first plants to arrive in Scotland; as they died they rotted to form thin soils which enabled small herbs and shrubs, adapted to the arctic climate, to gain a foothold. Their remains in turn added further humus to the soil and, as soil accumulated and the climate warmed, less well adapted southern and lowland species were able to colonise.

These were often ranker-growing and smothered the delicate arctic plants. They were followed, in turn, by taller shrubs and trees which completed the process. Increasingly the arctic plants were pushed out into areas where high altitude or northern latitudes created a climate similar to southern England during the Ice Age.

Many of these Ice Age survivors are found in Scotland today, usually in the high mountains where the climate is severe and late snow cover allows only a brief growing season. Most of these species also survive today high in the mountains of central Europe, or in Greenland, Iceland and the far north of Scandinavia, justifying the name for these plants: arctic-alpines.

Today the widest variety of arctic-alpines occurs at sites where the mineral rich rocks are so friable (crumbly) that they readily erode to produce rich, basic soils, like the primitive soils the glaciers left behind. The only Scottish endemics (species peculiar to Scotland) are a few hawkweeds and other so-called 'micro-species' – closely related species distinguished by experts on the basis of very fine details. However, the precise mix of species in the Scottish hills is unique, with arctic plants almost at the south of their range and alpine flowers at unusually low altitudes. The resulting plant communities are therefore of international scientific interest, and merit the most careful conservation.

THE ARCTIC-ALPINES

Perhaps the most famous site in Scotland for its arctic-alpine flora is Ben Lawers, a National

Nature Reserve (see Chapter 16) largely owned by the National Trust for Scotland. At 3,984 ft (1,214 m), Ben Lawers is the highest mountain for many miles and thus has a particularly severe climate. This, combined with an extensive outcrop of a rich and friable rock called Lawers schist, creates precisely the conditions in which arctic-alpines can flourish.

One stretch of cliff in particular probably holds more species of arctic-alpines in a small area than anywhere else in Britain. Its rarities include alpine gentian which, although often less than an inch high, is as intense a gentian blue as any of its larger relatives. Also here we find alpine forget-me-not, a widespread plant in the true Alps found at only one other site in Britain. Beside this grows the so-called alpine fleabane, a relative of the daisy, with tight purple flowerheads. Despite its name it is not found in the Alps but only in the Arctic, and Ben Lawers may well be the only site in the world where it grows side-by-side with alpine forget-me-not.

Despite the fame of Ben Lawers, outcrops of rock similar to Lawers schist occur throughout the Breadalbane hills. Many of these, as far west as Ben Lui, are almost as rich as Lawers itself, although the schist generally occurs at rather lower altitudes, excluding some of the most strongly montane species. Ben Lui does have one notable plant, apparently missing from Ben Lawers. This is alpine bartsia, a handsome plant with dark purple flowers reminiscent of toadflax. Apart from this area of the western Breadalbanes, this species is only found by the upper stretches of the River Tees in northern England, yet it is common and widespread in both the Alps and the Arctic – another mystery of Scottish plant distribution.

Eastwards of Lawers essentially the same band of lime-rich rock outcrops at a number of other very important sites. Ben-y-Vrackie, near Pitlochry, has a limited area of crag with a diverse arctic-alpine flora, including alpine milk-vetch with its delicate pale purple pea-like flowers. Further east the crags in Glen Loch are one of only two sites for yellow oxytropis, another member of the pea family, with clusters

of flowers the colour of parchment suffused with yellow and purple.

Continuing eastwards two attractive mountain grasses, alpine foxtail and alpine cat's-tail, flourish in snow-fed runnels beneath the imposing domed summit of Glas Maol. On the east side of the summit, dramatic crags plunge down into Caenlochan Glen, another rich site sharing many of the characteristic species of Ben Lawers. One acidic bluff of rock here is home for blue sowthistle, a tall member of the daisy family. In the Alps and Arctic it is a woodland species, but here deforestation and

1. MOUNTAIN AVENS: A CLASSIC ARCTIC-ALPINE

Mountain avens (*Dryas octopetala*) is a low creeping shrub which hugs the ground to avoid the worst effects of the winter winds. The name of its genus, *Dryas*, honours the oak fairies, or dryads, and refers to the oak-like shape of its dark, deeply veined, evergreen leaves. Its showy white flowers are well over an inch across and have eight petals. They are pollinated by flies and bees which are attracted by nectar and partly by the warmth trapped inside the flowers, which follow the sun like miniature satellite dishes.

Mountain avens grows commonly throughout the Arctic, in the mountains of central Europe and in the Rocky Mountains of the USA. In Britain it grows only where the severe climate excludes other ranker-growing species. In gardens it will survive only if competing species are removed by weeding.

It is found mostly in lime-rich mountain areas in the north and west Highlands. It grows at altitudes of up to 3,400 ft (1,000 m) in the Cairngorms, but in the far north it can come down almost to sea level, because the climate there is relatively arctic, even at low altitudes.

grazing by sheep and red deer have confined it to inaccessible mountain rock ledges, where Scottish Natural Heritage is now working to ensure its survival.

In the north, many of the arctic-alpines creep lower down the mountain slopes. On Skye the richest montane flora is found on limestone west of Broadford, or on the slumped crags and pinnacles of the Trotternish ridge, usually below 1,000 ft (300 m). At greater heights, one corrie in the Cuillin hills is the only British site for alpine rock-cress, otherwise widespread in both the Alps and the Arctic. The Invernaver National Nature Reserve, near Bettyhill on the north coast, has a rich montane flora almost at sea level, including purple oxytropis, while mountain avens (Box 1) forms extensive heathland at low altitude near Durness.

Shetland has one particularly remarkable site: a low rounded hill on Unst called the Keen of Hamar, where the exposed climate and a severe soil create an unusual flora including Shetland mouse-ear, a species unique to this small area.

The granite mountains of the eastern Highlands, centred on the Cairngorms, produce poor, acid soils which support far fewer species. Plants flourishing in this harsh habitat include trailing azalea (recognised by its delicate pink flowers and narrow, leathery leaves) and dwarf willow, a miniature tree that grows to only an inch or two in height.

The high tops of the Cairngorms have the most arctic climate in Britain, with snow patches lasting through many summers on some north-facing corries. Several particularly demanding species are restricted to these areas, including arctic chickweed, Highland saxifrage and hare's-foot sedge, named after the appearance of its oval grey flowerheads.

Many other upland sites around Scotland, although less rich, support arctic-alpine species, from the higher hills of Dumfries and Galloway to many areas around the Highlands and Islands. Alpine lady's-mantle is often a useful indicator of rich sites, easily recognisable by its frothy yellow flowerheads and fingered leaves edged with silver hairs. The commoner

mountain saxifrages may also occur here: purple saxifrage is the only one with purple flowers, which it produces soon after the snow has gone in March and April; starry saxifrage, with starry white flowers, often grows in mossy flushes where underwater springs enrich the soil; while yellow mountain saxifrage, which has yellow flowers and stems packed with narrow leaves, often grows beside mountain streams.

Many other species grace our Scottish mountains and reward the botanical hill walker. The best introduction to these is *Mountain Flowers*, by John Raven and Max Walters (1956). This describes a heady period in the early 1950s when three new mountain flowers were discovered in Scotland: diapensia in Inverness-shire (Box 2); Iceland purslane, a tiny

2. DIAPENSIA: AN ICE AGE RELICT

In 1951 a birdwatcher discovered an unfamiliar plant flowering on a windswept shoulder in the hills near Glenfinnan. Expert botanists identified it as *Diapensia lapponica*, a plant new to Scotland, in a family never before found in Britain.

Diapensia is a low cushion-plant related to heathers. It has narrow leathery leaves and creamy-white bell-shaped flowers. It normally flowers in May, although this can be delayed by bad spring weather. It is found throughout the Arctic but is restricted in Scotland to an acre or so of ice-shattered rock on a rather dull hillside. It was probably left behind there as the glaciers retreated, although the possibility of accidental or deliberate introduction by man cannot be ruled out. It is a mystery why it does not grow anywhere else in Scotland, but perhaps other colonies await discovery elsewhere in the Scottish hills.

Rowan sapling at Creag Meagaidh National Nature Reserve.

Scots pines and heather, RSPB reserve, Abernethy forest.

3. THE PINE OF SCOTLAND

An ancient granny pine tree is as potent a symbol of Scottish history as any historic castle. Our oldest pines, over 500 years old, would have been mature trees when wolves still roamed the Highlands.

Scots pine (*Pinus sylvestris*) is easily recognisable by the reddish brown upper trunk, where the bark has peeled off to reveal the heartwood, which is sold commercially as 'red deal'. A mature straight tree can be up to 160 ft (49 m) tall, and it would take five people to circle its trunk with linked arms.

The paired needles of Scots pine are bluish and about an inch long. In springtime, oval yellowish clusters of male flowers produce abundant pollen which is carried by the wind to the female flowers, growing in crimson tufts at the tip of new shoots. These develop by the following summer into soft green cones which become hard and woody, splitting to release the seeds in the third summer.

'Scots pine' is perhaps an inappropriate name for the most widely distributed conifer in the world: it is found from the Sierra Nevada of Spain to north of the Arctic Circle in Scandinavia, and east to the Pacific coast of the USSR.

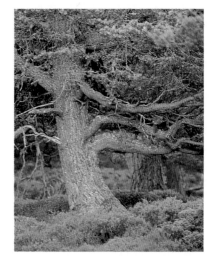

relative of docks, on Skye; and Norwegian mugwort, looking like a withered daisy, on the hills of Skye and Wester Ross. While the decades since have been less productive, those remarkable finds suggest that more species may await discovery by the dedicated botanist in the Scottish hills.

THE FORESTS OF CALEDON

About 9,000 years ago, as the climate continued to warm, trees began to colonise Scotland, finally swamping the arctic-alpine plants of the lowlands. The woodland spread gradually, with temporary retreats in periods when the climate became colder.

The first tree to arrive after the ice melted was birch, which is also the tree growing furthest north in the arctic taiga forest today. The birch spread rapidly, forming low patchy woodland often mixed with juniper and willow. It was succeeded in turn by Scots pine, which arrived in Wester Ross about 8,000 years ago and spread south-eastwards from there.

Then, as the climate reached its warmest about 7,000 years ago, oak began to spread from the south to form extensive forests in most of southern Scotland and the west Highlands. Ash, elm and hazel grew among the oak, with birch, rowan and holly where the soil was poorer. Ash established locally in limestone areas, while alder grew in the wetter areas and beside rivers. But oak was not suited to all of Scotland. Pine remained the dominant tree over much of the central and eastern Highlands while, north of this, birch woodland persisted. Most of the far north of Caithness and Sutherland was never fully covered by trees but remained as open moorland, patterned with peat-stained bog pools known as dubh lochans – an area now celebrated as the Flow Country (see Chapter 5).

The loss of tree cover from most of the rest of Scotland occurred partly as a result of human activity and partly through natural processes. About 4,000 years ago a colder oceanic climate developed, bringing stronger winds and increased rainfall.

In many northern and western areas the climate became so wet that the bog mosses expanded beyond their wet hollows to form widespread blanket bogs, swamping and killing many trees that grew there. These bogs eventually turned to peat, and the preserved

4. CORNCOCKLE: A VANISHING CORNFIELD FLOWER

Corncockle (*Agrostemma githago*) was a common weed of arable crops in lowland Scotland during the late nineteenth century. However by 1983 the last remaining Scottish site where it was found was in Moray; this decline was caused by the use of cleaner seed corn early this century and through the increased use of herbicides.

Corncockle was well adapted as a cornfield weed. It thrived in the same soil as cereal crops, and had fruits that matured around harvest time, and its seeds were so similar to grain in size and weight that they could not be separated in the harvest. In 1920 almost 2 per cent of oat crops were contaminated by corncockle seeds which gave flour a bitter taste and were poisonous in quantity.

There were obvious benefits in eradicating the plant from cornfields, although in the process we lost an attractive plant. A relative of garden pinks, it has showy pink flowers up to two inches (5 cm) in diameter and a tall stem with greyish, hairy, spear-shaped leaves.

It has apparently disappeared from the roadside verge on which it grew in Moray, but is now making a comeback elsewhere in Scotland. Increasingly, it is planted in wildflower gardens, both for its beauty and to attract butterflies.

remains of so-called bog oaks and pines are still unearthed from the peat today. Even where trees survived, the wet soil and strong winds killed any seedlings and, without young trees, the woods eventually died out.

Shortly after this change in climate the first signs of man's farming activity appeared on the landscape (see Chapter 7) as our ancestors cut down large areas of forest for land on which to grow their crops. In the lowlands, deforestation began in the Bronze Age, about 3,000 years ago, but even in northern Skye and Sutherland the dominant birch and hazel woodland began to disappear about 2,500 years ago. This has been linked to Iron Age clearances for agriculture and charcoal production.

Nevertheless by the time the Romans arrived, many parts of Scotland were still forested; their Latin name for the country, 'Caledonia', means 'wooded heights'. By about AD 400, however, woodlands were being felled across most of Scotland. By the sixteenth century almost all the forests of the central Lowlands had gone and the western oakwoods were much reduced.

The pinewoods of the eastern and central Highlands (see Box 3) survived rather longer, because of their remoteness. However, the introduction of sheep farming in the early eighteenth century accelerated their decline; the grazing of sheep and burning of undergrowth killed all young trees until eventually the wood died out.

The development of grouse moors in Victorian times further hastened this process. Modern grouse moors, dominated by ling heather, originated as the dwarf shrub understorey of pinewoods. Such moors today are thus a totally artificial landscape, created by tree-felling and maintained by regular burning. In theory, pine trees could re-establish if the burning stopped, but in most areas there are no mature trees left to provide seed, and red deer browse off any seedlings that do sprout.

The timber demands of the Napoleonic wars and two world wars brought the final demise of our extensive native woodlands, so that today only tiny fragments remain of the old woods of Caledon; and even these are threatened by the fast expanding red deer population.

TODAY'S WOODLANDS

The area of relatively natural pine woodland left in the Highlands today is less than 42 square miles (108 sq km). Fortunately the best remnant woods are protected either as nature reserves or as Sites of Special Scientific Interest (see Chapter 16). The largest area under active conservation management is the Abernethy reserve owned by the Royal Society for the Protection of Birds, with a total area of almost 50 square miles (130 sq km), although by no means all of this is native pine forest.

Other pinewood remnants include the Black Wood of Rannoch on the south shore of Loch Rannoch; an area beside Loch Maree in the Beinn Eighe National Nature Reserve; parts of Rothiemurchus in Speyside, Mar Lodge (now owned by the National Trust for Scotland), Glen Tanar near Braemar, and Glen Affric west of Drumnadrochit.

Many pinewood remnants gain extra appeal from the gnarled multi-trunked trees growing there – a natural variety of Scots pine called *condensata*. In a truly pristine wood they would be intermixed with other forms with straight, true trunks; but in most forests the straight trees have been selectively felled over the last three centuries for their high timber value. The pines we romantically admire as natural woodland may often be merely the rejects of forest harvesting.

The remnant pinewoods are characterised by pine trees of widely varying age, but also have birch, juniper and willow trees and a distinctive ground flora. Many of these typical flowers and mosses are soon lost if a wood is felled or heavily managed, and their presence is a strong sign of undisturbed woodland. They include creeping lady's-tresses orchid, and four species of wintergreen with oval glossy leaves and spikes of creamy-white flowers. Some of these pinewood plants also occur in birchwoods which, although often over-looked, were also an important component of the Old Caledonian Forest.

Semi-natural oak woodland is almost as rare as pine, with isolated examples in Kirkcudbrightshire, in the more inaccessible parts of the Upper Clyde Valley, on islands in Loch Lomond, and most notably around Loch Sunart in Ardnamurchan and Loch Sween in Kintyre.

Although we label them 'oak' woodland, such woods include a mixture of other trees and shrubs. Their ground flora is less characteristic than that of pinewoods, and many of the commoner species will also grow in plantations. Common species include dog's mercury, primrose, wood anemone, lesser celandine, dog violet, wild hyacinth (the bluebell of England), early purple orchid, bugle, wild garlic, wood cranesbill, wild strawberry, foxglove, and blaeberry (the Scots name for bilberry), together producing a glorious display in spring and early summer.

Many ferns also grow in these woods. Hay-scented buckler-fern is restricted to the far west, while filmy-ferns are only found in damp and shady, frost-free pockets of the same area. But perhaps the most important feature of these western oakwoods is the diverse and abundant growth of mosses, liverworts and lichens that grow on the trunks and branches of the trees, including several species unique to Scotland.

Although afforestation has been extensive in the Border and Highland hills since the Second World War, these plantations are a poor substitute botanically for the native woods. There are few places more dark and sterile than the floor of a thickly planted Sitka spruce forest. Even plantations of native Scots pine or broadleaved trees have a less varied flora than natural woods, because dense even-aged planting leaves little space for other herbaceous species to move in, and the inevitable management work disturbs and restricts the flora.

Primroses and bluebells in the woods of Kinloch Castle, Isle of Rum.

Poppies among the crops near Drem, East Lothian.

PLANTS AND FARMING

Early farming actually benefited a few wild flowering plants. Some plants set seed at the same time as the grain crops, and had seeds of similar size and weight; such seeds could not easily be separated from the harvested grain, and were therefore sown with the following year's seed crop. Cornflower (a beautiful blue-flowered relative of scabious), corncockle (Box 4) and bindweeds flourished in this way, but today's cleaner seed corn and herbicides have all but eliminated them from our fields.

Herbicides also poisoned other cornfield weeds that had adapted to the regular disturbance of ploughing. Poppies and the yellow daisy-flowers of corn marigold both declined dramatically under the chemical farming regime, as did redshank (a straggly relative of dockens), bugloss (an attractive plant with blue flowers and densely hairy foliage) and fumitories, which scramble over the surrounding vegetation with weak stems and have attractive, tubular, pink flowers tipped with crimson. These are common today only in the crofting areas of the north-west and the machair farmland of the Western Isles, where the intensive use of chemicals is shunned (see Chapter 5).

The seeds of many of these species can survive for decades in the soil and occasionally reappear when, for example, farmland is ploughed and abandoned prior to construction work. Suddenly an unexpected blaze of colour will appear as the long-dormant seeds burst into flower.

Roadside banks also serve as a last refuge for many of these weed species. Scrub and coarse grasses must of course be kept down by occasional cutting, but if the mowing is delayed until late summer when the plants have set seed, this can help spread the seeds and maintain a wide variety of wildflowers.

One Scottish habitat that has disappeared almost completely is wet meadowland. Once, these were common in marshes and along riverbanks, but drainage and farm improvements have converted most of them to drier, less attractive, grassy swards.

Wet meadows were the home of plants such as globeflower (a relative of buttercups with shining yellow, globular flowers); wood cranesbill (with showy purple flowers); and melancholy thistle (perhaps the true thistle of Scotland), which has lance-shaped leaves, white felted on their underside and solitary swollen purple flowers. Today these survive only in the few remaining fragments of meadowland; elsewhere they also grow on mountain ledges well beyond the reach of deer and sheep.

But human activity has also enhanced our flora, for better or for worse, by introducing a wide variety of alien species either deliberately or accidentally. Many of our commonest trees, for instance, are introductions – not just the plantation conifers such as Sitka spruce (from western North America), European larch and Norway spruce (from the European mainland), but also common species such as sycamore (introduced in the fifteenth or sixteenth century).

While these were deliberately planted, others arrived accidentally as seeds attached to sheep or their wool, which was imported as 'shoddy' for fertilising fields. Early this century Tweeddale was particularly famous for its short-lived flora of invaders from the southern hemisphere, and today seaports are the entry point for other invaders which rarely survive in our climate for long.

Most aliens, however, originated as garden escapes. Some of these can have a harmful effect by swamping native vegetation. Giant hogweed (Box 5), Himalayan and giant knotweed are particularly aggressive invaders. However, other alien plants have spread widely with little detrimental effect. Slender speedwell, with pale-blue flowers on thread-like stalks, is a native of the Caucasus but is now probably Scotland's commonest speedwell, while New Zealand willowherb, a low mat-forming plant with delicate pink flowers, was first recorded as a garden weed in 1904 and has already spread to the Outer Hebrides and Orkney.

THE COAST: A LAST WILD REFUGE

Seen in the context of the changes wrought by man in the landscape, the coast acquires a considerable importance as a natural habitat. This is especially so in Scotland. With the fiord-like sea lochs of the west coast and the myriad islands of the north and west, Scotland's coast-line is estimated at more than 6,000 miles (10,000 km) in all, 65 per cent of the total UK coast.

Sea-washed coasts are a severe habitat for plant life. Paradoxically the main difficulty is often a shortage of fresh water. Rain drains quickly from rocky shores and sand, while tidal floods exclude fresh water from salt-marshes for long periods. Sea water itself is highly damaging to most plant life because it upsets the balance of salts inside and outside the cell, which is crucial to the process by which plants absorb water. Many coastal plants are therefore highly adapted to cope with this harsh environment. On exposed windy coastlines, where the soil is thin and plants are regularly doused with salt spray, trees have never established and the vegetation is similar to that found on the mountain tops. Thrift, whose tufts of pink flowers are such an attractive feature of rocky coasts in May, is also widespread on mountain tops, growing, for example, above 4,000 ft (1,200 m) on Ben Nevis.

5. GIANT HOGWEED: AN ALIEN INVADER

Giant hogweed (*Heracleum mantegazzianum*) is one of the most impressive plants in the Scottish landscape, as its statistics show: it grows up to 12ft (3.6m) tall, with hollow stems 4 inches (10cm) in diameter, and huge rhubarb-like leaves over 3ft (1m) across. A member of the carrot family, it has tiny white flowers arranged in large umbrella-shaped heads.

Giant hogweed was introduced into British gardens from south-western Asia around 1893. From about 1930 it began to spread outside gardens and today it is common in most of Scotland.

Its typical habitats (the banks of rivers and railways) relate to its methods of dispersal. Its seeds are spread by the wind, and can travel 30 ft (9m) in strong winds before they settle and germinate; the slipstream of trains therefore helps spread them along railway banks. The seeds can also float in water for up to three days, allowing them to colonise riverbanks up to 240 miles (380km) away.

Giant hogweed has a bad reputation because its sap produces painful blisters on contact with the skin in bright sunshine. Merely brushing against the plant can cause blisters, by breaking the fine stem hairs and releasing the sap. Calamine lotion will soothe these uncomfortable symptoms but it is best not to touch the plant without gloves.

Perhaps even more harmful is the way in which giant hogweed swamps native vegetation, producing impenetrable jungles in some parts of Scotland. Efforts are being made to control its spread in most regions, but this can only be achieved by the repeated use of herbicides – a costly and time-consuming business.

Silverweed has adapted to life on the shifting sands.

Sea thrift at Elgol, Loch Scavaig, Isle of Skye.

Scots primrose in Sutherland.

6. SCOTS PRIMROSE: A SYMBOL IN DECLINE

The Scots primrose (*Primula scotica*) is a very special Scottish plant, found on the exposed clifftop turf of Orkney, Caithness and Sutherland. Although closely related to the Norwegian *Primula scandinavica*, it is now accepted as a unique species found nowhere else in the world – a truly Scottish endemic.

Usually it is little more than one inch (2.5 cm) tall, although it can reach four times this size. Its leaves are yellow-green above and mealy-white underneath, and hug the ground in a tight rosette for protection against gales. Its rich pink flowers appear in May and June, often with a second limited flowering in July and August. The flowers are half an inch (1 cm) across, with five notched petals united into a short tube, and a bright yellow 'eye' at the mouth of the tube to guide pollinating insects to the nectar at its base.

In the last century the Scots primrose declined dramatically as a result of agricultural 'improvement' of its clifftop habitat; in Orkney, for example, half of the thirty sites known last century have been destroyed. Recent research suggests that climate may also be implicated in this decline, with plants only flourishing in years with mild winters and infrequent summer gales. With the current trend towards colder winters in the north, this steady decline seems likely to continue.

Practical conservation can help the Scots primrose, and several colonies are protected within nature reserves or Sites of Special Scientific Interest. But the best safeguard for Scotland's only endemic flower would be for more people to appreciate the beauty of this gem of the cliff tops.

Similarly roseroot, a yellow-flowered relative of the stonecrops, which grows on rich ledges high in the mountains, is also found on sea cliffs around Scotland. It has thick fleshy leaves with a bluish waxy coating, which protects it both from icy mountain winds and coastal spray. Sea campion, common scurvy-grass, buck's-horn plantain, sea-spurrey, and sea-lavender are all widely distributed on sea cliffs, as are many lichens and ferns.

As its name suggests, Scots lovage is confined mostly to rocky Scottish coasts, although it just gets into England on Lindisfarne, and is also found elsewhere in north-west Europe. A member of the carrot family, it has spreading heads of white flowers and glossy, bright-green leaves.

Although sea cliffs themselves are largely untouched by human influence, farms increasingly encroach to their very edge. Maritime heathland, which once formed the landward margin of many cliffs, survives extensively along the north coast and on Shetland and Orkney, but even there it has shown a marked decline in recent years.

This heathland is dominated by various heathers, including crowberry, which has shining green needle-like leaves and glossy black berries. More open areas amongst the heath often produce glorious displays of spring squill, like a miniature blue hyacinth, together with the yellow pea-flowers of bird's-foot trefoil and kidney vetch, and carpets of thyme. The Scots primrose (Box 6) is found in open grassy areas on the clifftops of Orkney and Caithness.

More sheltered clifftops, especially on the east coast, are often dominated by gorse (known as whin in Scotland), which shelters woodland species such as wild hyacinth, red campion and lesser celandine. In Shetland the campion has particularly deep-red flowers, a stronger stem and larger seeds – useful adaptations to the severe northern climate.

Salt-marshes usually form in sheltered estuaries where mud accumulates; their typical plants are specially adapted to cope with flooding by sea water at the highest tides. The outer edge of salt-marshes is often fringed with glasswort, whose spiky cactus-like form is adapted for storing water. Inland of this zone we find sea aster (a relative of garden Michaelmas daisies), sea lavender, sea plantain, sea purslane and sea arrow-grass, along with thrift, scurvy-grass and a variety of true grasses. Salt-marshes are highly susceptible to human disturbance. Many have been damaged by grazing sheep or cattle, while others have been 'reclaimed' – planners still tend to see salt-marshes only as 'wasteland' that is ripe for development.

A remarkable plant found beyond the salt-marsh is eelgrass whose long leaves wave, snake-like, in the tide. It is the only truly marine flowering plant and forms extensive beds on muddy shores well below the low tide mark. Known as widgeon-grass in parts of Scotland, its seeds are food for widgeon and other duck. It declined dramatically in the late 1930s as a result of wartime pollution, combined perhaps with endemic disease. It now seems to be recovering, although it has yet to recolonise some former Scottish sites.

Scotland boasts some superb sand-dune systems, including Torrs Warren in Wigtownshire, Culbin in Moray, Tentsmuir in Fife, St Cyrus in Kincardineshire and the Sands of Forvie in Aberdeenshire, the last three of which are National Nature Reserves. These include few exclusively Scottish plants, although they are excellent examples of the succession by which a series of plants progressively stabilises the sand. St Cyrus is notable for several species which are adapted to milder climates and which reach their northern limit there, including clustered bellflower and wild liquorice.

Sand dunes, too, are often damaged by human activities. Recreational use often destroys their growing edge and opens up bare areas of sand which are then extended by wind action, while 'poaching' by grazing animals can have similar effects. In many parts of the east coast this erosion has been partly halted by planting sea buckthorn, a native of more southerly coasts, with some impact on the local vegetation.

Bogbean is common among the lochans of the Western Isles.

Perhaps the truly unique Scottish habitat is the machair of the western shores of the Outer Hebrides (see also Chapter 9, Box 1). Machair consists of short grassland enriched by shell-sand blown in from the sea by the prevailing winds, and kept open by traditional crofting agriculture. Each year the crofter turns over patches of machair so that the surface vegetation adds humus to the thin sandy soil allowing barley or potatoes to be grown. The soil is further enriched by the spreading of seaweed, which fertilises it and adds 'body' in a way no chemical could. However, the harvesting of a single crop scours the nutrients from this tenuous soil so that it has to be left fallow for several years to be refertilised by the natural vegetation. These fallow areas produce vast swathes of colourful wildflowers which are of enormous conservation value; but their survival depends upon the maintenance of the

Yellow Flag Iris survives on the croft lands.

traditional system of crofting agriculture.

The machair has no rare plants but produces some superb massed displays of flowers – an echo of the flowers that once brightened farm landscapes throughout Britain. Each piece of machair has its own character, but the commonest colours are the yellows of lady's bedstraw, bird's-foot trefoil, kidney vetch, yellow rattle and lesser meadow-rue, the blue of Scots bluebell (harebell), the red of clover, the purple of tufted vetch and the whites of yarrow and ox-eye daisy or gowans.

Around the edges of machair fields, poppies, bugloss, fumitory, sun spurge and corn marigold add a further blaze of colour while, inland, the wet machair supports yellow flag iris, red bartsia, eyebright and masses of ragged robin. This wet machair is also the habitat for one of the few machair specialities: the Hebridean subspecies of early marsh-orchid, recognised by its more deeply blotched purple flowers. The resulting explosion of flowers produces one of the finest botanical displays in Britain and ensures the machair international recognition as a unique plant habitat.

THE FLORA OF THE FUTURE

With large areas of semi-natural vegetation still remaining in Scotland, the threat to individual species is far less severe than in England, although the damage to plant habitats and communities is just as great. Of fifty-eight rare Scottish species listed in *The British Red Data Book: Vascular Plants*, most are threatened by the destruction of their habitat rather than individual pressures, although there are exceptions.

One of the rarest species, alpine coltsfoot, is confined to a single ledge in the Grampian mountains where it was discovered in 1814. Although it is abundant in the Alps there are scarcely two dozen plants in Scotland, and its origins remain mysterious. But its rarity has attracted large numbers of visitors to the site, causing erosion and threatening a landslide that could destroy the entire colony.

The network of protected sites across Scotland has helped preserve the best areas of vegetation, although many are still inadequately managed. The biggest problem remains heavy grazing by sheep and deer. Recent European Union measures have helped reduce the damaging densities of hill sheep, and there is a growing realisation of the need to control red deer numbers (see Chapter 4). Their population exploded from 155,000 in 1960 to around 300,000 in 1989, partly because estates, while shooting many stags, failed to cull sufficient hinds. The Deer Commission of Scotland has a new duty to protect the natural heritage, and deer management groups are starting to tackle the 'deer problem'.

The important role of farming and crofting in maintaining a diverse landscape is being recognised through support schemes to assist environmentally friendly farming. The new commitment to 'biodiversity' has helped forge new partnerships between government bodies, voluntary conservation organisations, fishermen, farmers and landowners to tackle the loss of species and habitats. Yet there is still a tendency to regard Scotland as underdeveloped and to impose inappropriate developments on the landscape, rather than building on the natural capital of the environment.

Plants remain a potent symbol for the future. Many people enjoy the colours of a wild flower garden or a meadow in full bloom, and it is heartening to see families with rucksacks and field guides enjoying the countryside. The tourist potential of our wild flowers is still largely unexploited, although far more people go to the Highlands in summer to enjoy the natural environment than go there in winter to ski.

If people can only be helped to understand the beauties of a wet meadow or the machair, the natural rock garden of a mountain cliff, the pattern of plants on a rocky shore or the intricate community of a native woodland, then the real value of these habitats will be recognised, and the future of Scotland's flora could be truly secure.

*Wildflowers of the Machair on croft
at Shader, Barvas, Isle of Lewis.*

Mountain hare in winter camouflage.

CHAPTER FOUR

The World of Mammals
Andrew Kitchener

In this chapter, Dr Andrew Kitchener, Curator of Birds and Mammals at the Royal Museum of Scotland, tells the story of how Scotland's wildlife has changed radically over the last 10,000 years.

More than 12,000 years ago, the eternal winter of the last Ice Age finally began to end. Revealed for the first time was a scarred and desolate landscape of mountains smoothed by moving ice, and valleys chiselled out by glaciers.

Only the south was free from the ice cap at any time during the last Ice Age, and even here on the permanently frozen tundra few mammals could have survived except possibly the polar bear, arctic fox, musk ox and reindeer – the kind of mammals we find in the Arctic today.

For a brief 1,000 years a warmer climate prevailed, and it was during this period that sedges, grasses and willows and, later, birch scrub began to green the landscape, encouraging the arrival of land animals such as collared lemmings, mountain hares and giant deer (Box 1), and birds such as snowy owls and ptarmigan.

But the Ice Age had not quite relaxed its icy grasp. Suddenly the whole of northern Europe was once again plunged into a new winter that lasted for more than a thousand years. This final freeze saw the extinction of the giant deer ('Irish elk') in the British Isles, and drove the rest of the fauna south into what is now England and across the dry North Sea to continental Europe. An ice cap spread over the western Highlands as far south as Loch Lomond, thereby earning it the name of the 'Loch Lomond Readvance' (see Chapter 1).

With the final end of the Ice Age the climate warmed rapidly and the sea level rose as the melting ice drained to the coastal waters. The last Ice Age had caused a drop in sea level of about 80 metres (260ft) leaving much of the English Channel and North Sea as dry land, so that the British Isles were an extension of the European continent. Now that the sea level was rising once more, those animals which migrate

1. THE GIANT DEER

Popularly known as the Irish elk, the giant deer (*Megaloceros giganteus*) was neither exclusively Irish nor related to the elk or moose of mainland Europe. Ranging from Ireland to Siberia it was dependent on a unique and vanished wildlife habitat known as the 'mammoth steppe'. Changes in climate at the end of the last Ice Age led to the disappearance of the mammoth steppe, and with it went one of the largest deer the world has ever seen.

The giant deer is famous for its huge, spade-like antlers, which are similar in shape to those of the fallow deer, its closest probable relative. Until recently these enormous bony structures were thought to have been used only for display purposes, designed to intimidate rival stags and attract females during the breeding season or the 'rut', as it is known; but a mechanical analysis of the antlers has shown that they are superbly designed for actual fighting: the giant deer was indeed a fighter, just like other deer.

Artist's Impression of Giant Deer fighting.

Below: The northern lynx disappeared as the forests were cleared.

The Mongolian (Przewalski's) Wild Horse at the Highland Wildlife Park, Kingussie.

2. THE REINDEER

There has been much argument about when the reindeer became extinct as a wild animal in Scotland. In the thirteenth-century Icelandic *Orkneyinga Saga*, an account of the Norse earls of Orkney, there is a reference to reindeer-hunting on the mainland of Scotland in the eleventh century; but it is now believed that the author confused reindeer with the native red deer. Recently, reindeer bones found in the Inchnadamph caves of Sutherland have been radiocarbon-dated; the results suggest that Scotland's last-known reindeer died more than 8,300 years ago.

There were some unsuccessful attempts to reintroduce reindeer in the eighteenth century, at Dunkeld and on Orkney. Two centuries later, in the early 1950s, a small herd of domesticated reindeer from Swedish Lapland was successfully established at Rothiemurchus in the Cairngorms. The semi-domesticated herd now numbers about a hundred and is maintained as an attraction for the tourists: although they could survive in the wild without much difficulty, they can hardly be classified as part of Scotland's wildlife as yet.

overland had limited time to recolonise Britain. Many animals from southern Europe simply did not reach Britain before it became an island again. Consequently, although Britain's animal wildlife is sometimes described as being impoverished or 'depauperate', it should really be called 'incomplete'.

The new warm phase heralded the first in a series of changing climax vegetations which in turn led to subtle changes in the animals that depended on them. The return of the birch saw the re-arrival of the reindeer (Box 2) and the mountain hare; but as the climate warmed further and the vegetation changed, conditions became unsuitable for the reindeer and it became extinct in Scotland more than 8,000 years ago.

The mountain hare, which turns white in winter, became restricted to the Highlands; it is still relatively common on heather moorland, particularly in northeast Scotland, but is also found on many of the Western Isles and in the Borders, where it was deliberately introduced in the nineteenth century. The warming of the weather must have been the main reason for its retreat into the higher mountain areas. The birch forests were being gradually replaced by Scots pine and hazels as temperatures continued to rise.

Another factor in the retreat of the mountain hare may have been competition from a new arrival, the brown hare, which probably became established naturally in Britain at the beginning of the warm phase when there was more open ground. However, if the brown hare did reach Britain then, it may have died out as the forests thickened and spread; it is thought to have been re-established by the Romans, some 7,000 years later, and is now widespread in southern Scotland as well as in the eastern half of the country.

Another animal whose distribution was clearly upset by the intervention of the last Ice Age is the weasel, a predator which is found nearly everywhere on mainland Scotland but on

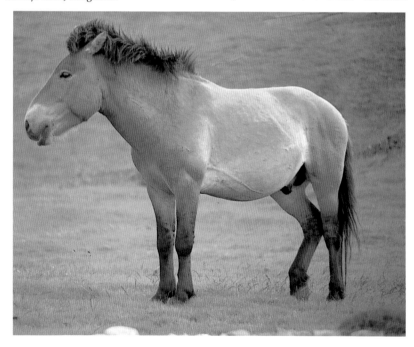

very few of the islands. In the north of Europe and in Asia the weasel changes its coat to white in winter; but, oddly enough, British weasels very rarely change colour, even in the colder climate of Scotland where they might be expected to do so. This is because our weasels are descended from animals from farther south in Europe where weasels never undergo a seasonal change of colour. The weasels from eastern Europe, which do change colour, could not recolonise Britain because of the barrier of the North Sea.

By 9,000 years ago, Britain's present-day mammals were all established: foxes, badgers, otters, stoats, weasels, wildcats, roe deer, red deer, hedgehogs, shrews, wood mice and voles were spreading through Britain's forests and moving northwards to Scotland. But there were also larger mammals which do not survive in Scotland today, including the lynx, the wild horse, the reindeer, the moose (elk), the wild ox (known as the aurochs or urus), the brown bear, the beaver, the wild boar and the wolf.

Humans also recolonised this virgin land after being driven out by the great freeze. Middle Stone Age (Mesolithic) hunters brought their dogs with them as they exploited the rich animal and plant life. They began to colonise Scotland from southern Britain more than 9,000 years ago. Less than 3 thousand years later the New Stone Age (Neolithic) farmers and their domestic livestock had at last reached Scotland from southern Europe (see Chapter 7). Until this period the animals and plants of Britain had been influenced almost entirely by natural events; but as soon as farming people arrived, the fate of Scotland's wildlife lay in the hands of our own species.

People's earliest impact on the environment was the clearance of forests for farmland to grow crops and provide grazing for livestock. The destruction of forests, combined with an increase in hunting, led to the early extinction of animals which depended most on woodland habitat; these included the lynx, the wild horse and the moose. The wild ox, an enormous creature that stood up to 6 ft (1.8 m) at the shoulder, survived to the Iron Age, just before

the Romans arrived; the last few animals in Scotland may have disappeared through inter-breeding with their domestic cousins from southern Europe. The wild horse may have suffered a similar fate, but much earlier.

THE FIRST STOWAWAYS

The Neolithic farmers did not just bring their livestock; they also accidentally added to the British fauna. The first of these stowaways were the ancestors of the common vole (not to be confused with the field vole) and the wood mouse on Orkney. In their isolation, Orkney voles had already evolved much larger bodies than the common voles of Europe by about 4,500 years ago. But why did they grow so much larger? One possible explanation is that, in the absence of ground-living predators, the right conditions were created for the natural selection of bigger voles that did not have to escape from anything by bolting into small cracks or holes in the ground. A further reason may simply be that, in order to survive in the open windswept islands of Orkney, voles need to be of a more robust build, and larger voles have evolved as a result.

But voles were by no means the only stowaways to reach our shores. Another early stowaway was the house mouse which, far from

The black rat brought bubonic plague to Britain in the fourteenth century.

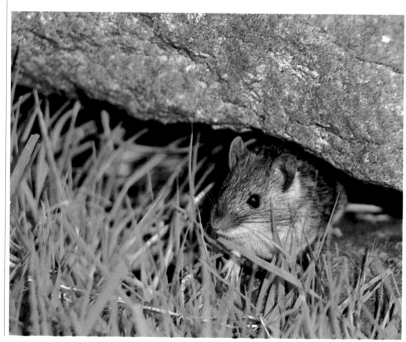

The St Kilda wood mouse.

being isolated on an island has spread throughout the length and breadth of the land with human help since at least the Iron Age.

Other rodents which are common on the mainland occur apparently at random throughout Shetland, Orkney and the Hebrides. For example, the common vole (i.e. the Orkney vole) is found only on Orkney, but the bank vole occurs only on Raasay, Mull and Bute. Another vole, the field vole, is found on the Uists, Eigg, Muck, Mull, Bute, Skye, Islay, Jura, Gigha and Arran, but not on Raasay, Shetland, St Kilda, Lewis and Barra. The odd distributions that we see today are now known to have been caused by a combination of natural events and human introductions.

The wood mouse seems to have made it to most of the islands. However, those that invaded Shetland, St Kilda, Fair Isle and most of the Hebrides are more closely related to Norwegian wood mice than to the animals of the Scottish mainland, whereas the wood mice on Mull and Colonsay are of Scottish descent. The clear implication is that the wood mouse first reached many of the Scottish islands with the Vikings and has travelled with the human population ever since.

The story of the St Kilda house mouse is a sad one. Its ancestors were introduced to St Kilda by the Vikings, along with wood mice, and they evolved into a unique island race that remained dependent on the human population. However, when the people of St Kilda were evacuated in the 1930s, they left the house mouse open to competition with the more independent wood mouse, and within a few years house mice became extinct. In less than a thousand years the St Kilda house mouse had evolved into a unique race, flourished, and disappeared into extinction.

The black rat, or ship rat, was originally an invader from Asia and was probably brought to our shores by the Romans. It would later earn itself eternal infamy as the carrier of the fleas that introduced the Black Death, or bubonic plague, to Britain in the fourteenth century. Today the black rat is faring badly. Competition from the more adaptable brown rat has left it

The red squirrel continues to decline along with its forest habitat.

3. THE RED SQUIRREL

Scotland is now regarded as the last stronghold of the red squirrel in Britain, but this has not always been the case. With the clearing of the ancient pine forests of the Highlands during the eighteenth century the red squirrel became virtually extinct in Scotland; it had already disappeared from the Lowlands by the early 1700s. Perhaps a few lingered on in Speyside, but to all intents and purposes the red squirrel had disappeared.

As extinction proceeded in the Highlands, re-introductions began in the Lowlands, starting at Dalkeith in 1772 and Dunkeld in 1793, using animals from England and Europe; by the end of the nineteenth century they were extremely common once again – so much so that they achieved the status of 'vermin'. The gradual spread of the re-introduced red squirrel coincided with the restoration of the forests, particularly in the Highlands, where the new plantations provided the habitat which the squirrels needed. At the beginning of this century, however, the red squirrel population crashed, probably due to disease.

Meanwhile the American grey squirrel, introduced into Britain from 1876 onwards purely because it looked nice, began to make inroads into red squirrel habitat and territory in England as the red squirrel died out. The commonly held view that the grey squirrel forced the red squirrel out of its territories is wrong; the evidence is that the grey only moved into areas after the red squirrel had disappeared.

Introductions also took place in Scotland, starting at Finnart, Loch Long, in 1892; the grey squirrel is now found throughout central Scotland, but it is still isolated from the rest of the British population.

Today, by an irony of history, the red squirrel is extinct in most of southern and central England and only survives in any numbers in Scotland. It is one of our most attractive and elegant creatures and Scotland may become even more important as its last stronghold. Large areas of coniferous forest may have to be specially managed to exclude the alien grey squirrel. Yet, by another irony, the current drive to encourage the planting of deciduous trees such as the oak may actually promote the spread of the grey squirrel into the Highlands, and assist its invasion into the remaining habitat of the shyer and less competitive red squirrel.

4. THE RED DEER

The red deer is Britain's largest surviving land mammal and its population has probably never been higher in Scotland than it is today, with at least 300,000 now roaming the Scottish hills. Originally a woodland animal, the red deer had to adapt to Scotland's increasingly treeless hills and glens; even today very few red deer are to be found in the new conifer plantations. Its enormous population increase has been due entirely to the management of deer as a game species to the point where there are now serious problems of over-population that need to be addressed urgently.

To the visitor the red deer epitomises all the grandeur and wildness of Scotland's mountain areas. Yet as a result of having to live on the over-grazed pastures of Scotland's deforested mountains for so long, the Scottish red deer has become one of the smallest and most malnourished in the world. When Scottish red deer were introduced to New Zealand in the nineteenth century, the rich food supply there produced a massive increase in body size in subsequent generations, until today New Zealand red deer are as large as their mainland European cousins.

Like Scotland's native wildcat (Box 5), the red deer also faces a threat from hybridisation – in this case from its close relative the sika deer, introduced from Japan and eastern Asia. These were first imported to Scotland as decorative and exotic parkland animals in the 1870s; later they were also brought in for sporting purposes. The population and distribution of sika deer increased considerably in the 1970s, and during the 1980s some cases of hybridisation between sika deer stags and red deer hinds were noted. It is not yet known how much of a threat this might represent to the survival of the pure-bred native red deer – but in south-west Scotland it is already very difficult to distinguish between the two species.

hanging on in only a few ports and docklands, where constant reinvasions from overseas probably bolster the population against ever more efficient poisons and keen competitors. Black rats now survive in Scotland only on the Shiant Islands near Skye.

The brown rat arrived in Britain from Asia in the early eighteenth century, but it was not commonly recorded in Scotland until the second half of that century, and it did not reach the Highlands until the beginning of the nineteenth century. It quickly displaced its longer-tailed cousin, the black rat, from many of the areas it occupied. Today the brown rat is found everywhere, from the sewers of our cities to the farms of our countryside. As the ultimate survivor it can live off human waste and garbage and anything else that comes to hand, making it one of the world's most formidably successful mammals.

LARGER MAMMALS

There were other comings and goings among our Scottish wildlife, mostly of larger mammals. The Romans admired the great Caledonian brown bears they found in Scotland and shipped many of them home to amuse the citizens of Rome in bear pits and the gladiatorial contests of the Coliseum. Eventually the brown bear in Scotland was killed off by human hunters and by the destruction of its forest habitat probably no later than the tenth century.

The fallow deer with its palmate antlers was probably introduced by the Romans, but it was only widely established following 1066 when William the Conqueror used it to stock many deer parks. Several parks were later established in Scotland; there have been many escapes into the wild, but it is much less common than the red deer or roe deer and is still considered a 'park animal'.

The Normans also brought the rabbit, which they kept in warrens where it was bred for meat and fur. It soon escaped and, although far removed from the sunnier climes of southern Europe, it spread and prospered. At first rabbits

Overgrazing by 300,000 red deer poses one of the most serious threats to the remaining native woodlands of Scotland.

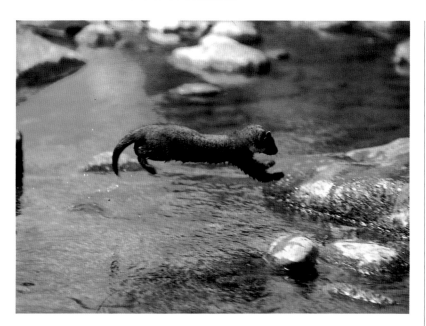

The pine marten is gradually recovering from former persecution.

were considered a luxury, jealously guarded for the rich. The rabbits in the Royal Warrens of King Alexander II of Scotland were protected from poachers by statute during the thirteenth century; and the Earl of Orkney's rent book records 1,200 rabbit skins as part of his annual rent at the end of the fifteenth century.

Rabbits on Scottish islands are often black or of other colour varieties because they are descended from domestic breeds that have escaped. However, despite their abundance in the Lowlands of Scotland, rabbits were not successfully established in the Highlands until the eighteenth century.

Their destructive effect on the regeneration of scrub and forest became clear in the 1950s and 1960s when the introduction of the myxomatosis virus decimated Britain's rabbit population. Areas that had been bare of woodland soon became covered with scrub and young trees. However, the rabbit population later became largely immune to myxomatosis and their numbers have increased again.

The beaver was prized for its luxurious fur and was also hunted for a glandular musk-like secretion called castoreum with alleged medicinal properties. This secretion actually contained salicylic acid, the active ingredient of aspirin (derived, no doubt, from the beaver's diet of willow bark), so its value as a medical

penacea may have had some foundation in fact. The beaver became extinct in Scotland in the sixteenth century. It has been suggested that the beaver could well be re-introduced to Scotland today, and Scottish Natural Heritage is currently investigating the feasibility of this.

The wild boar was another common woodland animal in Scotland until as late as the sixteenth century. It was an important food source and was greatly prized for hunting by the nobility. Hunting and destruction of its forest habitat eventually caused the wild boar's extinction. When it finally went, Britain lost one of the most important contributors to the natural regeneration of woodlands since, through its selective feeding habits, the boar assists forest growth. Today wild boar are kept for sport on a farm at Ben Wyvis and there have been various attempts to re-introduce them elsewhere, but without much success.

The wolf, which for centuries was the main predator of the forests, was hunted to extinction in Scotland sometime in the seventeenth or eighteenth century. It was not really a threat to people but became a very real threat to livestock whenever its natural prey, the red deer, became scarce. Several Acts of Parliament were passed to exterminate the wolf. The remote Highlands were its last refuge, and the Highland forests were often destroyed in order to drive the wolf out. According to tradition the last wolf in Britain was killed in 1743, in Moray.

THE RISE OF THE GAMEKEEPER

During the nineteenth century much of Scotland was turned into a sort of 'outdoor leisure centre' for the landed gentry (see Chapter 17). The red deer (Box 4), which had been taken for food in the past, was now carefully conserved for wealthy sportsmen to hunt. Heath and moorland were opened up by tree clearance and managed for red grouse by burning the heather. Mountain hares also benefited from this management of open moorland, and they were deliberately introduced to the Borders and some Scottish islands. The capercaillie (see Chapter 5) was re-introduced and protected from predators for the guns of the sportsmen. Trout and salmon fishing were also promoted on Scotland's rivers and streams by killing all fish-eating predators, including herons, ospreys and otters. The development of Scotland as a rich man's hunting ground resulted in a tragic change of fortune for many animals which suddenly became the gamekeeper's enemies.

With the rise of the gamekeeper no carnivore was safe. The belief that game could be best encouraged by destroying all predators was flawed, but it continues to this day. Polecats and wildcats suffered most because they were large and easily trapped or poisoned. However, the smaller stoats and weasels, as well as badgers, foxes, pine martens and otters, also suffered.

Birds of prey such as eagles, ospreys and peregrines also fared badly; as soon as they took to the wing they were blasted out of the skies. By the beginning of the twentieth century the carnage had been so relentless and efficient

that the pattern of Scotland's wildlife had been profoundly altered.

The elusive wildcat with its distinctive banded black-tipped tail (Box 5) only just survived in the western Highlands; it is a legally protected species now, but is still threatened.

The rivers and sea-lochs of Scotland are the last stronghold of the otter in Britain.

5. THE WILDCAT

The Scottish wildcat lived throughout Britain long before the domestic cat even existed; but its range has gradually contracted under the impact of the destruction of Britain's forests and persecution by gamekeepers, until it now survives only in a few Scottish strongholds. Even in Scotland it became virtually extinct, except in the western Highlands; but the wildcat is now a strictly protected species under the Wildlife and Countryside Act 1981, and a relaxation in the ceaseless persecution, combined with extensive reafforestation, has allowed the wildcat to extend its range.

Yet it is still far from safe. Although now found in many of its former Scottish haunts, the native wildcat faces a new and insidious threat from its domestic cousin. Domestic cats are descended from the African race of the wildcat and as such are closely related to Scotland's wildcats. First domesticated by the Ancient Egyptians 4,000 years ago, they were brought here by the Romans and have spread ever since. Beneath the benign disguise of your home-loving moggie is a ruthless predator quite capable of surviving in the wild as a feral animal.

The close relationship between wild and domestic cats, coupled with the recovery of the wildcat population, resulted in hybridisation between these two species. In common with many mammals, males recolonise areas first. Finding no wildcat females with which to mate, these males probably mated with local domestic females. The resulting hybrids have continued to mate with wild, domestic and other hybrid cats to produce a whole array of different shapes and sizes of cat belonging to the hybrid population.

One commonly occurring colour variety is the black Kellas cat, named after the Moray village where the first specimen was recorded. This handsome-looking animals is often thought of as a new species of cat in the popular press. Now that we have several specimens to study scientifically the situation is clear – they are no more than one of the complex hybrids between wild and domestic cats, although one animal appears to be Scotland's first black wildcat.

At this stage the threat of hybridisation to the pure-bred wildcat population is uncertain. It is hoped that current research can discover the extent of this threat and formulate a plan to preserve the Scottish wildcat for future generations.

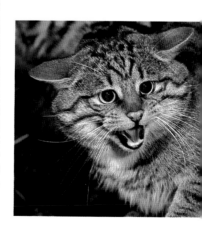

The Scottish wildcat is threatened by inter-breeding with feral cats.

Atlantic Grey Seal

The polecat was totally exterminated (see Chapter 15, Box 1); an attempt was made to re-establish it in western Scotland in the 1970s, but such attempts are probably doomed since it has now interbred with domestic ferrets that have gone wild.

The pine marten suffered severely from a combination of persecution, habitat loss and the near extinction of one of its favourite foods, the red squirrel (Box 3). The loss of its woodland habitat drove the pine marten out of the dwindling forests and up on to the rocky hillsides, particularly in Sutherland where it may have filled the niche left by the eradication of the polecat. Persecution by gamekeepers became intense in the latter half of the nineteenth century and it is something of a miracle that the pine marten survived at all. Now a protected species, it has extended its range very considerably and has recolonised woodlands even around the towns and cities of central Scotland, where the occasional animal has been spotted crouching observantly high in the tree tops.

The delightful otter, a larger member of the weasel family, suffered because it became fashionable to hunt it. Packs of otter hounds were specifically bred to hunt down this beautiful carnivore. This was not just good sport; gamekeepers believed that killing otters saved large numbers of trout and salmon for the game fisherman. In fact poaching by local people probably had far greater impact on fish populations. Apart from persecution by gamekeepers the otter is notoriously accident prone, and many otters are killed by drowning in lobster pots and fishermen's nets, or fall victim to cars. The otter has also been affected by pesticides and chemical poisons leaching into waterways and contaminating the fish stocks.

The otter is now a protected species. Its survival in many parts of southern Britain is still in the balance but, although it has declined in some areas of Scotland, it is happily still thriving in the western Highlands and Islands, and has recovered well in the Borders.

For many decades the gamekeeper's gibbet was heavy with the corpses of all these carnivores, slaughtered in order to demonstrate to estate owners that he was doing his job preserving game birds and deer. Cruel traps were supplemented with even crueller poisons

Bottlenose dolphins in the Moray Firth are threatened by pollution from sewage and industrial effluents.

in an attempt to eradicate all wild creatures that were of no value for sport.

The First World War brought much of this carnage to an end. After the human butchery on the battlefields of Europe, less than a quarter of the gamekeepers returned to Scotland's shooting estates and grouse moors. Much of the land was turned over to forestry. It was too late to save the polecat, but it helped to save the wildcat which has prospered and recolonised many of its former Scottish haunts despite continuing persecution.

SOME NEWCOMERS

There have been accidental introductions in this century, often of commercial species like the musk rat and the American mink which at first were confined to fur farms; unfortunately they escaped and became established in the wild in the 1930s.

In Scotland the musk rat became established for a time in the valley of the River Earn, from where it could have spread to have disastrous effects on our waterways. Fortunately a change in the fashion for its fur led to a vigorous extermination campaign which saw its demise by 1937.

The mink, on the other hand, has continued to spread and is now common in much of Britain. Its adaptability as a water-loving and ground-living predator means that it has often been regarded as a formidable enemy and destroyer of wildlife, particularly of ground-nesting birds such as terns and moorhens. Islands are no longer safe sanctuaries. Certainly in some areas the mink has devastated waterfowl and water voles, but in other areas wildlife populations seem unaffected by its presence. It is now official policy to ban the establishment of fur farms in sensitive areas and to do everything to keep mink off hitherto uninfested islands. Whether or not the mink is bad for Scotland's native wildlife, it is probably here to stay.

So far this chapter has concentrated largely upon land mammals, because birds are dealt with separately in the next chapter. But there have been two natural bird colonisations this century that demonstrate their advantage of flight as contrasted with the ground-living mammals.

71

One is the fulmar, which was once considered a very rare bird in Britain when it was confined to the extreme west and north on St Kilda and Shetland. However, it has spread southwards, starting from Shetland in 1910, until by 1970 it had spread throughout Britain. With a present population of **300,000** it is one of the most successful seabirds around our coasts, resilient and adaptable; there is even a unique inland colony of fulmars now nesting on the cliffs of Salisbury Crags on the slopes of Edinburgh's volcano, Arthur's Seat.

The collared dove, in contrast, came to Britain from south-west Asia in 1952. The first recorded nest was discovered in Norfolk in 1955. Within two years it had reached the north of Scotland, with a pair nesting in Moray in 1957. Within ten years the British population had soared to 10,000 birds, and it is now classified as an extremely common resident.

We are now entering a new stage of conservation, where bodies such as the Scottish Natural Heritage and the Royal Society for the Protection of Birds are attempting to restore Scotland's wildlife through selective re-introductions. Although the peregrine falcon, osprey and golden eagle have largely recovered from former persecution, others such as the sea eagle and the red kite have not. It will be extremely interesting to see how well the policy of reintroductions succeeds.

LOOKING TO THE FUTURE

Although its wildlife has been irrevocably altered by humans and natural events in the last 10,000 years, Scotland is still fortunate in being relatively sparsely populated; so there are large areas where wild plants and animals have been able to survive with little or no conflict with humans. However, we cannot be complacent; there are new threats facing the remaining fauna and flora.

Large areas of Scotland are still managed primarily for the benefit of game, which means that in some areas predatory birds and mammals still fall illegally to the gamekeeper's guns, traps and poisons. A better understanding of the relationship between wild carnivores and game animals would help us to develop new management techniques which avoid the recourse to wholesale slaughter: otherwise, despite legal protection, golden eagles, wildcats and pine martens will continue to be killed by traps and poisoned baits allegedly set for vermin.

As regards the marine environment, Scotland's seal populations are important in international terms. The grey seal population, in particular, is substantial, with Britain being home to about half of the total world population, most of which are to be found in Scottish waters. But their voracious appetite for fish brings them into competition with human fishermen and salmon farmers. It is claimed that grey seals eat the equivalent of half the tonnage of fish landed from the Scottish fisheries, although the fish which seals eat are not necessarily commercial species. Finding a resolution of this perpetual conflict will not be easy. The grey seal is a legally protected animal, although fishermen are allowed to shoot seals in the vicinity of their nets and salmon cages. But any attempt to reduce the seal population, by the culling of cubs for instance, is met with public outrage. The problem, as is so often the case, is that we simply do not have enough information on the true picture.

In 1987 a deadly disease struck the North Sea common seal population, killing more than 18,000 animals during an epidemic of the newly-discovered phocine distemper virus. Mercifully the Scottish population of common seals, which is found largely along the west and north coasts, was much less severely affected than that in other countries. We do not know why Scotland's seals escaped so lightly; but Scottish animals may become an important source of stock to repopulate the North Sea when the pollution problems, which may have reduced the seals' ability to resist this disease, are resolved.

But seals face new threats from a new and expanding industry. Salmon farmed in cages in the sea lochs are a ready-made food source for all fish-eaters, and this has brought seals, in particular, into conflict with humans. Investment in better protection for the farmed salmon could help to solve this particular problem.

Whales, dolphins and porpoises are also common around Scottish coasts, especially in the west. Inshore species such as porpoises and bottle-nosed dolphins have suffered greatly in recent years from pollution, waterside developments and disturbance by speedboats and jet-skis. Even now the sedentary population of bottle-nosed dolphins which survives in the relatively unspoilt Cromarty Firth is threatened by industrial expansion and the construction of a raw sewage outfall. We must look very carefully to balance human needs and wildlife needs: if we carry on as we are doing, the dolphin problem will cease to be a problem as the last dolphins disappear.

On land the banning of chemical pesticides like DDT and dieldrin in the 1960s was successful in helping the peregrine falcon and other raptors to recover from disastrous breeding results caused by eggshell thinning, and adult deaths caused by direct poisoning (see Chapter 5). But new threats face our wildlife. The infamous PCBs (polychlorinated biphenyls) are known to concentrate in the predators at the top of food chains; this means that hawks, dolphins, whales, seals, otters and other predators are at risk. We do not know what effect PCBs will have on carnivores in the future, or whether we can rid the environment of them; but the only safe thing to do is to stop them being released into the environment and to continue to monitor their presence in animals.

Not all Scotland's wildlife is on the defensive, however. Some animals have responded very well to the new urban habitats created by humans. Foxes, and now badgers, have infiltrated cities to take advantage of our wasteful food habits: one human's rubbish is clearly another animal's food. Safe from persecution, and with an assured supply of food, foxes and badgers can survive at higher population densities than their country cousins.

Sparrowhawks have also invaded the suburbs, despite their normally shy nature. They have exchanged their traditional woodland homes for parks and gardens as new hunting grounds. No doubt bird tables and garden nest-boxes have helped to ensure a good food supply.

Scotland's wildlife is basically in good shape – but what might happen in the future? Some people have suggested that the wolf could be re-introduced to control Scotland's huge deer population. This usually receives a swift and negative reply from sheep farmers, who see their stock as fair game for the big bad wolf. But if we can overcome our primal fear and hatred of the wolf, would it be such a bad thing? In Italy the wolf has somehow managed to survive, and active conservation has seen its population rise to over 400. In Italy attacks on livestock have been minimised by re-establishing the natural prey of the wolf, and a compensation scheme for both real and alleged kills made by wolves has proved very popular with local farmers.

The lynx is another predator which could conceivably be re-introduced to Scotland, but only with local support. Again, fears of sheep-killing weigh against this at the present time. Attempts to re-establish the lynx elsewhere in Europe have had varied results. However, it could be the beaver that returns to the Highlands first, if Scottish Natural Heritage is able to develop a successful reintroduction strategy.

Far more important than restoring lost species, though, will be to ensure that we keep what we already have, and we can only do this by protecting the habitat of the animals in question. It is up to us if future generations are to be able to appreciate, use and benefit from Scotland's unique wildlife heritage. Scotland's wildlife is very special; let us all do our best to keep it that way.

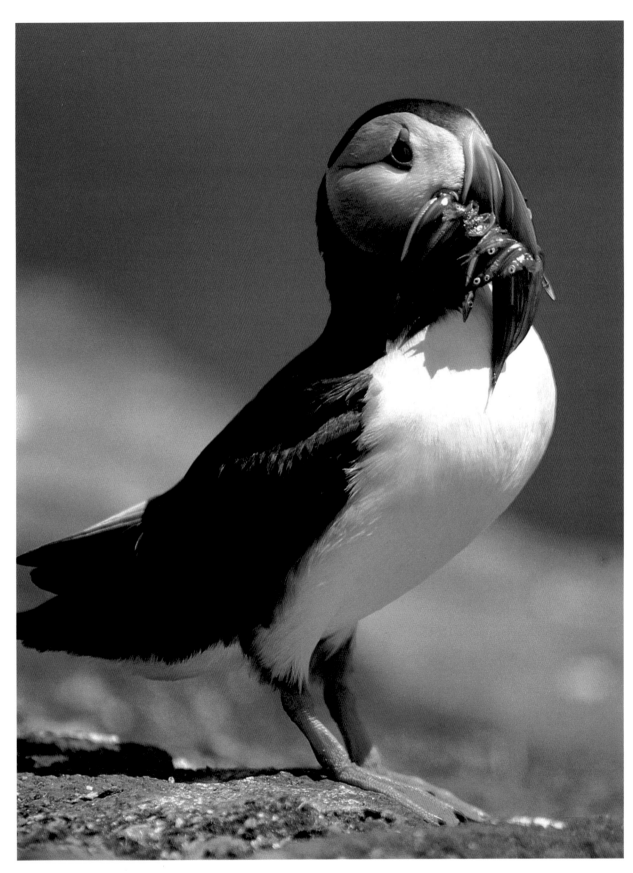

*Puffins need small sand eels
in order to rear their chicks.*

CHAPTER FIVE

The Birds and their Habitats

David Minns

David Minns, of the Royal Society for the Protection of Birds (RSPB) in Scotland, focuses on some of the problems facing Scotland's birdlife.

Of the 36 'red list' species of birds of greatest conservation concern in the UK, all but seven occur in Scotland, and around half are either exclusively or mainly found here. But that does not make them solely a Scottish concern; many of them winter or breed in other countries, and so we also have international obligations for them.

SEABIRDS

When we say seabirds we tend to think of gulls wheeling around our harbours and seaside towns or terns darting and swooping along summer beaches. But many groups of birds use the sea; some of them, like guillemots, razorbills and puffins use it all the year round; others only at certain times, like grebes and divers which winter on sheltered inshore waters but nest on inland freshwater lochs.

It is essentially for cliff-nesting seabirds that Scotland provides so many living places. Our towering cliffs may hold some six million birds in summer. Scotland is home to well over half of all the world's razorbills, more than half of the world's gannets and a high proportion of Europe's ground-nesting terns. The great skua, that splendid robber-baron of the northern seas, has its world headquarters in Shetland (where it is called the 'bonxie'); and Shetland is also home to many of Britain's arctic skuas and red-throated divers (Box 1).

All of these birds, and many human communities too, depend on fish, a resource which we have traditionally regarded as limitless. But as far as seabirds are concerned it is the smaller fish, hitherto not normally caught for human consumption, that have caused the most recent problems – in particular, the sand eel. The warning signs came in 1984, when the arctic terns on Shetland raised very few chicks. In 1985 and 1986 they failed again, almost totally: tern chicks were literally starving to death because their parents could not find any sand eels, their staple diet, to feed them with. The crisis grew and the tern population dropped by 60 per cent. Puffins and kittiwakes also suffered badly, since they also feed on sand eels near the surface of the water.

After several years' campaigning by the RSPB and others, commercial fishing for sand eels around Shetland was banned in 1991. Monitoring then showed a gradual recovery of both sand eel stocks and seabird breeding success, and the fishery was re-opened in 1995 with restricted catch and time limits.

WADERS AND WILDFOWL

Waders are among the most attractive and popular groups of birds in the world: long-legged and gregarious creatures that add vivid life to their wetland haunts. They breed in marshy tundra, moorland and grassland. They winter on estuaries and muddy or sandy seashores and can be found at freshwater margins chiefly on migration in spring and autumn.

Scotland has two areas that are of special importance for breeding waders: the machair

The gannetries of Scotland are of international importance.

Red-throated diver.

1. DIVERS

Britain has two resident species of divers, both of them confined to the north and west of Scotland – the red-throated and the black-throated. Of the two the black-throated is much the rarer, with only about 150 breeding pairs in Britain; the red-throated bird is particularly a denizen of Shetland where its 700 breeding pairs make up 50 per cent of the British population.

Divers are always listed first in bird books because they are considered the most primitive of birds. Their legs are set at the rear of the body in order to maximise their paddle-power, which makes them extremely ungainly on land. They are water birds par excellence and as such are wonderfully elegant and attractive.

The main difference is that the red-throated diver nests on small lochans but seeks its food in the sea, whereas the black-throated feeds in the freshwater loch where it nests. This makes it particularly vulnerable to the general deterioration in the upland environment – the removal of the natural vegetation of forest and scrub coupled with the problem of acid rain affecting the water of the lochs, and the plantations of conifers that acidify the watercourses.

Both divers are extremely shy birds and are easily disturbed from their nests, perhaps by fishermen. These nests are sometimes on the shores of a loch, but more usually on an island where the birds feel more secure. Some organisations, notably the Forestry Commission and the RSPB, are now providing artificial islands for nesting divers in our northern lochs. These may not solve the problem of declining populations; but they are a welcome step in the direction of trying to keep for Scotland some of our most hauntingly lovely northern birds.

land of the Western Isles and the Flow Country in Caithness and Sutherland.

The machair is found mainly down the west coast of the Western Isles and in a few other places like Tiree and small areas of Orkney and Shetland. The low-intensity use of the land and the very low levels of pesticides have resulted in exceptionally high numbers of birds.

To walk on the machair in summer is an amazing experience: the birds are everywhere, together with carpets of wild flowers such as are seldom seen nowadays except on nature reserves. Dunlin, ringed plover, oyster-catcher and lapwing nest here at some of the highest densities found in Western Europe. For example, in 1988 on the 1600 acre (650 ha) RSPB reserve at Balranald on North Uist there were no fewer than 178 pairs of oyster-catcher, 94 pairs of ringed plover, 288 pairs of lapwing, 93 pairs of dunlin, 60 pairs of snipe and 115 pairs of redshank nesting, as well as 125 pairs of ducks and eleven calling corncrakes! (Box 3).

The other area of enormous importance for breeding waders is the Flow Country of Caithness and Sutherland. Not many years ago this area near the top of mainland Scotland was virtually unknown, perhaps even to residents of these two districts who seldom had cause to go into it unless they were anglers.

'Flows' (from the Old Norse word *flói*, meaning 'marshy ground') are areas of blanket peatland for which Scotland is internationally important. From above they show a distinctive pattern of pools and vegetation in concentric arcs which appear to 'flow' across the landscape. The largest area, almost 1,500 square miles of east Sutherland and west Caithness, has been practically untouched by human hand for 7,000 years.

Until the end of the 1970s this land was largely grazed only by deer, together with some sheep, and was famed mainly for the high-quality fishing on its many lochs and rivers. It was also excellent for waders, with some 70 per cent of the European Community's breeding population of greenshank, as well as providing a home for 20 per cent of the Community's dwindling numbers of black-throated divers;

but there had been few proper bird surveys. The Flow Country was not regarded as threatened in any way.

In the early 1980s, however, several huge estates were sold off to a private forestry company. Between 1980 and 1986 it bought up nearly 100,000 acres (40,000 ha) at the amazingly low average price of £15 an acre. By 1987 some 35,000 acres (14,200 ha) had been sold on to private investors, in parcels averaging

2. THE GREAT AUK: SCOTLAND'S OWN DODO

The great auk (*Pinguinis impennis*) was once abundant and widespread throughout the North Atlantic, living in huge colonies on rocky islands. But it was flightless, like the penguin, and so became an easy source of food and feathers and fat for man. By the end of the eighteenth century the number of great auks had plummeted until they were close to extinction. The last Scottish great auk met its end on St Kilda in 1840 at the hands of people who did not know what it was and were actually afraid of it. The last two recorded birds anywhere were killed on a remote rock stack off south-west Iceland in 1844 in the cause of 'science', their bodies destined for the taxidermist. The great auk is now extinct throughout the world.

Nowadays the word 'dodo' is often used to signify someone who is stupid. But who was the more stupid – the flightless dodo in Mauritius or the men who, as with our own great auk, killed off a ready food supply and a charming species?

350 acres (142 ha). Tax relief was the main attraction because in those days people paying the top rate of 60 per cent income tax could, when the planting grant was included, have 70 per cent of their forest paid for by the taxpayer. This could amount to nearly £300 per acre which, over the average parcel of land mentioned, came to over £100,000. In addition, all timber sales would be tax free, making forestry the only industry subject to a 'double subsidy'.

By 1987 some 80,000 acres (32,000 ha) of prime flows had been ploughed up and drained. The ecological damage caused was incalculable, but sample surveys suggested that some 640 pairs of golden plover, over 300 pairs of dunlin and, rarest of all, over 120 pairs of greenshank had their unique habitat destroyed. Worse still in some people's eyes, a huge part of this pristine area of primeval country had been violated beyond redemption – and to no good purpose, because earlier experimental plantations by the Forestry Commission had indicated that the waterlogged windswept peat was totally unsuitable for forestry.

The RSPB, supported by the Nature Conservancy Council, launched a vigorous campaign against the whole project; the media responded with gusto, and in the 1988 Budget tax relief on forestry was abolished.

In the wake of the campaign The Scottish Office urged the Highland Regional Council to produce a 'land-use strategy' for Caithness and

Greenshank have lost much nesting habitat to afforestation of the Flow country.

A Great Auk, Scotland's own dodo, preserved for the National Museums of Scotland by taxidermist.

Once common in the lowlands, the corncrake survives in the Western Isles.

3. THE CORNCRAKE

The corncrake is more often heard than seen. It has a loud rasping call which can be imitated by drawing two notched bones across each other, which gave rise to its onomatopoeic scientific name, *crex crex*. The unmistakable voice of the corncrake sounding across the early summer meadows and hayfields at dusk evokes all the nostalgia of the countryside. And nostalgia it is, because the corncrake has declined greatly all over Western Europe throughout this century.

It is a summer visitor to Britain, arriving here to breed during late April or early May after spending the winter in south-east Africa. It is extremely shy and elusive, a solitary well-camouflaged creature that hides among long grass and other tall plants, betraying its presence only by that distinctive call in the evenings. When it takes flight the large bright chestnut areas on its wings catch the eye and mark it out from similar birds like the quail.

Today in the British Isles the corncrake is almost entirely confined to the Inner and Outer Hebrides, with a few surviving enclaves in Ireland. The reason for its catastrophic decline is that it has been unable to survive alongside intensive agriculture. The loss of hedgerows, hedgebanks and rough field margins has left the corncrake with ever fewer suitable areas for breeding; and earlier mowing of grass, especially for silage, has destroyed nests, thus preventing corncrakes from raising their young in hayfields.

Only where traditional methods of agriculture are still used, as in the crofting machair lands, does the corncrake have a chance. Its survival depends on how and when the farmer mows the hay. If mechanical mowers are used before the end of July working a field from the outer edge inwards, they will destroy the nest and the sitting bird, or drive any chicks towards the centre of the field where they are killed.

Hopefully, although the decline in corncrake numbers is still going on, sympathetic and concerted action by the farmer involved, supported by compensation schemes, can save it from extinction in its last refuges.

Sutherland, and the Nature Conservancy Council was set the task of designating large tracts of land as Sites of Special Scientific Interest (SSSIs). The Highland Regional Council's report eventually divided the whole of the two districts into four zones according to their availability for forestry, classified as Unsuitable, Undesirable, Possible and Preferable.

It was an uneasy compromise and the potential for conflict is still there; but at least the conservationists, having lost a lot of early ground because they were never consulted, were able to save what could be saved by their strong rearguard action.

GEESE

Huge flocks of geese spend the winter in Scotland – and their numbers are increasing. In September and October they migrate south from their breeding grounds in Iceland, Greenland and arctic Russia and stay in Scotland until March or April the following year (Box 4).

The geese which come to Scotland have nested on tundra during the short arctic summer. They nest in a hostile environment under precarious conditions; if the arctic summer is late starting, they may not rear any young at all. For geese, therefore, winter survival is much more critical for the species than it is for more prolific breeders such as our garden birds, some of which rear three broods a year.

The sight of skeins of these magnificent birds scything across the skies; the sound of their haunting voices as they call to each other for contact or in alarm; the view of a feeding flock seeming to form a rolling grey carpet as they move over the fields – there is no doubt that wild geese can, and do, stir the heart of even the most hardened city-dweller.

However, not everyone welcomes the return of the geese each winter, particularly in districts where the largest flocks gather. Traditionally geese wintered on stubble, rough pastures and unreclaimed salt-marshes; even then there was conflict as farmers needed the grass for their cattle and sheep. But farmers increasingly sow winter cereals which sprout from January to March, providing an unexpected feast for geese during their hardest months when food is in short supply. This new source of food in these critically cold months must have been an important factor in the increase in the numbers of geese now wintering in Scotland.

The island of Islay, in particular, has seen a large increase in numbers, particularly of barnacle geese, with around 45,000 now wintering on the island. The main goose areas, at Gruinart, Bridgend and Laggan, are designated as Sites of Special Scientific Interest (SSSIs) and farmers on such land can receive compensation for loss of crops to grazing geese and for managing in a particular way. Environmentally Sensitive Area (ESA) payments are also available on Islay.

The RSPB, for its part, purchased Aoradh farm at Gruinart in 1984 and manages it as a nature reserve to provide winter pasture for the geese and habitats for birds like corncrakes. The grass is grazed by cattle which keep it at the right length for the birds. The RSPB aims to attract as many geese as possible, thus relieving grazing pressure on other farmers' land.

The increase in numbers of geese on Islay has led to calls for the population to be reduced; the problem is deciding what level would be appropriate. There are those who point out that their numbers used to be much lower, and still they have survived, so why cannot they be reduced back to those levels? Against this can be put the difficult nesting conditions which these birds experience on the tundra; a late arctic summer can result in no young at all being reared that year.

Into this comes also the moral question of whether farmers should be paid substantial subsidies, increasingly linked to producing environmental benefits, and then be allowed to kill species which many of those paying for the subsidies would rather see protected. There are various compromises which could be reached over this issue, and the Government has issued a discussion paper to promote debate on the way forward. The results of this exercise are awaited.

BIRDS OF PREY

Scotland boasts a good selection of birds of prey, which enjoy varying fortunes. Some, like

4. WINTERING GEESE

Scotland is of international importance as a wintering ground for several particular species of wild goose, all of which have remarkably restricted breeding ranges.

The most common is the pink-footed goose, which has its largest breeding colony in the central hinterlands of Iceland and smaller colonies in east Greenland and Spitsbergen. There are more than 250,000 of them now. The elegant dark-headed pink-feet are cousins to the slightly larger greylag goose (the ancestor of our farmyard goose), whose numbers have also increased dramatically in the last thirty years, from 25,000 to more than 100,000.

The white-fronted goose (so named because of the white on the front of its head at the base of the bill) is the smallest of the 'grey geese' that come to Scotland – and the least common. It nests in Greenland and Siberia; the Scottish birds all come from Greenland, and are distinguished from other white-fronts by having orange bills. Of the 30,000 Greenland white-fronts in the world, some 20,000 of them winter in Scotland, where they concentrate on the green jewel of the Hebridean crown, the island of Islay; the rest winter in southern Ireland.

The smaller grey-black-and-white barred barnacle goose is the third of Scotland's important wintering geese; it was so named because people thought that they emerged from barnacles every year! Barnacle geese breed in the Arctic, where they form three distinct populations: the largest, from Siberia, winters in the Netherlands; another breeds in Spitsbergen and winters on the Solway coast; a third nests in east Greenland and spends the winter on Islay and a few other west coast islands. By the end of October there may be over 40,000 barnacle geese on Islay, feeding in tightly-packed congregations at a few choice locations. Under the protection of the law the world population of barnacle geese has risen from some 30,000 birds to more than 80,000 today.

Barnacle geese on the Isle of Islay.

the golden eagle (Box 5) and the osprey (Box 6), are thriving; others, such as the dashing little merlin and the fierce hen harrier, are not.

5. THE GOLDEN EAGLE

Ask most people which bird they think of when Scotland is mentioned and as often as not the golden eagle will be their first choice. It is a majestic bird, and few sights can be more thrilling than an eagle soaring and spiralling over its mountain territory. It is also Scotland's bird par excellence. There are some 400–450 breeding pairs in Britain, and all but one or two live in Scotland – the largest population in Europe apart from Spain and northern Scandinavia. But it is still extremely vulnerable. Eagles are long-lived birds which are slow to mature – they do not normally breed until five years old, and they normally rear only one young per year. Their habitat has been seriously reduced in modern times by forestry plantations and on top of all that they still fall victim to illegal poisoning.

For many decades man regarded birds of prey as a threat to his activities. Sadly, in many areas, the attitude still persists that any bird with a hooked bill should be exterminated. Traditionally, birds of prey were shot or trapped – and that still happens; but nowadays many of them are poisoned.

It is all too easy. A rabbit carcass is laced with poison and slung out on to the hill, supposedly to be taken by foxes and crows. But poison is indiscriminate. Many a carcass is spotted by a sharp-eyed bird of prey which promptly swoops down for a feed. Often the poison kills so quickly that the bird is found dead beside the bait.

The number of birds killed in this way is unknown, but illegal poisoning continues to be a serious problem in the countryside as the following numbers of incidents reported to the RSPB indicate: 1990 108; 1991 134; 1992 134; 1993 116; 1994 129; 1995 115. However, these are only the tip of the iceberg; poisoning is usually carried out in remote and sparsely populated areas where many victims perish unnoticed. In the last five years alone the RSPB has recorded some forty-five buzzards, ten other birds of prey and 156 other wildlife species, all poisoned; in addition, twenty-three dogs were killed in this way. In 1983 a gamekeeper actually died after ingesting a small amount of a poison called Phosdrin which he had been diluting in a cup. That chemical has been withdrawn by the main manufacturer, Shell, but it still turns up: in 1989 seven out of forty cases handled by the Department of Agriculture's Wildlife Investigation Service involved Phosdrin.

This continuous flouting of the law is a grave affront to everyone who has the nature of Scotland at heart. It has been suggested that poisons could be chemically 'tagged' so that they can be traced to the individual purchaser as a way of bringing him to justice. But perhaps the most effective weapons for the future will be education and the power of publicity. Estate owners realise that they cannot afford to have their image constantly tarnished by the law-breakers and there are now signs of change.

For far too many years there were hardly any buzzards in the Scottish Borders. I have travelled up and down in the Borders for over forty years and, until recently, never saw a buzzard. This contrasted markedly with areas such as Argyll and Wales, where buzzards are everyday sights in the sky. In the 1990s, however, the situation has greatly improved, so that by 1996 there were around 100 pairs of buzzards nesting in the Borders – and some 30 pairs in the Lothians. The birds' habitat and food supply have remained substantially unchanged, so the most likely reason for this welcome change is a reduction in illegal killing, whether by poison or shooting. Buzzards have also expanded their range in Aberdeenshire in recent years.

A longer-term success story is that of the peregrine falcon (Box 7). The peregrine occurs around the world, but in the 1950s numbers dropped disastrously and apparently without explanation. Eventually, after patient scientific detective work, it was found that the peregrine was being systematically, but accidentally, poisoned by the pesticides which man had been developing, specifically the persistent organo-

6. THE OSPREY

The osprey has been a spectacular success story for determined conservationists. Once upon a time the osprey bred freely, although not commonly, throughout the Scottish Highlands as well as in other parts of Britain. But throughout the nineteenth century it was severely persecuted by game-keepers, along with the red kite and the sea eagle. It was also the victim of Victorian collectors and trophy hunters who sought its beautiful skin and boldly-blotched eggs. By 1917 it was extinct as a breeding bird in Britain.

After an absence of some fifty years, single birds began to return to the lochs and pine forests of the Highlands in the breeding season; and soon attempts at breeding occurred. The news leaked out, and some early nests were robbed of their eggs by fanatical collectors. So in 1959, to enlist public support, the RSPB 'went public' over the successful hatching of three osprey chicks at Loch Garten – and invited the public to come and see them from a special observation hide at a safe distance from the eyrie. Within the next six weeks, while the birds were still at the nest, no fewer than 14,000 visitors came to see the osprey family.

Since then the nest has been guarded night and day. Hundreds of volunteers and RSPB staff have kept watch over the Loch Garten birds in 'Operation Osprey', and well over a million members of the public, who might otherwise never have seen these spectacular birds, have visited the osprey centre. Closed circuit television now brings the nest and its occupants even closer.

The focus of attention on the Loch Garten site has allowed a growing number of ospreys to nest undisturbed; there are now around a hundred pairs in Scotland, producing some 150 young each year. With prospects of recolonising England, ospreys can now be said to be out of danger in Britain.

chlorines such as DDT.

Chemicals like DDT had been used extensively during the Second World War against insects which transmitted diseases such as malaria, and had saved the lives of untold numbers of servicemen. After the war they were

7. THE PEREGRINE FALCON

The peregrine is the prince of all falcons, the consummate master of the air. Down the centuries it has been prized by falconers above all other birds for its speed. The hunting peregrine is one of the fastest birds alive, reaching 50 miles per hour (80km/h) in level flight with rapid shallow beats of its long pointed wings and stooping on its quarry with its deadly talons at speeds of up to 180mph (290km/h). It is also a great wanderer, or peregrinator as its name implies, and occurs throughout the world. It is everyone's favourite falcon.

Yet there was a time in the 1960s and 1970s when the Scottish Highlands held probably the only remaining healthy population of peregrines in the world. It was the time of the great population crash caused by chemical pesticides. But Scotland's birds survived. Because of the temperate climate there is less pressure on Scottish peregrines in the Highlands to migrate south in the winter; they simply move from the higher country down to farmland or to the coast. When the pesticide crisis struck, Scotland's birds were less affected than the populations of other countries, although their numbers did show a decline. They are now

The main threat to the peregrine is no longer pesticides but the robbing of nests by egg collectors.

The snowy owl occasionally ventures as far south as Shetland to breed.

The Sea Eagle, exterminated by game-keepers during the 19th century, was reintroduced to Scotland during the 1980s.

used against agricultural pests, and again were found to be extremely effective. But during the latter half of the 1950s reports began to come in of large numbers of seed-eating birds found dead in farming districts; the cause of their deaths was traced to the birds having eaten grain treated with some of the new insecticides. It was now only a matter of time before birds of prey such as the peregrine, at the top of the food chain, became affected by eating poisoned birds. As well as killing adult birds the pesticides also caused the thinning of eggshells, which broke when the birds tried to incubate

them. The poisons also caused adults to exhibit grossly abnormal behaviour such as eating their own eggs.

The scientific evidence presented by the RSPB and the British Trust for Ornithology was so strong that several chemicals for treating seed, including dieldrin, were placed under voluntary ban in the spring of 1962. The restrictions were extended in 1964 and, although DDT itself was not officially banned until 1984, its use declined sharply, probably because of the adverse publicity which had been incurred.

By 1967 the peregrine population began to pull out of its plummeting decline. By 1981 some 90 per cent of pre-war eyries were being occupied again. The saving of the peregrine, one of our most magnificent wild creatures, was part of the coming of age of the modern science-based conservation movement, and an object lesson that wildlife can act as a vital indicator of the health of our environment.

RE-INTRODUCTIONS

Even with the peregrine restored to its former eminence, and the golden eagle quartering most of the available territory in Scotland, there is still so much open space and open sky in Scotland that there is ample room for the other birds of prey which once flourished here. And there are two exciting enterprises under way to restore Scotland's portfolio of raptors to something like its former glory: one is a project

8. THE SEA EAGLE

The sea eagle is a magnificent creature. Its colouring is a light brownish grey, the feathers of the head and neck a lichen white, with a short, wedge-shaped tail of pure white (hence its alternative name) and a massive hooked bill of brilliant burnished yellow. The eyes are a pale honey colour, which has earned the bird the poetic Gaelic name of *Iolaire suil na greina*, 'the eagle with the sunlit eye'.

It is a huge bulky bird, with very broad wings and a wingspan of over seven feet (2.2 m), the largest of any British bird. It has a heavy flapping

flight as it hunts low over land and water, feeding on fish, seabirds and small mammals, and it announces its presence with a variety of barking calls.

Like the golden eagle the sea eagle does not mature for breeding until it is about five years old, but the courtship display is well worth waiting for. The birds grapple their talons in mid air and plummet cartwheeling earthwards in a spectacular frenzy. They nest on sea-cliff ledges, or sometimes in trees; these nests are guarded by Scottish Natural Heritage and the RSPB as if they were the crown jewels themselves.

to re-introduce the sea eagle, the other is an attempt to bring back the red kite.

The sea eagle (Box 8), or white-tailed eagle as it is sometimes called, used to nest round the rocky coasts of northern and western Britain and originally as far south as Cornwall; however, its main stronghold was always Scotland, with more than a hundred pairs nesting around the north and west coasts, although a few nested inland in places such as Rannoch. After a century of almost continuous persecution by shepherds and gamekeepers, when the Highlands were 'cleared' for sheep and red deer, the sea eagle finally became extinct in Britain early this century. The last known breeding attempt in Scotland was on Skye in 1916, and the very last bird, an albino (white) female believed to have been about thirty years old, was shot in Shetland two years later.

Fortunately the sea eagle breeds over a wide range across the northern hemisphere and, despite major declines in other European countries, it held on in Scandinavia. People waited in vain for it to recolonise Britain naturally, as the osprey has done: but our islands seem to be beyond wandering range of other sea eagles, which are less far-ranging than ospreys. There were two early attempts to re-introduce the birds, to Glen Etive in Argyll in 1959 and to Fair Isle (by the RSPB) in 1968 involving seven birds in all, but both projects came to nothing.

Eventually, in 1975, a more thorough programme was launched on the island of Rum, which is owned and managed by Scottish Natural Heritage as a National Nature Reserve. Over the next ten years, eighty-two young sea eagles from northern Norway were flown over to Scotland (courtesy of RAF Kinloss) and released on Rum. This was a joint enterprise involving the old NCC, the RSPB and a generous sponsor, Eagle Star Insurance.

The birds were kept tethered and provided with food for a while to accustom them to their new surroundings, and then released to fly free. The first nest was built in 1982, and in 1983 two pairs laid eggs but failed to hatch them. In 1984 there were at least four nests, two of them with

eggs, but still no successful hatching. At last, in 1985, came the breakthrough, when a Scottish-born sea eaglet took to the Scottish skies for the first time in almost seventy years. Since then there has been slow but steady progress: in 1989 eight pairs laid eggs, from which five young birds hatched. This brought the total up to thirteen young successfully reared in Scotland.

However, adult survival has proved lower than expected, and so in 1993 a further programme of re-introductions was begun, again bringing young birds across from Norway. This has helped the number of pairs laying eggs to reach twelve by 1996, of which seven were successful in rearing nine young. It has been a long, slow haul, but after more than 20 years the sea eagle looks as if it has secured a toe-hold in Scotland again.

The red kite is a beautiful, swallow-tailed, agile bird which was once very common but is now one of Britain's rarest birds of prey. Throughout the nineteenth century it was persecuted almost to extinction until, by the start of this century, only a few pairs were left hanging on in the remote valleys of central Wales. Kite protection schemes were started as early as 1904; but by 1989 there were still only fifty-three breeding pairs in Wales.

The hope has always been that they would spread out, but this has never happened, partly because of poor breeding success in Wales and partly because of the inevitable poisoning and shooting. So in 1989 another ambitious re-introduction project was launched jointly by the

The Scottish crossbill is the only bird unique to Scotland.

NCC and RSPB: six young red kites were brought across to Scotland from Sweden, where numbers are high, and released in a suitable part of the Highlands after the necessary period of quarantine and acclimatisation. They were fitted with lightweight radio transmitters which enabled RSPB researchers to track their movements for the first six months.

Tragically, after only five months of freedom in Scotland, one of the six was found poisoned, but the Highland re-introduction scheme has continued and by 1996 seventeen pairs produced 39 young – a very high production rate. The success in the north is most encouraging, as is the favourable response to the kites from the overwhelming majority of landowners, but it was calculated that it might take almost a century for this population to expand into the lowlands. A second re-introduction scheme has therefore been started in central Scotland, bringing young kites from Germany. It is hoped it will not be long before the kite, or 'gled' as it used to be known, is once again seen twisting and turning over places such as Gladsmuir in East Lothian, or even Gladstone's Land in Edinburgh!

PINEWOOD BIRDS

Our last group of special birds are denizens of one of the most threatened habitats in Scotland – the ancient Caledonian pinewoods, the fragmentary remnants of the great 'wildwood' that carpeted much of Scotland after the last Ice Age (see Chapter 3). Today there are fewer than 30,000 acres (12,000 ha) left: in the past 500 years we have destroyed over 99 per cent of our equivalent of the rainforests.

A whole community of birds lives in and around the remnants of the pinewoods, which provide a rich and diverse habitat for a marvellous assemblage of fauna and flora; but we shall concentrate on three very special birds.

The first is our largest grouse, the capercaillie. It is yet another of the birds of Scotland that was driven to extinction by a combination of habitat loss through deforestation and over-hunting: the last two cock capercaillie were shot in Aberdeenshire in 1785. Fifty years later the capercaillie was successfully reintroduced when a collection of thirty-two birds from Sweden was brought to the Breadalbane estates in Perthshire in 1837, and quickly became widespread again in many parts of Scotland. But there was a major problem, arising from a historical anomaly; although the capercaillie was clearly a game bird it was never classified as such because it had become extinct by the time the first game laws were drawn up; and its winter diet of conifer shoots and buds and young cones made it so unpopular with foresters that it was treated as a pest. It was only when it did become treated as a game bird by sportsmen that it began to thrive again.

Between the 1970s and 1990s, however, the population again declined, from about 20,000 pairs to only 2,200, despite a voluntary ban on shooting. Shortage of suitable habitat, particularly open pinewoods with abundant blaeberry, is presumably the main reason, but

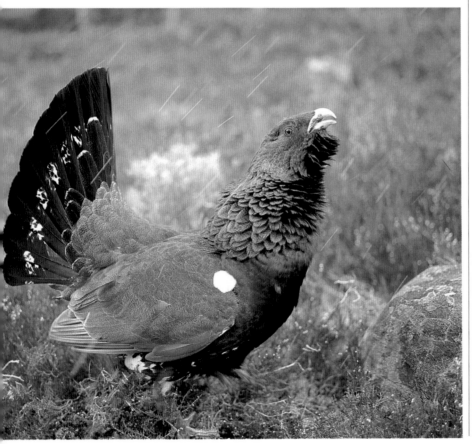

The Capercaillie, a giant grouse, displaying on the 'lek'.

collisions with deer fences have been found to kill up to 30 per cent of adult capercaillies on the RSPB's Abernethy Forest reserve. RSPB staff have removed all internal fences, and the Forestry Authority now recommend avoiding using deer fences in woods which hold capercaillies.

Our second special bird of the pinewoods is the delightful crested tit. This charming little black and white bird with a distinctive crest on the back of its head is so shy and elusive that it can often be detected only by its trilling call. It is widespread on the continent, but in Britain is only found in the Scottish pinewoods, and even there it is confined to just a few areas. Its main territories are found in the woods along the valley of the River Spey and those to the north in the catchment of the Beauly river; for some unknown reason it is not found on Deeside, to the east of the Cairngorms, even though there are some beautiful pinewood remnants there. But it is our hope that the bird will find its own way there one day, unaided.

Our third bird is the most special of all, because it is Scotland's only unique species: the Scottish crossbill. Originally it was regarded as a race of the common crossbill, which occurs much more widely throughout Britain and Europe but it has since been classified as a full species, *Loxia scotica*.

Whereas the common crossbill feeds mainly on soft spruce cones our endemic native bird depends largely on Scots pine, particularly mature trees. It has evolved a powerful cross-over bill to deal with the much tougher cones of the Caledonian forest; it holds the cone down on a branch with one foot while it prises the cone open in order to extract the seed with its tongue.

The male is a striking crimson red, while the female is a subdued olive green. They nest early in the year, often in March or even February while the snow is still lying deep, when the food supply is coming up to its peak.

There may be as few as 600 pairs of Scottish crossbill in existence although numbers are difficult to estimate because it is hard to distinguish them from common crossbills in the field. But there is considerable hope for the future: the indications are that our native pinewoods have at last reached the nadir of their fortunes and are now on the way up again. Increasingly, more and more people recognise the aesthetic and wildlife value of balanced forests of regenerating native pinewoods and associated broadleaves like birch and rowan.

THE FUTURE

The challenge as we approach the twenty-first century is whether we can finally discard the outdated idea that nature is only there to be conquered or tamed: to be exploited to the limit in order to meet our immediate short-term needs. Perhaps, instead, we can genuinely accept the idea that it is not only beneficial but essential to safeguard as many of our natural resources as possible.

There are three valid reasons for this.

First, for ecological reasons: as we destroy one part of the matrix of life, we inevitably affect other parts. Sometimes this may not matter too much; but if it is done on a large enough scale, as we have done with our pinewoods and our fish stocks, then we progressively impoverish the resources which sustain our own lives. Remember, too, that birds like the peregrine are valuable indicators of the general health of our environment because they are at the top of the food chain (like humans). They are also relatively easy to observe and monitor.

Second, for genetic purposes: we do not know if or when genetic material in plant and animal species, which at present has no apparent use, may prove to be of vital importance.

The third reason for conserving and cherishing our wildlife is essentially spiritual or aesthetic: birds give so many people so much pleasure. Who has not been charmed by the song of a blackbird or the sight of a robin? There are no urgent conservation reasons for giving full legal protection to such common birds: they are in no way endangered. But we do protect them, simply because we like them. It is up to us to demonstrate with our actions that we care for our world, our own habitat, much more than we have done in the past.

9. THE BIRDWATCHER

Sir John Lister-Kaye
Naturalist and President of the Scottish Wildlife
Trust

I found myself facing a steel dawn. Sharp stinging raindrops whiplashed into my face on a northerly wind as I turned up my tweed collar and I was pleased to climb into the Land Rover and slam the door.

I was out in the grey dawn to watch capercaillie, the giant grouse of the Caledonian pineforest, strutting defiantly on the lek, wattles gorged, fan tail spread and great secateur bill thrust arrogantly upward. I tiptoed closer on cushions of sphagnum moss beneath a wood of ancient gnarled pines, through which the great birds planed in, twisting and turning on down-curving pinions to parade and affect like popinjays.

I lingered on long after the show was over, head back against the orange jigsaw bark of an old pine as I craned my neck to glimpse the flash and trill of tiny goldcrests weaving amongst the highest cones. As I did so a troop of Scottish crossbills swung in. Suddenly my early morning silence was strident with the gaudy shrieks of green and scarlet courtiers haggling over cones, snapping, clicking, cracking with forceps bills to extract the feathery seed and tumble the ravaged cone earthwards. For a few minutes the forest rained pine cones and the trees were alive with riotous destruction – and then they were gone, their shrieks fading with each undulation as they swung away to a distant glade. I was alone with a single crestie, the tit which belongs to the pinewood, which trilled and fluttered around me in delicate contrast to the departed jesters.

For me the great prize of the Highlands is the golden eagle (Box 5) and its recently introduced cousin the sea eagle (Box 8). To witness these great birds spiralling upwards on huge open-fingered wings, or perched haughtily on a lonely crag, is to experience the very essence of wildness. Wildlife is there to be sought out in every season. In spring there are squelchy, muddy, bog-hopping days, tramping mountains of burnt-cork hue with red deer stags in brochure silhouette on the skyline and ptarmigan scuttling over lichen-patterned scree a few yards in front of you and,

forced into flight, belching like drunks as they peel across the corrie in a snow flurry of silver and white.

There are delicate dotterel on the high tops, absurdly tame and a sexual paradox as the drab male incubates the eggs while the stripey eyeshadowed female stands and watches.

Thin piping laments of greenshank and golden plover waft across these hills on wind which sings like surf, and snow buntings, the pied sparrows of the Arctic, lurk and flit among the great jumble of glacier-strewn rocks.

Far below in the glens lie the glinting cloud-filled lochs and burns. Here among the gurgling peaty runnels are dippers and grey wagtails, ring ouzels and pipits. A glance upward to the piebald hills will often reveal the crossbow shape of the darting merlin, our smallest falcon; or suddenly and unexpectedly, invisible at first against the blue of the sky and the distant hill, your ear is tantalised by strains of blood-tingling music. Slowly eye and ear converge on a broad chevron of whooper swans, whiter than the April snow with bills thrust ever forward to their arctic breeding grounds and their haunting calls echoing round the corries below.

On the loch you will find goldeneye ducks, now breeding successfully in Speyside, bright and buoyant as they dive and bob back to the surface in twos and threes. The osprey (Box 6), wild-eyed and hunch-backed, grips the bleached branch of a dead pine, its red-indian headdress a rattle of feathers all defiant and spiky as it picks at the fist-clenched trout. Once more it crashes into the loch in a shower of silver spray and grabs air on elbowy wings to fly over the pinewood to a family of five jammed into a foul-smelling nest.

Or yet again, on a smaller lonely loch, you can find one of Britain's rarest and most spectacular waterbirds, the Slavonian grebe, with outrageous marmalade eyebrows and glossy black satin jacket. These birds seem to have little fear of humans and sail breath-catchingly close if you sit quietly on the loch-side. When two meet they greet each other with elaborate sign language and display, eyebrows erect, ruby eyes sparkling, and the immaculately rehearsed grebe dance, upright, treading water to a high-pitched and penetrating trilling call.

On a few lonely northerly lochs you can find the

most exquisite example of divine engineering and virtuoso art: the black-throated diver (Box 1), the pearl-diver whose eerie call echoes back and forth through the sad, beautiful upland it inhabits. It is as close to design perfection as one could ever hope to find. From the tip of its aqua-dynamic lancet bill over its streamlined black velvet head and pyjama-striped neck, it seems that droplets of shining water, like a handful of pearls, have been sprinkled across its coal-glossy back. Below the water-line even its shin bones are moulded into knife blades for cutting water on the forward stroke, and maximum thrust when the powerful webbed paddles push back.

On the coast, Scotland offers great oceans crashing in slow thunder against some of the oldest cliffs in the world; towering high-rise slums where hundreds of thousands of guillemots and gannets crowd together in a haggling squalid tangle of bills, wings and jarring wailing calls. Or again great expanses of shimmering shell-sand, white and shining to the fluttering waves. Here waders stand about one-legged and drowsy, killing time while the tide turns: curlew, dunlin, lapwing, oystercatcher, godwit, ruff and reeve, and many more. Here one can witness scenes of great drama and thrill as a peregrine screams by, shattering the idyll and scattering frightened waders like chaff.

And, at the day's end, turning for home, from far out on the tidal mud come the calls of a thousand pink-footed and greylag geese to set the blood tingling and fix the unforgettable memory. They, too, head north to Iceland and beyond to far-off breeding grounds, up and away over the clouded hills. They will be back before the year is out; and so, for certain, will I.

The rare black-throated diver nests by a remote lochan.

The Peacock Butterfly

CHAPTER SIX

The Beauty of Butterflies
Richard Sutcliffe

Richard Sutcliffe is a Curator at Kelvingrove Museum, Glasgow. He is chairman of the Glasgow and South-West Scotland branch of Butterfly Conservation.

Scotland has only twenty-eight resident species of butterfly today in contrast with the sixty resident species found in Britain as a whole. The reasons for this are partly to do with the nature of Scotland itself in terms of climate and geology; but they are also closely connected with the great changes in farming practices over the past decades which have badly affected butterflies throughout Britain.

Climate has always been the major factor affecting the distribution of species, together with geology which determines the kind of food plants that grow in any area. The physical geography has sometimes isolated populations and has occasionally given rise to distinct subspecies, like the Meadow Brown in the east and the west of Scotland.

Butterflies have probably been present in Scotland for millions of years, apart from the gaps caused by the Ice Ages; there is no proof of this however, because no fossilised remains of butterflies have yet been found in Scotland. In fact we have no evidence of which species were present before recording started in the eighteenth century (Box 1); however, we can to some extent hazard a guess as to which species have been present since the end of the last Ice Age.

Pollen records indicate that almost all of the food plants required by the caterpillars of today's Scottish butterflies had probably reached Scotland soon after the ice retreated. Such pollen records cannot of course prove that today's butterflies were actually present at that time, but it is likely that many species quickly recolonised Scotland as the climate improved.

Since Britain was still connected to mainland Europe by a land bridge until about 7,500 years ago, it was relatively easy for continental butterflies to move into Britain, following the spread of their food plants as they moved northwards. As temperatures rose, the first butterflies to arrive would have been migratory species like the Red Admiral and the Painted Lady, although they would not have been able to become resident here owing to the cold winters. However, other species such as the Large and Small Whites may have become resident at that time.

These would have been rapidly followed by arctic and alpine species which could tolerate the cold conditions. Species from northern Europe would have moved in next, followed by the rest of the butterflies which we enjoy today. The last species to arrive would have been those whose caterpillars were dependent on trees for their food, such as the Purple Hairstreak which feeds exclusively on oak.

As the climate warmed, the arctic and alpine species probably died out or, like the Mountain Ringlet (Box 2), adapted to higher and cooler habitats. About 7,200 years ago there were probably twice as many species established in Scotland as there are today; indeed some continental species such as the Large Ringlet, Northern Wall Brown, Pearly Heath, Sooty Copper and Heath Fritillary may once have been quite common.

Apart from climate changes, man has had a major effect on our butterflies – but only in

1. EARLY RECORDS

The earliest surviving records of Scottish butterflies date from the 1760s and come from Dr John Walker (1731–1804). He recorded the Peacock from Dumfriesshire and Iona in 1766; the Scotch Argus (Box 3) in Drysdale, Dumfriesshire and what was almost certainly the Large Skipper from Bute in 1769. The first published description of a Scottish species came in 1793 when Johan C. Fabricius (1745–1808) described *Hesparia artaxerxes* (the Northern Brown Argus (Box 7)). The nineteenth century saw a large number of naturalists collecting Scottish butterflies, so that the distribution of many species was quite well documented by the end of the century. Remarkably, however, it was only in 1939 that the Chequered Skipper (Box 6) was first collected in Scotland.

From these old records it appears that some species recorded in the past are now extinct in Scotland. The Small Skipper was recorded from Edinburgh in 1811 and Alloa in 1845. The Grizzled Skipper was recorded from southern Scotland: Glasgow in 1857 and Cairnryan in 1896. There are records of the White-Letter Hairstreak in Dumfries in 1859 and near Dunoon in 1884; similarly the Duke of Burgundy in Dumfriesshire and Roxburghshire in the 1860s. The Comma and the Silver-Washed Fritillary certainly both occurred in Scotland in the last century but then suffered major declines. Many other species that have been recorded in Scotland were probably just vagrants and never became firmly established.

Johan Fabricius made the first recorded observations of butterflies in Scotland.

recent times. At first the coming of early people to Scotland may actually have benefited butterflies (see Chapter 7). Small-scale forest clearance by Neolithic farmers would have diversified the available habitats, allowing some species to expand into new areas. As the clearance of forests continued through the centuries it was the large-scale felling of trees to produce charcoal for the iron smelting industry during the eighteenth century which probably affected butterflies most. Today there are very few areas of truly natural countryside in Scotland and most butterflies are found only in modified or man-made habitats.

The growth of towns and factories during the Industrial Revolution, together with the accompanying pollution, resulted in the further fragmentation and destruction of many former butterfly habitats; their decline has been most marked in the Central Belt of Scotland during the nineteenth and twentieth centuries.

Most of Scotland is farmland and changes in farming practice have drastically affected many butterfly sites. Many fields have been 'improved' by drainage schemes; thousands of miles of hedgerows have been grubbed out; much of our native broad-leaved woodland has been destroyed and nearly all of our wildflower meadows and flower-rich hay meadows have been impoverished by herbicides. The massive increase in the use of fertilisers, herbicides and insecticides may have been healthy for farmers but it was extremely unhealthy for butterflies and other creatures which depend on natural habitats for their survival; chemical pesticides had the most damaging effect because they killed butterflies and other useful insects as well as the insect species for which they were intended.

As sites become smaller it becomes harder for some species to survive and local extinctions may result. The remaining sites become more isolated, making it increasingly difficult for butterflies to recolonise from surrounding areas as would have happened naturally in the past. Butterfly collecting, which like egg-collecting was once a popular pastime for vicars and schoolboys, probably did not have a great effect on butterfly populations, except where colonies had been reduced to critical levels by changes in climate or habitat. Today, however, there is very little justification for collecting Scottish butterflies, even though they are not protected by law as rigorously as are wild birds and their eggs. We can learn much more about butterflies by simply watching them, and taking photographs is far more rewarding than killing butterflies for display in a glass case.

SCOTLAND'S BUTTERFLIES TODAY

Although many of our butterflies are widely distributed they are often not commonly seen. Most people are only familiar with three or four different butterflies: the 'Cabbage White' (actually two species, the Large and Small Whites, which some regard as pests), the Small Tortoiseshell and the Red Admiral, which are often seen visiting flowers in town gardens. It comes as a surprise to be told of the considerable variety of butterflies to be found in Scotland.

Most of them have quite different food and habitat requirements which account for their distribution. The Dingy Skipper, for example, must have bird's-foot trefoil for its caterpillars to feed on; nothing else is acceptable and if the plant does not grow in the area the butterfly will not be found. But the presence of the correct food plant does not always guarantee that the butterfly, too, will be present. The main food plant for the larvae of the Small Pearl-bordered Fritillary is the marsh violet, a common plant found throughout much of Scotland; but the butterfly has a much more limited distribution than the plant.

Not only must the plant be present but it must be at the right stage of growth and in a position which receives the right amount of sunshine and at the right temperature for the eggs and larvae to develop. This means that only a small proportion of all the available marsh violets is actually suitable for the insects to lay their eggs upon.

2. THE MOUNTAIN RINGLET

At first glance this species is very similar to the Scotch Argus but it is smaller in size and lacks the white-pupilled eye spots. As its name suggests, it is an upland species, found mainly on south-facing slopes at altitudes of 1150 to 2950 ft (350 to 900 m). Found mainly in Inverness-shire, Argyll and Perthshire; an isolated population also occurs on Ben Lomond. The only other British localities are in the Lake District.

Colonies may cover large areas of ground and in some years the butterflies may be abundant. Males fly actively in search of females which often sit low down in the vegetation.

Recent research suggests that while most caterpillars complete their life cycle in one year, a proportion of the population may take two years to develop; a good stategy for surviving in a place with an unreliable climate.

One of the best places to see this butterfly is on the National Trust for Scotland's Ben Lawers Reserve on the northern side of Loch Tay, where it may be common in early July.

3. THE SCOTCH ARGUS

As its name implies, the Scotch Argus is restricted to Scotland apart from a couple of sites in northern England. In Scotland, however, it is widely distributed, especially on moorland over 300 ft (90 m) above sea level; the only exception seems to be central Scotland where it has not been found.

The Scotch Argus can often be found close to established woodland or young forestry plantations, or in sheltered boggy areas where there is an abundance of its larval food plant, purple moor grass.

When the butterfly is found, there are often very large numbers. It tends to hide in long grass in dull weather but sunshine will quickly bring it out to take flight. It is unmistakable with its bright red (male) or orange (female) eye-spotted bands on each very dark brown wing. It is the latest of all the Scottish butterflies to appear, emerging only in July, and can be found until September.

The Common Blue.

good years large numbers of these two species may appear anywhere in Scotland and often reach Shetland, the Western Isles and even St Kilda. Many of these butterflies may have travelled thousands of miles from north Africa and southern Europe, reaching Scotland as early as April. They may breed here, resulting in large numbers of 'home bred' individuals later in the year. However, very few manage to survive the cold Scottish winters and thus they cannot establish themselves permanently here. There is often a noticeable southerly migration of these species in autumn as they seek warmer

4. THE MARSH FRITILLARY

The Marsh Fritillary is in serious decline throughout Europe, and Scotland is probably one of its last strongholds. It is a generally sedentary species and even small barriers, such as hedges, arable land and woodlands, will often deter it from expanding into other areas. For this reason it tends to be restricted to distinct colonies, usually in damp meadows, rough pasture or moorland, where devil's bit scabious, its caterpillar's foodplant, is found. It is therefore particularly vulnerable to damage to and inappropriate management of its habitat and can quickly be exterminated from a given area. It is also prone to parasitism by an *Apanteles* wasp which occurs naturally in Marsh Fritillary colonies where it takes its toll of many caterpillars each year.

The Marsh Fritillary was once found in southern and eastern Scotland, but it is now almost confined to parts of Argyll, and some of the Inner Hebrides. Elsewhere in Britain colonies are disappearing at a rate of well over 10% per cent decade. Western Islay and the area around Taynish National Nature Reserve in Knapdale are regarded as key areas for this very attractive butterfly.

It is on the wing from the first week in June and can normally be found for about four weeks. It flies low over the ground, usually only in sunshine.

Some species such as the Marsh Fritillary (Box 4) and the Speckled Wood prefer a damp oceanic climate and tend to be found on the west coast. Other species, like the Small Heath and Meadow Brown, are much less particular and are found throughout Scotland.

Different butterflies pass the bitter winter months at different stages of their life cycle: the Purple Hairstreak overwinters as an egg, the Common Blue as a caterpillar and the Green-veined White as a chrysalis, while the Small Tortoiseshell and the Peacock both survive the winter by hibernating as adults. As a result each species is on the wing at different times of the year, usually between April and October. In addition a few species are able to complete their entire life cycle in a relatively short space of time. The Wall, the Speckled Wood and the Large, Small and Green-veined Whites are able to produce two and occasionally three broods of young each year. June is definitely the best month of the year to see butterflies and in a good year it is possible to see nearly all the Scottish species within that month if you are prepared to travel around a little.

A few species of butterfly migrate to Scotland regularly. The most common of these are the Red Admiral and the Painted Lady. In areas. The Clouded Yellow and the Camberwell Beauty also turn up from time to time, usually in very small numbers; However, in 1992 thousands of Clouded Yellows invaded Scotland – a rare and wonderful sight! Occasionally other species from the north of England may stray over the border into southern Scotland. The Holly Blue has turned up on the Solway coast and the Comma has been seen in the Borders.

It is possible that other species such as the Small Skipper may soon start to turn up from time to time.

THE FUTURE

The Orange Tip is one of the few real butterfly success stories of recent years (Box 5). In the 1850s it was probably found throughout much of mainland Scotland but it suffered a major decline in the second half of the nineteenth century. For many years the species was confined to two areas in the Borders and the north-east. In the 1950s it began to expand its range outwards from these centres, probably as a result of gradual climatic changes with reduced spring rainfall and more sunshine which appeared to suit it. By the early 1980s it was clear that this expansion was gaining pace and it was turning up in many areas where it had never been recorded before. It can now be found throughout most of southern, central and north-east Scotland, and large areas of the Highlands. It is still colonising new areas and is probably commoner in Scotland today than it has ever been since records began.

Other Scottish butterflies will benefit from climatic changes in the future. If global warming occurs it would probably lead to an increase in those species for which southern Scotland is the northerly limit at present, such as the Wall Brown and the Large Skipper. Unfortunately species like the Mountain Ringlet might find a warmer Scotland too warm and disappear. Recent work on Ben Lawers suggests that a 1°C or 2°C rise in mean temperature could reduce current suitable habitat for the Mountain Ringlet by as much as 40 per cent.

5. THE ORANGE TIP

The male Orange Tip is unmistakable. The fore-wings have a bright orange patch, tipped with black on the otherwise white upper surface. The female is more difficult to distinguish at a distance, resembling a Large or Small White at first glance. Both sexes are easily recognised when the under-sides are seen, as the hind wings exhibit what appear to be distinctive green marbled patterns. This is in fact an illusion: the green colour is produced by the combination of black and yellow scales on the wings.

The Orange Tip lays its eggs singly on a variety of plants but prefers lady's smock and to a lesser extent garlic mustard and dame's violet. The resulting caterpillars are cannibalistic so that only one will survive on each plant – a strategy which should ensure that there is enough food to satisfy the survivor rather than have several individuals starve. The caterpillar stage lasts about six weeks, after which it finds a suitable place to pupate. The pupa or chrysalis resembles a large thorn on the stem of a plant and the insect passes the winter in this state. The adults will emerge in May or June and will be on the wing for several weeks.

The continuing loss and fragmentation of habitats are the main threats to Scotland's butterflies in the future. Good areas for butterflies may be destroyed by new industrial or housing developments on 'green-field' sites. Misguided attempts to 'tidy up' areas of parkland or urban wasteland often destroy good breeding areas for many species of butterfly. On

6. THE CHEQUERED SKIPPER

The discovery of the Chequered Skipper in Scotland can be regarded as one of the great butterfly discoveries of the twentieth century. It was well known in the Midlands but its range extended only as far north as Lincolnshire and Rutland. The first definite Scottish sighting seems to have been made by Miss C. Ethel Evans near Loch Lochy in June 1939 but this fact was not announced until ten years later. In the meantime the butterfly had been independently discovered in western Inverness-shire in 1942 by Lt Col D. W. Mackworth Praed.

By the 1970s the Chequered Skipper was rapidly declining in its English haunts and it was decided to try to identify other sites where it might occur in Scotland. An SWT-sponsored survey turned up many new sites where it occurred in Inverness-shire and Argyll, showing that it was in fact far more widely distributed than had been previously thought. Although it has since been recorded from about fifty localities in the Lochaber area, there only appear to be ten main sites for it in the area.

The Chequered Skipper generally flies from the third week in May to late June. It prefers sheltered sunny sites, such as clearings and woodland edges. It requires purple moorgrass for the caterpillars and suitable nectar-giving plants, such as bugle, for the adults. Such areas can quickly become overgrown, and soon become unsuitable for the butterflies. Wayleaves created by Scottish Hydro-Electric to maintain access to their power lines are cut every seven to ten years. This regular cutting provides ideal conditions for the Chequered Skipper in areas such as Glasdrum National Nature Reserve. It is also well established along the shores of Loch Arkaig, to the north-west of Spean Bridge, where it can often be seen within a few metres of the road.

The Chequered Skipper is protected under the Wildlife and Countryside Act 1981, with respect to sale of specimens.

The species became extinct in England in 1976. Following extensive research and preparations, the butterfly was re-established at a site in the English midlands in 1995, using stock from France and Belgium.

the other hand, simple neglect may allow once suitable sites to become overgrown and of little use to most species. It is often very difficult to get the balance just right. Building motorways may actually benefit butterflies as they can act as corridors for the insects to move along, linking suitable sites; especially if their edges have been sympathetically planted with native plants.

In 1994 the Scottish Diurnal Lepidoptera Project was set up to study some of Scotland's most endangered butterflies and moths. Six species of butterflies, the Marsh Fritillary (Box 4), Chequered Skipper (Box 6), the Northern Brown Argus (Box 7), the Small Blue, Pearl-bordered Fritillary, and Mountain Ringlet were targeted. Known sites for each species were monitored and information about the habitats was carefully recorded. Even so, not enough is known about these and other Scottish butterflies to assess all their needs and promote their conservation.

Scotland is such a huge and diverse country with so many remote areas that it is not surprising that butterflies tend to be under-recorded. A species such as the Green Hairstreak is particularly elusive, since it blends in so well with the green leaves on which it rests. Similarly the Purple Hairstreak usually flies around the tops of oak trees and can often be seen only through binoculars; thus both species tend to be overlooked, even in areas where they may be quite common. It is vital that the changing status of butterflies is known and this can only be achieved through the regular monitoring of sites; this enables the results to be compared from year to year and from place to place so that any trends can be recognised before it is too late.

Such monitoring is carried out in various parts of Scotland by means of a 'butterfly transect': a surveyor walks a standard route once a week throughout the butterfly season and records the numbers of each kind of butterfly found along the route. The results can be used to help plan conservation strategies for particular species.

THE BEAUTY OF BUTTERFLIES

CONSERVATION

Several organisations are involved in encouraging the conservation of butterflies and other insects. Scottish Natural Heritage looks after a great many National Nature Reserves and Sites of Special Scientific Interest which contain important butterfly habitats. At Taynish National Nature Reserve in Argyll, for example, twenty-two species have been recorded, including Marsh Fritillary, Speckled Wood and many more. All butterflies on such a reserve are protected since collecting is not allowed, and a butterfly transect is monitored by the reserve's warden.

The Forestry Commission is also more enlightened today regarding the needs of wildlife in its forests, and in some areas it takes butterflies into account when planning for the future. At Mabie Forest near Dumfries an area has been set aside as a Forest Nature Reserve as a direct result of survey work which found at least seventeen species of butterfly in the area.

The Scottish Wildlife Trust (SWT) encourages butterflies on its reserves and in one case has actually purchased a reserve (Linn Dean in Midlothian) specifically because of the presence of the Northern Brown Argus. Almost all the Scottish species can be found on SWT reserves and in many cases areas are set aside and managed with butterflies in mind. For example, another SWT reserve in Tayside consists of an old railway line where the Small Blue is found; the area requires regular scrub clearance to prevent kidney vetch, the caterpillars' food plant, from becoming smothered by other plants. Careful attention is also paid to the amount of grazing by sheep and cattle which is allowed on some reserves. A certain amount of grazing is often beneficial since it prevents coarse grasses from taking over a site.

Too much grazing, however, may result in the complete loss of essential food plants for the butterflies. Careful management of this kind is vital nowadays to conserve many of our endangered species.

One society which specialises in the conservation of butterflies and moths, is

The Green Hairstreak.

Butterfly Conservation, whose aim is to encourage interest and awareness of butterflies and their conservation. The society has a network of over thirty branches throughout Britain, including three branches covering Scotland. Members do much useful recording work, and are actively recording the distribution of butterflies throughout Britain, to create a new butterfly atlas. They also do active conservation work, including scrub clearance, planting and, where appropriate, re-introductions – usually in conjunction with other conservation bodies. Above all they help to publicise the plight of our rapidly disappearing butterflies.

Some people would like to re-establish populations in areas where butterflies have become extinct. There is no doubt that properly planned and monitored butterfly releases can safeguard the future for some of our rarest butterflies. However, random releases, such as freeing surplus breeding stock, are to be deplored and in fact it is illegal to release non-native species. Butterfly Conservation has

7. THE NORTHERN BROWN ARGUS

Also known as the Scotch Brown Argus or Scotch White Spot, this delightful species was first discovered on Arthur's Seat in Edinburgh. It was described in 1793 by Johan C. Fabricius (Box 1) and so became the first Scottish butterfly to be recorded in the literature. In the early nineteenth century Arthur's Seat was the only known site and dealers employed local people to catch large numbers of specimens for sale to collectors. It was later found in much of southern, central and eastern Scotland in the mid to late nineteenth century. The butterfly finally became extinct on Arthur's Seat about 1870, probably as a result of habitat loss and over-collecting. Scottish Natural Heritage are hoping to re-establish the Northern Brown Argus on Arthur's Seat as part of their Species Action Programme.

The caterpillars feed mainly on rockrose and so the butterfly is generally to be found in areas where this plant grows, often on south-facing grassy slopes below sea cliffs. The adult butterfly, which usually flies from June to July, is very active in sunshine; males often return to settle on the same flower heads time after time as they patrol their territories.

produced a policy and code of practice on butterfly releases, with criteria which must be satisfied before re-introductions are attempted. The serious problems facing butterfly populations cannot be solved just by artificial introduction however, since the process of re-introduction is long and difficult and may not succeed.

WHAT CAN YOU DO?

One way that you personally can help butterflies is by growing suitable plants in your garden to attract them, but you don't have to fill your garden with nettles and thistles! The butterflies that may be attracted to a garden will very much depend on where you live in Scotland. However, if you plant aubretia, candytuft, lavender, scabious and of course buddleia (the butterfly bush), which are all good nectar sources, you may attract a good variety of butterflies to feed on them.

If you can also supply food plants for the caterpillars, such as stinging nettles, coarse grasses, bird's-foot trefoil and nasturtiums, or if you are prepared even to sacrifice a few cabbages in your vegetable plot, you may be lucky enough to have a few butterflies breeding in your garden as well. Of course many other plants are also suitable and the greater variety you have, the more butterflies you may attract.

It is hoped that several Scottish butterflies will achieve greater legal protection in the future, but it is no good protecting the butterflies if the habitats and the environment on which they totally depend are being destroyed around them.

Apart from being beautiful in their own right, butterflies are very sensitive to changes in the environment and as such are very good indicators of the general health of the countryside.

If an area has a good variety of butterflies it is very likely that it has a generally rich flora and fauna. It is to be hoped that Scotland's butterflies will continue to thrive in the future; but much will depend on what we as individuals and as a nation are prepared to do about it.

8. BUTTERFLY HOUSES

There is no better way to learn about the life history of a butterfly than to see it at first hand at a butterfly house. There are currently two butterfly houses in Scotland: Lasswade near Edinburgh, and Giffnock in Glasgow. They are usually open from Easter until October.

Butterfly farms are essentially large greenhouses maintaining hot and humid conditions similar to a tropical jungle environment. Paths wind their way among tropical plants, pools, waterfalls and mud flats, giving visitors the experience of being inside a jungle.

Many varieties of butterflies and moths from all over the world fly free within these enclosures. One can see iridescent blue Morphos from South America, Swallowtails from Africa and Asia, Monarchs from the USA, Common Crows from Australia, moths such as the Indian Moon Moth and even some British species such as the Red Admiral and the Comma.

Native Scottish species are encouraged in the areas around the houses by planting large numbers of suitable food plants and nectar sources for the adult butterflies. You are free to walk around and to approach the live butterflies as close as they will allow before flying off. Special areas are set aside to show the butterflies egg-laying, to show caterpillars feeding and pupating, as well as adults emerging from the chrysalis and drying their wings. However if you look carefully in the main flying areas you can see these activities taking place there as well.

A very popular feature is the 'Butterfly Pub'; many butterflies are strongly attracted to rotting fruit, so an area is set aside where they can feed on bananas, oranges, apples and other over-ripe fruits. Butterflies feeding on the fermented fruit actually become drunk and incapable of flying!

In addition to butterflies the farms exhibit moths, scorpions, Tarantula spiders and giant millipedes. Most of the livestock comes from the Far East, Central America and Africa; however this does not mean that all the stock is taken from the wild. On the contrary, many countries now breed butterflies in captivity to sell to European butterfly houses Thus it is in the interests of local people to conserve their butterfly habitats; as a direct result of this a few endangered species, such as Bird Wing butterflies from Papua New Guinea, have been brought back from the verge of extinction.

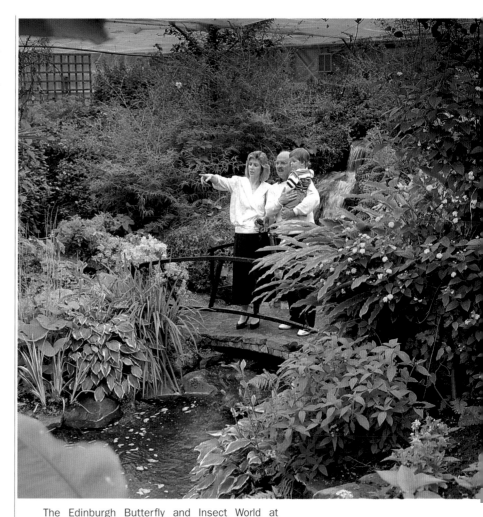

The Edinburgh Butterfly and Insect World at Lasswade has helped directly with butterfly conservation abroad. Members of staff have visited parts of Africa, funded by the World Wide Fund for Nature, to record what species are present in the ancient Korup rain forest of Cameroon. They have played a part in establishing breeding farms for butterflies there, which help to conserve butterflies and also create local employment, thus giving conservation a practical value in the local community.

The educational potential of butterfly houses is very great and school parties are always encouraged. Many children and adults get a terrific thrill when an exotic butterfly settles on their arm, allowing them to see such an exquisitely beautiful insect at really close range.

Edinburgh Butterfly World.

Pierced standing stone at Onich,
West of Scotland.

CHAPTER SEVEN

The Coming of Man
Anna and Graham Ritchie

Dr Anna Ritchie and Dr Graham Ritchie are a distinguished husband-and-wife team who have excavated many significant sites in Scotland. Anna Ritchie is a freelance archaeologist; Graham Ritchie is Head of Archaeology in the Royal Commission on the Ancient and Historical Monuments of Scotland.

THE HUNTER-GATHERERS

Archaeology has been unkindly described as the study of other people's rubbish, and there is more than a ring of truth to the saying. Our knowledge of the first folk to make their way into what is now Scotland is based almost entirely on the things they discarded. Such people made their way along the eastern and western seaboards as bands of hunters, at first making the journey north at certain seasons of the year before returning to a southern base-camp. In order to study the way of life of these people, archaeologists examine the scatterings of tiny flint flakes, the debris of a working place or refuse heaps of shellfish, the remains of gargantuan but monotonous limpet stews. These domestic middens can reveal more about the nature and culture of a people than the most sumptuous hoard of buried treasure.

The date at which people began to arrive in Scotland has been the subject of debate in recent years, with new evidence coming to light and objects found long ago being re-examined with more precise scientific methods. There is circumstantial evidence for the activity of hunting groups in late glacial times about 13,000 years ago, and there was probably a permanent population from at least 9,000 years ago. The bands of hunters may have had distinct territories and they probably had seasonal cycles of activity centered on fishing, gathering berries, digging up roots and hunting woodland animals.

An awareness of nature's seasonal bounty would give orderliness to a lifestyle we find hard to envisage. In addition the seas might occasionally provide an unexpected harvest, such as a small whale stranded on a tidal beach. Today such an event is just a mild curiosity; but to the hunters of early times the carcass would offer a wealth of food, oil and bone. For people who lived in tents or made temporary bivouacs in caves, the bones might have been used as weights around the sides of a tent made from animal hides.

An astonishing range of animals, birds and fish could be exploited: red deer, roe deer, boars, otters, bears and wolves, while the birds may have included guillemots and cormorants. But such hunting had only a limited effect on the natural landscape and its wildlife.

Excavations in Denmark have revealed what is so far lacking in Scotland: carefully deposited burials and elaborately decorated wooden objects show that early people may have had beliefs and interests beyond day-to-day survival, as modern hunter-gatherer societies demonstrate. In Denmark, adult males at this time were about 5 ft 7 in (1.7 m) tall and women averaged 4 ft 11 in (1.5 m) in height; their facial features seem to have been coarser than today. A life expectancy of between forty and sixty years bears testimony to a healthy way of life in Denmark as contrasted with the earliest farming communities in Scotland, where people seem to have died on average much younger. But then one American anthropologist has described hunting and gathering communities as the original affluent societies!

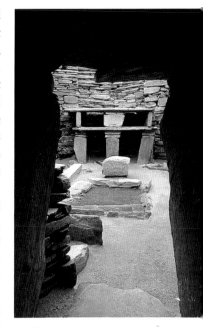

House interior at the ancient village of Skara Brae, Orkney.

Interior of Maes Howe tomb, Orkney.

Skulls from 'The Tomb of the Eagles', at Isbister were ritually buried with the bones of sea eagles.

THE FIRST FARMING COMMUNITIES

Around 4000 BC Scotland experienced one of the most significant episodes in her entire history – the introduction of farming. The idea of a settled life with permanent homes, cultivating plants and breeding animals, was a new and important development introduced into the British Isles by colonists from western Europe. This enterprising lifestyle spread quickly: using scientific dating, archaeologists have discovered that farming spread as far north as Shetland soon after its introduction into the southern parts of the British Isles.

Just why these early pioneers felt such compulsion to press on ever further is one of the unsolved puzzles of prehistory. It is as if every visible shore had to be explored. Shetland proved to be the northern limit of their island-hopping, for the next island group to the north, the Faroes, is well out of sight and would have presented an inhospitable prospect to any accidental visitors.

It is difficult to estimate the numbers of new farming settlers. But there is no doubt that there was a movement of people into Scotland rather than simply the spread of ideas, although in time the new way of life was also adopted by the existing population.

The farming pioneers brought with them seeds for cereal crops and young animals that were to be the start of their domestic herds, for these were resources that did not exist in Scotland. The incomers grew wheat and barley and bred cattle, sheep and goats, which were the most vital possessions that they brought with them from Europe. Other innovations could be carried in the head as knowledge and experience; in this way they brought knowledge of farming methods, how to build permanent houses, how to construct tombs of timber and stone, and how to make pottery.

The burial tombs were built to last and many have survived the intervening 5,000 years or more, some virtually intact. Their design varies from place to place, as do pottery styles, according to the tastes of the communities that created them, and this evidence shows the links between those communities. It is clear that the farmers who settled in Scotland came up the east coast from Yorkshire to colonies the fertile coastal plains and river valleys as far north as the Moray Firth and probably beyond. Others used the western seaways to settle Argyll and the Outer Isles, as well as northern Scotland, Orkney and Shetland.

Their transport for sea and river travel was probably by skin-covered canoe or the log-boat, made from a hollowed tree trunk, and possibly rafts for the livestock. The climate of those times was a little warmer than today and helped to ensure good harvests, allowing them to grow wheat and barley as far north as Orkney and Shetland. The good weather also made for calmer seas making journeys easier. The bones of red sea bream and corkwing wrasse have been found in Orcadian tombs, implying a slightly warmer sea temperature than today when both fish are rarely encountered so far north.

In the words of Stuart Piggott, 'Throughout Scottish prehistory echoes the sound of the woodman's axe'. Indeed the theme of forest clearance runs through every stage of social development in Scotland, from the earliest farmers to the charcoal-burners supplying the eighteenth century iron furnaces of Argyll. The prime concern of the early settlers was to clear land for agriculture, and by felling woodland they created the first dramatic man-made impact on the Scottish landscape. The timber itself had many uses, from boats, houses and stock-enclosures to platters for the family meal.

The axe was perhaps the farmer's single most important tool. In Scotland axe heads were usually made of hard volcanic rock, ground to a sharp cutting edge and set in a wooden haft. Many were of local stone, such as Shetland felsite, or the greenstone outcropping at Killin in Perthshire, but others were imported, such as those made of porcellanite from County Antrim in Northern Ireland.

A good axe was a prestigious gift. The role of the axe was so important that it was used as a status symbol; some axes are of exceptional beauty, meticulously crafted from rare stone, and were clearly only used for ceremonial purposes.

Once a suitable area had been cleared of trees the farm could begin to take shape. The house would be oblong or square with rounded corners, built of timber or a combination of stone and timber, and it could be of spacious proportions: the post-holes of a timber house excavated beside the River Dee in Grampian mark out a great hall fully 80 ft (24 m) long and 40 ft (12 m) wide. The house would be surrounded by a working yard, animal enclosures and small cultivated fields with open pasture beyond.

By 3000 BC the process of forest clearance and farming had even created sufficient grassland to allow the occasional stripping of large areas of turf and topsoil in order to build imposing burial mounds. The mounds were often built on top of old farmland, thus preserving traces of the agricultural methods used. Both the spade and a very simple form of plough were common.

The forests remained a major source of food as well as timber. Wild game was hunted but the native pigs were soon domesticated. Berries, crab apples, nuts, roots and fungi would have been gathered to enrich the diet (Box 1).

THE NEW TECHNOLOGY OF METAL WORKING

The early farmers began the long process of changing land-use, and their basic economy and lifestyle persisted throughout prehistory with the addition now and again of new technical developments.

They also embellished the landscape in a less practical way with public buildings. They altered skylines with the tombs of ancestors set beneath pale stone cairns; great slabs of stone were set up in circles, rows or pairs or as single mighty sentinels. Many of these monuments were central to the life of the community for a thousand years or more; some became the focus around which later ceremonial building took place and they remained sacred for many centuries more.

The first major technical innovation in Scotland was metalworking, again introduced into Britain from Europe. Unlike farming, however, the basic ingredients of copper, gold and tin were already available in the British Isles (iron-working was to be discovered later). Surface deposits of copper occur widely in Scotland though gold is less common. The knowledge of how to work copper and gold reached Scotland around 2500 BC, probably arriving with traders

1. THE PEOPLE

Fortunately for the archaeologist, ancestors seem to have been important to early people since they put considerable effort into building tombs to house the bones of their dead and modern excavations have yielded a reasonable sample of bones for analysis. On average, adults were only a little shorter in height than today's norm but their lives were considerably shorter. Of those who survived their childhood few lived beyond their twenties – and those few must have been vital to their communities in passing on knowledge, technical skills and traditions. From about 3000 BC some of those traditions were concerned with circles and alignments of standing stones, and there has been much discussion in recent years over the possible geometric skills and astronomical purposes behind the construction and use of such settings. The plain fact is that the observable level of technical expertise among the early farming communities is such that sophisticated knowledge of geometry and the universe is most unlikely.

Despite the overall youth of the population a very common health problem was spinal disease, usually osteo-arthritis, detectable as malformation of the bones. This was probably caused by the hard physical work of daily life, carrying very heavy loads and manhandling large timbers and slabs of stone.

Their clothes appear to have been made entirely from animal skins, for no spinning or weaving equipment survives from this period and the sheep probably did not produce wool suitable for textiles. The skins could be used either as furs or, with the hair removed, as leather. Virtually every part of the animal would be used, especially the bones for tools, beads, pendants and toggles. Furs were also essential as bedding, laid on top of straw or springy heather; furniture was made of wood or stone or even from the massive ribs and vertebrae of stranded whales.

Ronnie Simison, the farmer who excavated the Tomb of the Eagles on his land at Isbister, Orkney

The stone circle at Calanais on the Isle of Lewis, Western Isles.

The Ring of Brodgar, stone circle Orkney.

and craftsmen looking for new supplies of raw metal. Gold was fashioned into jewellery and copper into axe-heads; ownership of either would have been equally prestigious.

Few copper objects have survived, because people soon discovered that the addition of tin to the copper produced a harder and more useful metal, bronze. Tin could only be obtained from Cornwall or Europe, pointing to the far-reaching trade networks existing between communities. Later still, some time after 1000 BC, lead was added to improve the casting qualities of bronze.

Around the time that knowledge of metalworking reached Scotland a new wave of incomers appeared in the population; there may have been a link between the two developments but it does not seem to have been a simple matter of migrants bringing new technology. A type of pottery known to archaeologists as 'beaker pottery' made its first appearance in Britain around 2500 BC. Comparing the earliest Scottish beakers with those in Europe, it is clear that the new settlers came in small numbers to eastern Scotland across the North Sea from the Netherlands.

They buried their dead in single graves rather than communally as in earlier tombs, and they seem to have had broader skulls than the native farmers. They were buried with their personal belongings, often including bows and arrows and a beaker which, at least sometimes, contained a mead-like drink. These new people with their novel pottery and burial rites were soon absorbed into the existing population. Cremation became increasingly popular from about this time, and the large amounts of timber required both for cremating the dead and for metalworking led to more forest clearance. Peat was not a significant fuel until the major growth of blanket peat was under way around 1000 BC.

Peat formation was caused by a worsening climate, and the colder and wetter weather affected farming. Bad weather led to more frequent crop failures and it is also possible that the early farmers had exhausted the soil in some places. All these factors led to growing social pressures: there was less farmland to support a growing population and competition for land would have increased. The social effect can be seen in an increased production of swords and shields by the bronze industry and in the building of fortifications.

CELTIC SOCIETY

Few words evoke as many different reactions as the word 'Celtic'. It may suggest a style of modern jewellery with interlace and spirals; it may describe the family of languages that includes Gaelic and Breton; for many Scots it conjures up a green and white football scarf. In prehistoric terms it is used to describe a series of tribes active in central Europe and France from the sixth century BC who spoke a language that was ancestral to modern Gaelic and who did indeed have a distinctive art style, although they did not use interlace. Celtic society was composed of tribes with leaders, warriors, farmers and craftsmen in metalwork, pottery and wood. The Celts have recently been introduced to a far wider audience through the adventures of Asterix the Gaul and the village life of Vitalstatistix, Obelix and their friends.

The names of Celtic gods are known and their worship may have involved the ritual casting of objects into sacred pools and lakes. The introduction of certain aspects of this way of life into Britain, along with the adoption of the Celtic language, was once thought to be the result of a series of waves of invaders and settlers from the continent. In recent years, however, archaeologists believe that large-scale immigration was not the cause of the changes evident in the archaeological record of later centuries BC. Perhaps the arrival of small groups of people who gained a measure of political ascendancy was responsible for the introduction of the Celtic language, but trade

and other contacts may also have made the new ideas fashionable.

As we have seen, the farming communities of many parts of Scotland seem to have been subjected to social pressures which resulted in the building of defensive enclosures formed by stout palisades of timber.

Palisaded stockades and fortifications of stone with wooden frameworks required large quantities of straight timber beams for their construction and hastened the deforestation of upland Scotland. The building of one palisaded settlement in the Borders is estimated to have required at least 2,600 upright posts. Hilltop fortifications also needed large quantities of timber for their construction, as a criss-cross framework often stabilised the rubble walls. A stout timber gateway would have led into a bustling community living in timber houses, some set against the fort wall. One of the main industries, iron-working, would have required large areas of coppiced woodland in order to have a ready supply of charcoal.

Many hill forts caught fire either accidentally, as a result of attack, or most plausibly as a result of deliberate burning after a successful campaign. The wall cores fused into 'vitrified' lumps because of the great heat, but it should be stressed that this was not a deliberate constructional technique.

Left: The Broch of Mousa in Shetland.

Above: In cross-section Mousa Broch reveals the galleried walls which protected defenders against attackers.

The Bridgeness Slab from the Antonine Wall in West Lothian depicts a Roman legionary defeating barbarians.

103

The many fortifications found all over Scotland imply a way of life that involved raiding neighbouring tribes; in some cases such refuges are no more than a defended farmstead, in others the equivalent of small fortified towns. Security could be obtained by building a stout stone wall round the top of a small rocky knoll, but in many parts of Scotland people sought safety by building their homes on an artificial island or 'crannog' of stone and timber a little way offshore in a loch or perhaps in an area of marshy shallows. The timber and thatch houses built on these islands could only have been reached by boats or by causeways, making them easier to defend.

Many rural settlements can be detected as 'crop markings' on aerial photographs, the holes in which upright timbers were set appearing as darker marks in growing crops. The economic basis of society appears to have involved both grazing animals and mixed farming, the balance depending largely on climate and topography, much as today.

Broch towers, epitomised by the Broch of Mousa in Shetland, have captured the imagination of archaeologists and tourists for over a century. These drystone constructions, described as 'the only really advanced architectural innovation invented entirely within Britain', have in the past been seen as indicating that the west and north of Scotland were subjected to invasion, probably from the south-west of England following Roman occupation of that area.

Nowadays the architectural innovations of broch construction are seen to have an acceptable local ancestry, and large-scale folk movements were not involved. On the other hand the building of such powerful symbols of authority and prestige underlines the uncertainties of the times. It is perhaps not surprising that the name of the first north Briton to be recorded is Calgacus, or 'Swordsman'.

THE ROMAN ARMY IN SCOTLAND

With the march of two columns of Roman soldiers into southern Scotland in AD 79 we take that faltering step from prehistory to history. We know some dates, we know the names of two of the players on the stage – Agricola (the Roman general) and Calgacus (the leader of the Celtic army at the fateful battle of Mons Graupius) – but the bulk of our information, particularly about the environment, comes from archaeology.

The Roman period in Scotland has an unusual fascination for archaeologists and historians. Roman influence in Scotland was brief and only affected parts of the country, but the surviving remains are among the best preserved in the northern Empire.

In fact Roman troops were stationed in Scotland for only two periods, each of about twenty years' duration; the first at the end of the first century AD and the second in the mid second century AD. A further period of intense military campaigning took place between AD 208–11, when the Emperor Septimus Severus led a massive army into Scotland. Thereafter some measure of political authority was exercised in southern Scotland until AD 367. The economic impact on the native population is likely to have been considerable. The Roman army obtained supplies locally, and demands for grain and other foods as well as leather and wool for uniforms and clothing must have radically altered the former economic patterns of local exchange.

The frontier earthwork known as the Antonine Wall, built around the year AD 142 for the emperor Antoninus Pius, ran for almost 37 miles (60 km) from Bridgeness on the Firth of Forth to Old Kilpatrick on the Firth of Clyde. It was designed to control travel and trade rather than as a defensive work. The wall was in fact a turf rampart at least 10 ft (3 m) high and on average some 15 ft (4.5 m) wide at the base, and the stripping of such a large quantity of turf is itself testimony to the extensive areas of grassland available. A recent estimate has suggested that some 800–950 acres of land were stripped, and that to complete any breast work along the top about one million cubic feet of timber were needed.

The diet of the Roman soldier included bread as well as meat from cattle, sheep, pigs, red deer and chicken. Examination of plant debris in a cesspit at the fort of Bearsden has revealed some exotic additions to the diet, including figs, coriander, wild celery and opium poppy. Roman soldiers clearly also enjoyed the variety offered by local raspberries, brambles, strawberries and bilberries!

BRITONS, PICTS, ANGLES AND SCOTS

Life in Scotland altered little after the departure of the Roman army in the middle of the second century. On the domestic front rectangular houses became more popular, although circular designs (which had been the norm) continued to be built virtually throughout the first thousand years AD. In southern Scotland it is likely that the native British population received some new blood through intermarriage with Roman soldiers; but that blood was not truly Roman or even Italian but German, as a result of local recruitment into army units stationed in Germany before being sent to Britain. The most important effect of the Roman presence in north Britain was political: opposition to Rome seems to have fostered a degree of unity among the tribes beyond the frontier zone. The original small Celtic tribes appear to have gradually merged until, in the fourth century AD, the entire population north of the Forth – Clyde line was known by one name, the Picts.

This process of political amalgamation led, by the sixth century, to the emergence of distinct kingdoms in Scotland as elsewhere. There were three British kingdoms in southern Scotland: Gododdin with its major stronghold at Edinburgh; Strathclyde with a stronghold on Dumbarton Rock; and Rheged based on the

Interior of the south cairn chambered tomb at Nether Largie, Kilmartin valley, mid-Argyll.

2. THE KILMARTIN VALLEY

An exploration of the Kilmartin valley in mid-Argyll allows the visitor to appreciate the monuments of prehistoric and early historic times even though the setting has been much altered with the passing centuries. There is an impressive cairn at Nether Largie and you can still drop into the long stone-capped chamber and try to imagine the shrouded burials of members of early farming communities with pottery vessels laid reverently alongside. The stone circle at Temple Wood was used for rituals and burials over many centuries and was finally sealed with a cairn of stones; but look out for the double spiral decoration on one of the uprights.

Burial cairns laid out along a straight line give the impression of a cemetery of a local dynasty; several of the individual stone coffins or 'cists' (the Scottish word for a chest) can still be seen, some with carved decoration on the slabs in the form of axes – surely a symbol of status. Several groups of standing stones dot the valley, some decorated with cup-and-ring markings – mute testimony to forgotten rites. The great rock expanses at Achnabreck and Cairnbaan a little to the south are carved profusely with cup-and-ring markings and have puzzled antiquaries for years.

Shortly after 2000 BC peat began to form across the valley floor and covered several sites, including Temple Wood, until drainage and peat-clearance in the nineteenth century when the neat present-day fields were laid out. There are several forts and duns built on rocky knolls on the margins of the valley from the first few centuries BC onwards.

The climax of any visit to Kilmartin should be the rocky stronghold of Dunadd, one of the citadels of the Scots in the seventh and eighth centuries AD; it is however quite an imaginative feat to recreate the bustling fort with timber buildings set within the walls, blacksmiths and bronze-workers, and the feasting halls and domestic quarters of a chief.

On a rock surface just below the summit two carved footprints and a basin may betoken royal inauguration ceremonies, while an incised boar in a very Pictish style may even commemorate contact with their eastern neighbours in the seventh or eighth century.

The location of the present village on a little terraced apron set above the valley floor has, like the gravel terraces opposite, probably been a focus for settlements from earliest times. A carved cross, now in the church, shows that there was a Christian community here from about the tenth century; there is another fine cross of sixth-century date. Many fine grave slabs in the distinctive West Highland style show that Kilmartin remained a focus for burials in the later fourth and fifth centuries AD – as it had become so many millennia earlier.

Pictish carved stone with cup and ring markings at High Banks, Kirkcudbright, Dumfries and Galloway.

105

Solway Firth. In the meantime German migrants known as Angles (or English) had been settling along the coastal plains of Yorkshire and Northumberland, creating the Anglian kingdoms of Deira based on York and Bernicia based on Bamburgh.

The Britons of Gododdin and Rheged were the first to suffer from Anglian territorial ambitions in southern Scotland; Bernicia and Deira had been fused into a single powerful kingdom, Northumbria, in AD 605 and Anglian war-bands penetrated north and west, occupying British lands. Edinburgh was captured in AD 638 and much of Rheged was conquered during the rest of the seventh century. From this time on, the population of southern Scotland was to be of mixed British and Anglian stock until Lothian was taken over by the Scots during the late tenth century.

The Scots had come originally from Ireland and there was already strong Irish settlement in the Rhinns of Galloway by the sixth century, not mentioned in historical sources but detectable through place-names and archaeology. The documented settlement of Argyll by the Scots was on a grander scale. The 'Scotti' were an Irish tribe in County Antrim for whom the visible shores of Kintyre had long beckoned with the lure of new land; sporadic migration seems to have taken place over perhaps a century or more, until around AD 500 the ruling dynasty of the tribe transferred itself to a new kingdom of Dalriada in Argyll. In so doing, the Scots displaced Pictish political influence in the area but not the bulk of the population.

By the seventh century, Dalriada stretched from Kintyre northwards to Ardnamurchan, with major strongholds at Dunaverty at the south end of Kintyre, Tarbert, Dunollie at Oban, and Dunadd near Kilmartin (Box 2). Years of uneasy relations with the kingdom of the Picts led finally to a Scottish takeover of Pictland around AD 843.

None of these political developments had any long-term effects on land-use in Scotland. The various peoples shared a basic economy of mixed farming and a common settlement-pattern of princely strongholds and farms.

Political takeover was normally accompanied by the physical takeover of existing power-centres in order to demonstrate the new authority. We know from historical, place-name and archaeological evidence that the British fort at Dunbar was taken over by Angles, and similarly the Pictish royal centre at Forteviot in Perthshire became the palace of the Scottish king.

The various kingdoms were also linked through the Church. Key figures in the spread of Christianity were St Ninian, based at Whithorn in the fifth century, and St Columba, founder of the monastery on Iona in AD 563; and by the end of the seventh century the Church was a strong influence among Britons, Scots, Picts and Angles alike.

Monasteries were self-sufficient farming units. Secular power and ecclesiastical power were closely linked, with the same noble families providing the leaders in both spheres and craftsmen enjoying the patronage of both.

Pictish stone-carvers were renowned for their skill, and their repertoire of distinctive symbols was greatly increased by the addition of Christian motifs and iconography. The creation of elaborately decorated cross-slabs was a challenge to which Pictish sculptors responded to magnificent effect. It is thought that the eighth century high crosses of Iona were commissioned from Pictish master-sculptors and, after the union with the Scots, Pictish workshops continued to produce sculpture for their new masters (though without the symbols that had identified the old Pictish kingdom).

Carved stones must have become a familiar component of the man-made landscape from about AD 600 onwards; several hundred survive today, intact or in fragments, and more must once have existed. Some marked graves, some stood in the grounds of monasteries, some marked land boundaries, some were wayside prayer crosses; all were part of everyday life.

A favourite theme on these stones is the hunt, and this too was part of everyday life, though perhaps enjoyed only by a privileged few. We see horse-riders and their hounds in pursuit of fleeing hinds and archers crouched to take aim at charging boars. Horses are particularly well portrayed, with a real understanding of the animal and more than a hint of sophisticated training of a fine breed. Carvings of salmon perhaps indicate another preoccupation.

Unlike the Picts, the Angles had no tradition of stone-carving before their conversion to Christianity, with the result that Anglian sculpture in southern Scotland is purely church art, from high crosses to shrines carved to hold the bones of saints. The Church developed a network of contacts throughout western Europe, and Scotland was thus part not just of what was happening in Britain and Ireland but of early medieval Europe. Ships laden with jars of wine, mass-produced pottery from France and all kinds of exotic goods from further afield plied their trade all round the Irish Sea. People themselves travelled, especially missionaries and the craftsmen who created fine metalwork.

The influence of the Church could involve mundane matters as well as spiritual affairs. Among the innovations that Irish monks brought to Scotland seems to have been the horizontal corn-mill, a water-powered and larger version of the old hand-quern in which the paddles of the mill-wheel were set horizontally rather than vertically as became normal later. Such horizontal mills date from as early as the seventh century in Ireland and there is evidence on Iona for the use of similar mills there before the eighth century. Mechanised grinding machinery would have made an immense difference to the hard labour of producing flour from grain. Excavation of only part of the contemporary Scottish fort of Dunadd has yielded the remains of some fifty hand-querns, eloquent witnesses to the 'daily grind' in a place lacking the water-courses suitable for mechanised mills.

THE IMPACT OF THE VIKINGS

Contacts across the Irish Sea were disrupted in the final decades of the eighth century by Viking activities. Monasteries kept brief records or annals of important events and Viking raids

are mentioned from AD 793 onwards: 'Devastation of all the islands of Britain by the gentiles', wrote an Irish monk in AD 794, and the following year saw the pillage of Skye, Iona and several Irish monasteries. This pattern of swift and terrifying raids along the western seaway continued throughout the ninth century and it was one of the factors that encouraged the kings of Dalriada to look eastwards into Pictland for their political future.

The raiding Vikings came from Norway and it is likely that they had bases in the Northern Isles for their seasonal campaigns. The prevailing winds in the North Sea favoured a spring voyage westwards and an autumn return to Norwegian fiords. But the advantages of permanent settlement in the Northern and Western Isles were obvious; there was good land for the taking, close to the sources of rich pickings, and it was not long before Viking war-bands returned with their womenfolk and belongings to build farms.

From the evidence of archaeology, place-names and documents, it is clear that Pictland and Dalriada rapidly lost their northern and western fringes to the Norsemen during the first few decades of the ninth century. At one time scholars assumed that this process involved

The incised footprint carved in this stone on the summit of Dunadd fortress may have been part of the initiation ceremonies of the kings of Dalriada.

Viking houses, Brough of Birsay, Orkney.

important crop was introduced: flax. Fine linen tunics were essential to the affluent Viking wardrobe and special glass linen-smoothers were used to produce a good finish to the cloth. Fibres from the stem of the flax plant were spun into linen, and flax seeds have been found at Norse settlements in Orkney.

The Norsemen also breathed new life into the soapstone carving industry in Shetland; Norway has its own sources of soapstone (also known as steatite) and the Norse settlers in Scotland were accustomed to using bowls and lamps and other items carved from this relatively soft stone. In Shetland there was intensive exploitation of steatite outcrops in Norse times, on Unst and at Cunningsburgh, south of Lerwick.

The Scandinavian settlement of Scotland, from the ninth-century land-grabs of the far north and west to the tenth- and eleventh-century penetration of the south-west, was the last major influx of migrant people in early medieval times. Another new element was added to the population during the twelfth century, but it was considerably smaller in numbers and more peaceful in intent: these were the Anglo-Norman and Flemish families to whom David I and his successors gave grants of land in southern Scotland, Fife and Moray.

Their chief contribution to the landscape was dramatic for they built huge earthen mounds, or mottes, as bases for their timber castles. In many cases the motte was surrounded by an outer bailey, enclosed by a great ditch and ramparts, in which domestic buildings could be protected, and the whole enterprise represented a massive earth-shifting operation. The castle and other buildings required large quantities of timber to be felled. The fashion for mottes caught on among the Scottish lords and the number built is reflected by the surviving remains of more than 300.

A marked characteristic of Scotland in early medieval times was the rural nature of its settlement-pattern. There were no urban centres to emulate Viking Dublin or York, and Scotland lacked any coinage of its own until the twelfth century. There was certainly trading and

extermination of the local people, or at best dispossession and enslavement, but excavations over the last twenty years have uncovered a more subtle picture of what happened. The majority of Norse settlements were built literally on top of the demolished ruins of earlier native homes, which in most cases had been abandoned some time previously.

At the Brough of Birsay in Orkney, a large settlement of special importance both in Pictish and Norse times, the Viking-age houses were placed so that they occupied the same individual plots of land as their Pictish predecessors. In other words, we see the Norsemen establishing their authority and overlordship by taking over existing estates and land-patterns and occupying existing power-centres. For the local population this meant new masters and little more – some enslavement, no doubt, but slavery was already a familiar part of life among all peoples at that time.

The Norsemen acquired native equipment such as bone combs and pins, and they were prepared within a few generations to adopt the local religion, Christianity – there are few pagan graves after the end of the ninth century.

Norse farms were similar to those of the existing population, but at least one new and a degree of craft-specialisation, but the trade was based on barter and exchange, and the craftsmen were mostly itinerant metalworkers. A cargo of wine and fine glassware might be exchanged for slaves, furs or exquisite brooches, or in Norse times for silver bullion, carefully weighed on the folding scales found in pagan Viking-age graves.

Wine was for princes and warlords and most feasts were washed down with mead or ale, both mentioned in early documents. Diet could be quite varied, particularly for those living near the sea; excavations have yielded the bones of cattle, sheep, goats, pigs, deer and domestic fowl, along with a wide range of fish, shellfish, seabirds, seals and whales. Many of these provided more than meat of course, for they were sources of wool, skins and furs for clothing and bedding, and bones, antlers and horns for tools, as well as dairy products, eggs and oil. Crops such as barley, wheat and oats were processed into bread, porridge, bannocks and, in the case of barley, fermented brews.

Wild fruits and berries, nuts, roots and herbs were gathered. Peat had become an important fuel: Turf-Einar Rognvaldsson, a ninth-century Viking earl in Orkney, was so-called by his compatriots because 'he was the first man to dig peat for fuel, firewood being very scarce on the islands' – a wise man not slow to learn native ways!

In the north and west, stone remained the main building material, but both Picts and Norsemen used a wind-proof combination of stone and turf for the walls of their houses, with a good stone face on the inside and an outer cladding of turf. Turf on a timber framework was probably also used for roofs. South of the Moray Firth, timber was more widely used, and traces of early medieval houses are consequently more difficult to find.

Place-names incorporating the element *carden*, or copse, underline the prevalence of woodland in the landscape and its relationship to the Pictish settlement pattern between the firths of Moray and Forth. The crannog, familiar from earlier times, remained popular among the Scots and Britons of the west and south-west, who now built rectangular as well as round houses on their island-platforms. Crannogs used the surrounding water as a natural defence, and forts were similarly located on naturally defensive land sites such as isolated hills or coastal promontories. Both crannogs and forts made extensive use of timber, for the ramparts of early medieval forts were reinforced internally by wooden beams, as had been the forts of earlier times.

AN ARCHAEOLOGICAL HERITAGE

The people who made Scotland their home from the earliest agricultural communities of prehistoric times to the Anglo-Norman families of the twelfth century have left enduring monuments in the form of burial mounds or fortifications. Only a tiny fraction of such sites have been examined in detail by excavation and our knowledge about the dates or social contexts of the remainder is limited. The archaeological landscape of Scotland is known in detail only in a few selected areas; Orkney and Argyll for example, and many other parts of the country are as yet unsurveyed in any depth. The impact of modern development on the countryside from afforestation, opencast mining or land improvement places a burden on the sparse archaeological profession in Scotland to ensure that as little information as possible is lost.

The wealth of archaeological information in lowland Scotland which has been discovered as a result of a concentrated programme of aerial photography shows that many sites may potentially be at risk as a result of deeper ploughing methods or farm woodlands. No archaeologist would seek to halt inevitable changes in land management; indeed our study is one of constant change brought about by the demands of agriculture and timber exploitation. But by surveying and excavating sites in advance of change, and conserving sample areas of landscape illustrating a range of sites – cairns, field systems, houses (perhaps with some reconstructions) – the archaeological heritage of Scotland could be better understood and presented to Scots of today.

Norman motte at Bass of Inverurie, Gordon, Grampian.

*Highland cattle are hardier beasts
than modern breeds and can survive
the harsh northern winters and
poor grazing.*

CHAPTER EIGHT

The Farming of the Land

Alexander Fenton

*Professor (Emeritus) Alexander Fenton is Director of the
European Ethnological Research Centre.*

In April 1990 in north-east Scotland the air was filled with the cacophonic racket of a new phenomenon – the 'de-stoner', Reekie's 'Stone and Clod Separator'. Drawn behind tractors that dwarfed their drivers, these travelling riddles were at work on several farms, sifting and refining the soil and burying the stones they gathered, preparing seed beds that had the quality of garden ground. The drill-sown crops that followed would be potatoes, carrots and turnips; not the 'yellows'and swedes that had foddered the cattle in the winter byres for over 200 years, but smaller turnip varieties grown to suit the tastes of urban housewives who like the 0.5 to 0.7 kilogramme (1 to 1.5 lb) size, which growers then wax to make them keep until they reach the shops.

The coming of the 'de-stoner' may have been promoted by farmers moving to Scotland from England, attracted by currently cheaper land prices in Scotland. More certainly it marks one of the responses to central government,which is currently pressing for alternative forms of farming. In this case we see the emergence of a kind of 'supermarket gardening' to satisfy the food demands of a population increasingly distanced from the land.

From the viewpoint of the nation's heritage, the de-stoner sadly obliterates all traces of the archaeological record lying beneath the plough-soils of the last 300 years. Near the fields where I saw the de-stoner at work I have picked up flint arrowheads and a flint core from which flakes had been struck in Neolithic times (see Chapter 7); the plough has also taken the lid off a Bronze Age cist-burial which contained the remains of a bronze dagger, a pot, and the bones of a human being who could not have envisaged de-stoners in his wildest dreams. Change can damage the past as well as the future.

The de-stoner is a modern example of change and of the possible effects of change, not all of which can be foreseen and planned for unless we take a very broad view. The most obvious historical change has been demographic: the increasing concentration of people in the towns and industrial areas of the Central Belt of Scotland. In 1974 about 3.8 per cent of Scotland's total work-force was engaged in agriculture; today it is less than 1.5 per cent (see Chapter 10). Scotland's people are no longer based mainly in the countryside, as they were for most of the preceding centuries.

Also, in modern times, a real distinction has emerged between farming as a self-sufficient way of life (encouraged by governments during and after the two world wars) and agriculture as a food industry. The industrialisation of farming was characterised by mechanisation, a move away from tenancy to ownership and the subsidised production of crops. It has also created close relationships with the food-processing trades, and drawn support from interested groups like the National Farmers Union, co-operative societies and marketing boards. There is now a European drive to reform the structure of farming because of the pressure of too many on the land, the proliferations of holdings too small to be

Reekie's de-stoner at work in the fields of East Lothian.

viable, and the waste involved in excessive fragmentation under certain kinds of landholding.

Until the 1700s the countryside of Scotland was more like the rest of Europe in having a settlement pattern with farming villages, or 'ferm-touns' as they were called, predominating; these were farms worked jointly by the families living on them (Box 1). But around 1700, when most of Scotland's people still lived on and depended on the land, there was no real way to improve crop yields or intensify the system of land-use except here and there through spreading lime on the land; and even that was not enough in itself without the support of good drainage. The pressure to produce more food from the land had become irresistible. The need for change had become vital, though it came much sooner for the Lowlands than for the Highlands. What were the factors that brought about, and financed, such change?

AGENTS OF CHANGE

A main agent of change was the pressure from the towns – and the demand of their markets, particularly in the growth of the grain and cattle trades.

Lothian and Moray grain was being exported to the Netherlands, the Baltic, Norway and western Sweden in exchange for timber, and was also exported to England after the Union of 1707. The coastal trade in grain from the north of Scotland to Edinburgh increased substantially after about 1660 in response to demands from the capital's mills and breweries. Merchants offered landowners contracts for their annual crops, and annual rents were paid in the form of grain. The government put its finger in the national liquidity pie by controlling grain imports and putting a bounty on exports. There were strong pressures to increase the arable acreage of grain-growing areas, and the enabling Enclosure Acts of 1661, 1685 and 1695, as well as the Division of Commonties Act of 1695, can be seen as a government response under first James VII and II and then William and Mary.

Another factor in the growth of income was the role played by the celebrated 'black cattle' of the Highlands. From the early 1600s the pastoral Highlands had been supplying the Lowlands with cheese (some of which may have come from sheep's milk) in years of cereal scarcity; but the major economic resource, in national terms, lay in cattle. Before the Union of 1707, Scotland was already considered 'a mere grazing field to England', and Scottish beef helped to feed the city of London as well as the British army and navy. Scotland's unique banking system financed the growth in the cattle trade by facilitating cattle deals through loans to dealers from the south and elsewhere.

The droving trade had a marked physical effect on the landscape. The droving tracks became the progenitors of the road system (see Chapter 11) and by the 1580s grazing parks enclosed within stone walls or 'dykes' were appearing, for example near Edinburgh and in Galloway. Moreover, in the cattle-rearing hinterland of the Highlands, change was also becoming apparent in the traditional shieling or summer pasture system (Box 2).

The grain trade in the Lowlands and the cattle trade in the Highlands were not, of course, sufficiently profitable to fund the 'agricultural revolution' by themselves. Other factors, like the tobacco trade of Glasgow and the movement of capital (some of it from England) through the banks, have to be taken into account. By 1707, however, there seems to have been sufficient progress in agriculture to avoid the famine conditions of earlier years. But Scottish agriculture could not yet support a growing urban population or provide enough stocks of essential raw material. Since agriculture was the dominant sector of the economy, change was vital to strengthen the nation's weak exchange position if opportunities opened up by the Union of 1707 were not to be lost. Scotland's unimproved agriculture seriously handicapped the nation's opportunity to take part in a widening world economy.

THE NEW MONEY

At the time of the Union with England the landed interests had an infusion of new blood by recruiting merchants, bankers and lawyers to their ranks. They were willing and even eager to promote agricultural improvement and had a strong concern for the industrial aspects of economic opportunity, as shown by the industrial enterprises in most of the planned villages they established in the eighteenth century.

There had already been some investment, as

Runrig cultivation beds are still evident on Duddingston golf course, Edinburgh.

1. THE FERM-TOUN

The early ferm-touns contained up to a dozen households clustered in homes and steadings on the edge of their arable land, which was worked jointly by all the inhabitants. They were mainly organised on the runrig system whereby each family had several detached rigs (lengths of raised ploughed land) originally allocated by rotating lot each year, so that everyone would have a fair share of the more fertile land.

The arable land lay in strips and patches scattered amongst the heather and moor, the bog and waste ground, with rough grazing and moorland areas beyond. As the ferm-toun expanded (for instance by woodland clearance), single tenancy units came into being.

The use of the arable land was by 'infield' and 'outfield'.

The infield was the best land nearest the houses. It was manured regularly from every possible source available, including preying on the poorer land around. Dung from the byre and stable, household refuse, and turf from many sources (including composted earthen middens made from turf cut for the purpose) all went into the infield soil. The two staple crops were bere (a form of barley) and oats. In the best farming areas wheat was important since it produced cash from the sale of its white flour for the bread of the better off. Extensive parts of the surrounding land were continually being depleted to maintain the productivity of the relatively limited infield areas.

The outfield, or poorer quality land, usually lay a little further off. It was an essential complement to the infield, dedicated primarily to stock grazing and only secondarily to crops. It was a source of grassy turfs for many uses. Shifting cultivation was practised on the outfield with stock being folded on different parts in turn with those parts being used for crops for a few years, without further manuring, until their ability to produce crops was exhausted. It was on the outfield that new forms of manuring were first tried, such as salt (from the late 1500s) and lime (from the 1620s), sporadically at first but later with increasing frequency. By spreading lime the outfield could be brought up to infield quality. In lime-bearing areas such as the Lothians and Ayrshire this led to a great increase in land under the plough in the late 1600s and early 1700s.

The surrounding rough grazing and moorland, the peat bogs and the wet scrub-covered land were necessary service areas. They provided peat for fuel as well as turf for building and for making earthen middens. They were also grazed by sheep and cattle, watched over by the young folk of the farms, and sometimes provided famine food like dry sprigs of heather.

From the infield, the outfield and the moorland there developed a kind of ecological energy cycle. In good times this economy fed men and animals, provided seed for next year's harvest and created a surplus to cover the rent and the cost of smithy work for plough and cart. It might also provide a mart (an animal fattened for winter slaughter and pickling, so that a meat feast might be possible at the New Year and at celebrations like weddings). But if the weather was bad and the crops poor the system, already stretched to its limits with the increase of population, could not readily cope and had no built-in flexibility in the less-favoured areas.

Lime kilns at Esperton, Midlothian: lime was vital for improving the fertility of the land in the 18th century.

113

Descended from a race of Ingenious Mechanics,
To whom the Country, for ages, had been greatly indebted,
He steadily followed the Example of his Ancestors,
And,
By Inventing and bringing to Perfection
A MACHINE
For Separating Corn from the Straw,
(Constructed upon the Principles of Velocity
and furnished with fixed Beaters or Skutchers,)
Rendered, to the Agriculturists of Britain,
And of other Nations,
A more Beneficial Service, than any hitherto
Recorded in the Annals of Ancient or Modern Science.

Gravestone of Andrew Meikle, inventor of the threshing machine, at East Linton churchyard, East Lothian.

The mechanical reaper invented by Patrick Bell in 1827 revolutionised harvesting.

evidenced by the rebuilding of some tower houses in the sixteenth and seventeenth centuries and the erection of new mansion houses, such as Kinross House (1686–91) and Hopetoun House (1696–1701), around which extensive areas of parkland developed after the 1760s. Foreign writers have remarked that England was a country of parks, and by the eighteenth century Scotland was catching up on this tradition. Formally laid out parks were created as part of estate improvements and

these became elements in regularising the face of the countryside, with farmhouses and farms included. And part of the change they represented lay in the exotic trees and plants their owners introduced.

An enormous amount of our knowledge about the countryside comes from the estate plans which surveyors drew up to record the existing state of, and proposals for the improvement of, estates in most parts of the country. Something like 50,000 plans were made in the eighteenth century alone – a striking demonstration of intent concerning land management by aristocratic owners, lairds and bonnet-lairds (landowners who farmed their own land) alike, who in the 1770s controlled about 50, 40 and five per cent respectively of the agrarian wealth of Scotland.

Linked to such plans, three phases of eighteenth century improvement can be seen: a first generation thrust (1720–40s) by landowners and lairds who had capital to develop; a more businesslike set of team efforts

(1750–70s) between owners, surveyors, factors and tenants; and from the 1770s, input from large capitalistic tenants with the tenantry doing most of the improving.

THE CHANGING LANDSCAPE

Running through these phases, and affecting them, we see the new agricultural technology that was to alter the face of the ancient farming landscape almost beyond recognition.

The ploughing technique in most areas had consisted of turning the soil into a series of long raised 'rigs', or ridges, with drainage furrows in between. The ridges varied in width, the older ones being up to 36 ft (11 m) wide while more recent ones were between 10 ft (3 m) and 18 ft (5 m) wide. This system of ridge and furrow was necessary for surface drainage. Traditionally, the farmers ploughed along the length of the ridge; sowers walked along one half of the ridge, then back along the other as they spread their seed with one arm from a sowing-sheet knotted around the shoulder; at harvest time, reapers with sickles also worked along the ridges.

Remains of the old ridge and furrow can still be seen today. They show up well in slanting sun over light snow and can be found beneath woods planted in the early nineteenth century, on the lower slopes of hills and on golf courses created from farmland in Victorian times.

The new agricultural technology which emerged in the eighteenth century affected not only husbandry but cropping and crop-processing. It appeared first in the most basic of all agricultural implements: the plough. The early improvers looked to England for ploughs they thought better than the local type: they were men like Barclay of Urie in Kincardineshire, Grant of Monymusk in Aberdeenshire, and the Earl of Galloway, who had English plough types on his Orkney estates by 1747.

The Earl of Stair imported a Dutch plough in 1730 and sent a man to England to learn to make implements. But the real advance came with the plough developed in 1767 by the Berwickshire ploughwright, James Small. This combined the features of the northern English

Ploughing with oxen, from 18th century gravestone in Liberton kirkyard, Edinburgh.

Rotherham plough and the native 'old Scotch' plough, and use of the new hybrid plough spread rapidly.

A second major innovation was the threshing machine. Experiments to replace the centuries-old hand-threshing flails with mechanical beaters had been going on from at least 1732. By 1758 water-driven horizontally turning scutchers were tried, modelled on the flax mill. However, the real breakthrough came with Andrew Meikle who produced the first successful threshing mill by feeding sheaves of grain through rollers into a revolving drum. Meikle's mill was developed in 1786 and spread rapidly, at first to the larger farms and then to the smaller holdings throughout the country. Four decades later, technology revolutionised the back-breaking labour of hand reaping in the fields. In 1827 Patrick Bell invented the first practical mechanical reaper which quickly began to replace the sickle and scythe.

But the development which most radically altered the farming landscape was the spread of systematic underground tile drainage, along with the enclosing of fields, from the 1840s. Since ridges were no longer needed for drainage they were gradually levelled. It was then possible to work the flat land across the vanished ridges which no longer hindered the worker with the scythe, nor the horse-operated machine-reaper, nor the horsedrawn sowing-machines and rollers or any of the machines that soon became commonplace. It took only half a century to erase the shape of the old farming world by creating fields with level surfaces which have been familiar to us now for

2. THE SHIELING

The coming of the Blackface sheep hastened the end of the system of cattle grazing on the summer shielings.

The shielings were grazing areas to which stock were taken in the summer. For centuries the annual seasonal rhythm had been a movement in spring from the lower-lying village (the *wintertown*) to the higher-lying shieling areas with their clusters of huts of stone and turf or of wattle and turf (the *summertown*). Around the summertown the stock could enjoy the new hill grass while the new season's crop could grow to maturity in the wintertown. The stock was brought back to the lower levels after the autumn harvest when the village lands had been cleared of crops and were again thrown open to what amounted to common grazing.

But commercial pressures intervened to change the nature of the shieling system, both in the run up to the Act of Union of 1707 and afterwards. The use of the shieling areas was intensified as a result of the increasing commercial interest in cattle, particularly by lairds sending black cattle to the hills along with the stock of their tenants.

Such sharing, marking a period of co-existence under the conditions of cattle-trading, was rudely ended with the massive and widespread introduction of commercial breeds of sheep, Cheviot and Blackface, mainly in the nineteenth century. At this point the shieling areas were cleared and made into single farms for the use of sheep-farmers and sheep-men, many of whom came from the south of Scotland. Blue-slated farmhouses began to dot the lonely hills and, with the exception of Lewis in the Hebrides where shieling use ran on into the twentieth century, the 1800s saw the effective end, owing to economic pressures, of what had been a long-standing form of land-use in the more pastoral parts of the country.

nearly 150 years.

Although it did not happen overnight the change was irrevocable. Ferm-touns were replaced by consolidated individual holdings standing within their own enclosed fields on which crop rotation was practised, including sowing grass seed and allowing land to lie fallow in summer. Common grazing areas that had been allotted to owners were reclaimed and improved where possible as part of the spread of the new agriculture. Such former grazing areas were sometimes cultivated by using the lazy-bed technique for potatoes, a crop that spread from big house gardens to tenants' fields in the 1700s. The lazy-bed system involved planting on undug strips of soil using manure and soil from adjacent trenches as a covering and was good for cleaning the ground. With such enormous changes the whole appearance of Lowland Scotland, or at least the farming parts, altered dramatically.

In the Highlands a different kind of agricultural revolution was taking place, involving not mechanical innovation but a new form of land-use: sheep husbandry on a massive scale. The coming of the sheep produced the most spectacular change of all – the trauma of human displacement known to history as 'The Highland Clearances' (Box 3).

At the same time planned villages with their rural industries were appearing, turnpike roads and other smaller linking tracks were spreading and two-wheeled carts drawn by solidly-built horses proliferated. These changes made the transport of goods easier. The countryside was becoming more market-orientated by supplying food for the expanding villages, towns and cities to which increasing numbers of people were moving. Food production for a wider market was the key to the new economy as people moved inexorably away from the self-sufficiency of the old and isolated farming communities whose resources had done little more than allow them to survive.

The feeding of people and the foddering of animals were interrelated. By about 1740 turnips, which like potatoes had originated in the gardens of the rich, had become a field crop in the Lothians and the Merse and eventually elsewhere. Turnips enabled farmers to over-winter stock and to fatten cattle for the market. The spread of potatoes also led directly to an increase in pig keeping, especially in dairy farming areas where whey was available for use as swill. Even the Highlanders, traditionally opposed to eating pork, were feeding small swine on potatoes by the 1790s. They sold thousands of such pigs at the Kinross and Cupar markets to Lowland farmers, millers and distillers who had *draff* (the dregs of malt after brewing) to fatten them. By the mid-nineteenth century married farm-workers living in cottar houses had begun to keep pigs in sties attached to their homes, as part of their allowances; or they might get a couple of stones (12 kg) of pork in lieu. For a long time pork was meat for servants, as beef was for their Lowland masters and mutton was to the Highlanders.

Cereal crops also changed in character. Extension of the outfield areas expanded the oats acreage and gradually new varieties of oats came in. The growing of wheat spread northwards from the Lothians and Merse, often at first to coastal areas where seaweed manure was plentiful. The baking of white-floured loaves in the towns and of flour-scones and the like on farm kitchen girdles spread with the availability of wheat. The old cereal 'bere', with its four to six rows of ears, was replaced by the more productive two-eared barley. In fact oats had begun to replace bere in the Lowlands by the end of the seventeenth century and farm-workers bargained with their masters not to have bere-meal, but rather oatmeal, as part of the wages they received in kind.

Beef cattle like the Aberdeen Angus and the Shorthorn (a cross between native Scots and Midland English breeds) were fostered and became important items of trade. The Ayrshire, evolved in the second half of the eighteenth century, led to the establishment and spread from there of dairy farming, again in close support of the expanding urban populations. Plenty of winter fodder – turnips, hay and straw – and good summer grazings were needed to produce the quality of these animals and their produce, and the new farming was able to provide such fodder.

3. THE CLEARANCES

Sheep husbandry developed apace in the Borders in the eighteenth century. Through the use of sheep enclosures, selective breeding was facilitated. Turnips were also one of the bases for winter feed for sheep in the Border area. From here the Cheviot and Blackface sheep moved in their thousands with southern shepherds into the Highland areas.

In the Highlands the numbers of sheep and cattle were about equal in the 1750s but by 1800 sheep were dominant. Increases in the prices of wool and mutton after 1815 led to a major thrust from the south when farmers from the Scottish and English borders rented from Highland lairds shieling areas for the summer grazing of sheep as well as arable stretches for wintering at lower levels.

In this way commercial interaction between Lowlands and Highlands, at the time of the so-called 'Clearances', brought two worlds into conflict. It led to massive disruption of the traditional forms of Highland life and substantial migrations of people from the sheltered straths down to windy coasts, infertile peat-bog and moorland edges. Great numbers of people emigrated to the New World.

The kind of estate surveying that had long been proceeding in the Lowlands now reached the Highlands too, as lairds looked for ways of increasing profits. Sheep farming may have been the first inspiration for this but a secondary opportunity came after the 1870s through the establishment of deer forests, sometimes through conversion of former sheep-farms north and south of the Great Glen. By 1912 deer forests covered 5,800 square miles (15,000 sq km) of the Highlands, though 40 per cent of this was above the 1,500 ft (460 m) level in areas marginal for sheep grazing. In this way lairds in the Highlands were able to tap into the wealth of Victorian industrialists, some of whose profits now went into sport and recreation.

Such activities, however, effectively altered much of the landscape of the Highlands; the crofting settlements were left as a kind of fringe, reshaped in the nineteenth century, often in linear streets with individual fields running below the house to the sea and above the house to the head-dyke on the hill, beyond which the crofters' sheep still graze in common. The individual enclosure of the arable land of the crofts is, on the one hand, similar to what occurred earlier on the Lowland farms; but the survival of common grazing points back to the days of communal or joint farming that have long vanished from Lowland Scotland.

Ruined croft house, Isle of Rum.

ALL CHANGE

Throughout the country, improvements to fields, tools and stock were matched, with regional variations, by improvements in housing. New mansion houses and their surrounding parks started off the process in the late seventeenth century. Farm houses and steadings followed, the estate mains farm usually acting as a prototype. The actual scale and layout of units varied according to the type of farming practised – for example, a hill sheep farm did not need a barn and cereal-processing space as much as a Lowland grain-growing farm – but the new arrangements had some common features.

Most noticeable, marking the changing status between master and workers, was the separation of the dwelling-house from the steading: the house having its own separate garden, with the cottar house a little way off. Bigger farms were already being arranged around a square by the 1690s and this form (usually with the midden in the centre) continued. For smaller-scale places buildings were arranged around three sides or could form a right angle. Smaller farms and crofts continued in the old linear form with house, barn and byre and possibly other elements arranged in a row. But as a stage in modernisation, internal access between people and cattle slowly came to an end, although this 'long-house' tradition survived into the twentieth century in parts of the crofting countries. Probably the most remarkable of such survivals is the 'blackhouse' with its immensely thick walls and low-set thatched roof, well shaped to resist Atlantic gales; there is a celebrated survival, now a museum-piece, in the crofting township of Arnol in Skye. And the staple fuel was always peat (Box 4).

Such sequences of change, differing as they do in the Highlands and Lowlands, had a strong impact on the social structure of the countryside. In subsistence farming days a stake in the land, however minimal, was a form of social security. Improvements led to wage-labourers whose only link with the land was the work they did on it and the local produce they received in kind as part of their wages, whether they were single men in bothies or married men in cottar houses. A social gap came into being, marked among other things by the distancing of workers' quarters from the dwelling-house, the appearance of the farm grieve, overseer or steward as a buffer between men and masters, and a tendency to have food of different qualities. These changes were most common in bigger farming areas, although even the smaller farms were not without their symbolic status differentiations.

The nineteenth century north-east bothy ballad, *Auld Luckie of Brunties*, tells how the men supped their brose with spoons in the kitchen while 'ben the hoose' the knife and fork were wielded and breakfast included luxuries like tea and coffee, butter, eggs and cheese. In the crofting counties crofters and their families retained a land base, but because the 1886 Crofters Holdings (Scotland) Act froze their holdings at a level often too low to be fully viable in terms of producing a living, many had to supplement incomes by work not directly linked to the land.

THE HIGHLAND QUESTION

The cumulative effects of the immense changes in Scotland's land-use over the last 300 years have completely altered the appearance of the man-made landscape. Shared farms have become individual farms though some marginal survivals, like the farming township of Auchindrain in Argyll (now preserved as the Museum of Argyll Farming Life), remain as a pointer to earlier days. Tile drainage has levelled the corrugations of the old ridge-and-furrow system. Fences, hedges and stone dykes enclose Lowland fields within which grain, vegetable crops and grass grow in rotational sequences. Patches of arable farmland are no longer islands in great oceans of wilder moorland.

But the Highlands, which comprise one-sixth of Britain's land area, or 48 per cent of Scotland's (inclusive of the island of Bute), remain a problem area whose problems are only exacerbated by the pressures of European Community policies on Lowland farming as such. The real marginal periphery lies in the Western Isles, the north-west coast and Shetland; a transitional zone covers Orkney and Caithness; and there is a favoured inner zone arcing from Kintyre, Islay and Lorn through Speyside to the Moray Firth coast where conditions approximate closely to those of Lowland farming. Neither the Highland nor the Lowland areas are homogeneous but the effects of crofting legislation on the Highlands, from the time of the Crofters Holdings (Scotland) Act of 1886 onwards and including the activities of the Highlands and Islands Development Board (now Highlands and Islands Enterprise), have had a marked effect on the landscape everywhere.

Since agricultural use of these areas, other than pasture improvement, is inhibited by the century-old crofting system there is less emphasis on land improvement than on forestry and on the development of alternatives linked to sport, recreation and the sea. Industrial possibilities have also been promoted including seaweed-drying, knitwear, a pulp mill, aluminium smelting and, more recently, the oil-inspired Moray Firth developments. The likelihood (or danger, as many see it, see Chapter 9) is that the human landscape of the crofting counties will become increasingly frozen into a kind of three-dimensional photograph of the agricultural past – a tourist theme park in which the making of lazy-beds, the building of head-dykes and so on will add a flavour of the history of human toil to the scenic beauty that attracts tourists in the first instance.

PEOPLE AND THEIR ENVIRONMENT

Amongst all these changes perhaps the hardest to describe is the way in which the attitudes of people to their environment and to the creatures around them have changed over the last three centuries.

There was, for instance, a continual

Horses were used well into the 1950s on many farms.

broadening of personal horizons. An agricultural writer of 1797 observed how in Berwickshire the farm servants had

cast off the long clothing, tardy face and lethargic look of their forefathers, for the short doublet and linen trousers, the quick step and life of persons labouring for their own behoof, and work up to the spirit of their own cattle, and the rapid evolutions of the threshing mill.

Ministers of the church deplored the interest in expensive dress, including silk, among maidservants, the drinking of tea at breakfast, and the spread of whisky-drinking even among women of the lower class.

Such symbols of changing perceptions do not, however, affect the fundamental point that until well into the twentieth century the perceptions and attitudes of individuals still had a strongly rural basis. This is evident, for example, in the language of Lowland Scots, which reflects a picture of a relatively non-industrialised countryside whose inhabitants were on close terms with their environment and concerned with it in a way that is little known to the present-day majority.

Every detail of weather appears, sometimes as a prognostication. A halo or broch round the moon still means bad weather on the way: *a*

119

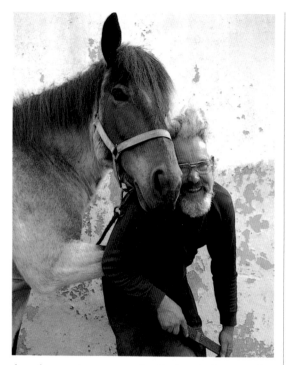

Blacksmith at Fort William maintains a traditional craft.

broch near is a storm far. Such a halo was also called a *cock's eye, fauld or gow,* illustrating the tenet that a multiplicity of names indicates a topic of importance to rural communities for whom the hourly and daily weather changes matter greatly.

The language of Scots also contains many echoes of pre-improvement conditions. Words like *rammel* and *rone* (brushwood), *scrogs* (stunted trees or shrubs), *etnach* (juniper) and *arnits* (pig-nuts) all point to untamed places and plants. Terms may survive locally long after peat clearance, drainage and the general processes of cultivation have completely destroyed the flora and fauna to which they refer. Words can become memorial stones to what has gone, and place-names act as pointers too. The farm name Bruntland (or *Brunties*) of north-east Scotland records places where mossy or peaty ground was regularly burned to fertilise the next crop. Natural features, all observed closely by country dwellers of the past, like *brae* (hillside), *cleugh* (crag), *drum* (knoll), *glack* (ravine), *heuch* (steep bank), *kip* (peak), *law* (hill) and so on have been immortalised in place-names.

Through words and place-names, Man's interaction with the natural world is held up as in a mirror. And the intimacy of such interaction is further highlighted by terms expressing character and physical attributes that liken people to creatures. Outcasts were symbolised as *bruits* (brutes), *cowts* (colts), *knappers* (ones who bite with their teeth, like animals, to drive off cats, etc.), or *tikes* (curs). Stupid folk were *anes* (asses), *gowks* (cuckoos), *hoolets* (owls), *mowdieworts* (moles), *nowts* or *stirks* (cattle) or *yowes* (sheep).

Time and again such words echo the reality of rural attitudes that contrast markedly with philosophical concepts of Man's superiority over the brute creation and of changing perceptions of scenery like those of Edward Burt in the 1720s. He saw Highland mountains as 'dismal brown', 'dirty purple, and most of all disagreeable when the heather is in bloom'; another unenthusiastic traveller, Dr Samuel Johnson, wrote in 1773 of 'this wide extent of hopeless sterility'. This contrasts vividly with the fashionable taste for romantic scenery largely initiated by Sir Walter Scott, whose *Lady of the Lake* (1809) 'sent visitors flocking to the Trossachs, and thus begat the tourist trade' (see Chapter 17).

Land-use is not just a matter of how farmers use the soil for arable and pastoral purposes. It is a reflection of a way of life that was that of most people until very recent times. In fact our landscape, buildings, language, attitudes and perceptions are still strongly conditioned or marked by the rural past to a degree of which most people are unaware.

The legacy of the countryside that lies both around the indwellers of Scotland and within their minds is at the same time the past in the present and a fundamental part of the present. Study of the details of this legacy can help us understand the path we have travelled from the past to the present. Such study provides us with a lens through which we can view the range and degree of contemporary change as the clank of de-stoners echoes across a countryside that contains fewer and fewer people, sounding a drum roll for the end of a way of life that will never return.

4. THE FUEL OF LIFE

For centuries the main fuel for the fires that warmed the kitchens, cooked the food and boiled the water was peat. Untold quantities have been turned to smoke and ash. Those unfortunate enough to live in districts where it had been used up were badly off and had to cut it expensively from neighbouring areas, or resort to using earthy turf (the cutting of which spoiled the grazing areas) or dried cow-dung (which meant loss of manure). Estates always tried to conserve their precious peat resource by regulating the use of turbaries. And no wonder: no fewer than fifty or sixty cart-loads were needed to keep just one fire going for a year, and this figure was repeated for every house, every year, for centuries.

Peat cutting has led to immense changes in the landscape, including settlement patterns and the associated forms of land-use and flora. Most of the Lowland Scottish peat has been exhausted, although former bogs can be traced by the extreme flatness of fields on their sites. Yet so much remains, especially in the Highlands and Islands, that ten per cent of Scotland's surface is still under peat.

Underneath that peat lies widespread evidence of earlier land-use by prehistoric farmers from the period before the climatic deterioration that led to peat growth; while on the peat surface a rich variety of plants and animals survives in a habitat that conservationists regard as unique. Herein are the roots of the present-day clash of interests between those who seek to preserve the heritage of the past and those who seek to exploit the peatlands by large-scale commercial extraction or by alien afforestation.

Women in East Lothian planting potatoes, circa 1920; machines have now replaced people.

Crofter cutting peat on the Ardnamurchan peninsula.

121

Crofting community,
Elgol, Isle of Skye.

CHAPTER NINE

The Way of Crofting
Frank Rennie

Dr Frank W. Rennie is a geologist by training who now lives and works as a crofter in Galson in the Isle of Lewis. He worked there as a scientific officer for the Nature Conservancy Council for four years and was the founding president of the 4,000 - strong Scottish Crofters' Union. He is now a consultant in rural development and adult education.

The stereotypes of the confident self-sufficient farmer on the one hand and the work-shy state-supported crofter on the other are just as nonsensical as the idea that every conservationist sports woollies and green welly boots on excursions from the city every weekend. But the mythology dies hard.

Crofting is more than a mere remnant of traditional peasant agriculture. It is neither a primitive nor an impoverished form of farming; rather it is a unique social system in which small-scale agriculture plays a unifying role.

The word 'croft' does not refer to a house but to a smallholding, the tenant of which (the crofter) pays rent to the landowner and shares the common grazing with other crofters in a village known as a crofting 'township'. An individual croft may be less than a tenth of a hectare (quarter of an acre) in size, more commonly two hectares (five acres) or so, but sometimes it can be the size of a small farm.

The crofting system grew out of the semi-feudal Highland land system in the eighteenth century under which the chiefs rented land to tenants known as tacksmen; these in turn rented smaller plots to subtenants, usually on poorer soils requiring reclamation. In effect the sub-tenant was required to create his own croft; but he had no security of tenure and could be summarily evicted at the whim of the estate factor.

The Highland Clearances of the eighteenth and nineteenth centuries (see Chapter 8) caused the eviction of huge numbers of crofters to make room for largescale sheep ranching and led to mass emigration to Australia and the Americas as well as to the industrial cities of Scotland. However, despite all the emigration, the Highland population kept rising, reaching a peak in the middle of the nineteenth century. This coincided with widespread poverty and destitution caused by disastrous harvests and the great potato blight. The poverty and despair of those cruel decades left a deep sense of historical grievance that has been slow to fade.

In 1886 Parliament passed the first Crofter Holdings (Scotland) Act, giving official recognition and legal protection to crofting as a system of land tenure. But crofts were not created as an act of generosity by landowners and politicians; the legislation was seen as a last attempt to stem the growing tide of civil disturbance that was spreading through the Highlands and Islands. The people in the rural areas were hungry, poor, landless and desperate. They had nothing else to lose and their obvious unrest was felt to be a subversive threat to the very existence of the nation.

The struggle for land at the end of the nineteenth and early in the twentieth century, one of the most radical periods of Highland history, has become popularly known as the 'crofters' war'. Indeed it is less than three generations since many peaceful crofters were fighting against the British army and the police force for their right to live and work on their native land. This link between the historical and the modern crofter is the key to understanding the motivations of the crofting community as a whole.

The history of my own village of Galson in

'Black house' with thatcher roof: Skye Cottage Museum, Kilmuir.

the Isle of Lewis is a microcosm of the history of crofting. The existing crofting village and our two neighbouring villages were destroyed by the landlord in 1863 and the people were cleared off the land. The villages were turned into one large farm with a single tenant farmer firmly installed in the only house. This situation continued until 1921 when ex-servicemen returning from the First World War began, not surprisingly, to look for the land they had been promised ('a home fit for heroes'), for which they had been persuaded to fight overseas.

The owner of the whole of Lewis and Harris at that time was Lord Leverhulme, founding father of the multinational giant Unilever. He had many grandiose plans for industrial development on the island but the idea of land resettlement was anathema to him. The pressures to redistribute land, however, became intense. Several farms were peacefully raided and occupied by landless families and eventually the government directed the Department of Agriculture to purchase a number of farms and divide them into crofting units. Today Galson has fifty-five crofts, several with second houses built by the second or third generation of the original settlers, and a thriving population of 146.

THE PATCHWORK LANDSCAPE

Under the original crofting legislation, crofting in Scotland is limited to the seven former counties of Shetland, Orkney, Caithness, Sutherland, Ross and Cromarty, Inverness-shire and Argyll. The entire region is now classified under a European Community directive as a Less Favoured Area (LFA) (see Chapter 10). It is 'less favoured' because in the crofting areas the soils are generally shallow and mineral-deficient, suitable at best only for marginal upland farming. It is no coincidence that these are some of the most sparsely populated and scenically beautiful places in Britain.

Within this area there are around 17,700 registered crofts, of which over 85 per cent are tenanted rather than owned, for although they

Shell sands at Smirisary, Glenuig. It is the calcium from these wind blown shell-sands that enriches the soil of the machair and produces the explosion of flowers, insect and bird life.

1. THE MACHAIR

One of the most striking features of the crofting landscape is the so-called 'machair', a Gaelic word for the stretches of low-lying meadow land near the sands of the seashore. The lime-rich machair grasslands occur on the west coast mainland and in the Western Isles, where they provide a habitat for a wonderful variety of wading birds and other species such as the increasingly rare corncrake (see Chapter 5). The machair lands are studded with millions of wild flowers and are a prime example of low-intensity farming methods that have produced a wealth of flowers, animals and birds as well as sustaining a rich human culture. The diversity of wildlife that makes the crofting lands so attractive to nature lovers stems directly from the nature of crofting land-use itself.

On the lime-rich machair grasslands of the Western Isles and west coast mainland cattle have helped preserve the wide range of wild flowers and plants; cattle are more selective than sheep in their grazing, tearing off only the tops of the grasses and plants while sheep graze right down to the roots. On

the hillsides the spread of bracken has been attributed to the decline of cattle; on the machair, cattle have also helped to keep out invading plants like butterbur (*Petasites hybridus*) by crushing the large leaves underfoot. It is evident that the spread of this plant is most rapid where cattle have been taken off the land. In addition to the beneficial effects of cattle on plants, their deep hoof-prints on the wet areas of the machair are often used for shelter by delicate wader chicks before they can fly.

have the option to buy, most crofters choose to remain tenants with very strong rights guaranteed in Acts of Parliament. Within the total land area of the Highlands and Islands only 20 per cent is croftland, mostly in the Western Isles, Orkney, Shetland and the north and west coasts of the mainland. These individual crofts are generally small discrete units with some arable cultivation, mainly producing sheep and some cattle which are then sold to mainland farmers to 'finish' for the market. Most crofters also have access to larger areas of rough grazing near their townships; some of this grazing has been improved by fencing and re-seeding with grass but mostly this is undeveloped moor and hill land. Many of them are sited on coastal machair land (Box 1).

On the arable and 'inbye' land of the crofting villages there is considerable variation in the use of the croft according to the quality of land, the size of the holding and the circumstances of the crofter. A common example would be a croft with some permanent grassland and some hay as fodder for a score or two of sheep. Potatoes, turnips and perhaps rape or kale may also be grown as additional fodder. So with such a variety on each croft, and with each village a patchwork of crofts, there is a much greater variety of habitat available for the wildlife. This is in total contrast to the agri-business of intensive farms which may have individual fields of cereal or oilseed rape as large as a whole crofting township.

Most crofts provide only spare-time or part-time employment and fewer than five per cent are able to support a household on the produce of the croft alone; these are usually the larger crofts on the relatively better-quality land of the east coast mainland.

It is the full-time crofter who is often the most disadvantaged; his croft is not big enough to compete on an equal footing with the larger farmers but the croft leaves him too little time to permit a regular (non-croft) job to supplement the croft income. The small level of croft income is neither derisory nor insignificant, however; the additional income gained from the croft is often important in enabling families to stay in

the rural areas of their choice despite the difficulty of finding alternative and/or adequately paid employment.

It would be a mistake to think that crofting has not changed in any way over the last century, but in comparison to the enormous changes in farming practice throughout southern Britain crofting is still very much a traditional system. One cannot really compare modern farming and traditional crofting, but to me there is no doubt whatsoever that the farming methods of crofting are very much more friendly to the natural environment than large-scale chemical-intensive agriculture.

The rich and varied patchwork landscape created by individual crofts ensures that a wide variety of wildlife habitats exists in a very small area. Croft land given over to permanent grass, turnips, potatoes, hay/silage and heather moorland all support subtly different communities of plants, insects and animals which in turn provide food and shelter for larger birds and animals. Many crofts have fields which are too small, or too rough, for tractors with spraying booms to be used; consequently crops are relatively free of the pesticides and

Traditional methods of hay making, as at Barvas on Lewis, enable the corncrake to survive in the Western Isles.

Hand shearing of sheep is still common in the crofting areas.

herbicides used on more intensive farms, making croft products healthier both for humans and for wildlife. Where weed-killers and fertilisers are used they are usually applied using knapsack sprayers and in such small quantities that there is no comparison with industrial farming techniques.

PROTECTION AND PROTECTIONISM

It has long been apparent that the policies and grant incentives offered by different government departments concerned with land-use are often incompatible. Agriculture, forestry, nature conservation and other economic developments obviously compete with each other for land and resources.

People who live in towns demand greater access to the countryside for walking, climbing, and many other recreational pursuits. This growth in countryside recreation and tourism has applied greater pressure on rural amenities and highlights the need to protect scenic and environmental attractions. The benefits to country people may be only marginal, for tourism tends to be seasonal, dependent on weather and the economic situation, and to provide generally low-paid jobs. Many people are concerned that tourist pressure is eroding the cultural identity of regional communities and destroying those cultural variations which attract tourists to the area. The choice is whether the

countryside should serve simply as a weekend playground for townsfolk or whether it should be a place for the people who live in the countryside to earn a decent living for themselves.

The major cause of friction between conservationists and people who live in the countryside has long been the designation of Sites of Special Scientific Interest (SSSIs) by the old Nature Conservancy Council (NCC) (see Chapter 10). These SSSIs are designed to ensure the protection of areas which are of national importance because of the wild plants, animals, birds and geological features found there, and they can vary in size from a fraction of a hectare to over a thousand hectares.

What usually causes the friction is not the principle but the manner of the protection of the site. The crofter or landowner will be notified of a list of 'Potentially Damaging Operations' (PDOs) which the NCC thinks would have an adverse effect on the site (see Chapter 16).

That is where the problem starts, for number one on the list of 'potentially damaging operations' sent to those with an interest in the site is 'cultivation, including ploughing, harrowing, and reseeding', followed closely by 'changes in the grazing regime', the 'introduction of stock', and 'the application of fertilisers and lime'. To most people who make their living from agricultural operations the effect of this letter arriving on the doormat is enough to raise their blood pressure to danger point.

Of course the list only refers to activities which are potentially damaging and need to be cleared by the NCC before any work is started, and in many situations there is in fact no real cause for concern; but it is the perceived lack of adequate information and prior consultation and of an independent appeals procedure which is the root cause of the farmer's discontent.

The system has created SSSIs as isolated islands of nature conservation dotted around the Highland countryside, and it is felt that this system is unduly restrictive and inappropriate for the protection of these areas. Much of the land surrounding these SSSIs is also environmentally sensitive and scenically beautiful, but the system seems to imply that while the SSSIs need to be protected the other parts of the Highlands and Islands do not.

The conflict and confusion surrounding the identification and designation of SSSIs may be resolved by paying greater attention to public information and encouraging greater consultation; however, the problem of the management of SSSIs is more pervasive.

Take for example an area of wet bog land; the high rainfall and shallow acid soils may mean that this area represents a loss of production to a crofter who wants to graze animals on it. The area may be quite small but in relation to the croft land available it may still be important to the crofter, who may even occasionally lose an animal in it. Consequently he may want to drain the land and improve it.

The bog, however, may be a very good site for wildlife – waterfowl and wading birds, for example – and conservationists may object to the crofter's plan to drain the area. Unless the bog is within a National Nature Reserve (NNR) or an SSSI there is apparently very little that the conservationists can do about it. Within an SSSI however, if the scientific value of the site would be damaged, and if no compromise plan can be worked out, the NCC can prevent the crofter from starting the draining operations. In such cases the law states that the farmer or crofter should be compensated for the loss of income which has resulted from the cancellation of the grazing improvement scheme (see Chapter 10).

The idea of getting payment for 'doing nothing', however, is alien to most crofters and upland farmers and does not rest easy with traditional notions of working the land. But there is another more serious complication, in that the management payment will be calculated according to an agricultural value, which is at best 'marginal', rather than for conservation value, which may be exceedingly high.

It is rather like offering £6.50 for a Van Gogh masterpiece on the basis that all you are paying for is a frame of wood, a square of canvas, and a couple of tubes of oil paint! Clearly this is absurd. In the same way no businessman would expect to pay only a few pounds for a piece of wasteland in the centre of London on account of

Crofter and tractor in South Galson; crofters may be engineers, journalists, fishermen or civil servants as well as farmers.

its dilapidated condition. What he would be paying for is the development potential of the site, and whether it is the potential for erecting a building or for maintaining a valuable ecological system the same standards should apply.

In reality crofters are not wanting to hold the nation to ransom by threatening the destruction of a valuable nature conservation site unless hefty compensation is paid to them.

This is no begging bowl mentality, nor is it a form of conservation blackmail, for most crofters have no thought of deliberately destroying the natural environment which surrounds them. For a number of years, crofters and the Scottish Crofters' Union (SCU) have suggested that, if the maintenance and protection of the natural environment are to be given a higher priority by the public, the public purse must be prepared to help pay for it.

A SUSTAINABLE SUPPORT SYSTEM

It is ironic that while recent changes of emphasis in European agricultural policies are pushing farmers away from intensive over-production and towards land management systems which are 'environmentally beneficent', the crofting communities have come full circle. The crofting communities have never contributed to the agricultural surpluses, but now those crofters and upland farmers (who by their very methods of working, operate in a

Fishing for lobsters off Pladda.

manner which is friendly to the natural environment) are being directed and controlled by the policy makers who wholeheartedly advocated industrial production methods that devastated the natural environment. Yet what these 'progressive' thinkers called 'uneconomic' systems or 'primitive' agriculture or 'unworkable' practices are the very systems which have safeguarded so much of the natural environment which was being lost elsewhere.

Many country people, including crofters, strongly resent the implication made by outsiders that 'development' (agricultural or otherwise) is a dirty word and that the land should be preserved in aspic as a large open-air museum in which country people themselves are among the living exhibits.

The people who live in the crofting areas may enjoy a wonderful landscape full of wildlife and scenic beauty but they cannot live off views and fresh air alone. The seasonal and low-paid nature of much of the available work often means that they suffer a lower standard of living. This makes it ethically difficult for conservationists to oppose appropriate local economic development on the grounds of minor environmental criteria unless they can offer other conservation-based ways of earning a living.

Obviously much depends on the definition of 'appropriate' development; for what may seem 'appropriate' to a crofter or hill farmer trying to maintain a decent living may be considered 'inappropriate' by an ecologist sitting at his desk in Edinburgh or London. Conversely the wholesale conservation of wild spaces, undrained wetlands and particular species of birds, animals and trees may seem to be an ill-affordable luxury to the crofter struggling for economic survival.

In the longer term we need to provide annual 'conservation management incentives' to all those land-users who engage in environmentally friendly farming, not just to those who have little islands of SSSIs within their land. The idea that environmental conservation must be actively managed rather than simply left to itself is not new and neither is the idea of conservation as a cash crop in itself. Unlike turnips or potatoes, however, the 'conservation crop' of a piece of land cannot be picked up and sold to consumers in a city marketplace. Some things simply cannot be bought.

Country people could be encouraged by direct tax incentives or by special payments to farm in ways which are agreed to be environmentally beneficial but which may not be considered 'economically feasible' from a purely financial aspect. The introduction of the voluntary Environmentally Sensitive Area (ESA) scheme in the crofting lands of Uist in the Western Isles was a welcome step in this direction (see Chapter 16).

Both crofters and conservationists have also been concerned about the rapid decline of cattle numbers in the croft lands. If a cash subsidy were introduced to encourage crofters to keep more cattle a better cow-to-sheep grazing ratio could be created. This would maintain the grazing in better condition than would be the case under sheep alone. A good grazing mix of one cow for every four or five sheep promotes a greater diversity of herbs and flowering plants in the pastures – a nice example of how nature can be enriched and sustained through man's creative exploitation.

In some parts of the country it is barely a generation since almost every crofting household had a 'house cow' which would provide the family with milk, butter, cheese and a calf to sell annually. Cattle are much more demanding of the crofter's time whereas shepherding fits more easily into the part-time nature of crofting. This is one reason, along with changing work patterns and standards of living, why cattle numbers have declined. There is general agreement that there is a need to get more cattle back on to the land, not in large herds but through hundreds of crofters owning two or three cows with calves. Such a change would require a shift in our priorities, and if the commercial market for cattle could not support such a socially desirable policy then social funding should be made available to encourage land-users to adopt such schemes of environmentally friendly land management.

The crofting system, with its more relaxed

and balanced approach to agriculture and development, could set the trend for the future of sustainable farming in Britain.

DIVERSIFICATION AND INTEGRATED MANAGEMENT

One of the main benefits of the crofting system is that it maintains a healthy level of population in the crofting areas of the countryside. The crofting communities of the Western Isles, Skye, or Shetland offer a stark contrast to the vast unpopulated areas of north-west Sutherland and the west coast mainland whence the people have long since vanished. Scarcely a house remains standing in these empty glens. This is not true wilderness but a devastated landscape cleared of its native people and emptied by human greed. Those of us who remain do not do so out of romanticism, nor purely for economic gain, but from a deep conviction that the quality of life here is better than that which we would have in a city.

The linch-pins of this social system are the rights of access to the land and security of tenure. Traditionally many crofts ran lengthwise from the sea, inland to the moor, in small clusters of scattered townships. The crofts were often further subdivided into narrower full-length strips among the surviving members of a family so as to give each descendant a piece of the moor, a piece of the good blackland, a piece of the machair and so on. This practice is no longer legal but it has left a patchwork of independent small family units, able to contribute to the family food supplies and, by selling the surplus, to the family income. Such crofts were never intended to support the household without additional employment, but this handicap has now changed from a curse into a blessing.

The reliance upon employment other than agriculture but with the security of land on which to put down roots, to build a family home and grow crops for income and food has become one of the pillars of the crofting community. It has allowed crofters to remain where they want to live and has enabled the development of a very wide range of skills.

Strips of croftland run down to the sea at Stoer point, Sutherland.

Here in my own village of Galson with its fifty-five crofts its population of 146 includes people who earn their living in catering, Harris Tweed weaving, civil engineering, publishing, the building trade, clerical work and a variety of other activities. All of these people are also involved in crofting.

One way in which the conservation movement could further help to reinforce the crofting system which has created and maintained this unique environment would be through the creation of conservation-related jobs for local people in rural communities. In this way the land-users (not simply landowners) would be able to act more effectively as custodians of the agricultural and conservation value of their own land.

This is well illustrated if we look at the IDP (Integrated Development Programme) for the Western Isles, which was launched a few years ago. The relative success of this development initiative has fostered several other development schemes in the Highlands and Islands. These have included an Agricultural Development Programme (ADP) for the Northern Isles, Skye and the Argyll Islands; an HIDB development scheme for the north-west Sutherland area; and an HIDB backed Township Development Scheme for the Western Isles. None of these new projects has caused the same degree of local tension nor the sensationalist headlines which greeted the start of the original IDP. The media exaggerations at the time included such gems as 'Imminent Destruction Plan' (in the RSPB magazine *Birds*), and 'a poisonous little plan' (in the *New Scientist*)!

Those fears were largely born out of ignorance of the economic and social realities of the crofting system. Local people who pointed this out were immediately branded as parochial and anti-conservationist by outside 'experts' who had by then developed an interest in the Western Isles.

Ultimately, however, the biggest worry for the future is the loss of croft land, for once it has been removed from crofting tenure there is no way under the present legal structure that this land can ever be returned to crofting. Just compare the diversity – ecological, social, and economic – of a thriving crofting community in Lewis, with a single land-use mainland estate, whether it is under-used or smothered with blanket forestry or kept as mile upon mile of grouse moor. With the continuing fall in farm profits there is now a good case for dividing some of these under-used estates and large farms into croft-sized units and encouraging families to settle on them.

By injecting such vitality into our rural communities we would be supporting the conservation of rural communities as well as their wildlife. Already some Scottish local authorities outside the crofting areas are seriously considering such a proposal.

If our rural communities become even more depopulated then the land will fall into disuse, and in many cases the wildlife will also suffer. In communities where croft land has been neglected or abandoned the resulting deterioration in the crofting system is often closely paralleled by a deterioration in the diversity of wildlife. Active resumption of traditional crofting practices and their modern equivalents will rejuvenate the land as well as the crofting community and the wildlife which depends on both for its survival.

2. THE ASSYNT CROFTERS

Bill Ritchie, crofter-fisherman from Achmelvich in Assynt, was one of the leaders of the crofters who acquired the North Assynt Estate in 1993. He is a member of the Crofters Commission and is chairman of the Scottish Coastal Forum and of the North Areas Board of Scottish Natural Heritage. He is a strong advocate of community empowerment to achieve sustainable rural development.

On 1 February 1993, a dramatic new chapter opened in the evolution of crofting in the Highlands. On that day 120 crofting families living and working on the North Assynt Estate in Sutherland took over full responsibility for the 21,000 acres of land they and generations of crofters before them had occupied as the crofting tenants of absentee landlords. These crofters, members of the Assynt Crofters Trust, became the first crofters to take total control and responsibility for their land: a land of spectacular mountains and coastlines, a poor land from an agricultural point of view but a land rich in cultural and natural heritage.

The crofters of Assynt have always been politically active and in many ways it is no surprise that this tremendous leap forward in the evolution of crofting should take place in Assynt.

Driving through the middle of Assynt today you cannot help noticing that, like much of the Highlands and Islands, the straths and glens are virtually empty: few cattle, few sheep and, more ominously, few people. Yet these are green and fertile straths. A closer look reveals the evidence of former townships: the remains of dozens of houses, the former homes to hundreds of native people. Only a few generations ago hundreds of people were driven from these straths and glens and crowded onto the coast on top of the already congested population.

At that time the Assynt Branch of the Land League demanded the restoration to the people of the newly created sheep farms and deer forest 'where there is plenty of provision for ourselves and our families...and [which are] in the possession of an English man in Glencanisp, while we at home are starving, and the land of our fathers lying waste'. But to no avail: Parliament failed to meet the principal demand of the crofters – the return of their land. The only escape from overcrowding and the lack of jobs lay in voluntary emigration. Meanwhile the 'land of our fathers' lay in waste.

The Assynt crofters continued their struggle; in 1887, in the township of Clashmore, after riots, the deployment of royal marines, arrests and imprisonment, some land taken from the crofters was returned. But it was a limited success. The fertile straths remained empty. In the century between the passing of the Crofting Act, 1886, to 1986 the population in the parish of Assynt dwindled from around 2,500 to a mere 800.

The Assynt crofters who stayed retained a strong sense of community and were not averse to 'managing' the 'natural resources' in their own way, albeit without the blessing of legal authority!

In 1989 the then 'English man in Glencanisp' sold the largest part of the croft lands to a Swedish partnership, SPS Ltd. Three years later SPS Ltd went bankrupt and the land went back on the market, in seven small lots. The land was never described as croft land; instead, it was advertised as a 'wildlife paradise' having 'sporting potential'. It was even described as a place 'where the people are perhaps alien' – in spite of the fact that the land had been occupied and worked by generations of Asaintich for thousands of years!

The ignominy of having to pay rents to foreign nationals and being described as 'alien' was too much for the Assynt crofters. In June 1992, believing passionately that the people belong to the land and not that the land belongs to people (especially not to anonymous international speculators), the Assynt crofters decided to act to prevent the break-up and sale of the land. They set about raising the money to buy the estate at a 'fair value'. SPS had paid over £1 million; the new asking price was £0.75 million; the crofters valued it at £0.25 million. And so began a high-profile campaign which was to last nearly six months – six months in which the resolve of the crofters would be severely tested.

But they succeeded. They received massive popular support. They also won the moral and financial backing of various public agencies which recognised an exciting opportunity to demonstrate their commitment to community participation and responsibility for sustainable development.

The real significance of this is not that the Assynt crofters now own their land but that, recognising that 'they belong to the land', they now for the first time in history have the opportunity and the responsibility to address the management of all of their resources – the land, the water, the woodlands, the minerals and the wildlife – in an integrated way which meets the needs of the present community without compromising the needs of future generations of crofters.

To meet that responsibility, the Assynt crofters are now embarked on a series of initiatives. In the belief that the people are the most important assets of all, the first initiative is working with the Crofters Commission and the Local Enterprise Company to help get young people into crofting by encouraging elderly or inactive crofters to give land to the young. To help lay the foundation for new economic opportunities the crofters are preparing a tourism development strategy, in parallel with a number of European Union (EU) partners, as part of a transnational initiative under Leader 11.

On the land the crofters have embarked on a major expansion of the native woodlands and are developing the wild brown trout fishing as a major economic resource. The crofters are also leading a major EU-funded telematics project with partners in four EU countries to develop the use of computers to assist sustainable management decisions on extensive ecologically sensitive lands.

In taking control of their own future the Assynt crofters have created an atmosphere of optimism and opportunity rarely experienced in the crofting counties. They are the first fully empowered crofting community. The Assynt crofters have not only opened a new chapter in the evolution of crofting, but have brought to the forefront the long-running debate on who owns, and who *should* own, the land throughout the Highlands and Islands. The importance of this for sustainable rural development has been placed high on the political agenda – thanks to the Assynt Crofters.

Bill Ritchie, Assynt crofter.

Anne Dunlop, Weaver of Stoer.

Above: Fishing school, Drumbeg, Sutherland.

Left: Organic garden on croft at Clashmore.

*Looking across to the Scottish
mainland from Ardvasar, Isle of Skye.*

CHAPTER TEN

The Managing of the Land
Alan Mowle

Dr Alan Mowle is a specialist in rural affairs and is currently Head of Corporate Planning and Information with Scottish Natural Heritage.

I sometimes think of Scotland's countryside as being a garden, and it's not really such an inappropriate metaphor. Almost every aspect of the land is managed and cared for to some extent, just like a garden; and if we are to sustain our wildlife heritage, the beauty of the landscape and the productive capacity of the land, our countryside has to be planned and tended, too – just like a garden.

Scotland is a very green place: almost all of the land is countryside, since less than 3 per cent of Scotland's 30,000 square miles (80,000 square kilometers) have been built upon. The land is also relatively empty of people because, although Scotland has about one-third of Britain's land area, it has only 10 per cent of the population. Moreover the population is heavily concentrated in the Central Belt, with nearly a third in the largest cities of Glasgow, Edinburgh, Aberdeen and Dundee alone. Only a fifth of the people of Scotland live in communities of fewer than 5,000 (the size of Dalbeattie or Huntly).

So the rural areas of Scotland are large, very thinly populated and, for the most part, free of the development pressures found in the south of England. Perhaps for these reasons, the countryside is where we feel that traditional values and a quieter approach to life may still be found; indeed, town dwellers are increasingly looking to the countryside for quiet recreation.

Country people have the same aspirations as their urban counterparts: we are all part of modern Scottish society and we all expect to share a similar standard of living. But the countryside means very different things to different people:

For farmers and foresters the countryside is a workshop, a factory floor, where they earn their living. They do not normally think of themselves as 'gardeners', although they are heirs to a long tradition of stewardship and husbandry. Their businesses are largely sustained by financial grants and subsidies from the rest of the community, channelled through a variety of government policy measures. One result of this has been the single-minded pursuit of farm and forest output at minimum cost which has damaged both social and environmental interests in the countryside.

For tourists, the countryside is a place of beauty and a source of inspiration. Most people visit the countryside for recreation purposes from time to time. Many country people derive part of their income from tourism, so they have an indirect dependence on the countryside beyond the direct dependence of farmers and foresters. But to date the tourism industry has contributed little to the management or conservation of the countryside on which it actually depends. For those who want to climb, walk or ski in the countryside it seems perhaps more like a park than a garden.

Conservationists tend to regard the countryside as a giant nature reserve where wildlife is protected and preserved. But we should never forget that most of this wildlife has survived by accident rather than as the result of deliberate management. The idea of 'gardening' may sound incompatible with the

Blackface sheep in Glencoe; more than two-thirds of Scotland's land is only suitable for rough grazing because of altitude and weather.

conservation of wild nature but, unless we start to tend the countryside with wildlife in mind, the destruction of habitat and loss of wildlife seen in recent years can only continue.

Of the three interest groups mentioned above, the management of the land and woodlands by foresters or farmers in their role as 'gardeners' has the greatest impact on the landscape and wildlife, and the relationship between the gardeners and the garden thus deserves closer examination.

FARMING THE LAND

A glance at the crude statistics shows that more than 80 per cent of Scotland's land area is devoted to farming. The way in which farming is carried out is of critical importance both for the land and for the community. Farming has been transformed over the last half century into a commercial business feeding urban markets.

The statistics conceal more than they reveal: more than 70 per cent of farmland consists of unimproved rough grazing in the hill areas.

Friesian dairy cows at Dalcross, Ardersier, near Inverness.

Fertile arable ground is concentrated up the east coast where less than 12 per cent of Scotland's farmland produces nearly 30 per cent of total farm output: crops to a value of £450 million per annum. In broad terms Scotland grows enough food to supply its population; and although there are shortfalls in horticulture these are counterbalanced by a large surplus of meat production.

But this impressive output is produced by a tiny labour force. There are only about 12,500 full-time farmers in Scotland (with another 9,000 part-timers), who between them employ roughly 17,000 full-time workers on about 8,500 holdings. Thus farming employs barely 1 per cent of Scotland's working population.

However, there are great contrasts in the size of farm businesses. A typical east coast farm will turn over more than £150,000 on an area of perhaps 350 acres (140 ha), mostly arable. At the other end of the scale a hill sheep farm may turn over less than £50,000 on a much larger area of over 3,000 acres (1,200 ha), more than 95 per cent of which is rough grazing.

Away from the east coast lowlands most farm businesses are small-scale and farm incomes are low. Nearly all farm output is in the form of livestock, mainly sheep and cattle, and the only crops grown on the farm are usually winter fodder for the animals. The European Union (EU) has designated most of Scotland a 'Less Favoured Area' (LFA) because of the natural disadvantage of its terrain, soils and climate; as a result special support measures are provided for farming in Scotland.

The principal support for LFA livestock farms takes the form of annual headage subsidies for each breeding cow or ewe; these subsidies cost the taxpayer around £200 million per annum. This financial support provides between a third and a half of the turnover of the farm business and without it most farmers in Less Favoured Areas could not survive.

Before 1992 the level of taxpayers' support for the cereal crops grown by arable farmers in Scotland was difficult to establish because it took the form of market price support through buying surplus crops and subsidising their export. Now this support is much more visible, paid directly to farmers who sell their crops on to the market at lower prices. The 2 million tonnes of these crops grown in Scotland represent a little over 1 per cent of EU production; they attract £200 million each year in the form of direct payments for every hectare grown and for Set-aside, where farmers are paid not to grow surplus crops. Without this support (see Box 1), Scotland's arable farmers would not survive either.

After arable and livestock-farming the third important sector is dairy farming, where over-production led to the introduction of milk quotas in 1985. Each farmer has an annual production quota, a quantity which must be sold to the milk board at a fixed price. The quota system controls milk production and maintains the broad structure of the industry. Simply reducing the price paid for milk would concentrate production on larger, more efficient, farms and eliminate dairy farming altogether in some parts of Scotland where farms are smaller and less productive.

Taken together the various forms of public subsidy for Scottish farming, channelled through a range of policy instruments, cost the taxpayer around £500 million per annum: that is to say, something approaching £2 million per working day. These subsidies have nearly doubled in size since 1990.

One effect of the high level of farm subsidies has been to inflate land prices. On the face of it this makes owner-occupier farmers rich; the land on the 350-acre arable farm described above may be worth over £350,000, but this asset can only be realised when the farm is sold with vacant possession. The down side is that these high prices make it very difficult for would-be farmers to buy, and rule out land purchase based on borrowed money. High prices are also maintained by an increasing interest in land for 'hobby farming', especially near urban areas.

These high land values and all the other economic pressures have pushed farmers on to a treadmill, forcing them to work the land more intensively, chasing higher yields through increased use of chemicals and larger machines.

Drenching sheep is easier with modern equipment.

1. Oilseed rape

The way in which the Common Agricultural Policy shapes Scotland's countryside is exemplified by the huge increase in the area of oilseed rape grown on the arable land on the east coast of Scotland. Oilseed rape is the crop with bright yellow flowers so prominent in the countryside at springtime. Hardly any was grown in 1981, but by 1995 the area under oilseed rape had increased to more than 170,000 acres. Why did this happen?

In the early 1980s the European Community (EC) reviewed the pattern of food production. The Community was almost self-sufficient in most food products; but for vegetable oils, used in margarine and cooking oils, it was very dependent on imports. Very little vegetable oil was produced by the Community's farmers apart from olive oil grown in the Mediterranean states.

The EC member states agreed to subsidise farmers to grow suitable oilseeds which could be crushed to extract the oil. A subsidy is paid directly to farmers, allowing them to sell to processors in competition with lower world market prices for imported seed. Each year this subsidy costs the European taxpayer about £200 for every acre of oilseed rape. Without this subsidy oilseed rape would not be grown.

Oil seed rape at Boghall farm, Pentland Hills.

Farmers who have resisted the pressure to join in have found themselves slowly squeezed out of business.

As farming has changed, so have the food processing and distribution industries with the development of supermarkets and increased processing of farm products for retail. One result of this is a decline in the farmer's share of the retail food price, adding to all the other pressures. Many farm businesses now carry significant overdrafts; the accruing bank interest eats into farm income and for a significant number their asset value declines year by year (Box 2).

Farmers find themselves with less and less freedom in their decision-making as their

2. FARMING TRENDS

Over the years farm incomes have been in long-term decline relative to the economy at large because, as living standards rise, we spend a smaller proportion of our income on food. Between 1970 and 1990 the value of farm production in Scotland was halved from 4 per cent to less than 2 per cent of our Gross Domestic Product (GDP). In fact the real value of farm output hardly changed over this twenty-year period, but the rest of the economy had grown correspondingly.

For many years farming has responded to this pressure by trying to increase the value of output per farm and per acre. This can only be done either by increasing total output, by reducing costs or by having fewer but larger farms. Technological advances have enabled farmers to increase total food output. For example, the area of cereals in Scotland increased by only about 10 per cent over this twenty-year period, but average yields went up by about 70 per cent. This improvement in yield was then undermined by lower unit prices.

The number of full-time farm workers in Scotland has fallen steadily since 1950, from around 100,000 to only 17,000 today, a decline which is continuing. Over the same period the number of farms in Scotland has fallen by more than a third, while the average size has increased as the land has been taken over by neighbouring farmers.

Looking to the future, the long-term pressure on farm incomes will continue. Many farmers will have to make part of their living outside farming if they are to maintain their living standards. Although people will continue to be attracted to live in the countryside, very few will be able to make their living on the land. The number of people directly involved in land management will continue to fall. All these changes will place continuing pressure on the Scottish countryside and its management.

The farmer's bill for chemical fertilisers, herbicides and pesticides often dwarfs labour costs.

dependence on outside resources is reinforced. Farmers are increasingly tied to their bankers, their accountants, their crop buyers and their suppliers of fuel, fertilisers and pesticides. Farming has become like any other industry but, unlike other industries, it happens to use most of the countryside as its main resource.

Farming is facing a crisis because there is simply too much food and the markets for produce are saturated. But farmers need to maintain their incomes like everyone else and will undoubtedly want to improve their crop yields in pursuit of ever greater efficiency and profitability; as a result it is probable that present levels of crop production could be maintained on progressively smaller and smaller areas of land. But with a saturated market there is no point in increasing food production – we do not need any more. Consequently large areas of land must come out of agriculture over the next twenty years if we are to limit food output to present levels. But which land will come out of farming?

One possibility is that marginal land in the hills will come out of farming as sheep and beef production is transferred to the more fertile lowlands. But since the level of stock which can be maintained per unit of lowland ground is much higher, most of the hill areas would have to come out of farming altogether in order to balance supply with demand!

Taking the most productive arable land out of farming would minimise the area that we need to lose but it seems illogical to cut production on the best land we have, and most farmers would resist such a move. The most likely scenario is that land of intermediate quality will come out of agriculture as attempts are made to strike a balance of economic, social and environmental objectives through a reorientation of policy instruments. The creation of new woodlands on such land would be an attractive option if appropriate policy tools can be devised.

FORESTRY

About 14 per cent of Scotland is covered with productive woodland, of which 92 per cent consists of plantations of exotic conifers. This contrasts markedly with Scotland in the eighteenth and nineteenth centuries when it was largely deforested. Nearly all Scotland's present-day forests have been created within the last century through the planting-up of bare ground.

After the last Ice Age most of Scotland below the treeline was covered by the ancient wildwood of native broadleaved trees, consisting of oak, ash and elm in the lowlands with the Caledonian pine forest north of the Highland line. A few rare fragments of the wildwood remain but the new plantations bear little resemblance to these original forests. They are composed of different, often introduced, species and have a very different forest structure; their large areas of uniform, even-aged, close-packed trees have earned them, understandably, the tag of 'blanket forestry'.

The creation of these commercial forests has been the largest land-use change in Scotland's countryside this century. The taxpayer has footed most of the bill for this exercise even though many of the plantations are privately owned. Most planting until the 1970s was carried out by the Forestry Commission, creating a state forest of over 2,000 square miles (5,000 sq km); but changing policy instruments have swung the balance since then to the private sector.

The private investor turned to forestry because he or she could use afforestation to turn taxable earnings into a tax-free capital asset over a period of years. In addition generous planting grants helped to pay for the cost of establishing the new forest (see Chapter 5). Increasing controversy led to the abolition of tax arrangements in the 1988 Budget. Although the planting grants have again been increased, private investors' interest in afforestation has fallen away and people with high taxable incomes have begun to look for tax shelters elsewhere.

The factors which led to planting of conifer forests in the uplands have now substantially changed. After the two World Wars the need for a strategic reserve of timber was matched by an equal need for increased self-sufficiency in farming; covering good farmland with trees under such circumstances would clearly have

Less than 1 percent of Scotland's original native pine woods survive today but the Millennium Forest project intends to reverse the decline.

3. THE SITKA SPRUCE

Sitka spruce is a fast-growing conifer native to the western seaboard of North America and well suited to the oceanic climate of Scotland. It is typically grown on hill ground and cropped after about forty-five years; only recently has harvesting started in earnest, because most plantings have taken place since 1950.

Before the 1950s upland planting involved a more diverse range of species and each planting scheme matched species to site characteristics of the area: larch for dry knolls, Norway and Sitka spruce for wetter soils, Scots pine for podzols, Douglas fir and other species for better soils. The predominance of Sitka spruce planting followed the introduction of deep ploughs, trailed behind crawler tractors, which created more uniform conditions across the planting site.

At the same time the objectives of forestry policy changed. The Forestry Commission was set up after the First World War to establish and maintain a strategic reserve of timber at the taxpayers' expense. A Treasury study in 1971 focused attention on poor financial returns; upland afforestation is inherently uneconomic, so the new concern with 'minimising losses' required a low-cost approach. Sitka spruce offers the highest yields for the lowest expenditure and Scotland's hills are now covered with this tree as a direct result.

Because Sitka spruce grows so quickly, its timber is light and relatively soft, even for a conifer; as a result it has only a limited range of uses. Much of the production from Scotland's forests can be used only for pulp, paper or reconstituted board; for high-quality timber we remain largely dependent on imports.

Sitka spruce has been planted in vast swathes across much of the Highlands and Borders of Scotland, creating a dark, sterile habitat.

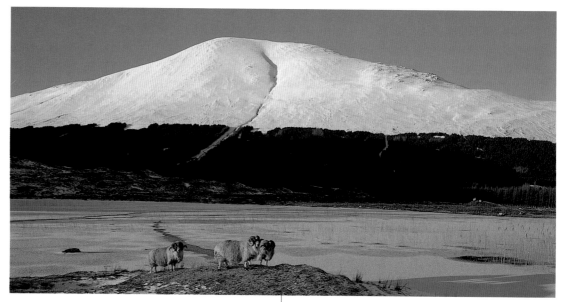

A tide of alien conifers creeps up the mountainside at Loch Lunn da Bhra, near Fort William.

been counter-productive. In the hills, however, unimproved land used for sheep grazing was cheap, reflecting its poor quality; so the uplands were planted with trees. As a result foresters adopted a low management-cost approach based on exotic conifers, principally Sitka spruce (Box 3).

Upland afforestation radically alters the landscape, and the impact can be made even worse by bad plantation design. If the lessons learned over the years are applied, many landscape problems can be avoided in present-day planting or in replanting after felling. But the ecological effects of afforestation are more damaging and more difficult to avoid.

In a sense, modern forestry is an extension of the intensive cropping methods of modern agriculture into the least developed corners of the countryside. During the 1980s more than 90 per cent of new planting in Britain took place in Scotland and about 62,000 acres (25,000 ha) of new trees every year displaced the wildlife which once lived on open moorland. Large areas of heather moorland were lost as a result, reducing habitat for birds of prey like the merlin and for waders such as the golden plover.

When large areas are afforested over a few years the water and drainage patterns of the catchment area are disrupted. Flash floods become more common as new drains and deep-ploughed forestry furrows increase the rate of water run-off; in addition the sands and sediments caused by erosion can damage fisheries by suffocating the gravel beds where salmon and trout spawn. Acid rain deposits are also known to concentrate in the dense foliage of the mature conifers; these deposits are then washed into the burns, destroying fish eggs and young fry as well as the invertebrate food supply of upland birds such as the dipper.

Therefore modern forestry, perhaps even more so than farming, is an industrial activity carried on in the countryside. Like farming it requires urban sources of capital, taxpayers' money, labour and fuel. Unlike farming, which still depends on a large number of one-man businesses, forestry is organised on a larger-scale industrial model with gangs of workers employed, often on a contract basis, under the supervision of professional managers. The type of employment offered by forestry is radically different from that in agriculture, and mechanised tree harvesting needs fewer and fewer workers.

During the 1990s the forestry industry has changed direction. There has been less of the upland afforestation which brought increasingly sharp conflicts with environmental interests. Instead there has been a shift of emphasis to new afforestation on lower, more fertile ground which may be coming out of agriculture. In the uplands the trees planted have increasingly been restocking recently felled plantations rather than planting up open ground.

The key to the future of forestry lies with the Forestry Commission, which has two distinct roles: that of a 'forest authority', disbursing planting grants and controlling felling, and that of 'forest enterprise', managing the state forest. As the original focus on timber production, to the exclusion of all other values, is replaced with a more balanced concern for social and environmental factors as well as economic objectives, the type and location of forestry must change.

Lowland forests using surplus farmland involve a wider range of native trees together with more varied designs and management. Now only 60 per cent of new planting takes place in Scotland, so there has been increasing planting elsewhere in Britain. We can never recreate the original wildwood but new forests in the lowlands can be more pleasing to the eye and much more environmentally friendly (Box 4).

THE PRICE OF WILDLIFE

Some 94 per cent of Scotland is in the hands of farmers and foresters, and they are the major custodians of our countryside heritage. But the ways in which they manage the land are largely dictated for them by the subsidies and other financial supports on which they depend; these economic constraints have had a serious effect on our wildlife heritage (Box 5).

Scotland has a crucial role in conserving Britain's rich heritage of wildlife. But the rich variety of native wildlife is unevenly distributed across the countryside. A few species such as the kestrel are able to adapt to the changes in habitat brought about by people, but most species are specialised and are relatively rare and restricted in their range.

Nature Conservation aims to protect and conserve our wildlife heritage by maintaining the range, variety and quality of habitats in the countryside; in particular it is important to preserve 'semi-natural' areas in which such wildlife can find refuge. In this way the wildlife typical of each place can continue to thrive

4. CREATING A LOWLAND FOREST

The debate about the afforestation of Scotland's upland areas has diverted attention from the opportunities for creating forests elsewhere; but the need to take large areas of countryside out of farming to combat surplus production creates such opportunities.

The Central Scotland Woodlands Project began nearly twenty years ago and has now been superseded by Central Scotland Woodlands Limited (CSW). It is an exciting initiative whose aim is to plant trees on about 250,000 acres of land between Edinburgh, Glasgow and Stirling, a bleak landscape scarred by 200 years of unplanned industrial development.

Although there is some high ground, most of the area is lower ground which is of higher quality than land normally used for conventional afforestation. This means that CSW can plant a wider range of trees, including native broadleaves. At present there is tree cover of about 25,000 acres (10,000 ha); the aim is to extend this to 75,000 acres (30,000 ha) over the next twenty years. This will not result in a 'blanket' of trees, as there would be tree cover on only about one-third of the land area – similar to that found elsewhere in Western Europe.

This new approach avoids the 'minimum cost' approach typical of upland forestry, and tackles wider objectives of environmental improvement, job creation and economic regeneration.

CSW was set up by the Secretary of State for Scotland in partnership with other public agencies, the private sector and the local communities involved. The company is not setting up its own forest enterprise; instead it facilitates tree-planting owned and managed by others.

A variety of planting schemes can be expected as the initiative gathers momentum. As most of the area is farmed, farm woodlands will make an important contribution. These could diversify sources of income for working farmers, or land could be sold to new owners who may be resident but whose main income derives from another source. There is considerable scope for reclamation of derelict land for use as woodland and for restoration of land following opencast mining. Another important objective is the creation of community woodlands, giving local people a direct stake in the management of their own environment.

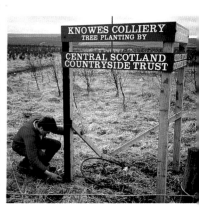

A new lowland forest could be created on derelict industrial land in the Central Belt.

Bluebells among oakwoods in Perthshire; roughly 25 percent of all ancient semi-natural woodlands in Scotland have been destroyed since 1946.

The barn owl has declined dramatically through loss of its traditional habitat due to changes in modern farming.

5. THE EROSION OF OUR NATURAL HERITAGE

How can we measure the changes which have taken place in Scotland's countryside over the years? Without a time machine this is difficult, but photographs can help us to explore what a particular place was like in the past, while aerial photographs of sample places taken at different times allow us to do this systematically and thereby estimate how the land has changed.

The National Countryside Monitoring Scheme (NCMS) has been doing this for each region in Scotland. Its first series of regional reports identified the principal changes from the 1940s to the 1970s; figures are now available for the 1970s to the present day. Although these cannot tell us everything about the changes which have taken place, they do quantify the most important.

The NCMS figures confirm that all over Scotland there have been serious losses of wildlife habitats since 1945. About a quarter of broadleaved woods have been converted to conifer plantations or cleared for agriculture. As much as half of the length of hedgerows and treelines along field boundaries has been removed. A third or more of heather moorland has been planted with conifers or converted to poor grassland because of overgrazing by sheep.

These major changes in land-use have been accompanied by more subtle alterations, shown by changes in key wildlife species. For example, populations of many farmland birds have fallen sharply over the last twenty-five years. Partridge numbers are down by three-quarters, skylark, linnet, bullfinch and reed bunting by half to two-thirds. Although increasing use of pesticides on farms may have contributed to those losses, research shows that this is not the only cause. Put simply, wildlife is being squeezed out of the countryside by loss of habitat and ever more intensive productive use of the land.

Such losses of habitats and species can be seen as further damage to the fabric of a countryside which lost much of its wild character long ago. Until the last millennium, wetland and woodland covered most of lowland Scotland; but these have been reduced to tiny fragments, and now even the small remnants are being lost or damaged. It is critically important that we protect what is left of these habitats for the benefit of the wildlife which cannot survive without them.

across its traditional range. Recently attention has been focused on key sites which are managed as nature reserves or protected by some form of designation such as Site of Special Scientific Interest (SSSI) (see Chapter 16).

However, these nature reserves and protected areas cannot, on their own, provide enough habitat to support viable populations of many plants, birds and animals. Over and above those key sites we need to sustain a much wider matrix of wildlife habitats throughout the countryside and to identify areas where the restoration of natural habitats can yield positive results.

But how are we to gain the active involvement and co-operation of the custodians of the countryside – the farmers and the foresters? The countryside requires positive and sensitive management, and merely banning activities which may damage the value of an area for wildlife would be quite ineffective. A far more positive and creative approach is needed.

On some designated sites management agreements are set up with farmers and landowners. In return for accepting restrictions on the management of land the farmer is sometimes offered compensation calculated by assessing the net profit which is foregone by managing the land for the benefit of wildlife. This approach seems reasonable but it is by no means perfect, because so many hypothetical calculations have to be taken into account in assessing the 'net profit foregone' by the farmer. The compensation payable is the difference between two financial forecasts: the first figure is the theoretical profit which the farmer could have made if no restriction had been placed on the use of the land; the second figure represents the reduced profit which might result with the restrictions in place.

The calculation for the hypothetical situation ignores all the risks taken by the farmer whenever a crop is planted; it is assumed that the imaginary crop will not be damaged by weather or pests, will produce good yields and will be harvested at a satisfactory price, and that no unforeseen expenditure will be incurred. In addition the calculation takes account of other forms of public subsidy as income. These factors tend to increase the apparent price of a conservation management agreement.

These compensation agreements have a place in some limited circumstances but, overall, they are cast in negative terms. They aim to pay compensation for farmers and foresters for not carrying out activities which may damage the countryside, but they do nothing to reconcile conflicting policy measures. We need an integration of policy measures so that conflict is reduced; and more importantly we need an approach based on positive management. Such an approach could well develop from the introduction of the system of Environmentally Sensitive Areas (ESAs) (Box 6). We must start thinking in terms of positive payments which encourage sensitive management and stewardship.

HOW ARE DECISIONS MADE?

It is an alarming fact that there is no single body or organisation with responsibility for co-ordinating the numerous decisions taken each day by public agencies which affect Scotland's countryside and its rural communities.

Each year huge sums of taxpayers' money go to support rural activities through a plethora of public agencies with little co-ordination. Each national agency pursues its statutory aims in deciding the application of the resources voted to it by Parliament and in deciding which projects should be supported or funded, all too often without reference to the work of other agencies in the field.

The result is that the actions of a public agency in one sector such as agriculture sometimes conflict directly with the actions of another, such as nature conservation. But there is simply no framework or explicit basis for co-ordination among the agencies either at local or national level. Even local authorities, which are more geared to local circumstances, can only tolerate the operations of the national agencies in their areas.

Not only is there no framework for consultation but many public agencies are only loosely accountable to democratic control. No rural public agency is directly answerable to the community whose interests the agency can sometimes dramatically affect. Consequently the people living in the countryside do not have the opportunity to participate in many of the decision-making processes which affect their lives. No wonder some of the public agencies are treated with distrust!

If the public agencies do not co-ordinate their policies or consult the rural community it is hard to see how collective, well-balanced decisions can be taken on issues such as which classes of agricultural land across Scotland should be given over to forestry. If the interests of landscape and wildlife agencies are to be taken into account as well as those of farming and forestry, the task becomes well-nigh impossible.

The need for some sort of co-ordination among the various agencies is becoming widely recognised. So far the attempts to break down the compartments between the agencies have resulted in little but confusion. Creating a framework which can balance these diverse local and national interests remains a major challenge for the next century.

WHO IS RESPONSIBLE?

These ingredients have set the scene for a real crisis in Scotland's countryside. There are many different agencies, interest groups and individuals, each with their own priorities and concerns; but there is no overall control and no integrated master plan. As a result the impoverishment of our wildlife heritage continues.

Most of the land is privately owned, a fact which is sometimes overlooked. What does this mean in practice? Some owners (fortunately a small minority) assert their right to do with the land as they wish; they make no distinction between land and other consumer goods which they own. But ownership of a washing machine does not carry with it any heritage or wider public responsibility, nor is there a framework of public policy and associated legislation and expenditure for the ownership and use of washing machines! In contrast, the ownership and use of land carries a variety of rights and public obligations which constrain the use of the land to a greater or lesser degree. Responsible landowners will decide how they use the land against the background of those rights and obligations.

At the same time there is a sense, far from trivial, in which all citizens feel they have a justified stake in the countryside and, when the scale of taxpayers' support for farming and forestry is appreciated, this feeling is strengthened. It is this which leads to confrontations of private and public interests and inspires some people to advocate simplistic solutions of legislative diktat and land nationalisation. The real debate should be to assess these rights and obligations to secure an appropriate balance of public and private interests.

Recent years have seen an increasing reliance on the workings of market forces in the countryside as elsewhere. But the scope for achieving protection of Scotland's natural heritage through the unguided application of market forces is extremely limited. However efficiently a free market operates in the countryside there will always be a residue of non-market activities and 'goods', of which countryside conservation is one of the most important. For this reason we can expect conservation measures of one kind or another to become more important determinants of public policy, with public money being directed towards private owners and occupiers.

For any landowner seeking to make a living from the land, government policies on agriculture and forestry dictate its management; but not all landowners make a living in this way. For example, there is a long tradition of landed estates in rural Scotland which rarely pay their way but which serve as playgrounds for the super-rich with an interest in field sports (see Chapter 17). More such 'playgrounds' can be expected as interest in the recreational use of the countryside continues to grow. For such owners, economic returns are a secondary consideration. Should such owners have access to incentives designed for struggling farmers on low incomes? If not, then how can the public interest be expressed?

As far as our countryside heritage is concerned, sensitivity in the continuing management

The Eildon Hills, designated as an Environmentally Sensitive Area (ESA) in 1988.

6. COUNTRYSIDE STEWARDSHIP

Scotland has ten Environmentally Sensitive Areas (ESAs), covering about 20 per cent of the countryside. Breadalbane (the largest, with 300,000 acres between Loch Tay and Loch Rannoch) and Loch Lomond were designated in 1987, as well as the Stewartry, Whitlaw and Eildon in the Borders, and the machair of the Uists, Benbecula, Barra and Vatersay. Five others were added in 1993–94: the Argyll Islands, Shetland, the Cairngorm Straths, the Central Southern Uplands and the Western Southern Uplands. These experimental designations were the first serious attempt to involve farmers in positive conservation management of the countryside.

ESAs stem from a 1985 European Community Regulation which was enshrined into UK legislation in the Agriculture Act 1986. ESAs identify wildlife, landscape and archaeological aspects of the environment and the management required to sustain them. The lessons from the early ESA designations have now been absorbed and it is recognised that *any* area of countryside is in some way environmentally sensitive. A similar approach is being adopted for the whole of the farmed countryside – the Countryside Premium Scheme.

Farmers voluntering to enter an ESA agreement must prepare a conservation management plan for their whole farm area. They receive payments in two tiers: the first relates to a number of general conditions applied to the whole farm and is calculated per acre; the second tier pays for the management of specified features of conservation value on the farm. The adoption of this plan allows each agreement to be tailored to a particular farm and to the ambitions of the individual farmer.

The general conditions aim to prevent farm operations causing damage to conservation aims and could perhaps deal with levels of stock, fertiliser applications and changes of land-use (for example, farm woodlands). The second tier payments are linked to management prescriptions for features of conservation value such as herb-rich grassland, wetlands and field boundaries (both hedges and drystane dykes).

ESA payments are not large and form only a tiny proportion (less than 1 per cent) of agricultural support; but they make a valuable contribution to farm incomes. They are not, and never will be, large enough to replace the income generated from farming, so they cannot become payments for 'doing nothing'. Instead they encourage the farmer to manage the land for a balance of objectives which include conservation of its wildlife and landscapes.

of the land is essential. The motivation of owners cannot be ignored; their co-operation must be secured. They must be offered various incentives with appropriate strings attached, securing their voluntary co-operation, with recourse to constraint by direction only as a long-stop against unreasonable behaviour.

AN EYE TO THE FUTURE

Many aspects of Scotland's natural heritage are threatened by the continuing changes in the countryside. These changes are driven by a combination of market forces and technology, modified by government policy and expenditure. Local communities are disenfranchised and have little influence over these instruments of policy. Meanwhile the urban majority is increasingly looking to the countryside for leisure and recreation and making its views heard through an increasingly vocal environmental lobby.

This increasing turbulence is exacerbated by the lack of any structure for co-ordinated action, and by a reluctance on the part of the various factions involved to yield individual freedom of action for any common benefit. Yet our examination of the needs of Scotland's natural heritage, and our exploration of the many threats to its survival, have shown that management for multiple goals must be the answer.

Market forces cannot provide a solution, however effective they may be as a mechanism for straightforward decisions on economic allocation. The many and unco-ordinated instruments of policy distort the market signals, persuading farmers, for example, to grow crops in European surplus by using methods which impose costs upon the natural environment.

More importantly, market forces can only work with cash valuations. They fail to recognise that 'man does not live by bread alone', that civilisation brings with it leisure and a search for fulfilment of the spirit as well as the body. Conservation of our natural heritage is not a marketable commodity; it is a resource whose protection requires intervention by government, steering market forces towards activities which are more sensitive to the needs of the environment.

Our response to this must come at three levels. First, at the practical level (on the farm), the adoption of a managerial ethic is essential. Land management must be more systematic, and taxpayers' support must be related to a farm plan (the cross-compliance principle). The business objectives of the farm need to be placed in context of an audit of the natural resources available and the quality of the natural environment, alongside the more conventional concerns with capital, technology and management skills. So the farmer or forester will demonstrate a willingness to work in a way which accommodates a wider range of interests, thus earning continuing support from the taxpayer.

Second, at the programme level, a structure of local and regional policy implementation is required which encourages flexibility of response and integration of purpose. 'Strategies' may help, if they spell out relationships between different interests and provide a basis for local interpretations of policy measures which are sensitive to conservation and development needs. It is at this level that the needs and aspirations of local communities must be drawn in along with those of other 'players' including owners, managers and lobbyists. There is no room for sectoralism at this level and it is here that the elusive 'balance' must be struck between local and national, personal and public interests.

Third, at the policy level, where overall goals are set and policy implementation is monitored, there is still a role for sectoral activity, as agencies representing the different interests monitor and evaluate what they see on the ground. At this level, environmental standards defining acceptable management in agriculture, forestry and other countryside activities should be set for implementation at the programme level.

As we have seen, reality falls a long way short of these ideals. But unless we find ways of 'managing the garden' at all three levels, Scotland's natural heritage can only continue its long decline.

*Stirling Castle dominates the
surrounding landscape.*

144

CHAPTER ELEVEN

The Paths of Progress
John Hume

*John R. Hume, Chief Inspector of Historic Buildings with Historic Scotland,
is a leading authority on Scotland's industrial archaeology.*

FROM PATHS TO ROADS

As soon as the first nomadic people began to settle in Scotland they began to create access routes to their sources of food and fuel, as well as to vital materials such as wood, stone, clay and, later, metals. These early pathways to the sources of such commodities became tracks which became more heavily used as communities grew. In places where ground conditions were difficult, or where the climate was poor, these routes could be critical to the survival and growth of individual settlements. In such circumstances water ways became more important and sites at the heads of navigable rivers, or with natural harbours, were particularly valued.

Such factors were already at work in prehistoric and early historic Scotland; places like Dumbarton, Dunadd (Argyll), Edinburgh and Stirling became important because they were sited near navigable water as well as having natural defensive heights. By Norman times water routes were well developed and land routes were becoming an essential part of social and economic life. The feudal system depended upon centralised political control which required good communications. Similarly the organisational structure of the Church – with its parishes, diocesan centres, pilgrimage churches and abbeys – relied upon inland transport and stimulated its growth in turn.

The economic dimension of this burgeoning society can be seen in the establishment of burghs as centres for trade and craftsmanship.

The growth of towns created central administration which, together with the religious function of the larger burghs, helped concentrate resources for the building of bridges, the laying out of proper through-routes and the construction and improvement of harbours. At a local level the building of corn mills by feudal lords also helped to create smaller trade networks.

In the later Middle Ages and in the early modern period these trends were complemented by the growth of industry and by the larger towns developing strong overseas links. During the seventeenth century successive Scottish

One of the best examples of a hump-backed Wade bridge. Built in 1732, it spans the River Fechlin on the east side of Loch Ness.

Field Marshal George Wade; painting by Van Diest.

145

1. THE A9

The A9 heads north across the Kessock bridge, Inverness.

Telford's girder bridge at Craigellachie.

Of all the roads ever constructed in Scotland the grandest in conception and execution is the A9 to the north of Perth. Its predecessor was for most of its length built by Thomas Telford as part of the government's policy of opening up the Highlands to stem the flood of people migrating south. In the far north some parts of the A9 still follow Telford's route, but since the early 1970s most of it has been completely rebuilt to carry more traffic at higher speed. This has involved major engineering work, dwarfing Telford's achievements in bridging the Tay at Dunkeld, the Beauly at Beauly, and in constructing the causeway across the Fleet estuary known as the Mound.

The most spectacular pieces of engineering are the great dual carriageway in the Pass of Killie-crankie which is carried on concrete legs, and the bridges over the Beauly Firth at Kessock and the Cromarty Firth at Foulis. These are immediately and obviously notable achievements, as are the smaller bridges at Bonar Bridge and elsewhere. What is less obvious is the care taken by the road's designers not just to build a road capable of carrying heavy traffic but also to make a road which is fit for the magnificent scenery through which it passes. Telford's road lasted for about a century and a half with minimal alteration; its successor may well be called on to do the same, in much more arduous traffic conditions.

administrations encouraged industrial growth, laying the foundations for the expansion of trade and commerce which followed the Act of Union of 1707.

The early and mid eighteenth century saw improved communications begin to transform the face of Scotland. Following the Jacobite Rising of 1715, General George Wade was ordered to construct a system of metalled military roads in order to police the southern Highlands. These roads opened up what was largely untracked land and required the construction of forty 'Wade' bridges built of stone. As an added bonus these roads allowed travellers access to the more remote parts of Scotland for the first time.

The growth of the cattle rearing trade in the Highlands, and the need to drive beasts south to market, created a network of drove roads through the glens and mountain passes. Many of them were simply tracks across unimproved ground, but wide grassy roads were also laid out in order to allow the cattle to graze on the surrounding land during the journey; this was especially so in the southern uplands.

Industry had grown considerably by the late eighteenth century, stimulating the demand for new and improved roads. Transport was making a visible impact on landscape and townscape by this time. But while the new roads may have made intrusive cuts through the landscape, nevertheless by channelling traffic they reduced the tendency of animals and vehicles to take a way round a miry track. Better communications encouraged land improvement and enclosure of common land. Enclosure, in fact, gave definition to the evolving road system by surrounding open fields with new stone walls and by planting boundary hedges and trees along roadsides.

Coach services were now being started but road surfaces were still very poor, making journeys long, uncomfortable and unreliable. However, coach services expanded rapidly and communication centres became more important as the wealthier classes began to travel for pleasure to a much greater extent. Landowners built inns for travellers on their estates and

146

writers and poets began to extol the aesthetic value of remote scenery and romantic ruins. These early literary tourists were the harbingers of today's mass migrations (see Chapter 17).

In the early nineteenth century Thomas Telford (1757–1834) revolutionised Scotland's road system; from 1801 he constructed more than 1,000 miles (1,600 km) of road as well as 1,200 bridges. It was Telford who built the prototype road which was to become the A9 of today (Box 1). With new road surfaces such as those developed by John Loudon McAdam (1756–1836) horses could pull carriages at high speeds provided that gradients were kept to a minimum; levelling of the road bed was achieved by the techniques of embankment, cutting and bridge-building. By 1830 Telford's roads had systematically opened up the Highlands, extending and improving the eighteenth-century military roads for the growing civilian traffic. Telford also built the major Glasgow – Carlisle Road as well as key bridges such as Glasgow Bridge, the Dean Bridge in Edinburgh, Lothian Bridge and Pathhead Bridge. Owing to the development of the railways, which absorbed a great deal of road traffic, most of these roads remained practically unaltered for a century.

The new roads undoubtedly improved travelling conditions but they were not used for mass transport of people and goods since they were expensive and could only cope with limited traffic. However, they proved vital for the transport of goods, postal communication and the middle-classes, since they created an integrated economy in Scotland for the first time.

Environmentally the easy lines, noble bridges and select clientele of the new roads made them relatively acceptable but, in addition, the economic possibilities which they opened up proved a powerful stimulus to the building of railways. However, before the railway boom came the heyday of canal-building.

THE WATERWAYS

Inland waterways had always provided a smoother and more reliable form of transport

2. THE CRINAN CANAL

Before steamships were invented, voyages by wooden sailing vessels round exposed headlands were fraught with danger. The voyage round the north of Scotland through the Pentland Firth was fearsome and so was that round the Mull of Kintyre, where vessels were exposed to the mountainous seas and high winds of the Atlantic. Additionally, in times of war, foreign worships and privateers could attack merchantmen without undue risk.

As commerce grew during the eighteenth century and inland waterways developed, the idea of cutting canals across narrow parts of Scotland emerged. The first planned canal was the Forth and Clyde (1768–90). The second, across the head of the Kintyre peninsula, which came to be known as the Crinan Canal, was projected by John Knox in 1784, as was the third, through the Great Glen: the Caledonian Canal.

The Crinan Canal was only nine miles long and was built relatively quickly. It was designed to take the small vessels engaged in the West Highland trade and was really promoted to benefit the people of the west coast rather than to make money. An Act of Parliament was obtained in 1793 and most of the capital came from private sources. It was completed in 1801 with a loan from central government and when it was in operation it came to rely on the state. It was formally taken over in 1848 and has been improved from time to time to take deeper vessels.

From the 1840s to the 1930s the canal was a link in a passenger service from Glasgow (later Gourock) to Oban, Fort William and even Inverness, the so-called 'Royal Route' after Queen Victoria used it in 1849. It was much used by puffers and still serves as a base for the VIC 32, the last operating steam puffer.

Today the canal's main importance is as a link for yachtsmen between the Clyde estuary and the west coast cruising area, perpetuating its original technical intention; and by bringing revenue to the coastal harbours of Argyll it fulfils something of the wishes of its promoters. It fulfils these functions quietly, efficiently and charmingly: Scotland's miniature canal.

Puffer on the Crinan Canal.

than roads, and from the late 1760s various schemes were advanced for canals and river improvements. Roads were much cheaper to

3. THE EDINBURGH AND GLASGOW RAILWAY

The cities of Edinburgh and Glasgow have been in rivalry for many centuries. For most of this period Edinburgh dominated as a centre of population, power and commerce. In the eighteenth century the Clyde became important owing to its relative proximity to North America, and its merchants were very effective in establishing trading links with what became the southern United States and with the West Indies. This stimulated the rise of industry throughout west central Scotland, creating a base for much larger-scale industrial growth in the nineteenth century. In consequence Glasgow grew to rival Edinburgh in population and to become the more important commercial centre. Edinburgh, however, was the seat of government, of the legal process and of banking, and thus there was a need for speedy communication between the two cities.

There were coach services from 1768, a canal link from 1822, and a part-rail part-canal route from 1840. But the Edinburgh–Glasgow route was an obvious choice for a first-generation mainline railway. As completed in 1842 it was superbly engineered, with three major tunnels, long and deep cuttings, lengthy viaducts and marvellous overbridges. Its curves were gentle and its gradients slight, except for a rope-worked incline at the Glasgow end.

Apart from an extension at the Edinburgh end and the abandonment of rope haulage from 1908, the Edinburgh and Glasgow Railway is virtually as built after nearly 150 years of operation. It remains a most noble and effective monument to the generous intentions of its promoters and to the capabilities of its engineers (Grainger and Miller). In its day industry grew round it but most of this has now gone, and its interference with the environment is minimal; indeed, as on railways generally, its cuttings and embankments are havens for plants and animals otherwise threatened. The Edinburgh and Glasgow Railway remains an effective argument for wise and generous provision of public utilities.

The viaduct over the River Almond at Ratho by David Octavius Hill.

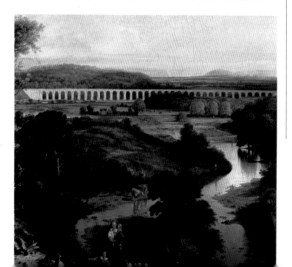

build, however, and the rate at which canals were built was restricted by shortages of capital and technical ability. The 35-mile-long Forth and Clyde Canal, from Grangemouth to Bowling, took twenty-two years to complete (1768–90) and a government loan was needed to pay for the final section.

The Forth and Clyde Canal, which was closed to navigation in 1962, was designed to allow coastal trade to cross the Central Belt of Scotland and was thus an important link in the shipping industry. The canal's own passenger and light goods trade was linked by road services to places much further afield. On the other hand the Monkland Canal from Glasgow to Airdrie and Coatbridge (constructed in 1761–90) and the Saltcoats Canal were primarily designed for the transport of coal.

The use of the early canals and river navigation encouraged the growth of towns, but after the first shock of the water channels being cut across rural landscapes their impact on the countryside was limited. Only one Scottish canal was built to serve agriculture and rural industry, namely the 18-mile-long Aberdeenshire Canal which ran from Aberdeen harbour to Port Elphinstone (1807), but it was not a commercial success. Some early nineteenth-century canals like the Crinan Canal (Box 2) and the 60-mile-long Caledonian Canal (built by Thomas Telford in 1803–22) crossed from sea to sea with little or no inland traffic; while others were just extensions of the Lowland canals system, like the Glasgow Paisley and Ardrossan (which reached Johnstone by 1811 but was never completed), and the Edinburgh and Glasgow Union (1822).

The Paisley Canal was historically important in pioneering cheap short-range passenger transport, enabling large numbers of Scots to use public transport for the first time. By that time, however, improvements in railway construction made further canal construction an unattractive proposition. Boats could only travel quickly on the canals if these were free of locks; but lock-free canals required level routes and the number of such routes in Scotland was very limited. The heyday of canal-building was over, and Thomas Telford was already turning his prodigious talents from the construction of waterways to the construction of road-systems.

THE RAILWAY AGE

The wooden rails of Scotland's early horse-drawn railways were exclusively built to carry coal from the mines to local consumer markets or to junctions with water transport for transfer to more distant customers. Thus the very first railway, built in 1721, was built to link pits at Tranent with the harbour at Cockenzie. But it was not until the 1770s, over fifty years later, that wooden railways became popular in central Scotland.

Horses could pull heavier loads on railways than they could on roads and this was the reason for using what were, in effect, specialised roads. The later invention of iron rails and wheels inspired new developments since they enabled horses to pull even greater loads and reduced maintenance costs.

Iron rails were first used in Scotland on the Kilmarnock and Troon Railway, which the Duke of Portland promoted as a coal-carrying line; this line used smooth wheels and flanged cast-iron rails, unlike today's railways, which conversely use smooth rails and flanged wheels. It became the first public railway in Scotland to pioneer passenger services using a steam locomotive.

Many schemes for railways were devised from the early years of the nineteenth century but it was not until the 1820s that improved technology produced a recognisably modern system. The critical invention was the wrought-iron rail, first produced in North-East England. It proved much better than the cast-iron tramplate and was used both on the famous Stockton and Darlington Railway and on the more modest horse-drawn Monkland and Kirkintilloch Railway (opened in 1826).

Even if steam locomotives had not been improved from their early nineteenth-century origins, railways would still have multiplied; but in 1829–30 the Liverpool and Manchester Railway successfully demonstrated that locomotives could haul speedy passenger trains as well as freight. The potent combination of steam locomotives and wrought-iron rails had a dramatic effect on the evolution of rail travel.

Within ten years central Scotland had a basic system of arterial railways and within twenty years the railway system had been extended as far north as Aberdeen, with three routes linking Scotland to England.

At first the locomotive-hauled railways had to be as level as possible, with cable-assistance on gradients if necessary, as at Cowlairs on the Edinburgh and Glasgow Railway (Box 3). But as steam locomotives became more powerful and reliable the massive civil engineering works required for the early lines became less necessary. By that time the advantages of railway communication were obvious, and although roads and canals remained important locally they were in all respects secondary to the railways. In the Highlands and some other areas railways were promoted primarily to improve communications rather than as profitable ventures.

The architects and engineers who built most of these pioneer railways considered it a matter of pride that they should design stations, bridges and viaducts as substantial and dignified structures. But the scars of large railway works aroused public antagonism and there were fears about the effects of steam engines on farm animals and the countryside. To minimise nuisance from smoke, only coke was burned in locomotives until the 1860s when improvements in boiler design allowed the use of coal.

Overall the effect of railways on the environment was complex and striking. They certainly encouraged the growth of towns and in the later nineteenth century were the main factor encouraging the spread of the suburbs. They also enabled the middle-classes to spread out from the industrial and commercial centres to commute from select dormitory towns such as Kilmacolm, Bridge of Weir and Troon in the west, while North Berwick, Gullane and Peebles became the equivalents in the east. Rail transport encouraged farmers to specialise in certain products – beef in the north-east, sheep in the Highlands and Borders, dairying in the south-west and cereals in the south-east. They made it easier to exploit coal, ironstone and oil-shale deposits over a large part of lowland Scotland and fostered the smelting of iron for processing into wrought iron and steel. Railway communications allowed the shipbuilding and heavy engineering industries of west central Scotland to develop on a very large scale.

From the early 1840s large numbers of people began to use the railways for excursions to the Clyde coast, and towns such as Helensburgh, Gourock, Largs, Troon and Ayr, along with towns on the east Fife coast, became popular resorts for day trippers. Rail travel enabled the more affluent tourists to visit Oban or to use the many golf courses which proliferated from the 1880s.

From the 1880s the railways became even more important in that they allowed cities to go on expanding. The price of this was the construction of expensive underground routes in Glasgow and the development of street railways (tramways); at first such trams were horse-drawn or steam-powered but they were later driven by cables and electricity. The construction of suburban railways resulted in the concentration of new houses and shops around stations; tramways encouraged ribbon development along tram routes as well as more intensive development of inner city sites.

The large number of horses which pulled the trams and other transport (especially in Lanarkshire) needed large amounts of fodder and increased the local demand for oats and hay. This altered the economy of some farming areas by creating a new market for native wheat which had suffered because of competition from imported wheat. Electric tramways eliminated this horse-economy although horses remained numerous in cities until after the First World War.

Electric tramways made mass urban transport both cheap and popular; routes were extended far from town centres, giving many people better access to the countryside. The publication of guides and travel booklets encouraged ramblers to take advantage of this new facility. More importantly the trams encouraged suburban development for the less well-off and gave both professional and labouring workers a wider choice of workplace.

STEAMING AHEAD

In parallel with the rise of railways and tramways, steamship services also grew and became locally significant. Although the first practical steamship in Europe – Henry Bell's *Comet* of 1812 – was not a commercial success, steamships quickly proliferated in the sheltered waters of the Clyde (Box 4). The size and power of such vessels grew rapidly and within a decade coastal services began to operate. From then until the 1840s, when long-distance routes were opened, steamers were increasingly important for passenger services around the coasts of Britain.

However, it was in the Clyde estuary and in the western Highlands and Islands that steamers proved permanently valuable. In the Clyde, steamers had two main effects: they allowed middle-class families to live permanently or seasonally in coastal resorts and they permitted large numbers of working-class excursionists to visit holiday places which catered for them. Rothesay and Dunoon became favourite 'Doon the Watter' destinations enjoying a popularity which we can scarcely imagine today.

Although at first steamers operated from the centre of Glasgow, combined rail-steamer services developed rapidly once the railways became integrated and by the later nineteenth century most steamships were operated by the three railway companies which served the area. The competition between the companies encouraged a high quality of both service and comfort. Faster steamers could work longer routes, enabling people to commute greater distances, but the development of large-scale coastal suburbs was confined to the upper Firth of Clyde and the island of Bute. The island of Arran would have been intensively developed but for the opposition of the principal landowner, the 12th Duke of Hamilton.

In the western Highlands and Islands the effect of the steamboats was different. Local communities were only marginally affected by incomers and commuters. Instead, steamers benefited isolated island and mainland communities by allowing them to develop and specialise. By providing cheap travel they encouraged people to move from remote areas to central Scotland but they also made lowlanders aware of conditions in the Highlands. Some lowlanders invested in land, with mixed results, but other more socially minded people tried to support the highlanders in their struggles with a harsh environment. The development of the whisky distilling industry on Islay, Jura, Mull and Skye was purely commercial, but the Harris Tweed industry was organised partly for benevolent social reasons.

Steamships greatly encouraged tourism in the southern Highlands; Fort William, Oban and Campbeltown all partly owed their economic rise to the tourist trade. And of course the rapid improvement of rail and steamer services gave a dramatic boost to another major aspect of the Highland environment: the sporting estates.

AFTER THE WARS

The First World War was a real turning point in the character of land-use in Scotland, as in so much else. The war began a process of democratisation of wealth and power and of control of the means of transport, which no administration since has been able to gainsay.

Many soldiers also gained experience in motorised transport during their service, and this encouraged the civil use of motor vehicles to expand rapidly in the 1920s and 1930s.

Immediately after the First World War bus and lorry services began to develop, linking urban communities with each other and with the country. Within twenty years the rural railways were dead or dying; electric trams had vanished from all but the four cities and a network of new

4. CLYDE STEAMERS

The Clyde estuary was a natural area for the development of steam navigation. In France and in the United States the broad navigable rivers provided something of the same stimulus but early experiments in France proved abortive. The line of development started in Scotland with William Symington (1763–1831), the Leadhills-born inventor and engineer, in the 1780s and was taken up in the United States on the Hudson River by the American engineer Robert Fulton (1765–1815). It resulted in the development of shallow-draught river steamers.

The physical topography of the Clyde, with its islands and long sea-lochs, created a need for water-based communication and its sheltered waters provided an ideal environment for the safe development of steam propulsion.

Henry Bell's 30-ton steamship *Comet* was built at Port Glasgow in 1812 as the first steam-propelled vessel to operate on a navigable European river. It began a process of evolution which culminated in transatlantic liners and world-wide commercial network of steamships; locally in the Clyde it led to the creation of a system of waterborne passenger transport without parallel in the United Kingdom. There was every kind of water transport, from short cross-river ferries, through bread-and-butter routes linking communities on the estuaries, to medium- and long-range excursions.

Steamers catered for all classes of society quickly, efficiently and quietly. It was a fiercely competitive business, as evidenced by the service from Ardrossan on the Ayrshire coast to Brodick on the island of Arran; here the Glasgow and South Western Railway and the Caledonian Railway challenged each other with fast boat trains and speedy steamers and all for minimal traffic rewards. At stake, ultimately, was control of the trade of Ayrshire; the Arran competition was merely a gambit – but what a glorious one. Both companies built fine, fast steamers for the trade. The Glasgow and South Western vessel, the *Glen Sannox*, was arguably the most beautiful Clyde steamer ever built. The fastest steamer time between Glasgow and Brodick in 1893 was 80 minutes; today, with the existing car ferry, the fastest achievable time is 115 minutes.

Henry Bell's Comet, *the first steam-propelled vessel on any European river.*

The first steamboat on the River Clyde by John Knox.

arterial and improved local roads had been built. These made motor transport much more attractive to the general public and greatly enhanced the use of the motor car.

Cars were glamorised in novels, in the cinema and by press advertising which encouraged people to buy them. The old bounds on large-scale settlement imposed by transport difficulties were burst and new suburbs came into being. Ribbon development, which had begun with the tramways, was extended by motor transport. Motor touring in buses and cars opened up more of the Highlands, hastening the decline of the Gaelic culture which was also being swamped by the English-language radio.

The Second World War did not have such a dramatic effect on the Scottish environment as the Great War. Scotland was strategically important during both world wars and the remains of military sites are still with us, some of them now recognised as important monuments to epochal events. So far as post-war developments were concerned perhaps the most important was the development of air transport which had started to make a small impact with internal commercial services in the later 1930s. In the years after the war

transatlantic aviation was at first centred on Prestwick airport; it led to a great increase in the number of American visitors, whose spending power had a definitive effect on the tourist trade, especially in the Highlands. It also encouraged government-sponsored investment in Scottish manufacturing industry.

The further expansion of aviation throughout the world badly affected the Scottish shipbuilding industry, which was further damaged by the concentration of freight into bulk carriers and container ships. The decline of Scottish shipbuilding was made even worse by the development of nuclear weapons which sharply reduced the demand for conventional warships.

Railways were badly affected by post-war trends, especially the increasing use of personal cars. Many rural railways were closed for passenger services during the 1950s and in the 1960s most of the remainder went as part of the Beeching cuts. Services to the north and west Highlands were subsidised for social reasons but elsewhere the cuts were severe, involving closure of almost all railways in the Borders and in Galloway. Further expansion of road transport through massive road improvement schemes since then has slashed freight traffic on the railways. However in the west of Scotland conurbation rail transport is still much used, and towns in the Central Belt which have good rail services have grown faster than other comparable settlements. In recent years the re-opening of passenger services on some lines and the building of new stations have been a notable feature; it may well be that the railway age is due for a revival.

Meanwhile Scotland has been gaining a very fine road network. This has allowed large numbers of people to move away from the inner cities to housing developments in suburban and semi-rural areas; this is especially so in west central Scotland. The mechanisation of agriculture and the dwindling population of farm workers released many buildings in the countryside for other uses, and in a 50–60 miles radius around cities many farm properties have been converted into homes for city commuters. Only strict planning controls have prevented large-scale building in the 'green belts' around the cities.

The pattern of shipping round the coast of Scotland has also been influenced by the dominance of motor transport; coastal freight services have almost all disappeared. Ferry services across sea lochs, once numerous, have now been eliminated, and even Skye is now linked by bridge to the mainland. Similarly what were once fully fledged shipping services to island and mainland piers have been replaced by car ferries on the shortest possible routes – if necessary with overland road links as on the Outer Isles service operated via the Isle of Skye. These changes have put more vehicles on island roads, creating considerable new traffic pressure.

But today's transport is in some ways more environmentally friendly than that of the nineteenth and earlier centuries. Aviation traffic, especially at peak holiday times, has brought with it considerable noise pollution on the flight paths into Glasgow and Edinburgh airports. But no palls of smoke hang over railway stations or harbours and the noises of steam engines and clanking wagons no longer disturb the sleep of town dwellers. On the roads cars have cleaner exhausts and are quieter.

As the millennium draws near there is increasing concern about the effects of motor transport and of intensive use of walking routes both on urban areas and in the countryside. The National Lottery's Millennium Fund is helping to address these problems by the creation of a network of long-distance cycle ways under the auspices of Sustrans, and by part-funding the Millennium Link, a scheme to re-open the Forth & Clyde and Union Canals to through navigation. These safety valves for both formal and informal recreation should reduce the pressure on established areas, and reduce the conflict between different road users. Cyclists are also being helped, in both Edinburgh and Glasgow, by increased designation of cycle lanes in urban streets, making it easier for journeys to work and for access to the countryside. In the countryside more cycle routes are being designated. The popularity of long-distance footpaths, however, continues to grow, causing erosion of fragile hillsides. Off-track motoring and cycling (both motor and pedal) pose further threats to hillsides with their vegetation cover (see Chapter 17).

Transport-linked development is also eroding the countryside fringes of all urban settlements. The decline of the nuclear family is creating a demand for more and more housing, and despite pressure from local and national government to use brownfield sites, house-building firms are putting increasing pressure on green belts. Out-of-town shopping, retail and business parks and stadia are also eating up countryside, and by their dependence on private transport putting enormous pressure on road systems. They are also, in areas close to urban centres, further eroding the viability of village shops and local bus services, encouraging the decay of rural communities, or their conversion into commuter suburbs. Deregulation of bus services has had an impact too. The low esteem in which the bus is held limits its usefulness. Railways are in little better case. It remains to be seen how privatisation of the railways will affect services, but outside the central belt rail

5. SCOTLAND'S TRANSPORT HERITAGE

The historical value of Scotland's inheritance of transport hardware is being increasingly valued. Hundreds of road bridges, tollhouses, canal structures, viaducts and railway stations are now on the Secretary of State's lists of buildings of Special Architectural or Historic Interest. Some are scheduled as Ancient Monuments, but perhaps the most notable schedulings are the surviving Scottish canals, which are all either scheduled or in the process of scheduling. Being identified as of special importance is, of course, no guarantee of survival. Many transport relics survive in use, or with minimal adaptation, even if their original function has gone. Others have been converted to other purposes, retaining much of their original character. Many disused railway stations, for instance, are now houses, and others are guest houses, restaurants, and even in one case a health centre. Whole routes have also been adapted as long-distance walks (notably the Speyside Way), as bridle paths, and as cycle ways. On the Speyside Way, former stations have been re-used as bunk houses.

In the early 1990s a number of important listed structures have been thoroughly overhauled to give them an expectation of life extending well into the next century. The Association for the Preservation of Rural Scotland has been active in repairing bridges on the eighteenth-century military road system. On an altogether larger scale, the Scottish Viaducts Committee has since its formation in 1985 been instrumental in securing funding for the repair of some half-dozen major viaducts. Grant aid from Historic Scotland, local authorities, European funds, and enterprise companies has secured the preservation of, among others, Laigh Milton Viaduct, Ayrshire, believed to be the oldest railway viaduct in the world. Similar partnership funding has secured the restorative repair of Wemyss Bay Station, probably the grandest surviving seaside station in Britain.

The railway preservation movement, now nearly forty years old, goes from strength to strength. The old-established 'firms' are the Scottish Railway Preservation Society, whose Bo'ness line runs partly through recreated countryside, and the Strathspey Railway, on a section of the old Highland Railway from Aviemore to Boat of Garten. It is currently being extended to Grantown-on-Spey. The Ayrshire Railway Preservation Group has long been developing at Minnivey, near Dalmellington, and is about to introduce train services to the Dunaskin site of Doon Valley Heritage. The relatively new Caledonian Railway runs from Brechin to Bridge of Don, and has refurbished the historic Brechin station. Not so much a preservation, more of an evocation, is the Lowthers Light Railway at Leadhills, a narrow-gauge line on the route of the old Leadhills and Wanlockhead Light Railway. Apart from their interest to railway enthusiasts, a journey on them, at relatively slow speeds, recaptures the once-familiar feeling of the train interacting with the countryside through which it passes: great experiences all.

services look increasingly marginal. Proposed expenditure of many millions of pounds by Railtrack on backlog maintenance, and on signalling renewal is, however, likely to create a rail network which is easier and cheaper to run.

One thing is certain. There is probably more interest in, and consciousness of, the importance of transport and communications in Scotland than at any time since the last war. The organisational and political changes of the recent past (especially privatisation), cut-backs in Government expenditure and local government reorganisation have significantly altered the decision-making map. One aspect of this is the recognition that roads should no longer be designed solely to speed up the passage of motor vehicles. Instead of bypasses (no longer affordable in many cases) traffic calming is being introduced for roads through rural settlements, and 'fitting roads' are being designed, which are tailored to the countryside through which they pass. The increasing sensitivity to the environment epitomised by these moves is born in part of the need to economise, but is very welcome to all those who love rural Scotland.

THE POST OFFICE – CONNECTING COMMUNITIES

Martin Cummins
Secretary to Scottish Post Office Board

The succession of revolutions in transport and communications has played a vital role in the evolution of modern society. Today the micro-electronics revolution has heralded the age of instant information and is bringing about change at work and in leisure which is more pervasive and rapid than ever before.

The Proclamation of Charles I in 1635 'for the settling of the Letter Office of England and Scotland', linking 'Edinburgh' and the 'City of London' in a return journey of five days, may be regarded as the start of a public communications service. But throughout the troubled seventeenth century and well into the next, all the post in Scotland was carried on foot, with the exception of the single route between Edinburgh and Berwick, en route to London.

The failure of the 1745 Jacobite Rebellion resulted in much official attention being given to roads and bridges in Scotland. These Highland roads and the march of the Turnpike Trusts paved the way for a major impetus to the development of posts. They also heralded the arrival of that most romantic of postal conveyances, the mail coach. The first arrived in Edinburgh from London in 1786; – and by the end of the century coaches also plied between Edinburgh, Aberdeen and Glasgow.

It was Robert Wallace, the member of Parliament for Greenock from 1832, who was instrumental in securing Parliamentary support for the sweeping reforms of the Post Office which were carried out by Rowland Hill. The most famous of these was the universal Penny Post of 1840, with mail being charged by weight not distance and prepaid by means of the 'Penny Black' stamp. The impact on public communications was immediate and dramatic. In 1839 just over 7.5 million letters were delivered in Scotland; the next year recorded 18.5 million letters and within ten years this figure had doubled. The mail coach could not have coped, but steam trains could.

As the nineteenth century progressed, so the rate of scientific and technological change accelerated. The age of steam was followed by electricity, with the telegraph being a splendid example of response to that change. But the telegram was doomed by the product of still newer technology: the telephone, destined to become one of the great icons of the twentieth century.

Now the digital integration of telephone, television, satellite and personal computer offers an amazing communications potential with almost unlimited access to information and the ability to publish, do business or communicate on a global scale more easily than ever before. The Post Office sees itself as part of this revolution, using technology to achieve greater efficiency for its letter, Postbus, parcel and retail services, but, ultimately, providing face to face contact compared with the impersonal world of cyberspace.

Post offices themselves gradually became the local representative of a state increasingly involved with the lives of its citizens. What with dispensing pensions (since 1908) and benefits, TV licences and more than 160 other transactions, including providing access to Royal Mail and Parcelforce Worldwide's international letter and distribution services, the 2,000 post offices in Scotland have a vital and central role to play – particularly where they underpin the viability of remote rural and island communities. The forthcoming automation of the nation's post offices will not only provide more efficient payment of bills or benefits but offer exciting opportunities for the provision of information and help keep them relevant to the complex and shifting needs of the twenty-first century.

River Dee near Braemar,
Aberdeenshire.

CHAPTER TWELVE

The Streams of Life
Peter Maitland

Dr Peter S. Maitland is a specialist in freshwater ecology and fish conservation, and runs his own consultancy based at the Fish Conservation Centre near Stirling. He has been on the staff of the Universities of Glasgow and St Andrews, as well as the Nature Conservancy and the Institute of Terrestrial Ecology.

The lochs and rivers of Scotland are famed all over the world in poetry and in song as a national resource of breathtaking beauty and inestimable value. The *bonnie, bonnie banks of Loch Lomond, Sweet Afton*, the *Silvery Tay* and many other references all conjure up waterside images of peace and beauty. There is a practical side too: pure water from Highland springs is an essential ingredient in the production of that other celebrated liquid, *uisge beatha*, the Gaelic for 'water of life' – Scotch whisky; and fresh Scottish salmon grace restaurant tables on every continent. In addition the mystery of Loch Ness and its alleged monster has drawn visitors from every part of the globe. No image of Scotland can be properly conjured up without including her lochs, her lochans, her rivers and her burns.

In times of critical water shortage in other parts of Great Britain, Scotland is fortunate in having vast amounts of high quality water: Loch Ness alone contains more water than all the lakes and reservoirs in England and Wales put together. Yet although we value Scotland's fresh waters highly for their beauty we often undervalue them as a key national resource; indeed substantial damage is being done to some waters by various human activities.

Much of the physical nature of the lochs and rivers of Scotland has been shaped by ancient land movements and in particular by the action of ice during the last Ice Age which came to an end some 12,000 years ago. The grinding action of huge glaciers which gouged out many of our loch basins and river valleys, the kettle holes left after the melting of huge ice blocks, and the damming of river valleys by terminal moraines – these all left behind a varied but barren landscape as the great ice cap finally retreated.

Many people think of Scotland as being a very wet country yet the rainfall in some parts of the east (Moray and East Lothian, for example) is low, with only about 20 inches (50 cm) of rain each year. Some parts of the west, on the other hand, make up for this and well over 80 inches (200 cm) of rainfall each year is common in some of the mountainous areas of the west coast.

Running water has formed much of our landscape as it is seen today and our freshwater resource in terms of the number of lochs and rivers is an impressive one. Recent counts have shown that Scotland has a total of well over 31,000 lochs and lochans and over 5,000 rivers and burns. These include some of the most

Water sculpted rocks and giant kettle-holes at Glen Orchy.

spectacular freshwater bodies in Great Britain as well as the largest: Loch Lomond (Box 1) is the greatest by area at 27 square miles (70 sq km); Loch Awe is the longest at 25 miles (40km), and Loch Morar the deepest at 1000 ft (300 m), while Loch Ness has the greatest volume – 26 billion cubic ft (735 million cubic metres). The River Tay (Box 2) is the largest river with an average flow of 5,614 cubic ft (158 cubic metres) per second, more than twice that of the River Thames.

1. LOCH LOMOND

Loch Lomond, famous for its scenic beauty and 'bonnie banks', is the largest area of fresh water in Great Britain (see Chapter 1). It is also vitally important for wildlife, and parts of the shoreline and islands have been protected as a National Nature Reserve for nearly three decades. The loch has been studied intensively for some time and the ecology is now quite well documented.

Several uncommon plants are found around its edge, the most notable being the Loch Lomond dock; a few rare invertebrates also occur. At the turn of this century a small worm discovered in the mud at the bottom of the loch was found to be a species new to science and was named after the loch: *Arcteonais lomondi*. It has since been recorded in Loch Morar but appears to occur nowhere else in Great Britain.

No fewer than nineteen species of fish occur in Loch Lomond – the largest number of species known from any Scottish loch. The rarest species in national terms is the powan. Second in rarity is the unusual black dwarf race of river lamprey which feeds mainly on powan. The combination of the powan and the river lamprey is unique in the British Isles. In the last ten years several new fish species have been introduced to the loch, including the ruffe; four of these are now established and abundant in some places.

Much of the loch's water catchment is natural moorland or woodland but some areas are substantially affected by farming and forestry. Fertilisation of the land has polluted local burns with nutrients which have eventually leached into the loch. In addition schemes to improve drainage by ploughing and ditching have caused more silt to be washed into the loch; they have also made burns more liable to sudden spates as well as causing them to be drier during droughts.

At the height of the last Ice Age no wildlife existed in Scotland and practically all our present plants and animals have managed to arrive over the last 10,000 years or so. Clearly this is not too difficult for plants with airborne seeds and for birds and flying insects, but the problems of immigration and dispersal are much greater for purely aquatic invertebrates and for fish. Actually fish are still slowly moving northwards to invade Scottish waters

There is now substantial demand for the water within the loch and its catchment, and considerable volumes are piped away for use elsewhere. Perhaps even more seriously, recreation is becoming a major industry on and around the loch because of its proximity to Glasgow; a wide variety of activities attracts increasing numbers of people. In summer thousands of visitors bathe in the loch, or picnic along the beaches. The resulting noise and litter are the main difficulties arising, but actual erosion of the shore is also evident.

Loch Lomond is an ideal centre for boating and, with more and more boats using the water each year, pollution from rubbish, oil waste and sewage has increased. Boats also cause problems because of noise and interference to wildlife as well as to anglers and bathers. There are increasing problems among boat users themselves, causing friction between, for example, water-skiers and anglers. Sport fishing is controlled by the Loch Lomond Angling Improvement Association which has about 1,000 members, many of whom have boats on the loch.

Loch Lomond is probably Scotland's most important loch. Its high amenity value should mean that changes detrimental to its water quality are opposed. However people with interests in tourism, camping, boat hire, cabin cruising, power boating, water-skiing, canoeing, bathing, picnicking, natural history, angling, research, conservation and water supply are increasingly involved in profound conflicts of interest. The problems can only be successfully resolved if a management strategy for the integration of different uses is developed for the loch and its catchment area. In addition it is vital that more effort goes into conserving the quality of the loch rather than simply attracting more people to the area.

perfectly suitable for them, which they have been unable to colonise as yet. People play an increasing role in transporting such organisms and there have been many changes in our aquatic wildlife in recent times.

2. THE RIVER TAY

Many fine waters could lay claim to the title of Scotland's premier river; but the one with most justification is probably the River Tay. Its catchment area of 2,000 square miles (5,000 sq km) is the largest in Scotland and it has the greatest flow of any river in Great Britain; this exciting water is at one and the same time a most attractive and valuable resources.

Rising as a small trickle at a height of 2,050 ft (620 m) in the west of the country, near Beinn Laoigh, the source water tumbles down the mountainside to join with other burns, forming the River Cononish. Further downstream, near Tyndrum, the Cononish becomes the River Fillan which passes into Loch Dochart and Loch Iubhair and emerges as the River Dochart; this flows east and eventually passes over the lovely falls at Killin to enter Loch Tay, one of Scotland's many large and beautiful lochs.

Emerging from the loch as the River Tay, at Kenmore, it flows down a magnificent wooded strath to Ballinluig where it is joined by the River Tummel, which doubles its size. Now a major river it flows steadily towards Perth, joined by the Rivers Braan and Isla. At Perth it becomes tidal as it enters the firth and is joined by the River Earn before reaching the open sea beyond Dundee. During their journey from Beinn Laoigh the waters have travelled 92 miles (148 km).

The river shows many ecological changes along this course. Starting as a cascading mountain burn with few nutrients and very few plants or animals, it slows to become a rocky Highland river full of mosses and other weeds as well as many invertebrates and fish. As it enters the strath it slows further and meanders, with many deep pools and extensive areas of gravel. This stretch, surrounded by farmland, is very rich and has an abundant aquatic wildlife. Finally it moves into the estuary and merges with salt water, providing yet another varied habitat for aquatic life.

An obvious feature on the river is Loch Tay itself, which forms almost one-sixth of the total river length and whose deepest point at 508 ft (155 m) is well below sea level. There are many other lesser lochs within the catchment (574 are shown on the 1 : 50,000 map) and several of the larger of these have been harnessed for hydro-power. As a result the pattern of flow in the river is somewhat erratic, being related to changes in power demand rather than immediate rainfall. Some of the water in the River Tummel has actually been transferred from the River Spey.

In Scottish terms the fish which live in the River Tay form a diverse community and the river's twenty species are of considerable conservation interest. There are no fish at all near the river's source, but trout soon appear downstream and are joined by salmon and eels, all of these occurring throughout the main river to the sea. Some thirteen species are common in the middle reaches but one species, the arctic charr, is found only in Loch Tay.

As the river moves into the estuary and salty conditions take control, some fish such as minnows disappear; but these are made up for by other species like sparling, which make up a varied estuarine community here.

The salmon fishery on the River Tay is a famous one. Huge numbers of fish are caught each year: formerly about 50,000 by the commercial netsmen near the mouth and 10,000 by anglers upstream. Commercial netting is at present being phased out. In the modern river, salmon making their way upstream must surmount several hydro-electric dams. Fortunately they are helped at each one by a fish ladder, and built into the ladder on the Faskally Dam at Pitlochry is a viewing chamber in which the public can see these magnificent fish move upstream (incidentally recording themselves on an electronic counter as they do so).

The largest salmon ever caught by rod and line in Great Britain was taken in the River Tay in 1922 by Miss Georgina Ballantine; it weighed just over 64 lb (29 kg).

As well as being a pearl among Scottish rivers the River Tay is also famous for its production of fine freshwater pearls. These rare lustrous gems are formed around stray particles of grit which lodge in the mantle of the pearl mussel *Margaritifera margaritifera*, once common in the River Tay and other Scottish rivers, but now becoming rarer owing to changing land-use, pollution and overfishing.

The flow volume of the River Tay makes it Britain's greatest river.

Loch Ness, the largest volume of freshwater in Britain.

WATERS OF HISTORY

Historically Scotland's fresh waters have been of critical importance to human settlement and culture. The words of the famous song *The Road to the Isles* ('by Tummel and Loch Rannoch and Lochaber I will go') show how the larger lochs and rivers were vital for transport at a time when there were few roads and much of the country was covered by impenetrable forest. The major routes across Scotland were, and still are, along the larger glens and river valleys, notably the lochs and rivers of the Great Glen and the Rivers Forth and Clyde in the central Lowlands. The value of these two routes was further enhanced by the construction along them of Scotland's two major canals: the Caledonian Canal and the Forth and Clyde Canal. Both were extensively used for transport at one time (see Chapter 11) and the latter is soon to be revitalised from Millennium Funds.

Water has also determined the siting of human settlements from earliest times, since

Atlantic salmon migrating upstream to spawn.

3. THE ATLANTIC SALMON

The life cycle of the Atlantic salmon, the largest British salmonid, is well established: adults return from the sea to spawn in the river of their birth around November in nests called redds (see Chapter 2). The eggs hatch in the spring to give young called alevins which quickly develop into small fry and then into well marked 'parr'. After two years or more these become silvery 'smolts' which migrate downstream to the sea and thence to their rich feeding grounds in the North Atlantic. There are approximately 400 different stocks, or local races, of wild salmon in Scotland.

The stocks of Atlantic salmon in Scotland have declined over the last few centuries. Whereas most river systems formerly contained populations of salmon, these disappeared from some rivers with the onset of the Industrial Revolution because of pollution and artificial barriers. However, in some places where salmon have been absent for decades, recent improvements in water quality have been such that stocks are recovering naturally (from adjacent stocks), as in the River Clyde.

Superficially at least the Atlantic salmon is economically the most important of our three native

salmonids (salmon, trout and charr) and it is certainly the one which receives most attention politically. New measures for their management and conservation have recently been proposed. Wild fish were formerly the most important; about 1,000 tonnes a year are caught by anglers and by commercial netsmen. However, the development of salmon farming has rapidly overtaken this and the production of farmed fish is currently about fifty times that of wild fish. Some netsmen have gone out of business in recent years; this trend seems likely to continue and eventually most wild fish will be taken by rod and line.

Attempts have been made at various times to estimate the value of the fisheries for Atlantic salmon and sea trout; these estimates vary widely according to the method used. One recent estimate gave a value of £50.4 million to the rod fishery (with 3,360 permanent jobs) and £1.8 million to the commercial fishery (with 390 permanent jobs). One of the highest values recently placed on Atlantic salmon was for the sale of fishing rights on a stretch of the River Beauly, where the value was assessed on the basis of £12,000 per fish caught annually.

almost all dwellings were built near suitable sources of drinkable water. In addition water was an important element in the defence strategy of early settlers who built their homes on small natural or artificial islands in lochs; these 'crannogs' were sited offshore for greater safety (see Chapter 7).

Salmon (Box 3) and sea trout migrating into Scotland's waters each year provided a marvellous and abundant source of food and it is evident that these were captured in various ways from earliest times. In some places they could be (and indeed still are) caught by hand but other methods were developed, including the use of spears, traps and nets. Wildfowl of all kinds must also have provided an important part of early Man's diet in Scotland.

Sources of water for power also affected the siting of later settlements and many derelict old mills and 'mill towns' all over Scotland are testament to this. Alongside them we find the mill dams, built of stone and earth, which held back the water in many burns and rivers and diverted it down a new water course (the mill lade) to drive a mill wheel. Several of these mills have been kept in working order and can still be seen today: Preston Mill on the River Tyne in East Lothian is an excellent example.

OUR AQUATIC WILDLIFE

One of the great features of our fresh waters is the marvellous variety of habitats they provide for wildlife between mountainous source and sea estuary. Up on the high tops of our mountains, where the ptarmigan and golden plover live, there are innumerable shallow peat pools and small burns. Most of them cannot support fish but they do have fascinating plants, like the carnivorous bladderwort, as well as many interesting invertebrates. The deep lochs of the mountain corries may hold isolated remnant populations of arctic charr. Lower down in the straths are larger lochs and rivers, which support important salmon and trout (Box 4) populations in addition to many other fish as well as a wide variety of plants and invertebrates, including the large pearl mussel.

Most of these waters are very pure chemically and naturally slightly acidic, but in areas of limestone (e.g. Durness or the island of Lismore) the waters are alkaline and so clear that light can penetrate deep, giving the lochs a lovely bluish appearance.

As they approach the coast the rivers reach their maximum size and flow into firths or estuaries where the animals and plants of the freshwater communities change dramatically to salt-loving ones. All round the coast are small saltwater pools and creeks with similar species.

There is a wealth of plants and animals above and below the surface of these undisturbed waters. Pondweeds and stoneworts grow in the depths, lilies float on the surface, while irises, marsh marigolds, bulrushes and many other plants add grace and colour to the banks. Bright damselflies dart among the rushes and dragonflies hover in the sun, catching other insects, while whirligig beetles and skaters slide around on the water's surface film. Beneath the surface the nymphs and larvae of dragonflies, mayflies and stoneflies, as well as water boatmen, shrimps and snails, provide ample food for fish. More than fifteen species of fish may be found together in some of our larger waters. Scotland has fewer species of freshwater fish when compared with countries further south in Europe. Nevertheless forty of the fifty-five British species are found here and the number is slowly increasing as more arrive from the south. Taking the starting point of our fish communities as the closing stages of the last Ice Age, the fishes of our estuaries, many of which come into fresh water to spawn, had no difficulty invading new waters as the ice receded. Thus sturgeon, shads, sparling, sea bass, gobies and mullets must have lived in our estuaries for thousands of years.

The only fish which were able to colonise truly fresh waters permanently as the ice receded were those capable of living in both salt water and in the ice lakes and glacial rivers of those times. There were probably no more than twelve species capable of this at that period; most notable among these were lampreys, salmon, trout, arctic charr, powan, eel, sticklebacks,

Dragonflies, damselflies and many other freshwater invertebrates are threatened by pollution and loss of habitat.

Brown trout; the two top fish have been crippled and deformed by acidification of their loch. The healthy fish is from a nearby burn.

4. TROUT

The brown trout varies enormously in form and colour and this has resulted in many local names. There are two forms, the brown trout proper and the sea trout; both spawn in fresh water in October or later and the young develop there, rather as salmon do, for a few years. Thereafter brown trout stay on in fresh water (often moving into a loch to mature) but sea trout become silvery smolts and descend to the sea. Here they feed in estuaries and coastal waters before returning to the rivers of their birth to spawn. The number of different stocks of sea trout in Scotland is probably only slightly more than that of salmon, but the different stocks of brown trout must number several thousand.

The rainbow trout was first introduced to Scotland from North America about a century ago and is now a very common fish in places. However, although rainbow trout have been released in many waters throughout the country, the species has become established in only a few places and most stocks are maintained by regular introductions for angling or by escapes from fish farms. All too many farmed fish escape or are released, whereupon they compete with native fish for space and food. Many farms, for both trout and salmon, have imported foreign strains of fish and are developing domestic races with characteristics unlikely to be advantageous in the wild.

There has been concern recently over brown trout but this has probably been over-emphasised, for there are still many thousands of individual stocks in Scotland and some at least are likely to be pristine. Nevertheless there have been many losses, and some extinctions are at present masked by substantial annual stockings from hatcheries. There have also been some recent losses due to acidification and there is no doubt that the current dramatic decline in the stocks of sea trout on the west coast of Scotland is real and substantial.

flounders and the vendace (now extinct in Scotland but the subject of a restoration project by Scottish Natural Heritage).

By 1790 only another five species had been added to the Scottish fauna, namely pike, minnow, roach, stone loach and perch. How they arrived here is uncertain; some probably came naturally, carried as eggs on the feet of wildfowl for instance, but others may have been brought by humans.

By 1880, ninety years later, another five species were known to occur in Scotland: brook charr (from North America), grayling, tench, bream and chub (all from England). The main agents of dispersal during this and later periods were people and there are many records of deliberate introductions of these and other species around this time. This was a very busy period for the translocation of fish and many landowners introduced new species to waters on their Scottish estates, including several from North America.

By 1970 another eight species were known to have become established in Scotland: rainbow trout (Box 4), carp, goldfish, gudgeon, rudd, orfe, dace and bullhead, and humans appear to have introduced all of them. The latest character in this saga is the ruffe, a small perch-like fish which appeared in Loch Lomond in 1982, probably introduced by anglers from the south. This species has thrived in the loch and is now one of the most common fish but its impact on the ecology of the loch is still uncertain.

Many other fish have been introduced over the last 200 years but without success; these included largemouth and smallmouth bass (introduced to Loch Baa by the 8th Duke of Argyll in 1881), and cutthroat trout released into a small loch on Shetland. Between 1920 and 1930 several foreign species were introduced to ponds on an estate in Fife, including the American lake charr, dolly varden, mudminnow, bleak, bitterling, Danube catfish (which can grow to a length of ten feet!), brown bullhead and pumpkinseed. None of these species is known to exist in Scotland today.

Thus our present fish are a mixture of natural immigrants from the sea and from

Arctic Charr from Loch Doon have survived since the last Ice Age but are now threatened by acidification.

Powan are now one of Scotland's rarest fish, being found only in Loch Lomond and Loch Eck.

further south, along with many more recent arrivals which people have brought from England, continental Europe and even North America. The situation is by no means stable and we can expect other newcomers in future years. These will certainly add to the diversity of our fish communities but may also bring with them the threats of disease, competition and predation on our more sensitive and valuable native fishes.

EXPLOITING THE WATERS

The ever-increasing standard of living in Scotland (and many other countries) has entailed heavy demands on freshwater resources and made conflicting demands on the available water. We urgently need to develop schemes for integrated water resource use on a regional and national basis, but it is a course which planners and politicians have been slow to take.

To make the best use of water resources, especially in areas with low or variable rainfall, adequate reservoirs for the storage of rain water have to be constructed. These form an important part of most water supply systems and in areas of Scotland such as the Kilpatrick

Rainbow over the papermill at Corpach.

resources for the production of hydro-electricity, namely a mountainous countryside and lots of rain, much of which falls in winter when demand for electricity is greatest. Many hydro-power stations have been built in Scotland, sometimes harnessing the water of natural lochs but more often damming lochs to enlarge them or creating entirely new reservoirs by damming glens. The water in these reservoirs is often augmented by supplies brought in from neighbouring catchments via aqueducts; such auxiliary supplies are also used at pumped-storage schemes at Foyers on Loch Ness and at Cruachan on Loch Awe (see Chapter 13).

Regular irrigation is practised only in a few of the drier agricultural areas in the east of Scotland; there it has proved useful for watering vegetables during the growing season and swelling new potatoes just before they are lifted. Water is usually pumped from a nearby burn, or a borehole, and sprayed over the fields. Most water used in this way is immediately lost by evaporation or transpiration by the crop and very little ever finds its way back to the burn. Irrigation requirements are usually very seasonal, but unfortunately demand tends to be highest in dry periods when rainfall and reserves are lowest.

Although people have farmed or cultured fish for food from ancient times it is a relatively new idea in Scotland. Many of the early efforts were centred on 'stew ponds' associated with the monasteries. Later, fish hatcheries were built to produce salmon and brown trout for the stocking of lochs and rivers. Fish-farming has expanded rapidly in recent years and the production of rainbow trout for the table and young salmon for rearing in sea cages has been especially rapid. The main requirements for salmon and trout farms are large supplies of cool high-quality water as well as an adequate area for ponds and reasonable transport to markets. More and more fish are being reared in floating cages in lochs (see Chapter 2).

The fish which live in Scotland's lochs and rivers, especially salmon and trout, give pleasure and recreation to many thousands of anglers each year and constitute a major

Hills, the Ochils and several other upland areas close to the Central Belt there are now more reservoirs than natural lochs. Unlike some of the enormous reservoirs which we see abroad, these artificial systems have usually merged well with the local landscape and ecology.

The availability of copious amounts of clean water played an important role in the development of the whisky, steel and paper industries, all of which use large volumes of water. In modern times it is not so crucial for industries to be close to the actual source, since aqueducts have been built to carry water from one part of the country to another. The pipelines linking Loch Katrine to Glasgow, and Loch Lomond to Grangemouth, are good examples.

Although historically important, few waters in Scotland are now used for navigation, apart from the Caledonian Canal, which is still used by fishing boats travelling from one side of the country to the other. However, many pleasure boats, particularly canoes and yachts, still use the old canal systems as well as lochs and rivers and a few of the larger lochs still have small pleasure steamers on them – an echo of Victorian times (see Chapter 11).

Scotland is very fortunate in having the basic

national resource worth many millions of pounds. Most of the commercial fisheries for salmon and sea trout do not take place in fresh water but in estuaries or the sea, when the fish are moving upstream into fresh water to spawn. In addition to salmon and trout angling there is also an increasing interest in fishing for perch, pike and other coarse species.

People's increasing leisure time places an enormous demand on the remaining areas of natural countryside; our lochs and rivers are the focus for a tremendous variety of recreational activities such as sailing, power-boating, water-skiing, fishing, wildfowling, birdwatching, bathing and general picnicking (see Chapter 17). It is unfortunate that the most valued waters for these activities are rarely found in urban areas; understandably, people prefer to enjoy themselves among clean lochs and rivers set in attractive countryside.

THE THREATS TO OUR WATERS

The unusually dry summers of recent years have certainly made many people more concerned about water supplies; not only were many lochs and rivers in Scotland shallower than normal but reservoirs were lower, gardens were drier and cars were dirtier as a result. Is there really a problem? How can there be, when we actually use only a small percentage of our valuable water resources directly? With all that available water there should be enough for every need; yet there is an enormous range of demands which often conflict with each other.

For instance we each use about 22 gallons of water a day for our domestic needs: drinking, cooking, washing, bathing, toileting and so on. Industry too has huge demands: the Grangemouth petrochemical complex alone uses 3 – 4 million gallons of Loch Lomond water every day. Hydro-electricity, fish farming, domestic sewage, recreation of all kinds – they all make their insistent demands on our water resources.

Naturally all these pressures bring problems; many of our waters have been so misused that they are unfit for either people or wildlife. We

Fisherman on Loch Na Keal, Isle of Mull.

do many things which affect water even before it gets into our lochs and rivers; land-users are particularly important in this respect. The use of fertilisers, herbicides and pesticides in agriculture and forestry means that many of these chemicals or their residues end up in nearby water courses; and the spread of pollution is often enhanced by the draining and ditching of land which causes water to drain faster.

Many lowland lochs such as Loch Leven have suffered algal blooms caused by over-enrichment from agricultural fertilisers; when these blooms peak, the algae die and their decomposition suffocates fish from lack of oxygen. Domestic and industrial pollution can be even more severe and may completely kill all aquatic plants and animals, as has happened in parts of the Rivers Clyde and Forth. These stretches of extreme pollution, devoid of oxygen or poisoned by chemicals, act as a barrier to migrating fish which cannot cross them to reach stretches of clean water further upstream.

Weirs and dams on rivers act as barriers in the same way. Airborne pollution, such as acid rain, can also have a devastating effect and several of our hill lochs which had healthy trout populations a century ago are now too acid for fish to survive. People have also created other problems, for example by introducing alien plant or fish species; and recreational activity by the waterside can destroy vegetation and

*Loch Duntelchaig Reservoir
near Inverness.*

disturb wildlife.

The larger waters often hold the limelight, yet one of the saddest things over the last hundred years is what has happened to our smaller lochs, burns and ponds, especially in the Lowlands. Virtually all the small streams in Lowland agricultural areas have been ditched, canalised and piped to such an extent that there are virtually no natural examples left. With small ponds the situation is even worse, for they

have been gradually drained and filled in over the last century or so and even the few which remain are degraded or threatened. There is an urgent need in many areas for a review of what still remains in order that the most important small waters can be saved.

LOOKING TO THE FUTURE

Surely with so many lochs, rivers and burns in

Scotland there are enough to go round? The real answer is yes, but there are many problems and conflicts to be resolved. Our present national planning is quite inadequate.

What we need is a national framework and planning policy for all our lochs and rivers. We must look at their distribution, quality and value in relation to the demands we place upon them. Some are clearly vital for major uses such as hydro-electricity or water supply, and this must be the overriding priority although minor uses may fit in with this. Other waters may be of such tremendous wildlife importance that their conservation should be paramount. Several of our largest waters are so nationally important that an individual management plan is needed for each one in order that the needs of recreational or agricultural users do not conflict with the primary aim of maintaining the quality and value of that water. In all these cases people who use our water resources must be prepared to compromise and even renounce their claims in some cases – if not on one water then on another.

Such a master plan for our waters could integrate national requirements with local needs. Given an appropriate national framework (probably relying on a computerised database of some kind) the extent, value and role of each part of our water resource could be assessed. Rational judgments could then be made about the best uses for each loch or river; these could range from 'wilderness waters', where no human activity would be allowed, to urban waters which people could use intensively. Some water activities are perfectly compatible with others, and on certain lochs or rivers one can plan different zones of use: for example at Loch Leven and Linlithgow Loch, boating, angling, nature conservation and recreational use of the water's edge are all satisfactorily integrated. However, on other waters, even ones as large as Loch Lomond and the River Tay, there are increasing conflicts among user groups and these problems can only be resolved by the introduction of sensible local management plans. The earlier such strategies are introduced the better so that Scotland can take full advantage of her natural heritage of abundant pure water.

*All electricity, whether
made from nuclear fuel,
fossil fuel or wind and
wave power, is ultimately
derived from the sun.*

168

CHAPTER THIRTEEN

The Power of Scotland
John Butt and John Twidell

Professor John Butt is Professor emeritus of Economic History at the University of Strathclyde; Professor John Twidell, formerly Director of the Energy Studies Unit at Strathclyde, now holds the Marmont Chair of Sustainable Energy Technology at De Montfort University. Separately, they have published a number of books on the industrial archaeology of Scotland and on energy.

Scotland's energy resources have always been formidable. The sources of energy are very diverse and include peat, oil, oil-shale and coal as well as wind and water power, which have all been exploited by the talent of her scientists and engineers. Nevertheless for much of Scotland's history the brawn of humans and animals was the main source of energy.

Until the nineteenth century, people in Scotland lived in close harmony with their immediate environment and their activities were strictly conditioned by the energy supplies available locally. Then the power of fossil fuels – coal, oil and gas – was released and exploited to such an extent that the environment itself has been drastically affected. We cannot of course turn the clock back but we must return to the practice of a 'sustainable' energy lifestyle, while endeavouring to maintain our quality of life but on a higher plane.

Conservation of energy has always played some part in the thinking of energy producers – if only for economic reasons; but today we live in an age which should be totally committed to energy efficiency aided by a full range of advanced modern technologies. For instance just as peasants once used the endlessly renewable energy of the sun to bleach and dry cloth, today we should be looking at 'solar friendly' buildings, using the sophistication of computer-aided design and microprocessor-based energy control.

Scotland's energy riches have been released as a consequence of human determination, inspiration and ingenuity. But nature's gifts have not always been so easily available as today; the environment and geology of Scotland have often contrived to make it difficult to harness the resource in question. Moreover political involvement with England since the Act of Union in 1707 has meant that for practical purposes Scottish energy has not been, and is not still, master in its own house. The development of Scotland's energy, therefore, is an exciting, significant and unfinished story.

PEAT

If ground temperature is less than 5°C, dead plants do not decompose as they would otherwise; in much of Scotland's cold, damp and largely treeless environment the old heather, mosses and bracken do not completely decay as in warmer latitudes. Instead they are compressed by their own weight to form peat: a

Peat cuttings near Lochinver with Suilven in the background.

wet, dark brown organic mass that excludes oxygen. Peat was laid down in Scotland over many thousands of years, forming beds several metres thick. Indeed some of the earliest remains of Neolithic man in Scotland have been found in peat bogs dated to 6000 BC.

Crofters in the west of Scotland normally cut peat with spades; the peat pieces are stacked for drying and then used as fuel. Commercially it is scraped or extruded by tractor-driven 'ploughs' today. This peat is exactly the same material as that which is sold in garden centres for improving the soil of suburban gardens.

Over the centuries peat has been used to roof houses and burned for domestic heating and cooking. But it has had industrial uses, too, such as for the commercial extraction of salt in the thirteenth century, for firing pot stills for the distilling of whisky, and for the production of iron in ancient 'bloomeries'.

In recent times there have been frequent attempts to exploit peat on a commercial scale. From 1951 to 1961 the North of Scotland Hydro-Electric Board developed a two-megawatt, peat-fired, gas-turbine electricity generating station at Altnabreac in Caithness. However, this project, like many others, was a commercial failure. The basic problems remain: the extraction is labour intensive (even with modern machinery); the peat beds are often remote from roads; the fuel must be dried before it can be burned, and even then its calorific value is low. Moreover the removal of vast amounts of peat has implications for ecology, since peat bogs are vital wetland habitats for rare plants and birds, and if the peat is removed the habitat is destroyed.

The laws of Scotland have always provided Scots with the right to obtain fuel for basic warmth and cooking. In the Middle Ages it was a common obligation for 'bondsmen' to cut and supply a prescribed amount of peat for their feudal lord. However, everyone still had the basic right to cut their own peat from designated areas of common land. Rights to property, pasture, peats and personal protection are essential components of Scottish traditional life. These laws survive in modern times in the Crofting Acts which safeguard property and peat-gathering rights throughout northern and western Scotland, including the Islands. The hereditary owner of a croft is allocated an area to dig peats sufficient for a continuing supply from year to year; and a week's hard work in the summer can provide a family with a year's supply for home use.

TIMBER

Scotland's forests and woodlands have been exploited from prehistoric times for timber and fuel. Oak was a favourite wood for construction, whether it was for the beams of a great hall in a castle, for furniture or for shipbuilding. Beech was also used, particularly for early milling machinery, while Scots pine found many domestic and industrial uses. Farmers took their toll of woodlands by felling in many areas but especially in the central Lowlands. The prevalence of goats, cattle, sheep and deer throughout Scotland made the survival of seedlings and saplings unlikely. The grazing of domesticated animals and wild deer had a major impact in clearing the land of trees and keeping it barren.

In early modern times vast amounts of timber were burned to produce charcoal for industrial users, particularly the ironmasters. Charcoal was the main fuel for industries where quality or purity of the product was critical to commercial success. But the destructive distillation of wood itself produced other useful products besides charcoal such as pyroligneous acid, blacking, resins and pitch. Moreover the armaments industry used charcoal as a basic raw material in the production of gunpowder.

The blast furnaces had an insatiable appetite for charcoal; indeed Scotland's relatively cheap timber caused English and other ironmasters to move their works to forested areas of the Highlands in the seventeenth and eighteenth centuries. If no suitable local Scottish iron ores could be found it was cheaper to transport the red Cumbrian iron ores to the source of charcoal in Scotland than to export the charcoal to furnaces near the iron ore mines of the Lake

District. Sir George Hay, one of King James VI and I's favourites, was closely involved in founding several ironworks: near Loch Maree at Letterewe, at Talladale and the Red Smithy. Other early ventures are associated with Urquhart in Inverness-shire, Edzell in Angus and Cameron of Lochiel's lands in Argyll.

Developments during the eighteenth century are easier to trace. In 1723 a blast-furnace was operating at Achray in the parish of Aberfoyle, fuelled by local supplies of birch wood, and it was still operational in 1738. The York Buildings Company, leasing Grant's woodlands in Strathspey in 1728, bought 60,000 fir trees and established a furnace and forge at Coulnakyle using ore from the Lecht just over a dozen miles away. Glenkinglass (1727), Invergarry (1727) and the much more significant Bonawe (1753) and Furnace (1755) are other instances of investment in the charcoal iron industry. The furnaces at Bonawe near Taynuilt remained 'in blast' until 1866 and operations in the area by the Lorne Furnace Company, as it became known, carried on until 1874.

There is a common notion that the furnaces of the English and Irish ironmasters and charcoal-burners consumed much of the ancient Caledonian forest. However, two factors cast doubt on this: first, many of the areas where ironworks were established remain heavily forested today – and this is not as a result of plantings by the Forestry Commission, extensive as they have been; second, ironmasters, according to recent research, were much more committed to coppicing of woodland than is usually supposed. Coppicing was the method the wood cutters used to harvest the young tree-growth on a five or ten year cycle; when they cut down the trees they left the stumps and roots in place to grow more coppice poles because young wood produced the best charcoal.

This system also required careful woodland management and regular replanting. Thus the longevity of the Bonawe furnaces simply does not square with the idea of wasteful exploitation of the forests. If the ironmasters had simply burned up the surrounding woods

1. NEW LANARK

New restored, New Lanark, 20 miles (32 km) south-east of Glasgow, is recognised by world heritage bodies as one of Britain's outstanding industrial monuments: a classic factory village, designed to produce cotton cloth in the first phase of Scotland's Industrial Revolution. The newly invented English cotton-spinning machinery of the late eighteenth century required water power, and the River Clyde was tapped by an extensive water-lade tunnelled through a hillside. When David Dale (1739–1806) and Richard Arkwright (1732–92), the patentee of the water-powered cotton-spinning frame, visited the area in 1784, Arkwright thought Lanark could be turned into a new Manchester.

The first mill was built in 1785–6 and spinning began in March 1786, but this building was consumed by fire before a second mill was completed in 1788. Undeterred Dale replaced it and ultimately built four mills as well as housing for the workers. This remained the world's largest water-powered cotton-mill complex until its closure 180 years later. It was a very substantial investment and New Lanark became the model for enlightened management under Dale and his son-in-law, Robert Owen (1771–1858).

Robert Owen's name is strongly linked with New Lanark because he combined profitability with scientific management and a concern for humanity, when these attributes were rare and usually regarded as incompatible. He was a pioneer of factory reform, education, enlightened labour relations and co-operation, and became a messiah of utopian movements in early-nineteenth-century Britain and America. The village where he worked and wrote *A New View of Society* (1813) is one of the most complete survivals from the era of early industrialisation. Using the opportunities of electricity privatisation and the refurbishment of an original mill race, a modernised megawatt-scale hydro-electric generator now sells electricity to the area grid.

The mills at New Lanark built by David Dale were the largest working water-powered complex in the world until they closed in the 1960s.

Preston Mill at East Linton restored to full working order by the National Trust for Scotland.

they would have gone out of business, so sustainable coppicing made perfect economic sense. The common goat and the Blackface sheep may have more responsibility for the destruction of young saplings and the disappearance of woodlands than the ironmasters ever did.

Hydro-electric power house at British Alcan, Fort William.

In modern times trees are planted overwhelmingly as forestry monocultures. Quick-growing softwoods are raised for paper production and the building trade. Landowners have received significant subsidies and tax benefits to create and sustain plantations over farmland, hillside and peat bog alike. However, these plantations are not natural forests and do not sustain common plants and animals. Even worse, unique wilderness areas of the countryside are being blotted out for the production of trivial newsprint. A recent sign of hope, however, is the growing interest in safeguarding the last remnants of the Caledonian forest.

WATER POWER

The technology for using water power as an energy source for milling grain was first brought to Scotland by the Vikings and later by the English. The earliest machines were meal-mills using horizontal waterwheels on a vertical axis. These were most common in areas where Norse influence was strongest and remains and restorations of such mills can be seen in Shetland and Lewis today. They were simple easily built structures and they served local purposes well. More complex waterwheels, with a vertical wheel on a horizontal axis, were built throughout the country and were probably introduced by the Normans. A few were tide-mills (usually known as sea-mills) but most used the power of freshwater rivers and streams.

The use of such mills for grinding corn

2. LORD KELVIN (WILLIAM THOMSON, 1824–1907)

Professor William Thomson of Glasgow University was made Lord Kelvin in 1892 in recognition of his outstanding contributions to fundamental physics and practical engineering. His prime concerns were the theory and applications of energy. His reputation has continued to grow after his death and he is now honoured world-wide as the most outstanding applied physicist of all time. The author of more than 600 technical papers, his name was given to the fundamental unit of temperature (the degree Kelvin), to the derivation of the Second Law of Thermodynamics, to the invention and commercial production of many instruments, to the beginnings of hydro-power engineering, to the first transatlantic communication cable and to the establishment of science for commercial engineering practice.

He was born in Belfast into a family of seven children and his mother died when he was only six years old. Two years later his father moved with the children to continue his work as a mathematics teacher and writer at Glasgow University. William was obviously of outstanding intellect and was tutored by his father in mathematics; by the age of ten he had entered the university himself, first graduating from Glasgow and then from Cambridge. After careful planning by his dominant father, he returned to Glasgow University as Professor of Natural Philosophy when he was twenty-two. He remained loyal to Glasgow throughout his life, creating the world's first modern physics laboratory just off the High Street.

His relationship with the technical and commercial cultures of Glasgow was profound and his patents and commercial inventions made him a wealthy man; the city stimulated him and he stimulated it. On his death in 1907 he was buried in Westminster Abbey, with his name ennobled throughout the world by his discoveries; his reputation brought honour to the name of Glasgow, the city in which he blossomed.

became widespread and one estimate suggests that about 4,000 of them were in active use in the two centuries before 1870, scattered throughout the country. Large mill complexes were created in the towns, including Glasgow's mills on the River Kelvin, Edinburgh's on the Water of Leith, and those at Perth which used an intricate city-centre lade system.

The textile industry also made use of water power; the earliest application, in the fourteenth century, was for the 'fulling' or softening of woollen cloth, known in Scotland as 'waulking'. It is probable that this technology was copied in the early paper mills which pulped rags for making paper. These mills were the prototypes for later developments in the flax, linen, cotton and woollen industries which began in the early eighteenth century and culminated in the great cotton factory villages of New Lanark (Box 1), Deanston, Stanley and Catrine. The classic feature of industrialisation, the concentration of production in large factories, represented an initial victory for water power.

There are many other instances of the application of water power during the early phases of industrialisation. Landowners developed sawmills to increase their incomes and improve their estates. Water engines were used to drain the early undersea coal workings at Culross in Fife, and the mining areas around the Forth provided the best opportunities for these expensive innovations. The crushing and smelting of ores, particularly in the lead-mining districts of Leadhills and Wanlockhead, also attracted state-of-the-art water power: water-driven stampers broke up the ore and the same installations drove the air-bellows at the smelting furnaces.

In the eighteenth century, water-powered machinery was to be found at the iron furnaces and forges, improving the blast and driving the trip and tilt hammers. After 1750 there were considerable improvements to the design of waterwheels and to their installation. The resulting improvement in efficiency supplied much of the increased power demanded by the Industrial Revolution – so much so that the

Hydro-electricity generation at Laggan Dam, Roy Bridge.

contribution to the Revolution attributed to the arrival of steam power has probably been overstated. In fact large and small industries in Scotland continued to use water power on traditional lines until relatively recent times.

The total power available from water resources increased dramatically with the coming of hydro-electricity. The generation of electricity from coils attached to a rotating shaft became realistic for public supply from the 1880s. The question was, what power source should be used to turn the shaft? The first generators in New York and London were driven by steam engines but in Scotland water power was an obvious alternative. At this time Glasgow was the 'second city of the Empire' and arguably the world centre for engineering and commercial development. Here Lord Kelvin exerted his dominant influence in science and engineering (Box 2) and was soon joined by other great engineers. Hydro-electric power was proposed not only for Scotland but also for north-eastern America, using the Niagara Falls. The first commercial electricity generated in Scotland was from hydro-power at Greenock in the period 1892–95; then, in 1896, Lord Kelvin was a key figure in the opening of the British Aluminium Company's hydro-electric plant at Foyers on Loch Ness and in the encouragement of hydro-electricity as advancement for rural populations.

The use of hydro-power to generate electricity for urban areas on a significant scale required the creation of a national distribution grid. In 1927 Central Scotland was the first area in the UK for such transmission, providing power from a series of lochs in Galloway which in 1935 became Britain's first large hydro-power system with a capacity of 100 megawatts. The capital cost was £30 per kilowatt capacity and the electricity output generating cost was 0.11 old pence per kilowatt hour (kWh). Fifty-five years later the scheme is now operated by Scottish Power; the generating stations still function efficiently and have a long life expectancy. The generating cost decreased in real terms to about 0.3 new pence per kWh, classically proving the importance of investing in sustainable, pollution-free energy sources. Since electricity privatisation and the Scottish Renewables Obligations of 1995, new and relatively small private generators are installing new plant to sell electricity via the grid.

A further bonus was the success of the original consultant engineering companies in large hydro-power schemes world-wide.

The next significant hydro-power development produced a system of ten times greater capacity from the North of Scotland Hydro-Electric Board's construction schemes from 1943 to the 1960s. During the Second World War the socialist Secretary of State for Scotland, Tom Johnston, persuaded the Westminster government to create Britain's first nationalised power Board and to initiate the capital intensive programme needed to harness the water resources of the Highlands.

The 1943 Act establishing the Board was noteworthy in several respects: first, it was the forerunner of the 1947 Act, nationalising 300 separate companies and co-ordinating electricity supply throughout the UK; second, it had a long-term vision of economic development in the Highlands and Islands; third, it was the last major Act of Parliament relating to the 'right' of citizens to receive energy: section 2.3 of the Act, the 'Social Clause', made it a duty of the Board to supply new consumers in rural and island areas as a requirement 'for economic development and social improvement' at rates which would otherwise be uneconomic. In 1990 this requirement for social service, rather than

profit making, ceased with the privatisation of electricity supply.

The 1,064 megawatt hydro-electric capacity of the North of Scotland Hydro-Electric Board (now Hydro-Electric plc) is based on nineteen main power schemes and several smaller generating stations in the Highlands and Islands. In addition the Board had 700 megawatts of pumped storage at two stations. Care has been taken to protect the environment despite the obvious ecological disruption of water dams in blocking salmon runs; however, small run-of-the-river schemes are less disruptive. The network is now almost entirely linked by overhead and undersea cables which merge the electricity from hydro-power with energy from the gas-fired station at Peterhead.

The cable network also integrates the pumped storage dams of Loch Awe and Loch Ness with wind power on Orkney and with the rest of Britain's national grid. Before privatisation there were already about fifty private generating schemes, all of small capacity, which sell their excess power to the competing Hydro-Electric grid. Since privitisation such private suppliers are increasing in numbers, encouraged by the Scottish Renewables Obligation, which forces the utilities to purchase such private power. The Mackenzie Report of 1962 foresaw a total hydro-electric potential in Scotland of more than 1,964 megawatts. This would represent a 70 per cent increase over our present hydro-electric generating capacity, so the story of electricity from water power is far from over.

WIND POWER

The windmill was a relatively late arrival in Scotland and the earliest reference we have is to a mill at Largo in Fife during the mid fifteenth century. The idea was probably introduced from the Netherlands, or from East Anglia, where windmills were common. Many were constructed in the mid and late seventeenth century but the greatest building activity took place in the late eighteenth and early nineteenth century when a book on cereal production

The 60-metre diameter wind turbine at Burgar Hill, Orkney, generates more than three megawatts of electricity.

3. ENERGY ON AN ISLAND

Nothing concentrates history as much as the analysis of a small island. North Ronaldsay is the most northerly and nearly the smallest of Orkney's inhabited islands. The seas around it produce riches from oil but life on the island has had to follow its own way. In 1529 the priest John Bellenden noted that the islanders' only fuel was dried seaweed and cattle dung, having no local peat beds or woodland. In the nineteenth century various mills were used, including small household windmills; a large windmill that became the last traditionally operating post-mill in Britain when it ceased rotating in 1905; horizontal horse-driven mills; and even some hydro-powered mills that obtained a head of water despite the island being so flat. Around 1900 coal became a staple fuel imported during the annual visit of the steamer, affectionately called the 'puffer' throughout all the islands of Scotland.

Lighting in homes was usually derived from oil. From early times until the 1850s imported whale oil and natural oils were used in wick lamps. Then paraffin oil from mainland Scotland became available. Small battery-charging wind turbines were used in some houses by the 1930s before small diesel engine generators became the norm in the 1970s. These engines are still kept for emergencies even though the island was connected to the Orkney electricity grid in 1983.

Today the island has a 'low energy house', and Bird Observatory hostel, built by the local general practitioner, Kevin Woodbridge, which are thoroughly warm. These buildings, part of the North Ronaldsay Bird Observatory, depend for warmth on the use of thick insulation, the capture of solar energy (especially into the large south-facing spaces), forced ventilation heat recovery and, most importantly, the use of modern wind turbines to generate electricity for heat. The internal temperature stays above 20°C all year, proving that there need be no fear from the eventual exhaustion of fossil fuels, and electricity is generated for household power.

stimulated technical developments in milling.

By 1850 steam-driven mills, operating mainly in towns, had begun to eclipse the Scottish windmill. A few survived by converting to steam, for example at Carluke, and a few more resisted modern pressures until the early twentieth century. Survivals indicate a technical progression from the simple post mill to a variety of increasingly sophisticated tower mills. Most were constructed by local millwrights and masons, and the more limited the use the more simple the design. There were possibly no more than a hundred Scottish windmills of which the great majority were in the east of Scotland, stretching as far north as Orkney.

Windmills were more expensive to build than horse-mills or watermills and were rarely a sound economic proposition in a country where both water and horses were plentiful. Most commonly windmills were used for threshing and grinding grain, peas and other cereal substitutes; a few were used for pumping water or drainage, as for example at Strathbeg; one at Leith was used to grind metal ores brought from the Earl of Hopetoun's mines at Leadhills; and another at St Monans pumped sea water into storage tanks for the saltpans.

Modern wind turbines are very different from the historical windmills described so far. Today's wind turbines are used almost entirely for generating electricity although very occasionally they are used to pump water for cattle troughs. The idea of using electricity for lighting, and later for power, arose from the scientific discoveries and engineering developments of the late nineteenth century. In the 1880s, while Lord Kelvin opted for water power to drive electricity-generating turbines, and others used steam engines, James Blyth considered wind power.

Professor James Blyth was an engineer at Anderson's University in Glasgow (soon to become the Royal Technical College and later Strathclyde University). Blyth designed and built what was possibly the world's first patented wind turbine for generating electricity. His patent of 1891 was for a 16-metre (52 ft)

Energy efficient house at North Ronaldsay bird observatory, Orkney, uses maximum insulation, wind power, solar heating and heat recovery systems.

diameter machine, constructed at his family home in Montrose; this produced electricity for twenty-four years until the First World War, when Blyth had to stop work. After the war the development of wind-power generators ceased apart from the use of very small machines such as the Lucas 'Free-lite' which was used for battery charging for lighting on remote farms. Such machines were used through the 1930s and 1940s and the remains of some can still be found in the Highlands and Islands.

The next significant wind-power development in Scotland was the 100 kW, 14-metre (46 ft) diameter experimental turbine built on Costa Head, Orkney, in 1951. Commissioned by the North of Scotland Hydro-Electric Board, it was constructed by John Brown's of Clydebank, who also built the great liners, *Queen Mary* and *Queen Elizabeth*. Yet as many established engineers have found, wind power is not as straightforward as shipbuilding. The experiments continued for six years until the machine was dismantled in the face of the competition from cheap diesel fuel. The development could have continued but the rapidly falling price of oil in the 1950s and 1960s prevented further interest. It took the shock of the 1973 OPEC oil price rise to cause a renewal of activity.

When looking for alternative energy supplies, it is not difficult to realise that Scotland has the best windpower potential in the whole of Europe. The writer W.H. Murray has described life on the Western Isles as being akin to living on an aircraft carrier in mid-Atlantic! In the light of this potential, UK government and industry co-operated with the North of Scotland Hydro-Electric Board from 1982 to develop other machines on Orkney. These include the large 60-metre (197 ft) diameter, three-megawatt turbine on Burgar Hill which can produce more power than any other windmill in the world because of Orkney's strong winds. Three machines of this type could supply electricity to satisfy all of Orkney's needs (Box 3).

Elsewhere in Scotland modern wind turbines are used for commercial power. Some are manufactured in the UK while others have been imported from Denmark or the Netherlands. They all use modern composite materials and microprocessor-based controls. The wind turbine on Fair Isle, Shetland, erected in 1982, produces power for about 80 per cent of the lighting, cooking and heating needed by the island community. Other early machines in Scotland are used on fish farms and conventional land farms where farmers can earn extra income from selling electricity. Since the first Scottish Renewable Obligation in 1995, conventional wind farms are generating commercial power. The first was at Haggs Hill, south of Glasgow, and is owned by Scottish Power plc.

Throughout Scotland great care is taken to protect the environment and so far the careful siting of wind turbines has not caused complaint. However, despite the large wind-power potential and the success of wind farms in other countries, notably Denmark, only a few machines have been installed in Scotland. This is because we have so much surplus generating capacity from coal-fired, gas-powered and nuclear power stations; this surplus of electricity is also reflected in the very low price offered to small private generators.

However, wind power and water power create none of the pollution associated with coal-, oil- and nuclear-powered generating stations, and they are sustainable for as long as we have wind and water. These factors are now appreciated as we may see the beginning of the full development of Scotland's wind- and water-powered potential.

COAL AND STEAM POWER

The continuities in the development and exploitation of energy resources are nowhere more evident than in the story of the coal industry. As we have already heard, steam engines were used for water drainage at some collieries and Newcomen's steam engine, later radically improved by James Watt (Box 4), was used at a few others.

Most of the leading coalmasters in 1750 were also owners of saltpans and the Firth of

4. JAMES WATT (1736–1819)

James Watt was an inventive genius whose ideas transformed society throughout the world during his own lifetime. Born in Greenock in 1736 into a moderately prosperous family, and educated at the local academy, he demonstrated an early aptitude for making and repairing mechanical devices.

After training as an apprentice in Glasgow and London he became the 'Mathematical Instrument Maker to the University of Glasgow' in 1757. Staff and students interested in science and mechanics gravitated towards his workshop, since all the latest discoveries were discussed there. Watt made lifelong friendships with many professors, including Joseph Black, the theorist of latent heat, and John Anderson.

To illustrate his lectures Professor Anderson had a model of a Newcomen steam engine, as used to drain mines. However he could not make it operate successfully, and it was this failure in 1763 which changed the course of Watt's career and thereby the course of world engineering. A full-scale Newcomen engine functioned by creating a partial vacuum in a cylinder below the piston. First the cylinder was filled with steam, then cooling water was sprayed into the cylinder to condense the steam and create a partial vacuum. The model stimulated Watt to try to understand the working principles, so he began careful measurements for a quantitative analysis. As a result he became the first scientist to measure the energy (the latent heat) required to turn boiling water to steam and

realised how large an amount of energy this is (about six times the energy needed to heat the water to boiling point).

Watt realised that the heat losses from the small-scale model were proportionately much greater than from the full-scale Newcomen engines, so the model would never operate efficiently. In thinking about the essential inefficiency of cooling the whole cylinder at each cycle of movement, he realised that the steam should be condensed outside the main cylinder in a separate condenser. Thus the cylinder could be kept hot, resulting in greatly improved efficiency. Transferring this idea back to full-scale engines Watt embarked on his lifetime work as the developer of the modern steam engine.

The Watt engine took ten years to perfect and was manufactured as a significantly more efficient and reliable engine than Newcomen's. Watt's patent was obtained in 1769 after trials at Dr John Roebuck's colliery at Kinneil near Bo'ness. Roebuck's financial difficulties led Watt to seek a new partner in 1774, and this he found in Matthew Boulton (1728–1809) of Birmingham. The technical efficiency of Watt's engine depended upon accurately machined cylinders and other components, and over the following years Birmingham workmanship and Scottish engineering made the fortunes of Boulton and Watt. Further inventions and modifications greatly extended the practical uses of the steam engine, laying the foundation for much of Britain's pre-eminence as the workshop of the world in the nineteenth century.

Forth was the major area for the production of both coal and salt. The demand for coal diversified greatly in the next hundred years: household use increased very considerably and industrial demand grew even more. The population growth of Edinburgh and Glasgow – and the general spread of towns – after 1780 provided secure but fluctuating home markets for collieries in surrounding areas.

Many landowners and tenant farmers were improving their soil by spreading lime which was produced in local coal-fired kilns. The development of the glass and chemical industries, including town gas, required huge amounts of coal-gas as did the expansion of the

breweries and distilleries; the great growth of the coke-based iron industry, beginning with the foundation near Falkirk of the Carron Company in 1759, also demanded a constant supply of coal.

Coal production was approximately 460,000 tonnes in 1700 but had possibly reached two million tonnes by 1800. In the nineteenth century coal was king as the heavy industries of the West of Scotland came to dominate the economy. By 1850 output had climbed to about 7.6 million tonnes, the peak being reached in 1913 when 43.2 million tonnes were mined.

From 1800 to around 1870 the ironmasters determined the commercial fortunes of the coal industry since they tended both to own the collieries and to be their own best customers. Coatbridge, dominated by the ironworks of Bairds of Gartsherrie, was a stereotype of classic industrial pollution in the age of coal:

> dense clouds of smoke roll over it incessantly, and impart to all the buildings a peculiarly dingy aspect. A coat of black dust overlies everything....

David Bremner,
The Industries of Scotland, 1869

After 1870 the expansion of output was dependent on changing markets for coal; overseas exports increased from 1.4 million tonnes to 10.6 million tonnes by 1913 and ships' bunkers took about 3 million tonnes, while demand from the ironworks stagnated at just over 2 million tonnes. The railways and the merchant navy brought steam power to the fore and there was a close association between the design and manufacture of the world's locomotives at Springburn in Glasgow (Scotland's railway-building capital) and efficient marine engines for the Clyde's great shipbuilding firms.

From 1913 the path of the coal industry and steam power was ever downward. By 1945 output was just over 21 million tonnes. Deep mining was fraught with all the problems of a 'robber economy': the more coal was extracted, the more costly it became to extract the remainder. When the Scottish coal industry was nationalised in 1947 it was employing 81,000 miners, working 237 collieries, with an output of 25 million tonnes per year. However, in the 1980s it became increasingly apparent that Scottish deep mines were in decline owing to the difficult geology of the narrow coal seams and the shrinking of Scottish heavy manufacturing industry. There was also competition from bulk deliveries of cheaper imported coal and from nuclear power.

Moreover gross pollution of the air and the land became a severe handicap for all coal production industries. From the 1950s there were increasing restrictions on the use of ordinary coal for domestic heating and industrial purposes in cities and towns. During the same period North Sea gas became available – offering a cleaner fuel without the polluting gases of sulphur and nitrogen oxides which arise from coal burning.

So by 1988 output from 2,000 miners in the three remaining deep mines had dropped to 2.4 million tonnes per year; and this was almost entirely for use in coal-fired power stations. The deep-mined output had been overtaken by increasing opencast mining output from sixty-two sites, forty-nine of which were privately owned. It was the closing of an age for Scottish mining.

SCOTLAND'S OIL

Scotland has a unique place in the modern story of the exploitation of oil, mainly because of the discovery of huge oil fields in the North Sea. However, in the 1850s Scotland had established a land-based mineral oil industry based on extraction from oil shales; this shale-oil industry developed the technology from which modern methods of refining have evolved, and which will forever be associated with the name of James 'Paraffin' Young (Box 5).

Natural oils had of course been used by Scots from prehistoric times, principally for lamps, but industrialisation created a large demand for new lubricants since whale oil and vegetable oils tended to fail when used on hot fast-moving machinery. James Young established a new oil industry, at Bathgate originally, which quickly spread into other areas in the 1860s during what became known as the 'Scottish Oil Mania'.

American petroleum became a serious competitor in that decade and the later exploitation of major finds at Baku in the Caucasus area of southern Russia, and in the Middle East, ushered in the age of the giant multinational oil firms. Yet the Scottish shale-oil industry survived through a combination of scientific efficiency, diversification of products and its proximity to raw materials and markets.

5. JAMES 'PARAFFIN' YOUNG (1811–83)

James Young was born in Drygate, not far from Glasgow Cathedral. James first worked in his father's carpentry business and attended evening chemistry classes at Anderson's (now Strathclyde) University.

In 1837 Young moved into industry at St Helens on Merseyside. Lancashire was the major centre of the chemical industry at that time, and there were many opportunities for bright young men to advance their careers.

His opportunity came when a natural oil spring occurred at a coal mine in Derbyshire; Young was called in as consultant and in 1848 he set up the world's first oil refinery to process petroleum for lubricants and lamp oil.

The scale of the Derbyshire oil seepage was never large enough to make Young's fortune but it did lead him to question its origins and thence to distil coal. After two years of experiments he finally managed to produce oil from selected *cannel* (candle) coals. His friend Hugh Bartholomew, manager of the Glasgow City and Suburban Gas Company, sent him a barrel of the newly-mined cannel coal, known as Boghead, which had been discovered on the Torbanehill estate near Bathgate. Boghead coal turned out to be the richest oil-

bearing mineral ever discovered – neither a true coal nor an oil-shale, but a unique geological freak which had characteristics of both.

In 1851 Young moved to Bathgate and began Scottish oil production there, armed with his patent of 1850. Despite Young's attempts to keep operations secret the profitability of this operation became known, which constantly tempted businessmen to infringe his patent. Fortunately Young won all his court battles to defend his monopoly.

However, the oil-shales of the Lothians, which gave much lower yields than Boghead coal, were gradually exploited from 1859, particularly near Broxburn. When Young's patent ended in 1864 there was rapid investment in the industry and ninety-seven firms were soon established. Young meanwhile had created a new plant at Addiewell and his firm remained the largest public company.

Despite intense foreign competition large-scale exploitation of Scottish oil-shales continued. In the 1890s, for instance, more than two million tonnes a year were being mined and processed into saleable products. The major achievement of the industry, however, was the creation of the refining technology which led to the development of the world's petroleum industry.

The last plant only closed in the 1960s when the exploitation of the North Sea's oil fields was about to occur. 'Paraffin' Young's shale-oil industry has left us with the imposing landmarks of the great red shale bings which scar the landscape of West Lothian and the Central Belt of Scotland.

The first fossil fuel to be discovered offshore from the UK was natural gas in the southern part of the North Sea. This was in the early 1960s when the northern sea off Scotland was not expected to yield any supplies. Then in 1969 the Phillips Petroleum Company struck oil about 250 miles (400 km) due east of the Firth of Forth. This was the Ekofisk field, where drilling had to be carried out under 400 ft (120 km) of stormy sea.

Thereafter all the UK's oil finds were off the east and north-east coasts of Scotland, especially off the islands of Shetland. The

names of the fields read like a Scottish roll of honour: Duncan, Clyde, Montrose, Buchan, Claymore and Ninian amongst them. British oil was, in territorial terms, Scottish oil.

When the 1973 oil crisis was triggered by a doubling in price of Middle East oil it was clear that these Scottish resources would provide not only all the UK needs but would also, with Norway, ensure the supplies of Western Europe. By 1984 Scottish oil production was running at 2.5 million barrels per day (125 million tonnes per year). This bonanza provided ten per cent of the UK government's tax revenue and five per cent of the UK total business output, and the excess production of 0.5 million barrels per day (25 million tonnes per year) above national consumption was a major export earner.

In addition natural methane gas, often associated with oil production, has been an economic resource of great importance. A

*Oil production platform,
North Sea.*

History will probably see Shetland as the community that has best succeeded in taming the oil barons for its own benefit. In 1974 the Zetland County Council Act gave the Council the rights to charge taxes on oil developments and shipments. With a resultant income of more than £50 million per year the 20,000 citizens of the Shetland community have had the benefit of capital development and special programmes for elderly and disadvantaged people. Throughout the islands, houses were restored or newly built, school finance and staffing prospered, roads were widened and surfaced, harbours were improved and the fishing fleet strengthened. The falling oil prices in the late 1980s cramped the style of the council, who may never see the full realisation of their heady dreams of the early oil bonanza. Nevertheless as the price of oil increased again in 1990 the hopes returned.

NUCLEAR POWER

The commitment of the Scottish electricity boards to nuclear power has been distinctive and total. By 1990 over half of Scottish electricity was being generated from nuclear power stations; moreover the reactors used to produce the power are of unique British design: the Magnox and the Advanced Gas-Cooled Reactors (AGR). The ownership and the operation of the reactors were the responsibility of the pre-privatisation South of Scotland Electricity Board (SSEB). However, the North of Scotland Hydro-Electric Board cooperated with financing and with agreements to buy the power as a priority.

The first reactors in Scotland were built by 1964 at Chapelcross in Dumfries-shire (41-megawatt capacity) and Hunterston in Ayrshire (360 megawatt); these were of the Magnox design. The very considerable over-capacity of electricity generating plant in Scotland by 1989 resulted in electricity from Chapelcross being diverted to England before privatisation, and the Hunterston-A station was closed down as uneconomic in 1989 towards the end of its life.

The main nuclear stations have been the

national grid of gas pipelines fans out from North-East Scotland, supplying both homes and industry as well as a major power station at Peterhead and a huge chemical works at Mossmorran in Fife. Tragically the revenues derived from the use of these capital resources have been frittered away by the Westminster governments without any express purpose. Only Shetland and Orkney, whose councils had the wisdom to obtain special Acts of Parliament, have managed to turn these non-renewable resources into buildings, roads, sports centres, schools and other long-term developments.

Aberdeen became the oil city of Western Europe in the 1970s and was transformed from a city with a fishing and regional business economy to an international centre of subsea oil exploitation. However, without any special Act of Parliament the long-term effect on Aberdeen's economy is difficult to predict for, when the oil price dropped in the late 1980s, Aberdeen's economy quickly suffered, with little sign of any intrinsic strength that could have been developed in the preceding years of substantial oil wealth. Recently, oil reserves have been found off the Western Isles of Scotland, and we await developments.

later AGR installations. The first of these was also built at Hunterston, the B reactor (1,320 megawatt), and the second at Torness (1,364 megawatt). The Hunterston-B reactor has proved to be one of the most efficient nuclear power stations in the world and the Torness installation is one of the most noteworthy. In deciding to build Torness the SSEB stated their faith not only in more nuclear power to the detriment of coal but also in the British design as against the American Pressurised Water Reactor (PWR) design favoured in England.

We have yet to see whether the SSEB's predictions of the costs of nuclear power are fulfilled. Originally nuclear power was thought to offer the cheapest electricity costs after hydro-power and potentially to be the main strength of a privatised industry. However, when privatisation was being planned, the City financiers decided otherwise and refused to contemplate buying the reactors for the privatised electricity companies. They had decided that by the standards of commercial accounting, and with the need to charge for decommissioning and waste treatment, nuclear electricity was the most expensive form of power. Therefore Scottish Nuclear remained a nationalised company until the AGR reactors.

The UK Atomic Energy Research Establishment decided to build its most developmental nuclear reactor – the Fast Breeder Reactor – far away from major population centres, near Thurso in Caithness. Hundreds of nuclear physicists and engineers came to settle with their families at Dounreay looking across the Pentland Firth to the inspiring cliffs of Hoy on Orkney. The creation of this new community was for several years extremely successful, so much so that when the closure of the Fast Breeder Reactor and its associated 300-megawatt electricity station was announced in 1989 few families wanted to leave. This closure was another casualty of the reality of electricity privatisation and Dounreay had to diversify or perish. Having faced closure of the reactor research, reductions have occurred despite diversification.

THE FUTURE

The future development of energy supplies in Scotland is handicapped, surprisingly, by an embarrassment of established sources. The capital supplies of offshore oil and gas meet ten times Scottish needs by supporting the whole UK. Sadly nothing of this wealth is being garnered to prepare for the future when the treasure has all been sold. Over-capacity of electricity-generating plant discourages both small generating companies and private individuals from selling electricity. England does not have such an excess of conventional resources and the government has encouraged major plans for more renewable energy supplies, for greater use of gas and for the generation of energy from waste materials. Similar activity was continually delayed in Scotland, and only occurs at about 10 per cent of the capacity of the English developments.

Yet we know that Scotland has even greater resources of clean and renewable energy and the technology for the efficient use of energy. Scotland has Europe's greatest potential for wave and wind power and there is still more hydro-electric and tidal power waiting to be exploited. In addition landfill-gas (methane from rubbish), combined heat and power, forestry waste and passive solar heated buildings are all poised for sustainable economic benefits. The sum total of all these 'rational' forms of energy utilisation means that the energy needs of Scottish homes and industry can be sustained indefinitely if we use common sense, moderation and advanced technology.

Thus the ultimate future is exceedingly optimistic if only the present income from the North Sea capital assets is used to develop the technology for harnessing renewable energy resources. At the moment we are 'selling the family silver' and using the income for temporary benefit. It is imperative that we invest quickly in technology appropriate to the lasting value of Scotland's natural and human environment.

Turbine hall, Torness nuclear power station.

181

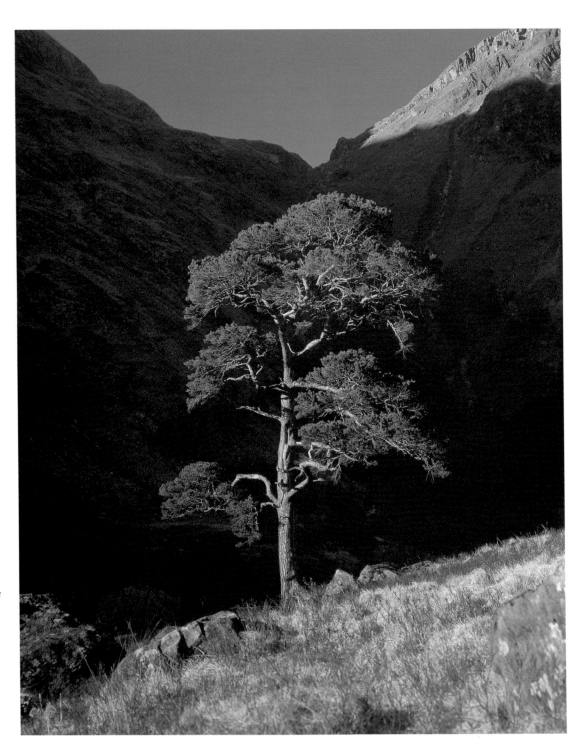

Caledonian Pine, upper Glen Nevis, near Fort William.

CHAPTER FOURTEEN

The Conservation of Nature

Alistair Sommerville

Dr Alastair Sommerville is the Head of Conservation at the Scottish Wildlife Trust.

ORIGINS

Wildlife conservation, as we know it today, is a very recent development which has its origins in the nineteenth-century legislation to prevent the commercial exploitation of wildlife. In particular the Victorian concern over the slaughter of wild birds at home and abroad led to a whole series of bird protection Acts being passed from 1869 onwards. At the same time some women activists, who were aware of the volume of egret and grebe feathers used in hats and fashion accessories, formed a pressure group to stop the trade. In 1889 this group became the Royal Society for the Protection of Birds (RSPB) which eventually achieved a ban on the importation of plumage for the millinery trade in 1921. Continued pressure from the voluntary sector led to full legal protection to British birds and their eggs by 1954.

The concept of Nature Reserves, to protect the places where wildlife lives, is even more recent (Box 1). The Society for the Promotion of Nature Reserves (SPNR) was founded in 1912 and set their members the task of surveying Britain and identifying the sites which should be conserved. The original idea was to persuade the National Trust to buy and manage the land concerned but it took until 1926 and the formation of the local Norfolk Naturalists' Trust before any reserves were established. After the Second World War the Yorkshire Naturalists' Trust was formed which led to the gradual spread of 'County Naturalist Trusts' throughout the UK. The Scottish Wildlife Trust was founded in 1964 with a Scotland-wide remit and is now one of the 49 which make up the 'Wildlife Trusts' partnership.

OFFICIAL NATURE CONSERVATION

Based on the pioneering work of the voluntary conservation movement it was not until 1949 that the government's own agency, the original 'Nature Conservancy', was created. This body became the Nature Conservancy Council (NCC) and then, in 1991, the Nature Conservancy Council for Scotland (NCCS) when it was split off from England and Wales. Today it is Scottish Natural Heritage (SNH) formed by a merging of NCCS with the Countryside Commission for Scotland in 1992.

The NCC's early remit focused on a duty to set up and manage a series of National Nature Reserves (NNRs) which would preserve some examples of the wide range of habitats found in these islands, together with the animals and plants which live there. A second task was to prepare a much longer list of sites, called areas of special scientific interest, as nature reserves 'in waiting'. This was to include all the remaining wildlife and geological areas of national importance.

Over time this statutory and systematic cataloguing of the wildlife resources of the British Isles was coupled to a programme of research into what was needed to manage effectively the wildlife outwith the NNRs in an increasingly exploited countryside. Fuelled by the demands of war, there had been an increasingly technological approach to farming. There was a dramatic boosting of the productivity of farms through the development and use of chemical fertilisers, pesticides and herbicides delivered by increasingly sophisticated and powerful machinery. This also resulted, however, in the destruction of huge areas of habitat through the grubbing up of thousands of miles of hedgerows, the filling in of ponds, the draining of wetlands and the ploughing up of meadows, marginal hill sides, heaths and bogs.

By the 1960s there was growing awareness of the huge impact which agricultural intensification had had on wildlife and on the ecological system itself. The story was being repeated throughout the world, but it took the book *Silent Spring* (1962) by the American ecologist Rachel Carson to give the warning that something was terribly wrong with the chemical farming methods. The chemicals which were killing wildlife were also affecting people, and something had to be done about it. The European Year of the Environment in 1970 brought much of the story to the attention of the public and initiated the next, more scientifically informed, stage in wildlife conservation.

A MASS MOVEMENT

By 1977 the NCC had produced *A Nature Conservation Review*, which described in detail the most important wildlife places in Britain. Unfortunately the wildlife legislation at the time meant that very little could be done about their conservation. The breakthrough came with the passing of the Wildlife and Countryside Act in 1981. This Act, which had been significantly improved through vigorous lobbying by the voluntary bodies, gave the NCC real powers both to designate Sites of Special Scientific Interest (SSSI) and to control the land-uses on them through a formal procedure of giving consents. The new survey work and documentation associated with the requirements of this Act has resulted in the SSSI system becoming the foundation of the government's approach to wildlife conservation.

However, it has become increasingly obvious that many of the threats to the wildlife of Scotland are the result of large-scale ecological problems. Intensive agriculture, marine pollution, acid rain and global warming have all demonstrated that the earth is a single fragile home for all of its living creatures including human beings. In 1980 a series of world-wide discussions on this topic was undertaken by the top environmental scientists from many countries. The end product was the seminal document 'The World Conservation Strategy'. This enunciated the now familiar concept of 'the sustainable development of renewable resources', that the resources of the planet are finite and need to be very carefully managed if they are to sustain economic activity, and therefore society, for forthcoming generations. This strategy was intended as nothing less than a global plan for conservation: a blueprint for

Waders at Aberlady Bay, East Lothian.

1. SCOTLAND'S FIRST LOCAL NATURE RESERVE

Aberlady Bay, on the Firth of Forth, is an extensive muddy and sandy bay with large areas of sand dunes, salt marsh, marsh and grassland. These habitats support a huge range of waders, geese and ducks in the winter, and terns, wildflowers and butterflies in the summer. This very popular site with naturalists and the general public is privately owned but through an agreement is run by East Lothian Council as a Local Nature Reserve (LNR). This designation has enabled an increasing number of local authorities to make major contributions to the practical conservation of wildlife. Currently there are 23 LNRs in Scotland.

the way in which man can ensure his own survival through the protection of the planet, its wildlife and ecological systems. Each country which helped with the preparation of the plan prepared a smaller, national version for action by its own people and government.

This international movement developed considerable momentum culminating with the World Summit in Rio in 1992. A number of common problems were addressed collectively there, including the environmentally based Agenda 21. However, from a wildlife point of view the most significant outcome was the signing of the Biodiversity Convention where the majority of countries of the world agreed each to draw up plans to ensure the long-term future of the biodiversity for which they were responsible. In the UK this has led to the refocusing of effort to produce Species Action Plans for many of our rare and endangered animals and plants, which has resulted in looking afresh at their biology, their distribution and the threats to them. There are also local Biodiversity Action Plans (BAPs) which identify the 'on the ground' actions required to safeguard the species and habitats at the local level. All of these Plans will together form the Biodiversity Action Plan for the UK.

A DOMESDAY BOOK FOR TODAY

The more effort which goes into planning the conservation of wildlife the more it becomes obvious that accurate information about habitats is an essential baseline for conservation, both to evaluate the resource and to detect changes to it. Success relies first and foremost on the accurate gathering of information from observations in the field. This surveying of plants and animals has always been a problem in Scotland because of its size and its relatively few skilled 'naturalists'. A lot has been done, principally by SNH and its predecessors using professional surveyors, but also by a dedicated band of amateurs and staff from the voluntary sector. As early as 1975 the Biological Recording in Scotland Campaign (BRISC) was launched to encourage people of

all sorts to help with recording. This has been achieved through promoting various local and national recording schemes to investigate the status of groups such as butterflies or wild flowers or to take up the special Scottish challenges such as the distribution of the pearl mussel and the red squirrel.

Several special methods have been developed to improve the quality, consistency and value of recording. These have resulted in major national efforts ranging from the Common Bird Census, which virtually monitors the general environmental health of the UK, to Butterfly Transects which provide valuable evidence for global warming.

Based on this type of information several countrywide analyses have been done to show the trends affecting the wildlife resources over the last decades; these include the Ancient Woodland Inventory (which compares woods

Grey Heron.

Landsat photograph of the inner Moray Firth.

2. SCOTLAND FROM SPACE

By analysing the different wavelengths of light reflected into space from the earth it is possible to work out what sort of vegetation is growing on the ground. Because of the variations with seasons and between years there always needs to be some 'ground truth' confirmation of the results. However this method does have the potential to map very accurately large areas of relatively inaccessible uplands as well as the better known lowlands.

3. WOODLANDS REBORN

With Scotland's native woodland cover reduced to 1 per cent of the land area, there have been many recent initiatives to restore the habitat which would naturally dominate a country with our climate. Grants from the Forest Authority have put a special emphasis on both planting and naturally regenerating birch, oak and pine woods. Even the role of wildlife is now recognised and a conservation aim can replace the previously only choice of timber production. The Millennium Forest for Scotland project provided a special impetus and extra cash to mobilise all kinds of groups to do more about the woods, or lack of them, in their area.

on current maps with those on the oldest available), the National Peatland Resource Inventory (drawn up from air photographs and field surveys), and the National Countryside Monitoring Scheme (in which samples of recent and old air photos were compared for changes in land-use: see Chapter 10). The most recent dataset is the Land Cover of Scotland which has mapped and measured a huge range of habitat types from air photographs taken in 1987–89.

Techniques are improving rapidly both in the collection of information, for example by remote sensing via satellite (Box 2), and in the storage and analysis of the resulting data, for instance by using computers and Geographical Information Systems (GIS). These advances are essential at the local level where survey information of all kinds can now be collected, collated and analysed thanks to computers and assistance (where they exist) from the network of local Biological Record Centres. These Centres, of which there are eleven main ones in Scotland, are normally run by local authorities in partnership with SNH and the voluntary wildlife organisations.

The conclusion drawn from processing this complex mix of survey data is that wildlife habitat in the lowlands represents a very small percentage of the land cover. Even in the uplands, native woodland and scrub generally exist in only fragments of once extensive forests. Scotland, which represents 32 per cent of the UK, has around 1,400 SSSIs covering about 11 per cent of the land surface, although most of this is made up of large sites in the uplands. There are also some 4,000 non-statutory Wildlife Sites, chiefly in the lowlands, which have been identified by the Scottish Wildlife Trust or the relevant local authority.

WORKING FOR WILDLIFE

Despite the amount of information which has been gathered about the wildlife of Scotland there are still major groups of animals, and even whole habitats, whose present status is completely unknown. Even worse is the blunt fact that most of them need to be managed if they are to survive, whether we understand them or not.

In theory an ancient woodland which has been in existence for 10,000 years should need little management interference; but in most cases it will have been cut over several times, planted with trees from other countries or invaded by plants dumped from local gardens. Parts of it may have been used as a rubbish dump. To 'put things right' may require the protection of the remaining old trees, the felling of a plantation of conifers, the eradication of rhododendron, and the cleaning-up of litter, to be followed by some new fencing.

All habitat and all species have their own management requirements even if they are already dependent on humans. A pond dug for agricultural purposes 200 years ago may now be rich in wildlife but threatened from the polluting effects of modern agricultural fertilisers and pesticides, from drying out as a result of the natural accumulation of water weeds over the years, or simply from being filled with junk and human rubbish. A meadow full of rare orchids created by cattle-grazing over the centuries can be lost in a few years if the cows whose grazing kept the grass short are removed, allowing the dominant tussocky grass to take over; the same meadow could be lost in one afternoon as the result of a single application of herbicides.

A mountain top or a seabird cliff may not need much physical attention but most of Scotland is intensively used and great care is required to balance the use of the land by man and by wildlife. The huge questions of lowland intensive agriculture, upland overgrazing by sheep and red deer, afforestation, fish farming and overfishing at sea still require a major breakthrough in policy if there are going to be any large-scale improvements to wildlife.

There are only about 250 nature reserves in Scotland, including National Nature Reserves (run by SNH), Local Nature Reserves run by the local authorities, Forest Nature Reserves, and the various reserves or equivalents run by the Scottish Wildlife Trust, the Royal Society for the Protection of Birds, the Woodland Trust, the National Trust for Scotland and the John Muir Trust. Within most of these the management of the habitats and their wildlife is carefully planned and a great deal of resources are devoted to carrying out the work required.

Outwith these areas the emphasis on the management of wildlife will normally take second place to agriculture, forestry or industry. There are, however, exceptions which are increasing in number. More owners of SSSIs are being encouraged to enter into positive management agreements with SNH; in this arrangement they are paid to carry out the essential work required to look after the wildlife on their land. In certain important areas of Scotland, designated as Environmentally Sensitive Areas (ESAs: see Chapter 10, box 6), there are agricultural grants to help farmers look after the special habitats, landscape and archaeology characteristic of their ESA. In 1997 this idea was extended to certain habitats throughout Scotland under the Countryside Premium Scheme, which offers various scales of payment which can be made to farmers to look after, or even create, specific habitats appropriate to farmland. In forestry the idea of wildlife management is recognised as part of the eligibility of the Woodland Grant Scheme; forestry management grants are available to owners to manage their woodlands

for the benefit of wildlife (Box 3). There are even a few examples where planning permission for industry has included a Section 50 requirement to retain, manage and/or create habitats on the proposed site, although in practice this chore is frequently off-loaded to a conservation body.

Ultimately some body with the appropriate technical know-how has to put significant resources into the care of wildlife. A deer fence will keep out deer and allow young native trees to grow, but a better solution would be to manage the deer numbers to a level which allows regenerating trees and deer to live side by side. The conservation ideal must be to build wildlife-friendly practices into everyday land-use management for agriculture and forestry.

Meanwhile, positive conservation action is creeping into all kinds of initiatives. Where wildlife management work requires to be done on private land the practical conservation teams from the Scottish Wildlife Trust or from the Scottish Conservation Projects Trust (SCP) can be brought in to do the specialist work. In most cases, however, the habitats for wildlife have been so severely damaged (or even destroyed) that it is a matter of creating habitats where none existed before. Habitat creation can involve planting wild flowers, grasses and trees on an industrial tip or making water bodies out of exhausted gravel works and allowing them to be re-colonised by freshwater plants and animals. These 'new' habitats all have their merits but it is essential to realise that they do not, and cannot, without hundreds of years of maturing, replace the original versions. A raised peat bog, for example, has taken 10,000 years to grow and for its communities to develop, which makes it irreplaceable in the short term.

However, several bodies have habitat creation as a part of their work, particularly the Farming and Wildlife Groups (FWAG) which have pioneered the methods needed through their advisory service to interested farmers. There are also many other local organisations involved including the various River Valley initiatives around Glasgow. Even private companies such as Scottish Coal or government departments such as the Roads Directorate of The Scottish Office are now becoming experts at creating land for wildlife to replace what was there before. It is also possible to get the necessary expertise from a small but increasing number of consultants specialising in wildlife and its management.

THE THREATS

The wildlife of Scotland is still under severe threat today. The entire country bears the scars of the original forest clearance; of the incessant grazing of sheep and deer; of the intensification of chemical agriculture in the lowlands and of the expansion of roads, industry and housing in the Central Belt; and the damage continues. Vast areas of the uplands have been planted with 'monocultures' of conifers, which drastically transform the landscape. Where this has happened the rarer birds of the open hill, such as the golden plover, are lost and replaced by some of the common woodland birds and mammals. Inevitably these plantations can only be poor imitations of the rich complex of plant and animal communities to be found in a native woodland. In addition the dense conifers mop up some of the acid rain produced by industry and transport and carried hundreds of kilom tres from its source. In the south and west of Scotland, where the ground is already acid, this additional input has sterilised lochs and rivers of their fish and birds. Even otherwise 'safe' areas of rural southern Scotland are now being exploited on an enormous scale by opencast coal mining and, on a smaller but growing scale, the mining of barytes and gold in some of the quieter parts of Perthshire.

The sea has fared no better than the land. Scotland's coasts have vast expanses of sheltered sea lochs, muddy estuaries, rocky shores, sandy beaches, underwater cliffs and reefs, kelp forests, tidal races and sandy plains. Most of this underwater world is still unexplored, but we know that it contains all manner of unfamiliar communities of brittle stars, of lime-encrusted algae, of forests of kelp, of sponges and sea squirts as well as the largest colonies of breeding grey seal in the world.

In these same waters the productive sea-bed sediments are regularly churned up by trawl nets disrupting or destroying the complex marine communities living there. Our very special west-coast sea lochs have been taken over by salmon fish farms which release huge quantities of nutrients and toxic pesticides into these sheltered waters whose ecology we barely understand. Even these very new industries may well be superseded in the next few years by cod farming or seaweed harvesting, each with its own ecological impacts. The open sea is already threatened by an increasing number of sophisticated pollutants and, in places, enrichment. However, the impact on the ecosystem of the intensity of fishing is only recently being appreciated. The wholesale removal of entire generations of mature fish of certain species has contributed to major changes in the balance of the food chain.

The very size of Scotland means that the impact of each threat differs dramatically from place to place. The most severely hit parts are inevitably the urban areas of the lowlands. Here the pressure from housing and development is still intense in a landscape where the effects of previous industrial exploitation are still all too obvious. The few remaining wildlife areas are often already too small to be viable in the long term yet are under increasing pressure. Housing, with its resultant roads, slices up the remaining countryside and fragments what is left into smaller and smaller pieces. Recent work on the badger in the Central Belt demonstrates the frequency with which this protected animal is moved out of its sett and/or separated from its feeding grounds. There is, of course, bound to be pressure to drain the remaining wet ground, to build as close to the river valleys as possible and to use the cheap areas of 'waste ground' as prime targets for opencast coal mines and rubbish dumps. Without positive action both to save and to expand these remaining wildlife sites the quality and quantity of wildlife-rich green spaces will continue to decline.

Of course, there are some gains as old railway lines, bings (coal tips), abandoned factory sites and neglected farmland are recolonised by the natural regeneration of trees and scrub, although they will never develop the wealth of species which could be found in a natural habitat.

CONSERVATION AS A FORCE

In the face of large-scale land-use changes, it is essential that the voice of conservation is properly heard and understood. Scottish Natural Heritage (SNH), as a Non-Departmental Public Body (NDPB), is the Government's advisory body on the natural heritage. It identifies SSSIs and administers their statutory controls; it has similar responsibilities in advising the Secretary of State for Scotland on European and other international designations and obligations; and it provides wide-ranging guidance on wildlife conservation and its interpretation, backed up by a grant-giving role. SNH also offers advice and opinion on a range of land-use changes including forestry, fish farming, agriculture and planning, but it is often limited in how far it can press its views.

Luckily in Scotland there is a close working relationship between SNH and the voluntary wildlife conservation organisations. The Scottish Wildlife Trust (SWT), the Royal Society for the Protection of Birds (RSPB) and the World Wide Fund for Nature (WWF) are the main bodies concerned with the wider issues involving wildlife.

Of these three main bodies only the SWT is entirely Scottish. Founded in 1964 it is a single Trust covering all aspects of the conservation of all plants, animals and habitats throughout Scotland via a network of branches and groups. The principle of the SWT is to involve local members in practical nature conservation and to survey and monitor the wildlife in their area (Box 4). Today the SWT has over 15,000 members, 116 nature reserves and 1,000 children in its junior WATCH club (Box 5).

There are, of course, many other

4. WORKING FOR WILDLIFE

Even the most unpromising urban sites can become important wildlife areas. Bawsinch lies along the shore of Duddingston Loch in the heart of Edinburgh; it was a vehicle scrap yard when it was bought by the SWT but it has been transformed into of superb woodland, scrub, grassland and wetland habitats. Over the course of twenty-six years volunteers have planted trees, dug ponds, maintained grasslands and monitored the wildlife to produce one of the finest city wildlife sites in Scotland.

Bawsinch wildlife reserve in the heart of Edinburgh was once a vehicle scrapyard.

organisations in Scotland which are more specialised but have a real involvement with wildlife and its conservation. These include natural history societies, badger, squirrel, otter or butterfly groups, botanical societies and many others which specialise in such things as marine issues, woodlands or environmental education. Mountaineers, ramblers and the various countryside groups also form an important sector which includes the conservation of wildlife as part of a broader remit. Almost all of these societies and groups successfully co-operate to discuss environmental issues of the day through membership of Scottish Wildlife and Countryside Link (SWCL).

5. THE WATCH CLUB

Getting children directly involved in the environmental issues at a very young age is seen by an increasing number of parents and schools as an essential part of a balanced education. The WATCH club, the junior SWT, has a long history of pioneering work in mobilising young people in monitoring and understanding their local environment and pooling their findings at a national or even international scale. Such investigations include the ambitious Ozone Project to measure air pollution and River Watch which detected and monitored water pollution.

The 'common' frog is increasingly uncommon in many parts of Britain due to water pollution and draining of ponds and wetlands.

6. THE COMMON FROG

Frogs are still common and widespread in Scotland despite the dramatic reduction in their numbers in parts of England. However their habitat has been decreasing, especially in Lowland Scotland, as ponds are drained, filled or polluted by chemical run-off from farmland. The presence of the humble frog and its tadpoles is therefore a valuable indicator of the health of our remaining freshwater habitats.

A WINDOW ON THE FUTURE

Other chapters in this book illustrate what Scotland's environment was like in the past, but it is equally important to have a vision for the future and to work towards achieving it. The basis of any such vision must embody the principles of sustainability and integrated land-use. This simply means that natural resources must be used in such a way as not to deplete the total available and that the best way of doing this is for the many different interested bodies to work in close co-operation.

An integrated approach involving these groups might, for example, mean a decision not to plan a conifer plantation on an area of grassland rich in wild flowers alongside a river. However, as the site will still need to be grazed it will act as a buffer to decrease the effect of the trees on water quality. This in turn will ensure

7. WATER POLLUTION

Industrial complexes such as Grangemouth on the Forth estuary have serious problems in disposing of their waste products. However, many companies now realise that they must set more stringent standards for environmental pollution and are using their own technical expertise to find new ways of reducing the amount of pollution they produce. The European importance of Scotland's estuaries has resulted in conflicts by all of the interested organisations through such bodies as the Forth Estuary Forum.

that there are plenty of fish for anglers to catch.

On a local scale the concept of 'favourable conservation status' is used throughout Europe as part of the innovative Habitats Directive (see Chapter 16). This has as its main objectives the conservation of the special key wildlife areas through Special Areas for Conservation (SACs) and Special Protection Areas (SPAs), and the long-term viability of the habitat or species concerned. In practice this means that anything which adversely affects the site must be tackled directly even though its source may be remote. Making the health of wildlife the measure of success means that there is a greater emphasis on conservation rather than simple protection.

For wildlife to flourish in the countryside outwith designated areas we need a sensitive and ecologically based approach to all developments (Box 6). Crucial to this is the concept of Environmental Impact Assessment where the many possible effects of any proposal on the environment are examined scientifically and thoroughly. This professional and unbiased assessment, although rarely carried out to the desired standard, informs a considered judgement on whether the development should go ahead. It also indicates what, if anything, can be done to lessen the adverse effects. The best examples of such an approach to planning include notable cases of 'planning gain' where extensive areas of native woodland have had to be planted to offset the loss of ground to a factory.

On a larger scale, strategic planning can contribute significantly to wildlife conservation through a number of positive approaches. These can include river catchment planning of the water resource, establishing 'corridors' along the course of rivers and keeping them free of development, reinforcing small areas of habitat by extending the sites and joining them together through habitat creation and by encouraging public recognition of the economic value of natural landscapes and their wildlife.

THE NATURAL SYSTEM

Wildlife is part of the entire ecosystem which supports us all, and damage to any part of it can affect our environment as much as the natural habitats. It is now recognised that industry, through pollution of land, water and air, has had and continues to have a major impact at both a local and global scale (Box 7). The role of pesticides in the food chain was publicly exposed when it was shown that DDT, a product of the chemical industry which was used to control insects on crops, accumulated in lethal concentrations in sparrowhawks and peregrines. The long-distance effects of acid rain, generated from the burning of fossil fuels, show that Scandinavian trees have been killed by factory chimney discharges in Germany. More recently the damage caused by chloro-flouro-carbons (CFCs) to the ozone layer of the upper atmosphere and the build-up of the 'greenhouse gases' have painted a gloomy picture of the future, darkened by fears of global warming. But, even now, we are only just beginning to appreciate the potential impact of the distribution of complex chemicals to every corner of the earth.

Although it has been left perilously late, there have been several international and national initiatives to reduce discharges into the air, into rivers and into the sea. Strict standards set by European Union legislation, coupled with the reorganisation of the regulating bodies in the UK, have made significant improvements to the monitoring and regulation of discharges to the environment. The concept of integrated pollution control is a particularly important idea which will ensure that waste can be tracked accurately from source to final destination. The creation of the Scottish Environmental Protection Agency (SEPA) in 1996 brought together a number of existing agencies to ensure that the responsibility for controlling pollution to land, fresh water, sea and air was dealt with by a single body. The concept of 'the polluter pays' is also being brought into the available range of practical tools. This penalty increases the pressure to reduce the pollution at source – the only effective way of making progress. The Landfill Tax, set up in 1996, levies a charge on each tonne of waste dumped and is expected to exert real economic pressure

8. ST ABBS HEAD

This superb site on the Berwickshire coast illustrates a unique partnership between the Scottish Wildlife Trust, who first set up the reserve, and the present owners, The National Trust for Scotland. St Abbs is famous for the vast numbers of seabirds which nest on the cliffs but it also lies within the St Abbs and Eyemouth Voluntary Marine Reserve. The rich and varied sea life found in the clean waters is protected by the collaboration of fishermen, conservationists and divers, all working together.

St Abbs Head provides nest sites for many thousands of kittiwakes, guillemots and razorbills.

to make manufacturing and other processes more environmentally friendly.

The philosophy of collective responsibility for the environment and ultimately for its wildlife is gradually seeping into statutory bodies, their various departments and projects with some signs of a spin-off effect on businesses. Government's Round Table on Sustainable Development has been encouraging this thinking although the stimulus has been Agenda 21 – the world agenda for the twenty-first century – which was a main plank of the 1992 Rio Convention. This approach has injected awareness of the issues into the workplace and has resulted in all kinds of 'green' Charters and environmental policies being developed (Box 8).

In the future, nature conservation itself

Great Sundew, a carnivorous plant of peatlands.

9. A PLACE FOR WILDLIFE

Today lowland peat bogs are particularly vulnerable not only to commercial extraction of peat but also from opencast coal mining, drainage, afforestation, fire, overgrazing and even rubbish dumping. Raised bog is a European Priority Habitat because of the destruction of peatlands throughout the world. Despite the fact there is not one undamaged example left the best examples are found in Scotland and we have an extra responsibility to ensure their restoration and long-term conservation.

should also be a natural part of every proposed development which would be supported by local and national government, national agencies and private companies alike. Based on the local Biodiversity Action Plan, which itself is an integrated part of the UK-wide BAP, it will be accepted that wildlife is a core element of the quality of life. In Scotland not only will the current remaining resource of natural and semi-natural habitats be conserved but they will be reinforced by the creation of extensive native woodlands and other types of sophisticated habitat creation and management techniques, maintenance of wildlife corridors, anti-habitat fragmentation measures, and habitat 'networks' and linkages (Box 9).

This is not a Utopian ideal. All it requires is the will to achieve the goal. If people believe passionately enough in the need to conserve Scotland's natural heritage for future generations and become actively involved towards that end, it is a crusade which cannot fail.

WHAT YOU CAN DO

Awareness of the urgency to conserve the environment both locally and globally has been the result of the persistent campaigning of a relatively small number of individuals. Of course, the large conservation and environmental bodies do have a huge influence today but the role of the individual is still a vital part of the process. The fate of the world is in our own hands, and taking personal action is an essential and effective way of influencing what ultimately happens. Anyone can help wildlife by taking on one or more of the challenges listed below.

● Get to know your own local area well. Looking after the wildlife around you is the basic step because your local knowledge may well be the vital element required to initiate action. Look at your local map, go for walks, talk to your neighbours and discover what is special about your area. Whether you live in the Highlands or in the inner city your environment may well be valuable not only for humans but for wildlife as well.

● Fight for your own green spaces. If there is a threat to any of the wildlife areas known to you, you can do something about it. If it is a planning matter which requires the local council to initiate public consultation, make your feelings known and encourage your friends to do the same. Even if the site is on agricultural ground it can sometimes be resolved by talking about it to those concerned. Damage is often done to wildlife sites by people who are quite unaware of the results that their actions might have and who would be quite prepared to accept a compromise if one were offered.

● Learn more about the natural world. For example, understanding the way in which the habitats 'work' is a real help in influencing what is happening over your local conservation issue. There are many very readable books available to explain the ecology and natural history of our native wildlife. A better knowledge of the subject will give you confidence and add authority to your views and suggestions.

● Make your views known. Public pressure is a most effective way of getting both local and national government to take notice: every voice counts. There are more and more opportunities to take part in the decision-making process itself through community involvement as part of Local Agenda 21. However, if this achieves nothing then letters to the newspapers and even to the Secretary of State can still be effective.

● Understand environmental issues. Most of the major newspapers and the 'green' magazines devote much space to local and national environmental issues. Many of the conservation bodies can also help by supplying detailed information, expert opinion and even direct help with local disputes and planning issues.

● Join a local wildlife conservation group. Actions speak louder than words: involvement with your local conservation group will make it more effective and will give you a focus for your own energies. You might choose to take on physical work like planting trees or clearing out an overgrown pond. It can be equally valuable to help with counting butterflies, watching bats emerge from a roost or even rattling a collecting box. All of these activities add up to making the British conservation movement the envy of the world.

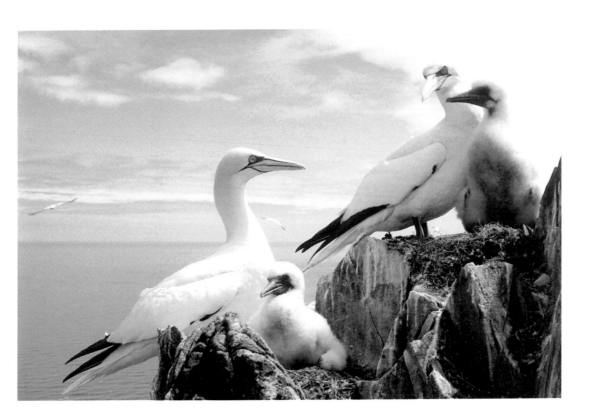

Gannets on the Bass Rock.
Scotland has an international
responsibility for the
conservation of many species
of sea-birds.

SIR FRANK FRASER DARLING (1903–79)
Profile of a Pioneer, by Dr J. Morton Boyd.

Any account of nature conservation in Scotland must include the story of one of the pioneers of the ecological movement in Scotland. Frank Fraser Darling was an Englishman, but he always felt himself to be half-Scottish. During his student days he had travelled in Scotland and fallen under the spell of the country and its people and he conceived a desire to make his professional mark as a scientist in Scotland.

So he came to Edinburgh to see F. A. E. Crewe, the Professor of Genetics there, whose work he greatly admired, and was offered a PhD studentship to work on the fleece characteristics of Blackface sheep. It was a hard decision to make for he already had a wife and child to support; but Fraser Darling seized the opportunity eagerly.

After graduating PhD he became Chief Officer of the Imperial Bureau of Animal Genetics at Edinburgh but he soon became disillusioned with administrative work. He had just spent three years with the sheep in the uplands and islands and had imbibed the rough beauty and freedom of these solitudes; but there were no opportunities now for ventilating the enormous enthusiasm for active research which had brought him to Scotland.

So he abandoned the comfortable salaried life in Edinburgh and took to the mountains and islands, complete with family. He wrote industriously for a living: *A Herd of Red Deer* (1937), which brought him a DSc from Edinburgh University, was both scientific and romantic in style. By choice he occupied the area between ecology and animal behaviour; his quest was for the underlying truth in natural processes. His main bid for a breakthrough in 'hard' science was in the studies of bird flocks. He

developed a hypothesis of a mechanism which drives gregarious behaviour but he was not quite able to demonstrate it from the meagre data he assembled from gull colonies in the Summer Isles. None the less, students of animal behaviour and physiology still feel that such a mechanism may exist; and in biology textbooks it is called the 'Fraser Darling Effect'.

It was through his books, *Island Years* (1940) and *Island Farm* (1943), taken almost verbatim from his journals of life in the islands, that he first made his name with the general public. They were charming idylls of family adventure, laced with science and philosophy, in the glorious settings of Coigach, Treshnish and North Rona. But his aspirations in 'hard' science were ended by the outbreak of the Second World War, when he returned to his 'island farm' on Tanera in the Summer Isles.

The war years saw a change of direction which brought him to the path of conservation, which he followed for the rest of his life, in Scotland, the USA and Africa. He became the great exponent of 'nature in the round'. His agricultural training and his natural instincts made him unusually sensitive to the relationships between man and nature, and his interests shifted from Wildlife *per se* to the impact of human beings on natural resources. With his island croft as his working frame he wrote a series of articles for the local press publicising his theories on self-sufficiency; later these articles were published as *Crofting Agriculture* (1945), which remains a little classic.

National recognition came in 1943–4 with his appointment to a Scottish National Parks Committee and its subordinate Wildlife Conservation Committee. The outcome was the setting up of National Parks in England and Wales, but not in Scotland (to his intense disappointment), and the establishment of a Nature Conservancy for the UK, *inter alia* to set up and manage National Nature Reserves.

He also became Director of the West Highland Survey to study the causes of population and economic decline there. Although the survey was completed by 1950 the report was not published until 1955, mainly because of a deep difference of

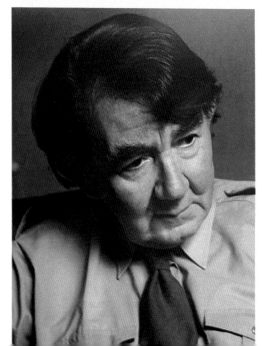

Sir Frank Fraser Darling, ecologist and conservationist (1903–79).

Loch Beinn a Mheadoin in Glen Affric.

opinion with officials in the Scottish Office who could not come to terms with his perception of Man's responsibility in the sorry tale of land-use in the Highlands. The sub-title of the report – West Highland Survey: An Essay in Human Ecology – betrayed the thrust of his thinking.

In the 1950s Fraser Darling was living in the south of England but kept in touch with Scotland as Director of the Nature Conservancy's Red Deer Survey, which led to the Red Deer (Scotland) Act 1959 and the setting up of the Red Deer Commission. But he had fallen from favour in Britain and was now active in the newly-formed International Union for the Conservation of Nature and Natural Resources (IUCN, now the World Conservation Union), where he became a dominant figure at international conventions throughout the world.

His main endeavours were now devoted to surveys in the US National Parks, the Game Department of Northern Rhodesia (now Zambia), and the Masai-Mara game Reserve in Kenya. In these surveys he saw a restatement of the travesties of Man's misuse of the environment, and spoke out vigorously in exposing greed and self-interest. He could be tactless to a fault when it came to presenting the facts as he saw them. His uncompromising report on the US National Parks was well received, but those from Northern Rhodesia (Zambia) and Kenya were not, and ran a similar gauntlet as the West Highland Survey had done at the Scottish Office.

In the 1960s he spent much of his time in the USA as a vice-president of the Conservation Foundation in Washington DC – an ambassador extraordinary for nature conservation throughout the world. In the many situations he looked at, from tropical Africa to arctic Alaska, his instinctive perception of Man's interdependence with nature took him straight to the core of the problem. Red deer in Scotland, caribou in Alaska, elk in Washington and elephant in Tsavo all had a different ecology but a common place in the human mind; and having perceived the guiding principle he was able to communicate it to the common man.

It was that gift of communication which came to the fore when he was invited to give the Reith Lectures of 1969. To those who knew him in his early days, when he was afflicted by a shuddering stammer, his delivery of the lectures was well nigh unbelievable. It was symbolic of his entire life, which he described as 'the hole out of which I have climbed', that in the end he should emerge so triumphantly into the sunshine. The lectures were published as *Wilderness and Plenty* (1970), and in that same year he was knighted.

He retired to the Laigh of Moray where he looked back with melancholy on the battles he had fought (and mostly lost) in the face of the implacable self-interest of his fellow man. In a man-centred world he saw nature as the elemental stuff of which we are made – sacred beyond compare, yet debased by us on a colossal scale. What he had to say is even more relevant to the conservation of nature today.

Dr J. Morton Boyd is a former Director of the Nature Conservancy Council in Scotland (1971–85). He knew Fraser Darling well, and is the author of many books, including *Fraser Darling's Islands* (1987) and *The Hebrides* (1990).

The poet, Dugald Stewart's monument, Calton Hill, Edinburgh; with the Old Town and Pentland Hills beyond.

CHAPTER FIFTEEN

The Greening of the Cities
Graham White

*Graham White is the founding Director of The City of Edinburgh Environment Centre
and a writer and broadcaster on environmental issues.*

Unlike human beings, plants and animals can make no conscious distinction between town and country but simply colonise any habitat which sustains them. Certainly, the abundant wildlife of our towns affirms Spinoza's aphorism that 'nature abhors a vacuum', since every space from the attics of our houses to the sewers beneath our streets, is home to some plant or animal. Foxes pad the granite streets of Aberdeen at night, while kestrels scour the embankments of Edinburgh's ring road by day. Peregrine falcons stoop above the spires of Glasgow University and may one day nest there, as they do in Prague. Every human development, from motorway to tower block, creates potential niches for wildlife, and since the history of urbanization is only a few hundred years old, evolution has barely begun to exploit these opportunities.

Of course, many plants and animals require specific rural habitats like peat bogs, sand dunes or ancient pine-woods. But other more adaptable species thrive just as well on the mortar of a brick wall, the asphalt desert of a school playground, or the clinker screes of an old railway. Paradoxically, as farming's chemical arsenal of herbicides, pesticides and fungicides imposes an increasingly mono-cultural countryside, Scotland's towns, with their intricate mosaic of parks, private gardens, railways and canals, offer relative sanctuary for many wild flowers, insects, birds and animals. And as the Common Agricultural Policy induces an ever more uniform agricultural landscape, the ecology of urban areas appears comparatively diverse.

It is perhaps inevitable that we tend to value the rarer animals and plants of the countryside and are complacent of those 'common or garden' ones which we find in the town. But human value judgements about wildlife are often highly subjective and sometimes, with hindsight, fatally mistaken. John Muir was twelve years old in 1850 when he first saw passenger pigeons in Wisconsin, where vast flocks darkened the sky from horizon to horizon. The myriads of roosting birds were slaughtered for pig feed, ploughed-in as fertilizer, and valued, if at all, only for the pot.

Foxes have adapted well to life in towns and are now common in Scotland's cities.

197

The idea that those uncountable hosts could ever be brought to extinction seemed impossible. But on Christmas Eve 1914, the day of Muir's own death, the last survivor of those teeming millions died in the Bronx zoo and an entire species passed into oblivion. We seem compelled to apply the quantitative values of the marketplace even to wildlife; if a species is common it is of little worth, but once it becomes rare it has infinite value. For centuries the red kite and polecat were common urban species and were tolerated in Scottish towns, but eventually they were declared vermin and hunted to national extinction; ironically, now that they are rare, endangered and singularly 'rural' species, we commit funds unstintingly to try and reintroduce them. Wildlife simply does not conform to these human stereotypes of 'town' and 'country' and crosses such notional boundaries with ease, traversing the planet on journeys which dwarf our tourist excursions. The Red Admiral butterfly in your town garden may have flown a thousand miles from the maquis covered hills of the Mediterranean, and the swifts which scream around Edinburgh's spires travel from Morrocco's High Atlas to build their nests on the Georgian sea-cliffs of the capital's tenements.

The plants of our towns are just as nomadic and arrive from around the world: the exotic purple buddleia (a plant from northern China), the pink rosebay willow herb (an American invader) and the golden Oxford ragwort (from Sicily's Mount Etna) blanket the gap-sites of our city centres. Their seeds cross oceans on the jetstream or by container-ship, and are spread by car tyres and the soles of shoes.

But until the late 1980s most nature conservation bodies in the UK seemed to view the world solely through rural spectacles; nature conservation was almost synonymous with the preservation of wildlife habitats in the countryside. Conservationists were not overly concerned with towns or cities, because the plants and animals which lived there were just 'common or garden'; they did not focus on the human environment as such, and saw little evident connection between nature

Oxford Ragwort and Rosebay Willowherb sprout from granite setts at The Shore, Leith.

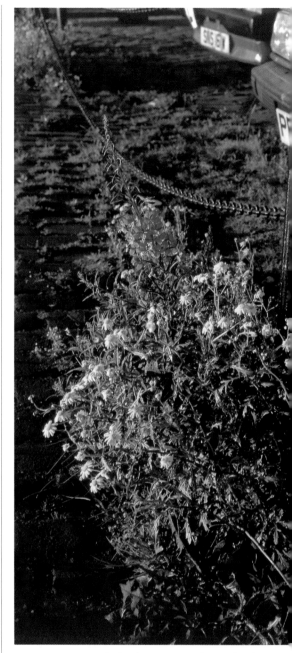

conservation and the human quality of life in towns. Indeed for most of us the words 'nature' and 'wildlife' still evoke that pristine landscape which persists in our imagination, somewhere out there, beyond the green belt and the barley fields, among the mountains, rivers and sea-lochs of Scotland. This prejudicial association of the words 'wildlife' and 'environment' with the countryside is deeply fixed in our minds, and has important implications for conservationists, planners and teachers.

Sadly, the policy of trying to conserve our natural heritage by simply putting a fence around rural wildlife oases and keeping people out has proved a national strategic failure, with 30 per cent of key wildlife habitats having been damaged or destroyed since 1949. In 1984 the Nature Conservancy Council published *Nature Conservation in Great Britain*, which catalogued the loss of ancient woodlands, heaths, herb-rich meadows, lakes, fens, bogs and grasslands, together with the extinctions, or near extinctions, of dozens of plant and animal species since 1945. There is now a consensus that any conservation strategy based solely on isolated Sites of Special Scientific Interest (SSSIs) will not of itself conserve species. If we are to conserve and enhance Scotland's biodiversity we need a mosaic of connected habitats, linking urban and rural sites via the nature corridors of woods, hedges, rivers, canals, disused railways and other wildlife migration routes. Consequently, towns and cities occupy a vital crossroads in the national jigsaw of wildlife habitats. Ironically, many of the urban creatures which we now dismiss as 'common or garden', were once admired as rare and exotic (Box 1). We seldom stop to consider that every town species must once have been exclusively a country dweller. Even the blackbird of our parks and gardens is a recent urban immigrant and only became common in gardens during the mid-nineteenth century. The city starling, often regarded as a mere pest, was once an admired rarity: in a letter to *The Times* dated 1894, a proud ornithologist claimed first sight of a pair nesting in London's Hyde Park; roosts of 50,000 or more birds soon became common in the capital as the birds forsook their traditional habitat of countryside meadows for the richer pickings of our parks and playing fields. Our rural prejudices are not just confined to birds. Some people dismiss the golden Oxford ragwort as just an exotic weed; like the Chinese buddleia, it is 'not native' and is an 'alien immigrant' to boot! In our botanical xenophobia, we often forget that every plant was once an alien immigrant, and that all

1. WHAT WAS ONCE COMMON IS NOW RARE

The red kite, or 'gledd' as it was known in Scotland, is a beautiful bird of prey that the Royal Society for the Protection of Birds (RSPB) and Scottish Natural Heritage (SNH) are reintroducing to Scotland (see Chapter 5). The kite was once a common scavenger in the streets of Edinburgh and Glasgow, as it was in London at the same period. Sadly, in Scotland, it was condemned to extermination in 1457 when King James II decreed that 'gledds' were among the birds of prey which should be destroyed. However, in London at the same time, people were prohibited from harming kites because of their value as street cleaners. The extinction of the red kite in Scotland is linked to farming improvements in the eighteenth century, when smallholders and gamekeepers killed any bird of prey which threatened their poultry or pheasants.

The polecat is also extinct in Scotland but it, too, was once familiar in the streets of Edinburgh and Glasgow. Until the 1860s it was the most common member of the weasel family in Scotland and was widely distributed in towns and villages, where it preyed on rats, mice and voles. Records from the Dumfries Fur Market in the *New Statistical Account of Scotland* state that in 1833 so many thousands of polecat skins were offered for sale each week that they were 'a drug on the market'. But the agricultural improvers and gamekeepers classed them as vermin and began a systematic extermination. By 1847, the *New Statistical Account* notes that their skins were available 'only in small numbers', and by 1858 they were 'very scarce'; the last one offered for sale was in 1866. In less than three decades the most common carnivore in Scotland had been exterminated by fur-trappers, farmers and gamekeepers.

The RSPB has successfully reintroduced the red kite to remote sites in Scotland, but poisonings and persecution continue.

arrived in Scotland within the last 10,000 years. The new urban colonists are of course recent arrivals; their impact is dramatic and often detrimental to previously established species, but they are undoubtedly here to stay. However, it all depends on what timescale one applies: the 'Scots' pine is almost a national symbol these days, but 10,000 years ago it was itself an alien invader, supplanting trees which failed to adapt to the developing climate and habitat of Scotland.

We sometimes envisage nature as a flowing river of dynamic, ever-changing species and relationships, or a shimmering web of inter-dependent life forms. John Muir used the metaphor of time and the river: 'Nature is for ever at work, creating and destroying, keeping everything whirling and flowing, in rythmical motion, chasing everything out of one beautiful form to another.' But our limited perception and lifespan means that we can only glimpse fleeting snapshots or abstractions from this epic flow; and we should never mistake scientific abstractions for reality.

To summarise: we conceive an artificial split between town and countryside; we tend to undervalue plants and animals that are common, and overvalue those which are rare; we distrust that which is 'alien' or new, and cherish that which is 'native' and old. We tend to see ourselves as being independent of 'nature' rather than as an integral part of the natural ecosystem, on which we are totally dependent for our survival. In short, we project all our human prejudice and parochialism on to the natural world. But even if we value the wildlife of the countryside above the natural heritage of the town, it is nevertheless clear that, for most of us, our first experiences of the natural world occur in the town where we live.

Many can still recall some childhood epiphany when the love of nature first blossomed: feeding crusts to mallard at the local pond; a jam-jar, glinting with silver sticklebacks; fingers trawling jellied frog spawn in the old canal; stravaigs along the old railway, hands stained with blackberries; a ladybird's scarlet carapace poised for flight on a fingertip. Such formative contacts with nature are of deep and lasting significance; they are not an optional extra, but an enduring human need.

As John Muir wrote:

'Everybody needs beauty as well as bread; places to play in and pray in, where Nature may heal and cheer and give strength to body and soul.'

THE VALUE OF GREEN OPEN SPACE IN TOWNS ('GREENSPACE')

Scotland is a very spacious country but more than 80 per cent of the people live within the small triangle of Edinburgh, Glasgow and Stirling. The vast majority of us are born, attend school and spend our working lives in towns. Thus, the area of green open space (greenspace) which survives within urban areas is a crucial factor influencing the quality of life which we enjoy, or suffer, in towns. Such greenspace comes in many forms: school grounds, playing fields, parks, nature areas, disused railways, riverbanks, canals and cemeteries. All are valuable for recreation, for aesthetic and spiritual inspiration and for the wildlife and biodiversity which they support within the city. Increasingly, the quality and area of greenspace in a city is regarded as a key influence for its economic prosperity and general quality of life. In April 1997 the Scottish Wildlife Trust published a report entitled 'The State of Scottish Greenspace', which analysed the urban nature conservation strategies of five Scottish cities: Aberdeen, Dundee, Edinburgh, Glasgow and Stirling (Box 2). But it could not review the twenty large towns in Scotland which lack nature conservation strategies of any kind.

The report concluded that urban greenspace is as vital for human happiness as it is for wildlife survival; but such areas are under increasing threat unless planning authorities can resist the clamour to develop them. The authors highlight the need for a co-ordinated strategy on the part of central government, local authorities and all public agencies, to sustain and enhance Scotland's urban greenspace. Specifically, they urge that all Local Agenda 21 initiatives should promote the protection and enhancement of urban greenspace as a central policy.

Finally, they ask local authorities to emulate Dundee by incorporating Urban Nature Conservation strategies into the Local Plan.

Much of our greenspace consists of nineteenth-century parks and gardens, but although valuable for recreation, these offer little sustenance for wildlife. Wide expanses of mown grass provide little food for birds or insects; such municipal prairies are often sprayed with herbicides to suppress 'weeds' (or wild flowers), and may be drenched with insecticides, poisoning bees and butterflies as well as the intended aphids. In addition exotic shrubs, such as rhododendron offer little food for native wildlife. By contrast, the unplanned and accidental wildlife parks which have evolved along disused railways and canals, on city wasteland and in neglected cemeteries, offer rich living space for plants, insects and birds. In *The Wild Side of Town* (1986), Chris Baines, highlighted this 'unofficial countryside' of the towns, and argued that urban life would be richer if we actively promoted such wild areas.

NATURE CORRIDORS: CANALS AND RAILWAYS

Many of Scotland's canals and railways no longer carry freight or passengers but they have acquired new value as urban greenspace (see Chapter 11). They have become urban wildlife corridors: the Union Canal flows into the very heart of Edinburgh, while the Forth and Clyde Canal runs through Glasgow's Maryhill. Along with the Caledonian Canal these comprise part of the 150-mile length of Scotland's industrial waterways which constitute our largest unofficial nature reserve. Rangers have documented 400 species of land plants, 100 of water plants, 500 types of insect, 15 different fish, 130 resident or migratory bird species, 15 dragonflies or damselflies and 30 visiting or resident butterflies. Millennium Commission funding will allow the canals to be reconnected and opened to navigation once again, but their great value as urban nature reserves and wildlife corridors will undoubtedly persist.

The Beeching cuts of the 1960s left many miles of disused railways, radiating from town centres out through the green belt into the countryside. The rails were torn up and the stone ballast was left for nature to reclaim; the rail beds now sport dense thickets of birch, willow and elder, which provide homes for

2. GREENSPACE IN SCOTLAND'S FIVE CITIES

	Aberdeen	Dundee	Edinburgh	Glasgow	Stirling
Urban Area	5,300	5,957	12,000	20,267	1,319
Population	211,000	172,000	418,000	674,820	36,000
Greenspace	1,380	1,314	4,545	4,574	172
% City Area	26	22	38	23	13
m² per person	65	76	109	68	48
Nature Areas	277.25	433.38	1234.4	1,612	122.58
% of city area	5.23	7.28	10.29	7.95	9.29
m² per person	13.14	25.2	29.53	23.89	34.05

Source: *The State of Scottish Greenspace*, Scottish Wildlife Trust 1997.
Note: A hectare of land is a square 100 metres by 100 metres.

hundreds of insect and bird species. By the early 1980s, many councils had begun to resurrect these dead railways as cycle-paths, walkways and green open space, at very little cost. Such nature corridors link the town with the countryside, enabling the migration of birds, insects and plants across the landscape, and enriching the biodiversity of our towns.

Edinburgh's original Botanic Garden, the Physick Garden at Trinity Hospital, in Edinburgh's Old Town (shown here at the bottom left of this illustration).

201

URBAN DEVELOPMENT AND ENVIRONMENTAL HISTORY: EDINBURGH

Early Scottish towns were not planned in the modern sense; they grew organically as streets and houses spread across the natural landscape, often clustering around a defended height. Buildings have often blurred the original topography beyond all recognition, but remnants of the primeval landscape still persist as wildlife habitats within our towns and cities. Rivers may have held their course for a thousand years, and oases of crag, wood and moor still survive as wildlife bastions against the rising tide of concrete and cars.

We cannot consider all of Scotland's cities, but Edinburgh presents us with a temporal microcosm of Scotland's urban development, since the environmental history of the capital illuminates many of our national attitudes to the town, the country, urban parks and wildlife.

The citizens of Edinburgh in the eighteenth century still lived very close to nature; engravings of the time depict the houses of the Canongate, each with its vegetable garden or orchard, sloping from the whaleback of rock to the fields and forests below. The defensive ridge of the Royal Mile overlooked extensive wetlands, with today's Princes Street Gardens flooded by the Nor' Loch and the Borough Loch inundating the area of today's Meadows. These lochs attracted some fairly exotic wildlife:

'. . .in the year of our Lord 1416…a pair of Storks came to Scotland, and nested on the top of St Giles [Cathedral] of Edinburgh and dwelt there throughout a season of the year; but to what place they flew away thereafter no one knows'.

(*Scotichronicon*)

The drainage of the bogs and lochs of Edinburgh's environs reflected similar improvement schemes nationally; as wetlands were drained to make way for agriculture and roads, the storks, ducks and herons migrated to wetter wilds, and as Edinburgh's ancient forest of Drumsheugh was axed, the wild boar, red deer, wild cats and wolves faded into legend.

The human ecology of Edinburgh evolved, along with the natural ecology. The Old Town was not planned as such but grew organically, like a vast honeycomb of stone, as more and more tenements were added to house the growing population. Conditions within the walled city became increasingly cramped and unsanitary throughout the seventeenth and early eighteenth centuries, spawning epidemics of cholera, typhoid and even bubonic plague. Lacking a piped water supply or sewerage system, the gutters of the Royal Mile literally ran with the filth and ordure of the overcrowded town.

Thankfully, the end of wars with England after 1745 meant that the town could at last expand beyond its defences, and Lord Provost George Drummond and the City Fathers rose to the challenge. In 1752 their *Proposals for Carrying on Certain Public Works in the City of Edinburgh* were published; they would relieve the overcrowding by building a great bridge across the Nor' Loch, giving access to the broad ridge of land to the north, which would be developed as a spacious 'New Town'.

A competition for the layout of the development was announced; James Craig's design was chosen and he was granted the Freedom of the City and a gold medal as his reward (Box 3). As the Georgian buildings rose there was a gradual exodus from the medieval city. The nobility and professional classes forsook the foetid closes and tubercular wynds of the Royal Mile for the airy gardens and spacious promenades of Queen Street and Charlotte Square, with their piped water and engineered sewers. A dramatic contrast ensued as the Old Town fell deeper into squalor while the New Town flourished, giving birth to the Scottish Enlightenment. Indeed, the epidemics of cholera, typhoid and plague which carried off thousands from the Canongate barely touched the citizens of Princes Street. The environment of the Royal Mile continued to decline until recent decades, when the growth of modern town planning and tourism heralded a civic renaissance (Box 4).

EDINBURGH: A CAPITAL ENVIRONMENT

Edinburgh today is often granted the accolade of having the highest environmental quality of life of any city in the United Kingdom. The legendary beauty of the capital with its classical architecture and views of the Forth, and the volcanic topography exhibited in the crags of Arthur's Seat (Box 5), the castle-rock and Calton Hill, all helped secure the Old Town's designation as a World Heritage Site; but the abundance of urban greenspace and wildlife sites was undoubtedly an influential factor. About 418,000 people inhabit the capital's 12,000 hectares; over a third of this area (4,500 hectares) is designated as 'greenspace' and of this 1,230 hectares enjoy the even higher classification of 'Nature Area'. Each Edinburgh citizen thus enjoys 109 square metres of personal greenspace, within which he or she has 30 square metres of Nature Area (see Box 2).

Edinburgh is today promoted as Britain's greenest 'festival city', which inevitably attracts more and more people. This has resulted in strong pressure for house building (9,000 new homes by 2020), a massive growth in traffic, and a virtual tourist invasion; all of which degrades the very environment which people flock to enjoy. Councillors struggling to balance the issues of economic development, job creation and house building, face the dilemma of how to do this sustainably, without eroding the environmental assets of the city. Since this book was first published in 1991, the capital has experienced waves of development on an unprecedented scale: the first was the building of

James Craig's winning plan for the New Town of Edinburgh.

3. EDINBURGH'S NEW TOWN

James Craig's plan for the spacious New Town included gardens in St Andrew Square and Charlotte Square as well as proposals for two formal parklands for the areas now occupied by Princes Street Gardens and Queen Street Gardens. The later additions to the New Town emulated these enclosures of private garden spaces, following the *rus in urbe* principle at the heart of Craig's plan; today there are no fewer than sixty private or council-owned gardens in the New Town Conservation Area. The legacy of eighteenth-century greenspace within the city has bolstered Edinburgh's reputation as having the 'highest quality of environment' in Britain.

At the time of the building of the New Town the land to the north of Queen Street was open fields,

and the boundary between the town and the country was gradual and diffuse. Lord Cockburn wrote in his *Memorials*:

> How can I forget the glory of that scene! . . .
> on the still nights in which I have stood in
> Queen Street and listened to the ceaseless rural
> corn-craiks, nestling happily in the dewy grass.

This reveals a very rural Edinburgh even after the building of the New Town and it is fascinating that the corncrake was a common bird of the meadows which at that time extended from Queen Street to the hamlet of Stockbridge. The corncrake is now an endangered species, even in its remaining stronghold of the Western Isles and it is hard to believe that it once nested right in the heart of Edinburgh.

Selective herbicides have erased poppies from the barley fields but they still thrive on the verge of the A1 near Tranent.

construction of the giant retail park at the Gyle and the adjacent business complex at Edinburgh Park, both on the western periphery of the city. These, the largest developments in the capital's history, have generated new waves of car-borne shoppers and commuters. They have also affected the neighbouring community of Corstorphine, where high street shops lost more than £20 million retail business in the first year.

A further giant retail park is currently expanding on the eastern edge of the city at Kinnaird Park on the A1 corridor, and a third retail park has been allowed just off the central bypass at Straiton. The tides of traffic which wash in and out of such peripheral shopping centres and the promotion of 'mall-culture' which results, makes any civic discussion of 'sustainability' simply absurd. If development is permitted on this scale and at this speed there is little hope for the survival of Edinburgh's green belt, its historic environmental quality or much of its existing greenspace.

the city bypass, which slashed through the protected green belt and was predictably soon flooded with traffic; the second was

4. SIR PATRICK GEDDES (1854–1932)

The name of Patrick Geddes shines like a beacon in the environmental history of Edinburgh as the champion for the improvement of social conditions in the Old Town. The pioneer of modern town planning, Geddes was a 'synthesist' who pioneered many ideas which today we would recognise as ecology, sociology and environmental education. He believed that people needed green open spaces, fresh air and daily contact with nature, just as much as warm houses, wholesome food, proper sanitation and meaningful work. Born in Ballater, the youngest of five children, he studied botany at Edinburgh University. However he found the system restrictive and moved to London to study under the radical biologist T.H. Huxley, 'Darwin's bulldog'.

After later studies at the Sorbonne and in Mexico, he worked for the next ten years as a demonstrator in the botany department of Edinburgh University. Remarkably, he moved his family back into the slums of the Old Town, where they set up home in the Grassmarket and later in James Court. Appalled at the environmental conditions of the Old Town, Geddes set about rehabilitating tenements, and annexed greenspaces for flower and vegetable gardens. He developed the Outlook Tower on the Royal Mile, an early attempt to merge ideas from sociology, town planning and ecology into what we today would call 'environmental education'. Geddes was one of the strongest advocates of 'greening the city' and carried out the first open-space survey of the Old Town, documenting seventy-six open-spaces on the Royal Mile. He believed that education should be centred on direct experience and study of nature, and organised local school children to create gardens on twelve of the sites. One open space survived below Johnston Terrace and in 1982 the Scottish Wildlife Trust restored this as an urban wildlife garden.

Geddes achieved fame as Professor of Civics and Sociology at the University of Bombay in 1919, but Scotland has never honoured him as the pioneer of environmental education and town planning, as the rest of the world has. A Patrick Geddes Centre has been established in Edinburgh's Outlook Tower, linked to an educational trail which runs the length of the Royal Mile, interpreting sites connected with him. It is interesting to reflect on what Geddes would think of our car-choked streets, filled with trucks, noise and noxious fumes; he might feel that his planning legacy had been wasted.

Some local authorities have taken a stand on 'sustainable development', which is arguably an oxymoron. Oxfordshire County Council was the first authority in the UK to identify green belt and greenspace as essential for the economic, social and environmental sustainability of the city:

The special character of Oxford does not just involve the university heritage areas, the 'dreaming spires' etc. but a much broader vista including the countryside around the city. Character also includes a concept of the overall scale of economic activity, since any considerable growth of the city will generate more activity, more traffic and more pressures for development, which are likely to threaten the nature, character and setting of the city.

(*1983 Structure Plan*)

5. HOLYROOD PARK: A MICROCOSM OF SCOTLAND'S ENVIRONMENTAL HISTORY

Arthur's Seat and Holyrood Park represent the survival of a unique wildlife habitat within the heart of a capital, and the history of the area offers useful environmental lessons. King David I (1124–53) kept the area as a royal hunting reserve, since at that time Edinburgh was surrounded by thick woods of oak, birch and alder. As late as the twelfth century, these forests harboured red deer, wild boar and wolves. During the Middle Ages the town of Edinburgh expanded and many oaks were felled to provide the beams for the wooden houses of the Canongate.

In 1541 King James V enclosed the area of Arthur's Seat and Holyrood Palace within a stone wall, creating the first Royal Park. We know that sheep were introduced shortly afterwards, because the court annals of 1556 record the conviction of one Thomas Bullerwell, who was banished for 'the steling of certane scheip fra the Quenis grace furthe of hir Park of Edinburgh'. As elsewhere in Scotland the grazing of sheep caused rapid environmental degradation.

From the moment they were introduced into the park they would have destroyed any seedling trees, and the landscape would soon become treeless. In 1966 more than 2,000 sheep still grazed in the park which they had kept treeless for over three hundred years: to echo the words of John Muir when speaking of Yosemite valley, the 'hoofed locusts' had swept everything away.

In 1977 Napier College carried out an ecological study which showed that the diversity and numbers of flowering plants, butterflies and mammals had declined markedly over the previous century; there had also been erosion of paths due to pressure from thousands of tourist feet. The Napier study recommended that the sheep be removed and that the original habitat should be restored by planting birch, oak, alder, ash and other trees. The sheep were excluded and grasses and flowering plants left to regenerate naturally; a visitor management scheme was also adopted, to channel people away from more sensitive sites and erosion areas.

Arthur's Seat remains a unique urban site and is designated as a Site of Special Scientific Interest (SSSI) because of its geological and botanical interest. It is home to a rare colony of urban fulmars, which have flown three miles inland to nest on the lava cliffs of Salisbury Crags.

The effects of the new management of the park are already apparent and visitors can look forward to a richer, more attractive landscape in coming years as the trees and shrubs mature and the birds, insects and animals return. The environmental history of Holyrood Park serves as a model of Scotland's past, and the regeneration of the park's landscape and ecology offers a positive example for the restoration of the environmental quality of Scotland's towns and countryside.

The Arthur's Seat volcano is a unique survival of an ancient landscape within a modern city.

Lord Cockburn
(1779-1854)

6. LORD COCKBURN (1779–1854)

For the first twenty two years of his life, Henry Cockburn lived on the south side of the Meadows, in open country which stretched away to the Pentland Hills. After a successful legal career he was made Lord Advocate in 1834 but in public and in private he devoted his life to preserving the amenity and beauty of Edinburgh. He fought for the highest standards in architecture, civic amenity, open space, natural heritage and the conservation of the unique topography and beauty of the city. In 1849 he wrote a letter to the Lord Provost entitled: '*The Best ways of Spoiling the Beauty of Edinburgh*'.

In this letter he railed against eight current development threats including: speculative building on the north castle slopes, the railway company's annexation of Princes Street Gardens for stations and goods yards, the loss of the city's trees, and the proposed building of houses along the south side of Princes Street. Cockburn believed passionately that Edinburgh's primary asset was its environmental quality and that this could only be defended by an enlightened and involved citizenry. His letter pre-dates Local Agenda 21 by almost 150 years but his concerns for landscape, wildlife, town planning, community participation and local democracy lie at the very heart of the Rio Summit.

In 1849 he wrote prophetically:

'*How will Edinburgh look in 1949 or 2049? Periods far off to us; they will arrive; . . . How will it look one hundred years hence? I hope well. But I see hurtful temptations at many points. Our danger has always arisen, and will ever arise, from three plain and intelligible causes:*
1. From unfortunate incompatibilities between private and public interests.
2. From that bad taste (that is ignorance) in proprietors, which leads them wrong even when they are disposed to go right.
3. From the inconsiderate use made of their power by public bodies and chiefly by public authorities. They are the administrators of the largest portion of the most important ground; what they do is generally done on a large scale; and their better judgement is apt to be tormented by absurd schemes and claims. The only remedy, besides public control, for this, is that they should work the principle, that the beauty of the town is paramount to every other consideration, into the very fabric of their official hearts. If they cannot direct themselves by this star, forego inferior objects and become impenetrable to the demonstrations and seductions of selfish projectors [lobbyists], they are unfit for their places. I am not aware that anything can be done to counteract these tendencies, except to instruct the taste, and to direct the attention of the people.

Pride in the beauty of the place should be the Genius Loci. *But in Edinburgh the power and the right are chiefly in the hands of the Town Council, or the public bodies where the town councillors prevail. Let us hope that the true friends of the city will always find a cordial ally in that body. This is a matter not concerned with party, or polemics, or anything that ought to irritate. It has the strongest claim on our municipal guardians. It brings its own, immediate and visible reward.*'

Edinburgh's Cockburn Association, founded in 1875, continues the fight to sustain the beauty and amenity of the capital from its home in Trunks Close on the Canongate.

This planning vision highlights the environmental quality of the city as its primary wealth and the economic exploitation of this as strictly secondary.

Edinburgh's Cockburn Association hopes that such planning policies might inform the development strategy of Scotland's capital, as did Lord Cockburn, writing in 1849 (Box 6).

THE GROWTH OF URBAN NATURE CONSERVATION IN SCOTLAND

The Nature Conservancy Council (NCC) played a seminal role in the birth of urban nature conservation when in 1978 it published *The Endless Village*, documenting a survey of open spaces and wildlife in the city of

Birmingham and the Black Country. This proposed that the plant and animal communities of the city should be identified; that the entire area of public land, parks and recreational spaces should be improved and managed for wildlife; and that derelict land reclamation projects should be used to create new urban living space for wildlife. Crucially the report stressed the need to interest local people in their wildlife heritage, and the environmental quality of their lives in towns.

In the late 1980s a change was also taking place in Scotland; by 1987 the NCC had funded ecological surveys of open spaces and wildlife habitats within the cities of Aberdeen, Dundee and Edinburgh (boxes 7 and 8). Every open space, public garden, disused railway, cemetery and derelict site was classified by habitat-type. In the same year the NCC published *Planning for Wildlife in Metropolitan Areas*, which advocated the inclusion of wildlife and the natural aspects of urban environmental quality for unitary development plans in England and Wales. Additionally, the Department of the Environment and the Welsh Office issued Circular 27/87 entitled 'Nature Conservation' which noted:

> Local authorities are required by section 11 of the Countryside Act 1968 'to have regard to the desirability of conserving the natural beauty and amenity of the countryside'. This duty embraces the conservation of flora, fauna, geological and physio-graphical features and extends to urban as well as rural areas. Councils are particularly urged to ensure that, where they own or hold land for any purpose, their own estate management practices take nature conservation considerations fully into account.

The 1986 Act imposed a duty on local authorities in England and Wales to take conservation into account in urban areas. However, this Act did not apply in Scotland, and the corresponding Scottish Development Department Circular 1/1988 made no reference to nature conservation in planning. However,

7. DUNDEE URBAN NATURE CONSERVATION STRATEGY

Dundee was the first city in Scotland to undertake an urban wildlife survey and to publish a corresponding Nature Conservation Strategy. In 1987 the City of Dundee District Council and the NCC set up the Dundee Urban Wildlife Project, and within a year an Assessment of the City's Greenspaces had been produced. Fifty sites from the Derelict Land Register were mapped and surveyed; a list of all plant species for each site habitat was prepared and any interesting insect or bird species found were also recorded. The sites were rated for their amenity value, their educational potential and the general richness of the site in terms of habitat and rare species.

Dundee is to date the only local authority in Scotland which has adopted an Urban Nature Conservation Subject Local Plan as a means of giving its Nature Conservation Strategy the full force of local statute. In doing so it has created a national example for other local authorities to emulate.

Kestrels have adapted well to urban life and hunt the verges of city motorways.

8. EDINBURGH'S NATURE CONSERVATION STRATEGY

During the mid 1980s the Planning Department of Edinburgh District Council became concerned that it did not have an up to date survey of open greenspaces within the city. There was no overall strategy for the conservation of the birds, animals and plants which survive in the city's parks, gardens, disused railways and watercourses. Developers increasingly target these marginal spaces and gap sites for housing and offices and the planners found they had little environmental information on which to assess the impact of proposed developments.

In 1987 the Edinburgh Wildlife Survey was launched by the Environment Centre working with the Scottish Wildlife Trust. The project aimed to find and survey every green open space within the City of Edinburgh. More than 965 sites identified from aerial photographs were mapped and surveyed. The resulting report formed the basis for the preparation of a city-wide Nature Conservation Strategy, by the District Council. It is hoped that the Edinburgh Nature Conservation Strategy will guarantee the capital's reputation as having the richest and most diverse urban environmental quality in Britain.

Kingfisher on the water of Leith at Canonmills, Edinburgh.

Children at High School Yards Nursery, Edinburgh, created this educational garden with support of teachers and parents.

9. GROUNDS FOR LEARNING

Grounds for Learning is a national education initiative supported by Scottish Natural Heritage, Learning Through Landscapes Trust and Amerada Hess Ltd. The project was created to address the fact that many of Scotland's school grounds could best be described as asphalt or grass deserts: ecologically sterile, recreationally limited and aesthetically impoverished.

From its Stirling office the project supports a national network of teachers and local authorities who have set out to improve the environmental quality of school grounds for the educational and recreational benefit of all children. The simple aim is to enrich children's educational experience through daily contact with plants, animals and birds and to foster their recreational, social, aesthetic and spiritual development through a more biologically diverse, colourful and stimulating school environment.

since its inception in 1992, Scottish Natural Heritage (SNH) has strongly supported a wide range of nature conservation and education initiatives in urban areas, in green belts and in the 'Countryside Around Towns' programme. A key initiative has been SNH's support for the Grounds for Learning scheme, which promotes the development and enhancement of the natural heritage aspects of all school grounds so that many thousands of Scottish children can now enjoy plants, flowers, insects and birds within the school grounds (Box 9).

ENVIRONMENTAL CHARTERS AND LOCAL AGENDA 21

A broader approach to promoting environmental quality in towns was initiated during the 1990s by Friends of the Earth, namely a Charter for the Environment. Such charters had a strong impact on council policies relating to traffic, pollution, recycling and the conservation of green open spaces and wildlife in towns.

Various local authorities in Scotland appointed Environmental Charter Officers to promote such agendas across all departments. As a result many councils now have proactive policies on issues such as the recycling of paper, glass, metals, textiles, oil, refrigerants and garden waste; pollution control for air, land and water; the conservation of wildlife through ecological management of parks, open spaces and roadside verges; the development of environmentally friendly transport policies and of environmental enhancement strategies for public open space. However, Environmental Charters were largely superseded by the World Summit on the Environment, held in Rio de Janeiro in 1992.

The central concept which emerged from this summit was Sustainability: the common sense policy that nations should only exploit the earth's natural resources in a sustainable manner. Governments agreed to common agendas, including ones on biodiversity and, crucial to the present chapter, Local Agenda 21. At the heart of this is the conviction that sustainability can never be achieved without the democratic participation of all groups in society. The UK Government promoted Local Agenda 21 as a blueprint for civic participation in all planning, resource and development issues in every community. Each local authority was asked to draw up a Local Agenda 21 programme, in consultation with its citizens, taking sustainable development as the guiding light. As a result some Scottish local authorities have appointed Local Agenda 21 officers, but many observers will only be convinced that councils have truly embraced the spirit of Agenda 21 when they witness significant shifts towards sharing power, budgets and decision-making with local communities.

The priceless environmental quality of Scotland's cities with their green open spaces, wildlife heritage and classical architecture, are the gift of history, of generations which fought to preserve the amenity and landscape of their towns. Today's councils and business sector inherit environmental assets which, if managed sustainably, can generate economic and tourist prosperity and a decent quality of life for everyone. But if this environmental capital, garnered over centuries, is exploited unthinkingly, sold to the highest bidder, or sacrificed for short-term gain, then a historic tragedy will ensue. The challenge, as Lord Cockburn wrote in 1849, is for councillors to take the long view, resist the pleadings of the self-interested lobbyists, and place the beauty, amenity and environmental quality of the town above every other consideration. No stronger plea for environmental sustainability has ever been made and it is to be hoped that the urgency of the millennial agenda implicit in Local Agenda 21 will be understood and wholeheartedly adopted by Scotland's councils and councillors.

The Gyle retail park, the largest single development in Edinburgh's history, has generated massive traffic increase and makes a mockery of council policies on 'sustainable development'.

*The Allt Coire Tholl Bruach
rushes to join the River Shiel
near the Cluanie inn.*

CHAPTER SIXTEEN

The Protection of the Land
John Arnott

John Arnott is an amateur naturalist and a former editor and manager with BBC Scotland. As Vice Chairman of the Countryside Commission for Scotland (CCS) he chaired the panel which led to the CCS report on the conservation and management of 'The Mountain Areas of Scotland' in 1990. He is a former member of the Committee for Scotland of the Nature Conservancy Council and of the South East Regional Board of Scottish Natural Heritage.

All land is protected for one reason or other. Historically, ownership of land gave the exclusive right to exploit the land, and the plants and animals it supported, without interference from anyone else; and the exhortation to man in the first chapter of the Bible to subdue the earth and have dominion over all living things in it is sometimes followed to this day.

Over the centuries the forests were cleared to the extent that Dr Johnson on his visit to Scotland with Boswell in 1773 could say: 'A tree might be a show in Scotland as a horse in Venice'. The Industrial Revolution and its aftermath scarred the countryside. Rivers ran with pollution. Intensive grazing by sheep and deer prevented regeneration of trees and created erosion. Urban settlements sprawled. From the early nineteenth century much of the uplands passed into sporting estates where game birds were protected by wholesale slaughter of golden eagles, hen harriers, peregrines and other 'vermin'. Attempts were also made to defend the land against people who wanted to seek recreation in the countryside.

Balanced against this rather stark view of the relationship of people and the land is the fact that some land-use was in fact beneficial to both landscape and wildlife, as well as being profitable. After the eighteenth-century enclosures, mixed arable and livestock farming produced small fields bounded by hedges and drystane dykes, giving cover for birds, insects and wild flowers. Shelter belts and hedgerow trees restored variety, and designed landscapes in private estates brought amenity woodlands and attractive parkland. Indeed, the Scott Report on 'Land Utilisation in Rural Areas' in 1942 declared roundly that 'there is no antagonism between use and beauty' and made the proposal, which was accepted by government, that farming and forestry should be excluded from the forthcoming town and country planning legislation on the grounds that they could do no harm to the countryside. The major threat was perceived as being the prospect of built development.

The 1942 Scott Report, and others, brought new concepts of collective responsibility to bear on the relationship between society and the environment. Before that, only a few enlightened landowners had made any efforts to conserve the countryside simply for its natural qualities. Post-war legislation led to the creation of a framework of new controls and mechanisms, including the setting up of government agencies and other bodies charged with safeguarding a selection of areas for their beauty or their 'scientific' (wildlife) interest. The Wildlife and Countryside Act 1981 was another landmark in nature conservation, which gives greatly increased protection to many of these areas.

By the 1980s, however, there was also a growing realisation that, in the face of increasingly intensive agriculture and afforestation, and development and recreational pressures, the whole of the countryside, not just samples of it, needed greater protection. Since the 1940s more than half the hedgerows of Scotland had disappeared. A quarter of the heather moorland and of broadleaved woodlands had been lost, together with nearly half the lowland peat mires. After thousands of years of human exploitation, which accelerated rapidly throughout this century, much of Scotland was presenting an impoverished and degraded landscape.

Yet this landscape represents one of the nation's great assets, both for the quality of life of its own people and for its commercial value: tourism currently brings in an annual £2.4 billion to the Scottish economy. Surveys have indicated that 86 per cent of overseas visitors rate 'scenery' as the main attraction of Scotland.

There are wider considerations, too. There is increasing awareness that the whole world has finite resources which are under ever greater pressure, whether tropical rainforests or North Sea fish stocks. A whole new vocabulary has sprung up: 'conservation', the wise management of resources, was a new word to most people only a generation ago, followed by 'ecosystems', the inter-relationship between living things and their surroundings. 'Sustainable development' made its appearance in the Brundtland Report in 1983: 'Development which meets the needs of the present without compromising the ability of future generations to meet their own needs'.

'Biodiversity', the richness and variety of and within species, came into prominence at another landmark conservation event, the Earth Summit at Rio de Janeiro in 1992 which set out an Environmental Agenda for the 21st Century (Agenda 21). Along with more than 150 other countries the United Kingdom signed up to the Summit's Convention on Biological Diversity and agreed to draw up a national programme (Biodiversity: the UK Action Plan 1994) to implement the Convention's objectives.

These new words such as 'sustainability' and 'biodiversity' are not just airy abstractions. They have practical implications for every organisation and every individual person in the country. Protection of the land is everybody's business.

NATIONAL WILDLIFE DESIGNATIONS

The principal agency concerned with the country's landscape and wildlife is Scottish Natural Heritage (SNH), which was formed in 1992 by the merging of the Countryside Commission for Scotland (CCS) and the Nature Conservancy Council for Scotland (NCCS). It is funded by The Scottish Office Agriculture Environment and Fisheries Department (SOAEFD) and its Board members are appointed by the Secretary of State for Scotland.

SNH has two main statutory mechanisms for safeguarding specific areas of wildlife value. One is the National Nature Reserve (NNR), in which the conservation of nature is itself the primary land-use (Box 1). There are seventy of them, totalling about 113,000 hectares, and they range in size from 26,000 ha in the Cairngorms and 10,000 ha in the Island of Rum with its Manx shearwaters and much-studied red deer, down to only 5 ha at the spectacular gorge of Corrieshalloch near Ullapool.

The other statutory mechanism is the Site of Special Scientific Interest (SSSI). The Wildlife and Countryside Act 1981 requires SNH to identify and notify to the owners a representative selection of all the different types of areas of particular wildlife and geological importance. There are more than 1,400 SSSIs in Scotland which cover about 11 per cent of the land surface. Some of them are very extensive, and cover huge areas of mountain, moorland and estuary; some are only a hectare or two. Others protect sea bird colonies or flower-rich meadows or outstanding geological features.

The 1981 Act required owners and occupiers of land notified as SSSI to inform SNH of changes in the way they manage the land which might have a damaging effect on the wildlife interest. It also introduced the novel and potentially expensive principle of 'compensation for profit foregone' in cases where SNH felt that the wildlife interest would be damaged by any such proposed changes.

This system has had a mixed reception from the 8,000 landowners involved, many of whom (like landowners everywhere) resent interference from outside. Territory is an emotional, highly charged subject. Some owners have been paid large sums of money under management agreements whereby they were compensated for not using the land in the way they wished. The problems of this approach were highlighted when tax concessions for conifer afforestation increased enormously the potential value of wide tracts of country. This led to public concern about the scale of compensation to such landowners or occupiers.

The tax concessions were stopped in 1988. Management agreements now put emphasis on positive benefits for wildlife in the use of the land by working in partnership with the owner (rather than by merely paying compensation). In practice, however, most sites continue to be managed as they were in the past, without the need for compensatory payments: about 90 per cent of notified changes of practice are given consent, 9 per cent result in agreed modification, and only 1 per cent require compensation.

The SSSI thus provides formal protection on a scale which had never been previously seen, but it cannot afford complete protection. Damage to the nature conservation interest still happens, either deliberately or by accident. Major developments such as a new road may be allowed to go ahead in the public interest after a ruling by the Secretary of State, or owners might carry out damaging operations without notifying them to SNH. As a result of this some sites are marred and a few have even had to be denotified.

INTERNATIONAL DESIGNATIONS

The national statutory designations of NNRs and SSSIs help to enable the UK Government to fulfil international Directives and Conventions.

The 1979 European Community Directive on the Conservation of Wild Birds (the Birds Directive) and the 1992 EC Directive on the Conservation of Natural Habitats and Wild Fauna and Flora (the Habitats Directive) are

1. BEINN EIGHE

The National Nature Reserve of Beinn Eighe (pronounced 'Ben-Ay') in Rose and Cromarty, in the north-west of Scotland, was the very first to be established in Britain, in 1951.

The land was purchased by the Nature Conservancy Council to preserve Beinn Eighe, with its classic geological formations, as a splendid example of the mountain and moorland habitat of the northern Highlands, and in particular to conserve the fragment of native woodland, Coill na glas Leitire ('wood of the gery slop') overlooking the southern shores of Loch Maree.

This pinewood was recognised as an important remnant of the 'Great Wood of Caledon' which once clothed most of Highland Scotland (see Chapter 3). Beinn Eighe provides as good an idea of what a primeval forest was like as any other woodland scene in Britain; this was Scotland's original 'rain forest' one might say. The trees at Beinn Eighe are up to 350 years old, and to stand amongst them is to feel the nature of Scotland's past.

Native pine wood at Coille na Glas Leitire, Beinn Eighe, Britain's first National Nature Reserve.

designed to establish a network of protected sites throughout Europe to be called Natura 2000. The safeguards afforded by SSSIs provide the main statutory basis by which the UK Government will fulfil these Directives; but Natura 2000 sites will have an additional tier of protection.

There are more than 130 Special Protection Areas (SPAs) proposed under the Birds Directive, spread across the country from the Loch of Spiggie in Shetland to Castle Loch by the Solway Firth. More than 100 sites are being considered as Special Areas of Conservation (SACs) under the Habitats Directive, covering areas such as Glen Coe and the machair island shores of Coll and Tiree.

Some of these overlap with another international designation devised by the Ramsar Convention (not another acronym, but the place in Iran where it was drawn up in 1971) which was ratified by the UK in 1976. This seeks to safeguard marshes and wetlands, particularly those which are of importance to migratory birds. More than sixty SSSIs have been proposed as Ramsar sites, of which thirty-four

Creag Meagaidh National Nature Reserve where over 5,000 red deer have been culled in order to allow regeneration of the woodlands.

have to date been designated by the Secretary of State, for example at the Loch of Strathbeg near Peterhead and the Montrose Basin, both famous for their wildfowl. Biosphere Reserves, a designation of the United Nations Educational, Scientific and Cultural Organisation (UNESCO), are applied in Scotland to nine of the NNRs.

BROADER PROTECTION

The Wildlife and Countryside Act 1981, which introduced the SSSI, also extended throughout the whole of Scotland a general level of protection for almost all wild animals and plants. It is perhaps not widely realised that uprooting any wild plant is a criminal offence. Heavy penalties can be imposed for damage to specially protected plants and animal species, and these have been meted out in some cases involving the theft of peregrines' and ospreys' eggs.

The sight of a peregrine flashing by or an osprey swooping down on a loch to take fish, or the colours of an ancient pine-forest with its junipers and blaeberries and red squirrels, are very much a part of the enjoyment of the natural beauty of the landscape.

Compared with the welter of designations and legislation for the protection of specific animals and plants, landscape is rather a poor relation. Not only is the beauty of a tract of country less easy to quantify than communities of birds or flowers, but its protection is not always pursued as vigorously by those with the powers to do so.

LANDSCAPE DESIGNATION

There is only one government designation in Scotland for outstanding landscape – the National Scenic Area (NSA). There are forty NSAs, ranging from the awesome cliffs of St Kilda and the fantastical shapes of the Assynt mountains, through the windswept semi-arctic Cairngorms to the more accessible scale of the Trossachs, the Kyles of Bute, and the Eildon Hills beside Melrose. Altogether they amount to about 13 per cent of the country.

Within these areas proposals for several types of development (such as the hill tracts for deer stalking which criss-cross so much of the mountain country) have to be notified to SNH

ENJOYMENT

and if, contrary to the view of the planning authority, SNH considers the development unsuitable for these special landscapes, the decision is referred to the Secretary of State. The NSAs also have the general effect (some would say the insufficient effect) of drawing attention to the importance of protecting these exceptional areas.

ENJOYMENT

Much of the work done by SNH in protecting and enhancing the natural beauty of the countryside throughout Scotland, and facilitating people's enjoyment of it, is by a mixture of advice and grant aid: to local authorities, voluntary bodies and private landowners, and by its own innovative projects. It provides much of the funding for the Countryside Ranger Service, which helps to resolve conflicts between recreation and other land uses. But the land needs protection from recreation, too; many of the most popular hills are scarred by walkers' paths. The mountains look robust but they have a fragile skin, and millions of pounds are needed for the laborious work of footpath repair. Wild country

untouched by roads is a diminishing asset in western Europe and there are some moves now to promote the 'long walk in', discouraging access by cars.

OTHER SPECIAL AREAS

It was pressure from walkers which was instrumental in securing another protective designation for the rest of Britain. Scotland is one of the very few countries in the world which does not have National Parks, even though they were proposed by the Ramsay Committee in 1945 and by the Countryside Commission for Scotland (CCS) in 1990. These proposals were not accepted by government for a variety of reasons including cost, landowner resistance and the reluctance of planning authorities to make over any of their powers.

The two areas considered to be most in need of this high level of protection and funding were the Cairngorms, and Loch Lomond and the Trossachs. Following the 1990 CCS proposals the government set up Working Parties for each of these areas. Consequently, in the Cairngorms, a Partnership Board was

St Kilda has a host of designations: SSSI, NNR, NSA, NTS Inalienable, RAMSAR, and World Heritage Site.

Dawn breaks at Loch Achtriochtan in Glencoe National Scenic Area.

established by the Secretary of State for Scotland, which draws together all the many interested parties to devise a management strategy for a large area including not only the mountains but the straths and settlements round about them. The intention is that this strategy will be implemented on a co-operative basis by everyone concerned. In time the Cairngorms may become the first recipient of a new designation, Natural Heritage Area (NHA), which was introduced in the Natural

Heritage (Scotland) Act 1991 and is the only statutory national designation which relates to the natural heritage as a whole.

The Working Party on Loch Lomond and the Trossachs proposed a development of the existing Regional Park (RP) as a joint committee of local authorities, with an extended area and an increased budget. In an annex to its report it also recommended in the longer term a local authority joint board which would take over planning powers for the area.

LOCAL AUTHORITY DESIGNATIONS

Alongside this statutory network of special areas of national importance, local authorities play another crucial role in the protection of the land. Loch Lomond is the largest of Scotland's four Regional Parks – large areas of hill country close to population centres and designated by local authorities (and confirmed by the Secretary of State for Scotland). In these Regional Parks existing landownership and farming continue but, by agreement with the owners, there is an extensive system of public access, aided by a ranger service. The other

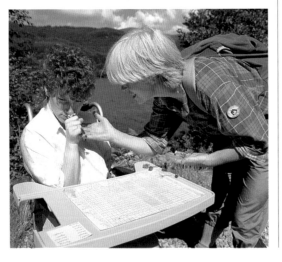

Countryside Ranger with a special needs visitor near Fort William.

three Regional Parks are at the north end of the Pentland Hills beside Edinburgh, in Fife centred on the Lomond Hills, and at Clyde Muirshiel in the hills between Greenock and Largs.

On a smaller scale there are thirty-six Country Parks near towns and cities, mostly owned and run by local councils, giving townspeople places in the country where they know they are welcome to walk or take part in informal sports. The parks are not very extensive, averaging under 200 ha and ranging from 675 ha at John Muir Country Park near Dunbar with its 13 km of shoreline, to just 16 ha at Clatto on the outskirts of Dundee which consists mostly of a reservoir used for water sports. The Country Parks are among the few areas in the countryside where public recreation is acknowledged to be the primary land-use, but for that purpose they act as a protection in a double sense: by conserving their natural amenity and by taking visitor pressure off more vulnerable areas. It is estimated that they receive about a quarter of the 40 million day-trips made to the Scottish countryside each year.

The locally elected unitary authorities are now responsible for both systems of parks, taking over some of the tasks from the former Regional Councils in 1996. They are also at the centre of one of the most comprehensive systems for protection of the land through their planning and development control powers. Apart from farming and forestry and some smaller exceptions, virtually every construction and every change in land-use throughout the whole country is subject to their scrutiny and to compliance with their Structure and Local Plans. Though only half a century old, and although planning consents are sometimes controversial, these measures might be said to have provided more protection for the land than any other mechanism.

Within the general planning system local authorities are allowed by a 1962 Scottish Office Circular to identify particularly fine landscapes as Areas of Great Landscape Value (AGLV) which may also be part of NSAs and can be given a variety of titles. They provide an additional safeguard against inappropriate

Coire an Lochain in Cairngorms National Scenic Area (NSA).

development. There are more than 170 of them, covering about 19 per cent of the country.

Taking their cue from the UK Biodiversity Action Plan's recognition that 'biodiversity is ultimately lost or conserved at the local level', local authorities have been taking the lead in preparing Local Biodiversity Action Plans.

Starting in 1996, this is a collaborative effort involving a partnership between local government, the public and private sectors, the voluntary bodies and, it is hoped, everyone in the community. The plans will require further surveys not just of rarer species and habitats but of common birds and plants too. It is a long-term project aimed at a cultural change, a common understanding that the richness and

Harvesting barley in the Lomond Hills Regional Park, Fife.

variety of living things needs good stewardship everywhere, in gardens, farms and woodland of every sort, lochs and shorelines, and not only in specially protected areas.

But special areas still have a role as well. Since the 1960s green belts have been designated by local authorities around the four Scottish cities of Aberdeen, Dundee (which later replaced it in 1978 with a separate countryside policy), Edinburgh and Glasgow, and around Ayr, Clackmannan and Falkirk. Stirling is committed to introduce one in 1997. They were set up to stop urban sprawl, and on the whole they have served that purpose well. They face ever-increasing development pressure; over the next ten years Scotland will need an additional quarter of a million homes.

The positive side – that of rehabilitating land which is highly marginal for farming and where farmers have in some cases given up in the face of falling income, vandalism and litter – is not so easy to implement. Various initiatives have been taken to tackle this. In the Glasgow green belt, which extends for 100,000 ha from Greenock to Cumbernauld and Carluke, several projects have been set up under the Countryside Around Towns (CAT) programme initiated by the former CCS. These bring together a partnership of local authorities, SNH, voluntary bodies and the private sector to improve the appearance and the enjoyment of the open country most accessible to the built up areas. To the east a similar project has been set up in the Edinburgh Green Belt Trust.

Between the green belts of Glasgow and Edinburgh lies an area of marginal farming country where the CCS initiated a pioneering project, now Central Scotland Woodlands Ltd (see Chapter 10, Box 4), which aims to plant millions of trees, largely for amenity purposes, to create a central Scotland forest. Its target is to double the woodland cover across 1,600 square kilometres from West Lothian to East Dumbarton. Part of this is funded by the Millennium Forest of Scotland Trust which by 1996 had disbursed over £11 million of National Lottery money to seventy-seven projects across the country from Orkney to the Borders. These

are all for restoring native woodland.

Councils are also enabled by the 1949 National Parks and Access to the Countryside Act to set up Local Nature Reserves (LNRs), of which there are twenty-three in Scotland. The first (and the first in Britain) was at Aberlady Bay in East Lothian in 1952. These designations often overlap. Montrose Basin in Angus, for example, is an LNR and also an SSSI and a Ramsar site, as well as a Scottish Wildlife Trust reserve.

Two local authority mechanisms relate to trees. One is the Tree Preservation Order for small areas of high amenity woodland or even individual trees. The other, on a much bigger scale, is the Indicative Forestry Strategy.

FORESTRY DESIGNATIONS

The Indicative Forestry Strategy concept arose in the 1980s from the outcry over the scale of afforestation in the Flow Country of Caithness and Sutherland, probably the most extensive expanse of blanket peat bog in the world.

When the then Nature Conservancy Council (NCC) proposed notifying large areas of the Flow Country as SSSIs, at a time when there were plans to cover much of it with conifer plantations, the then Highland Regional Council brought everyone concerned round a table, including those who saw valuable job opportunities in forestry, and together they worked out a strategy which indicated where forestry was more, or less, appropriate.

Strathclyde Region took up the idea and, with Scottish Office support, most Councils now have Indicative Forestry Strategies. These divide countryside into 'Preferred', 'Potential' and 'Sensitive' zones according to the number of constraints operating on them such as NSAs, SSSIs or Ancient Monuments. They do not in themselves provide protection from inappropriate forestry, but they do give an indication of where most opposition is likely to arise and can be helpful in reducing controversy over the location of new forests.

Scotland has about 14 per cent of its land under trees, compared with 27 per cent in France and 30 per cent in Germany. It has only one native conifer, the Scots pine, but its moist climate favours quick-growing North American conifers like Sitka spruce and lodgepole pine. They grow best for timber production when closely planted. The exclusion of red deer (which eat young trees) involves installing miles of expensive straight-running fences, and there is a larger return if planting runs right up to the fence. The result throughout Scotland has been the hard geometrical blocks of so-called 'blanket forestry' of even-aged single-species plantations: man's handiwork writ large on the landscape.

Antipathy to this was compounded by a widespread feeling that fiscal advantages and doubtful economics were resulting in taxpayers subsidising landscape blight. An increasingly vocal and articulate lobby expressed this feeling. But complaints about serried rows of Sitka spruce were given a frosty reception by foresters. For generations they had been doing what they had been asked to do: produce timber. It is society which has moved the goalposts.

The Forestry Commission (FC) is a government agency with two parts: the Forestry Authority (FA), which grant-aids private sector planting and issues felling licences, and Forest Enterprise (FE), which grows its own trees. The public and private sectors each have just over half a million hectares of forest. The Commission was set up after the First World War to replenish the forests cut down for the war effort and to build up a strategic reserve of timber. It pursued these objectives with single-minded determination, both at its own hand and by grant-aiding private landowners, almost trebling the tree cover in Scotland since it was founded.

During the late 1980s, however, the Forestry Commission's policy of maximising timber production was tempered by wider environmental considerations, with better forest design and more broadleaves among the conifers. Felling of first generation forests gives opportunities for varying the age structure of plantations, protecting the landscape from uniform crops.

Forests are attractive to walk in and can absorb large numbers of people without appearing at all crowded. The Forestry Commission has long welcomed recreation on its properties. It has five Forest Parks (FPs), the first dating back to 1935 in Argyll, with others in the Trossachs, Glenmore, Glentrool and at Tummel, where marked paths and other facilities are provided for visitors. Some of the best wildlife sites have been designated as Forest Nature Reserves (FNRs), where conservation is the prime management objective. There are forty-six of them in Scotland, from the sand-dune forest of Culbin and the pine forests of Glen Affric and the Black Wood of Rannoch, to smaller sites like the Dalavich oak wood at Loch Awe.

The great expansion of the Forest Enterprise estate has now stopped, and some of its forests have been sold off (raising fears about reduction of access for recreation); the main drive for new planting is now in the private sector, assisted by the Woodland Grants Scheme (WGS). This pays £700 per hectare for 2,250 conifers and £1,350 per hectare for 1,100 broadleaved trees – a considerable incentive. To qualify for grant, proposals must satisfy increasingly high standards of design, landscaping and species mix, and safeguards for wildlife interest, archaeological sites and public access. There is more consultation now with local authorities and others. Objections to planting proposals may be referred to the Forestry Authority's Regional Advisory Committees and there are further appeals beyond that. Under a 1985 Act the Forestry Commission is required to

Mass conifer planting in the Caithness Flow country.

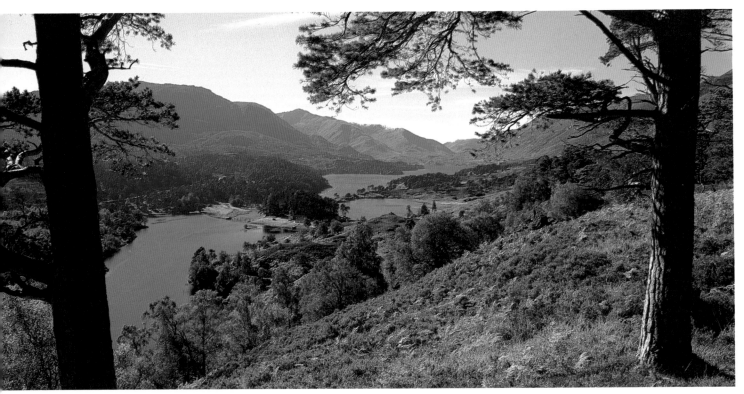

Glen Affric Forest Nature Reserve (FNA).

maintain a 'reasonable balance' between timber production and landscape and wildlife conservation. There are several other grant schemes aimed at improving the environment, for native pinewood planting and natural regeneration, for improving woodland biodiversity, for community woodlands and even for planting woody shrubs like hazel or juniper.

Largely for reasons of land tenure, much of the countryside having been owned in large estates, Scotland does not have the same tradition of small-scale farm woodlands as is found in comparable Scandinavian countries. The Farm Woodland Premium Scheme, run by SOAEFD, is designed to encourage the creation of new woodlands on farms, both to enhance the environment and as a productive alternative land-use which gives farmers annual payments.

AGRICULTURE

Farmers have traditionally been the stewards and protectors of the countryside with a vested interest in a fully sustainable use of it. In the critical years of the Second World War and subsequent years they answered the call for more home-grown food by increasing production. This was achieved through radical reform of traditional farming practices – reforms given a further boost by the incentives offered by the EC Common Agricultural Policy (CAP).

The changes to agricultural practice which brought about increased output had environmentally damaging effects, however: the wholesale removal of hedgerows and trees creating huge fields dedicated to a single plant species; the drainage of wetland; the heavy use of artificial fertilisers, insecticides and herbicides; and the loss of employment as expensive machinery took over. By the 1980s the pendulum had swung the other way, when over-production of food created an embarrassment of riches at enormous expense to the taxpayer. In 1992 aspects of the CAP were reformed in order to reduce food surpluses and costs. A 20 per cent cut in farm subsidies over the years 1995 to 2000 was included in the 1993 General Agreement on Tariff and Trade (GATT, now known as the World Trade Organisation).

Alongside this, the adverse environmental

effects of intensive farming are being tackled through the gradual development of the Agri-Environmental Programme. This began with the Environmentally Sensitive Area (ESA), which was introduced in 1987–88 in five places where the effect of intensive farming was less severe than elsewhere (see Chapter 10, Box 6).

The scheme is voluntary, but crofters and farmers who join it are required to agree to farm in ways which help protect and enhance the conservation value of the land. For this they receive payments based on the area of their holdings, and additional payments for many specified improvements, such as hedge and tree-planting, dyke repairs and, in the Uists, the traditional use of seaweed as fertiliser.

A new element of the Agri-Environmental Programme is the Scottish Countryside Premium Scheme, launched in 1997. This gives grants throughout the whole country for creating and managing nearly a score of different types of habitats for wildlife, from heather moorland to grass margins and beetle banks, and from cropped machair to extended hedges. It also provides capital grants for a dozen purposes including pond creation, bracken control and drystane dykes.

The consequences of CAP reform have affected both arable and pastoral farming. Most of the good arable land in Scotland is found on the fringes of the east and south-west coasts. Here, farmers are required not to cultivate a proportion of their land in order to reduce production, through Set-aside. Increasingly, this is being designed to bring environmental benefits. But in the higher, poorer land which comprises most of the country, hill sheep farming predominates. Under the CAP 90 per cent of Scotland is classed as a Less Favoured Area (LFA), sub-divided into Disadvantaged Area (DA) and Severely Disadvantaged Area (SDA).

These classifications allow extra payments to be made as Hill Livestock Compensatory Allowances (HLCAs) for cattle and sheep, mostly the latter. The result of encouraging so much grazing has been the suppression of the natural regeneration of the tree and shrub cover

which would otherwise occur over most of the upland country. Reform of HLCA is mooted, but it is primarily a social payment, for without these subsidy systems great swathes of the Highlands would be virtually unpopulated.

The Breadalbane hills Environmentally Sensitive Area (ESA).

THE DEER COMMISSION FOR SCOTLAND

Besides sheep, the other great nibbler of young trees is the red deer. A forest dweller by choice, it has adapted well to life in the bare mountain country. The red deer population in Scotland has soared to 350,000 across its range, encouraged by the sporting estates and untrammelled by any of its traditional predators like the wolf. Stags are stalked in the autumn as trophies and bring revenue and employment to many estates, but the much more numerous hinds are difficult to cull in mid-winter. Under new legislation in the Deer

221

Native pine woods, the preferred habitat of the red deer in Scotland.

(Scotland) Act 1996 the Deer Commission for Scotland has been given powers to ensure that numbers are controlled, not only to prevent agricultural damage, as was previously the case, but also in the interests of the natural environment.

THE SCOTTISH ENVIRONMENT PROTECTION AGENCY

The hills of the deer range are largely composed of acidic rock which contributes to low productivity of the soil. In more recent times acid rain has increased this ancient acidity – on the lower ground too, especially in the south-west. Other industrial pollutants have diminished but fertiliser run-off from intensively farmed fields has led in some places to the eutrophication (unnatural enrichment) of lochs, killing fish and unbalancing the natural order.

The Scottish Environment Protection Agency (SEPA) was set up in 1996 by the Environment Act of the previous year to tackle the problem of protecting the land from pollution. It took over some of the responsibilities of local authorities, and also the duties of the seven former River Purification Boards and Her Majesty's Industrial Pollution Inspectorate. SEPA has wide powers relating to water and air quality, waste disposal and radio-activity. So far as water is concerned, it is off to a good start; a 1990 survey showed that 97 per cent of Scotland's 46,452 km of rivers, lochs and canals were unpolluted.

THE VOLUNTARY BODIES

Dealing with the problem of air pollution from vehicles is a bigger difficulty, and one in which some of the voluntary bodies have had a leading role in publicising its extent. These Non-Government Organisations (NGOs) have an important role in protecting the land and caring for the natural heritage. They are widely involved throughout the country in managing nature reserves, and there has been an enormous increase in their membership over the last two decades which has given them considerable clout in environmental lobbying. Some, like the World Wide Fund for Nature (WWF), Friends of the Earth (FoE) and the Association for the Protection of Rural Scotland (APRS), work largely through education and campaigning. Some have large landholdings bought with money raised by their members, with gifts, or with grants from government agencies such as the National Heritage Memorial Fund (NHMF) and the National Lottery.

The largest of the Scottish NGOs is the National Trust for Scotland (NTS), which has 230,000 members. It holds over a hundred properties across the country, from Fair Isle to Threave Castle beside the Solway, and from St Kilda to Provost Ross's House in Aberdeen. Some are huge, like Torridon with the beetling cliffs of Liathach and the Mar Lodge estate in the Cairngorms, some are grand houses like Culzean with their imposing grounds, a few are domestic, like the crow-stepped houses of Culross.

The NTS is enabled by its founding legislation to hold property 'inalienably', which means that it can only be taken out of the Trust's care with the consent of Parliament. Its 1938 Act also enables it to enter into Conservation Agreements whereby owners of outstanding landscape voluntarily accept binding agreements, which are passed on to their successors, that nothing will be done to mar the property in future. Some 24,000 ha of Scotland are protected in this way through more than 600 agreements. (In a government provision with similar objectives, some owners of heritage landscapes may obtain conditional exemption from Inheritance Tax for them, so long as they safeguard them.)

For its wide tracts of mountain country, the Trust's objectives are the same as for its other properties: to hand them on to the next generation in at least as good a condition as it found them. This has created some controversy about the extent to which access should be made easier by signposting and path building: one of the Trust's principal benefactors in the past, Percy Unna, requested that the land should be kept as 'primitive' as possible with unrestricted access but no new or improved paths. He could not have foreseen the pressures which were to come and which necessitated the elaborate and costly path building projects in Glen Coe and on Ben Lawers and Ben Lomond, but the Trust has done its best to maintain the wild quality of

these areas, at least away from its visitor centres.

The Scottish Wildlife Trust (SWT), founded in 1964, has a membership of over 15,000. It manages 116 reserves, with a quarter of this land owned and the rest leased or managed by agreement with the owners. They include Ben More Coigeach and part of the Island of Eigg with open access, and at the other extreme a tiny cave in the Trossachs used by hibernating bats which do not welcome any visitors.

Wildlife conservation is the primary objective of the reserves, most of which are SSSIs. Many of them require active management; without it, rhododendrons invade woodlands, shading out the ground plants, and broken fences let in sheep and cattle. Members are encouraged to put on their wellington boots and help with the practical work, or explain to the public what can be seen from the visitor centres at, for example, the Falls of Clyde or Montrose Basin.

The largest voluntary conservation body in Europe is the Royal Society for the Protection of Birds (RSPB), based at Sandy in Bedfordshire, which has over 900,000 members throughout the UK, including 64,000 north of the Border. In

Native pinewoods in the Abernethy forest RSPB reserve.

223

Scotland it manages fifty-seven reserves, of which it owns about four-fifths. They range in size from a very extensive property in the Cairngorms running from Loch Garten with its ospreys, through Abernethy and Glen Avon to the summit of Ben Macdhui, down to the little island of Inchmickery in the Firth of Forth.

Although the emphasis of its royal charter is on birds, the RSPB is interested nowadays in protecting whole habitats for nature conservation, and it brings a large professional staff to bear on the management of its property. It has demonstrated in the Abernethy pine forest (as SNH has done on the open slopes of its NNR at Creag Meagaidh) that a major cull of red deer encourages natural tree regeneration and obviates the need for fencing. With the resources provided by a huge membership, coupled with special appeals and grants from NHMF, and government agencies, the RSPB has been able to deploy millions of pounds in land purchases.

Operating on a more modest scale are several trusts and societies devoted to safeguarding the natural beauty and wildlife of the countryside. Among them is the John Muir Trust which has more than 5,000 members and which takes its name from the Dunbar-born naturalist and writer who played a prominent part in the development of the United States National Parks at the turn of the century. The Trust owns more than 14,000 ha in Skye, Sutherland and Moidart which it aims to preserve in a wild state without development nor promotion of public access, but with some rehabilitation of run-down countryside and support for local communities to live in harmony with wild places.

Restoration of woodland lies at the heart of the work of the Lincolnshire-based Woodland Trust. It has over 3,000 of its 65,000 members in Scotland, where it owns eighty woods, the biggest of which is at Glen Finglas. The Wildfowl and Wetlands Trust holds a reserve at Caerlaverock on the Solway where 12,000 barnacle geese from Spitsbergen winter each year.

ACCOLADES

In addition to all these protective measures and systems operating within Scotland, there are two designations which do not themselves add any safeguard except that, as an accolade, they give international recognition to the fact that an outstanding area has been adequately protected, and can therefore cause opprobrium to be mobilised on a large scale if the site is unexpectedly threatened. World Heritage Sites (WHSs) are designated by UNESCO; the St Kilda group of islands (NTS inalienable, NSA, NNR, SSSI, SPA, SAC) is the only natural site in Scotland so far. European Diploma sites are awarded by the Council of Europe and are not related solely to nature conservation. They are renewable every five years provided adequate protection still exists, and Scotland's two sites are Fair Isle (NTS) and Beinn Eighe (SNH) (see Box 1).

The international dimension is an important one; it reflects a greater worldwide understanding that life on earth is a fragile creation. Since the 1970s there has been a growing public interest in wildlife and in the importance on a global scale of protecting it 'for its own sake' as well as for its attractiveness and usefulness.

Many people find the apparent complexity of environmental designations bewildering and ask: 'Why can't we just have one designation covering the whole country?' That indeed is the direction in which we are starting to move in the 1990s. The Scottish Office carried out a national heritage designations review in 1997 with a view to simplifying the system, but it will be a long time before the whole of the countryside receives the same level of care as its most cherished areas.

But natural heritage protection is not only a matter of wildlife. The rural communities of Scotland with their rich cultural history peaked in the early nineteenth century. Since then there has been a steady decline, either through forced or voluntary emigration. Depopulation of the Highlands has now been stemmed, but the people who live there and elsewhere in the

The Cuillin ridge of Bla Bheinn from the John Muir Trust's land at Torrin, Isle of Skye.

countryside have the same aspirations for a higher standard of living as town-dwellers do. Attempts by 'outsiders' to place amenity or conservation above jobs are understandably resented. It is sometimes said that it is people who are the most endangered species in the Highlands.

The problem of bringing together land-use management and protection of the environment is one of reconciling a host of conflicting demands. The problem is fundamentally insoluble, perhaps, at least to everyone's satisfaction. There is a finite area of countryside, and over the coming years a potentially infinite variety of pressures will be brought to bear to change it in somebody's interest, mostly by introducing man-made objects into a semi-natural landscape.

In the end it is for society to decide what it wants of its countryside, where its priorities lie and how much it is prepared to pay for them. It has to place values on such unquantifiable assets as a magnificent view, or a patch of Alpine plants, or a traditional rural way of life. They all have an intrinsic value; and simply because they exist they also have a value for the 95 per cent of the population who do not experience them most of the time.

We may all become affected by global warming and ozone depletion and other world-wide effects, but conservation of the nature around us – that is to say, the wise long-term management of all our natural resources in a sustainable way – starts at our own front door wherever we live on the planet. It is all inter-connected. As John Muir put it, 'Try to take anything out by itself and you find it hitched to everything else in the universe.'

225

*A climber heads for the
Cuillin ridge, Isle of Skye.*

CHAPTER SEVENTEEN

The Playground of the Future

Roger Smith

Roger Smith is a freelance journalist who has specialised in environmental issues for many years and was the first editor of Environment Now *magazine.*

It was a glorious September day as the party climbed slowly up Carn a' Chlamain, above Glen Tilt, following a well-made path. Some were on ponies, some on foot. The men wore Highland dress or tweeds and most of them carried rifles. Bringing up the rear, two sturdy ponies carried essential provisions.

The lively young woman at the centre of the group was clearly enjoying herself. As every turn revealed a new view she exclaimed with delight, wishing that she had time to stop and sketch the beautiful landscape all around her. After a while they descended, eventually returning to Blair Castle by moonlight after a long but wonderfully rewarding day; and that evening the young woman recorded her impressions in purple prose in the diary she was to keep for nearly seventy years. The year was 1842 and the young woman was Queen Victoria, at the beginning of her long love affair with the Highlands of Scotland. On the way back from that first long trip she recorded that 'the English coast appeared terribly flat'. Further visits followed until 1848, when she and Prince Albert acquired Balmoral estate and built there the castle we see today.

After Prince Albert died, the Queen was persuaded to allow parts of her diaries to be published. The first volume, *Leaves from the Journal of Our Life in the Highlands*, appeared in 1867, with a further volume following in 1883. Both were bestsellers and both helped to draw still more people to Scotland, to see the land which had so enchanted their sovereign.

Queen Victoria was thus a most definite influence on the development of the tourist industry, which she further encouraged by her regular attendance at the Braemar Highland Games. She was not, however, the first person to influence the development of the tourist industry. In 1810 Sir Walter Scott published his epic poem, *The Lady of the Lake*. It was a tremendous success – the more so because it was set in a real landscape in the Trossachs, which people could visit, thus bringing the characters closer to reality. *Rob Roy* (1817) and other novels had a similar effect. Scott's publisher, Robert Cadell, recorded that 'the whole country rang with praise of the poet. Crowds set off to view the scenery of Loch Katrine and, as the book [*The Lady of the Lake*] came out just before the season for excursions, every house and inn was crammed with a constant succession of visitors.' It sounds like all the Scottish Tourist Board's dreams come true!

Before Scott immortalised the area in prose and verse there had been other notable literary visitors, including William Wordsworth and his sister Dorothy, another inveterate diarist. They all swallowed the romantic legends of Rob Roy. I can't help wondering what the real Rob Roy MacGregor, who knew every cattle-thieving trick in the book, would have made of it all – and indeed of the large Rob Roy Centre in Callander; I think the idea of depriving the tourists of as much money as possible would have appealed to him.

There is no doubt in my mind that we can use the word 'recreation' in relation to the early

Queen Victoria and her Highland retainer John Brown, Balmoral 1863 by George Washington Wilson.

tourists who followed Wordsworth, Scott and Queen Victoria to the Highlands. Until the coming of the railways in the latter part of the nineteenth century (see Chapter 11) their tours were adventurous and often quite strenuous. They wanted to experience 'rude Nature' and were prepared to rough it, to some extent, in order to do so. These early visitors were necessarily from the moneyed and leisured classes; working-class folk had few holidays and would never have thought of using them to visit the Trossachs or Deeside. But a pattern was being set, and into that pattern fell, quite neatly, inns and hostelries which had long been established on cattle-droving routes or as change-houses. Many of them still welcome visitors to this day.

Recreation can mean many things. To most people it probably means visiting, touring, seeing and enjoying; to others it means more active pursuits, and we shall look closely at some of these later in this chapter. To a few, often accorded the epithet 'privileged', it means the pursuit of game on land, in the water and in the air: 'if it runs or flies, shoot it!'

The nineteenth century saw changes in both land ownership and land-use in Scotland. The arrival of royalty on Deeside meant that the Highlands were 'in', as rich industrialists from the south found that they could buy land cheaply. At the same time, influenced by continental trends and by Prince Albert's German background, wild animals which had always been hunted for food were transformed into 'game' to be hunted for sport and trophies, with any food thus provided being only a

'Dead Stag and Eagles': sketch by Charles St John from a 'Tour of Sutherland'.

1. CHARLES ST JOHN (1809–56)

Charles St John typifies the Victorian sportsman/naturalist. We know more about him than about most of his contemporaries because of three fine books he wrote, of which the best known is *The Wild Sports and Natural History of the Highlands*. The title gives a clue to the approach favoured in those days, a century and a half ago.

St John lived in Scotland from 1833 to 1853; during that time he toured the Highlands extensively, recording what he saw in his detailed notebooks, which give us an accurate picture of the natural history of the Highlands in the mid nineteenth century. But, in common with others of his time, St John saw nothing wrong in pursuing wildlife as well as recording and writing about it. Any bird of prey was fair game for the gun. Both golden and white-tailed eagles were especially prized, as were ospreys and peregrines. Eggs of all these birds were commonly taken for collections. It is fascinating to try to imagine what Charles St John might think if he returned today. He would probably be dismayed by the loss of species from the Highlands and surprised at the measures required to protect those which remain. If he and his fellow hunters of the nineteenth century had been equipped with cameras instead of guns, we might enjoy a much richer wildlife today.

secondary benefit.

There was no thought of profit in this. Landowners, whether of the aristocracy or the nouveau riche, invited their relatives, friends and associates to their estates to stalk and shoot almost anything which ran, flew or swam. In this they were aided by the knowledge, hillcraft and skill of their staff: the stalkers, keepers and ghillies who managed the game under the guidance of the estate factor.

Major landowners, such as the Duke of Sutherland, had their own private railway stations built, as a condition of allowing the lines to cross their land. Many of these people took a keen interest in wildlife and would have been taken aback by any suggestion that by their sporting efforts they were hastening the decline of a species (Box 1).

The obsession with hunting game led to the complete exclusion of the public from many estates. Sir George Bullough and his family, for example, purchased the Inner Hebridean island of Rum and ran it as a sealed estate with no uninvited visitors allowed for many years. He built there the extraordinary and extravagant Kinloch Castle and paid his workers (many of whom came from Lancashire) extra wages to wear the kilt.

Right up to 1945 there were problems of access to the land on the big sporting estates. In more recent years there has been a truce over access, albeit slightly uneasy, between estates and walkers, and this has to some extent been formalised in the Access Concordat (see the section, Freedom to Roam, below). Estates still wish to restrict public access during the main deer - and grouse-shooting seasons.

The reasons for this are self-evident. Sportsmen from other countries, notably Germany, Italy and Belgium, will pay large sums of money for the right 'bag'. In 1989, according to one report, a million pheasants, 300,000 grouse and more than 60,000 red and roe deer were shot as part of an industry which is worth about £30 million to the estates. Fishing is also extremely valuable to many estates and choice 'beats' on salmon and trout rivers change hands for very large sums.

Without this income, many large estates would struggle to survive. They provide employment in areas where there is little alternative, and have big houses to maintain. After rising sharply during the 1980s, estate land values have fallen again; a Highland estate is still, in some circles, 'the thing to have', but the new owners are much more varied than previously.

They may be pop stars, sports stars, business people or rich people from abroad. Scotland is one of the very few countries which has no restrictions on land purchase by foreign nationals and we have seen large areas bought by Arab royalty, European aristocrats and companies registered in Liechtenstein, the Virgin Islands or other tax havens. Many of these people have no knowledge of Scottish culture or traditions of public access and, although they may bring money in, some may also want to keep the public out.

Those who shoot, hunt and fish certainly see themselves as taking their recreation in the Scottish countryside. Whether you regard it as 'sport' to shoot driven birds, reared for that purpose, or wild deer bred on the hill, is a matter of individual taste. I find it strange that it is valued so highly in monetary terms. While it is, much of Highland Scotland will continue to be dominated by large sporting estates and those estates will want to ensure that the income derived from the recreation of their owners and clients is paramount; this aim can lead to conflict with other, more peaceful, recreational pursuits.

UPWARDLY MOBILE

Mountaineering in Scotland will always be associated with the name of Sir Hugh Munro – the man who, in 1891, published a list of Scottish mountains which top 3,000 feet in height (Box 2).

The first 'Munroist' was Rev Aeneas Robertson, who completed the list with the ascent of the summit of Meall Dearg above Glencoe in 1901. Robertson was a fine all-round mountaineer and a great hill man. He spoke

Gaelic and often stayed with shepherds and keepers in remote areas. He was also an accomplished photographer at a time when cameras were heavy and difficult to use in the mountains, and he was very knowledgeable about old tracks, drove roads and the like.

In the days of Munro and Robertson, mountaineering was a pursuit for the gentry. The Scottish Mountaineering Club, founded in 1889, organised yachting trips to Skye for its early meetings. Most of its early members were professional people, and some, like Hugh Munro, were titled. They were people with leisure time at their disposal – Aeneas Robertson could take two months off from his Rannoch parish and spend them in the hills.

Things began to change after the First World War: the youth hostel movement arrived in Scotland in 1931, providing inexpensive accommodation in the mountain areas, and there were hiking clubs as well. But it was the Depression which brought the most profound change. Hill-climbing became not just a hobby but a way of escaping the poverty and slums of the cities. By that time, many of the 'classic' routes on Scottish mountains had been climbed by great pioneers such as W. W. Naismith, Harold Raeburn and Norman Collie; Shadbolt and McLaren traversed the Cuillin ridge on Skye in 1911, taking fifteen hours. But the new breed of climbers were less interested in first ascents than in simply being outdoors, almost regardless of the location.

Since 1945, mountaineering and hillwalking in Scotland have become much more egalitarian pastimes, enjoyed by countless thousands of

2. SIR HUGH MUNRO (1856–1919)

Sir Hugh Thomas Munro, Baronet, the man who gave his name to Scotland's 3,000-ft mountains, was born into a comfortable life as the son of Sir Campbell Munro of Lindertis, the eldest of nine children. He was a great traveller and collector from childhood and began mountaineering while still a student at Stuttgart in Germany. After a spell in business in London he went to Africa and saw action in the Basuto war; he then returned to manage and, in time, inherit the family estates at Kirriemuir in Angus.

Munro was a founder member of the Scottish Mountaineering Club (SMC) in 1889, by which time he was already familiar with the Scottish hills; he was also aware that there were far more hills over the 3,000 ft mark than had previously been recognised. His list of 'Munros' (some 277) appeared in the first volume of the SMC journal in 1891. He has given us a century of fun in trying to climb all the hills he listed – a list which many people feel should never have been amended, as it has been over the years. The difficulty presented by the challenge of climbing all the Munros is shown by the fact that he failed in this goal himself, never managing to scale the 'Inaccessible Pinnacle' on Skye, despite several attempts. He died of pneumonia at the age of sixty-three and is buried on the family estate.

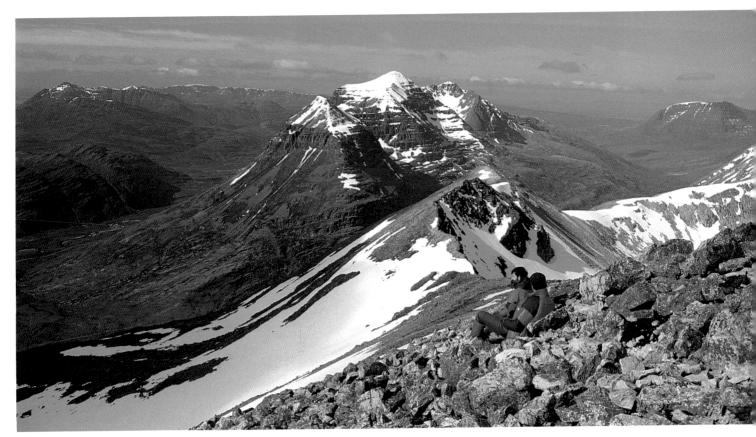

Mountaineers on the Beinn Eighe ridge look west across to Liathach.

people from all over Britain and abroad. Modern road and rail communications are vastly better than they were and today few areas can be classed as remote. The Munros have remained under assault, with well over a thousand people now claiming to have completed ascents of all 277 of them. Their lesser brothers, the Corbetts (hills between 2,500 and 2,999 feet), have become almost as popular.

Climbing has also reached out to new frontiers: climbs of ever greater severity have been established in Glencoe, in the Cairngorms, on Ben Nevis and elsewhere, with new locations such as Sron Ulladale on Harris being exploited. However, the vast majority of hill-goers are content with humbler achievements. They may climb ten or twenty Scottish hills; or they may climb one or indeed none at all, being content with walking the superb rights of way through the glens. Long-distance paths such as the West Highland Way and the Southern Upland Way attract large numbers of walkers, and further routes are under development. Scotland has thus far proved capable of accommodating them all, whatever their desires or aspirations.

Scotland is a country which, despite its relatively small size, truly has something for everyone. People have come to expect to be able to take their recreation in Scotland's hills and glens at most times of the year, untrammelled by restrictions. But that is not the true situation. As ever, economics are the root of the problem. Hillwalkers and climbers do not pay directly for their recreation (although it can be argued that through their taxation they contribute via such government agencies as Scottish Natural Heritage). Many put something back in the form of voluntary labour or through schemes financed by bodies of which they are members, such as the Mountaineering Council for Scotland, the National Trust for Scotland, Scottish Conservation Projects and so on. There have been suggestions of a 'boot tax', or a levy on equipment sales, and indeed the purchase of Ladhar Bheinn (the fine west coast Munro) by the John Muir Trust was partly funded in this way.

231

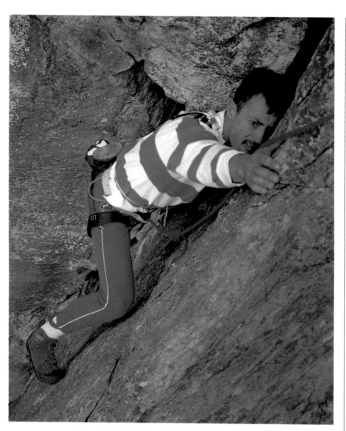

Rock climbing continues to grow in popularity.

Since the mid 1980s extensive research and survey work on mountain footpaths in Scotland has been carried out by Dr Robert Aitken, among others. His report, 'Scottish Mountain Footpaths', outlined the problems caused by heavy recreational use of the hills. This pioneering work led to the creation of Pathcraft, Scotland's first full-time professional pathwork specialists. Increasing amounts of money are now spent on path repair and restoration each year, but much more is still needed. Techniques of construction have improved dramatically, and the work carried out on Scottish hills is as good as that seen anywhere in the world. All of this has to be paid for, and the argument that those who use the hills should make a more direct contribution is growing in strength.

In the years ahead we may have to face up to the needs for some (it is hoped voluntary) restrictions on access by the visitor to the hills, not for shooting or stalking but for conservation purposes. It is all a far cry from the days of Hugh Munro and Aeneas Robertson, but it is a reflection on the very heavy recreational use of our hills today – a use which has arisen from their relative ease of access.

FREEDOM TO ROAM

The idea of free and open access to the Scottish mountains dates back over a hundred years, but has gained more force with the growth of walking and mountaineering as recreations since the 1940s. Before the Second World War there had been considerable obstacles to freedom of access in Scotland. Such incidents as the so-called 'Battle of Glen Tilt' in 1847 and the lawsuit over Jock's Road in Angus in 1886 are well documented. The Jock's Road case arose after a visit by a deputation from the Scottish Rights of Way Society, a body founded in 1845 as the Edinburgh Association for the Protection of Public Rights of Roadway in Scotland.

This society has done much to ensure that ancient rights of way have remained open and freely walkable, and still pursues the same objectives today. It was especially active in the 1880s, the decade which also saw the first attempt to legislate for 'freedom to roam'. This came in a parliamentary Bill introduced by James Bryce, Liberal MP for South Aberdeen, a very capable mountaineer with world-wide experience and the first president of the Cairngorm Club. For twenty years Bryce repeatedly strove to press the case for free access to the hills. He never succeeded in gaining sufficient Parliamentary time, not least because the opposition was strong and well organised. The access movement in England and Wales finally achieved limited success with the National Parks and Access to the Countryside Act 1949, but in Scotland the issue of access and National Parks was put to one side at the time – except that this Act was the starting point for statutory nature conservation through the UK (see Chapter 16).

In the absence of legislation, however, a complementary atmosphere of mutual understanding and tolerance developed between walkers and landowners in Scotland. This itself was a substantial step forward from the atmosphere of the 1920s, when stalwarts such as Ernest Baker risked prosecution in their widespread stravaiging. Baker's book, *The Highlands with Rope and Rucksack* (republished in 1942 as *The Forbidden Land*), clearly shows what a grip the great sporting estates had at that time. Mountaineers and walkers were barely tolerated, and some areas were effectively closed to any kind of access.

After 1945 public opinion would not accept such a situation. National Parks were being set up in England and Wales, and increasing numbers of people wanted to enjoy the simple freedom of walking the hills and glens, which after all represented everything they had fought and risked their lives for in six years of war. The National Trust for Scotland, established in 1931, had within six years acquired Glencoe, largely through the efforts of Arthur Russell, their law agent (who was also secretary of the Scottish Rights of Way Society for many years), and of Percy Unna; Unna was president of the Scottish Mountaineering Club, who organised the donation of funds by the mountaineering fraternity and also gave substantial sums himself to aid the acquisition not just of Glencoe but later of Kintail, Ben Lawers and Torridon (Box 3). Unlike England and Wales, where the situation regarding access is closely controlled by law, the mutual tolerance evident in Scotland in recent years is based on the *de facto*, not the *de jure*, position. Popular belief sometimes assumes that there is no law of trespass in Scotland; but the strict position is that there is no right to be on land, although trespass itself – the act of going on another person's land – carries no penalty; however, the visitor can be required to leave on request. Either damage or persistent nuisance must be legally proved for there to be an actionable offence leading to damages payable to the landowner and, as far as hillwalkers or others taking informal recreation are concerned, the position is largely untested in the courts.

Many of those who regularly walk the hills of Scotland have accepted the need for restraint during the peak shooting season from mid-August to mid-October. Outwith that period it has been generally felt that access should be freely available. This is the basis on which *Heading for the Scottish Hills*, a booklet published jointly by the Mountaineering Council of Scotland and the Scottish Landowners' Federation, was prepared. It asks people going to the hills during the peak shooting season to check with the estate first to see if shooting is in progress or is planned, and to be prepared to alter their route if necessary. Most landowners have, in turn, recognised that many people legitimately wish to take their recreation in the countryside and have placed few obstacles in their way.

During the 1980s there were signs that the situation was deteriorating; attempts were made in some cases to restrict access during the deer-calving season from mid-May to late June – one of the very best times of the year for walking. On some estates, notices were put up asking people to keep off the land from July through to February because of shooting. The number of notices which could be described as intimidatory, rather than informative, was increasing. More recently all those with an interest in the land, whether as owners, occupiers or for recreation, have come together in the national Access Forum led by Scottish Natural Heritage. The result was an agreed Concordat on Access to Scotland's Hills and Mountains, published in 1995.

In this Concordat the landowning bodies accept that access should be freely available at most times of the year, and the recreational bodies accept that responsible behaviour is needed, together with a reasonable amount of restraint during the peak shooting season. Another development is an experimental Hillphone system, introduced in some popular walking areas in 1996. Through this system a single telephone number for an estate or a group of estates provides information on stalking intentions, updated daily. The first year of the experiment has been judged to be reasonably successful and the trial is to be repeated in 1997. It is to be hoped that these measures will introduce an element of calm into the situation.

There has been much political discussion about the possibility of introducing legislation in the form of a 'Freedom to Roam' Bill for Scotland, and the Labour Party has declared it to be one of their priorities. Few organisations want legislation, however, although this is the declared ambition of the Ramblers' Association (both nationally and in Scotland). The Scottish Landowners' Federation is certainly against such legislation, fearing that it would only lead to greater confrontation.

A further development during 1996 was the launch of a national Paths For All project by SNH. This large-scale scheme aims to improve public access to the countryside around Scotland's town and villages on foot, by cycle and horseback. It was launched with the ambitious aim of setting up forty path networks by the year 2000, and a hundred networks within a decade. Research has shown a great need for better public access not so much to the wider countryside of hill and mountain as to the areas around settlements, most of which is farmland or woods.

The century therefore looks like ending on a fairly positive note as far as access in Scotland is concerned, with a recognition of the need for all interested parties to work together.

SKISTERS TO PISTERS

Skiing in Scotland is far from being a new sport. The Scottish Ski Club (SSC) was formed as long ago as November 1907, although at that time, and for some years thereafter, cross-country skiing was simply used as a practical means of getting about in the mountains during winter. Downhill or 'piste' skiing for recreational purposes and competitive sport had to await the development of reliable ski-tows. The Scottish Ski Club lay dormant from 1918 until 1929 when it was reformed. As with walking and climbing, access had been transformed by increasing car ownership, and ways were soon found of attaching skis to the roof or running board. Equipment too was much improved, with better and lighter skis and clothing being developed in the Alps. There was still much ski-

Percy Unna (1878–1950) formulated the 'Unna Rules' in order to preserve the wild qualities of the mountain land which he donated to the nation.

3. PERCY UNNA (1878–1950)

Mountaineers and all those who love the grandeur of the Scottish hills owe a great debt to Percy Unna, a civil servant of Danish parentage; but the debt has only come to light in recent years. In 1937 he was President of the Scottish Mountaineering Club (SMC) when it was learned that the 11,600 acres of Dalness Forest, in Glencoe, was for sale. Unna took the initiative and organised an appeal among all the mountaineering clubs in Britain to raise the purchase price of £9,000 so that the National Trust for Scotland (NTS) could acquire the land. He gave most of the money himself, anonymously.

In providing the funds to purchase Glencoe, Unna also put before the Trust a set of management guidelines which both he and the SMC wished to be followed. These stipulated that there should be no new paths made, no shooting for sport, and the very minimum of man-made structures; and that generally the hills were not to be made easier or safer in any way. Unna also provided most of the funds for the NTS to purchase Kintail in 1943, and money from the Mountainous Country Fund went towards the purchases of Ben Lawers, Torridon and Goatfell on Arran. Many people feel that Unna was a true visionary who foresaw the great increase in recreational pressure which was to come and wished to conserve some areas in as natural a state as possible by laying down guidelines for their future management. The National Trust for Scotland has on occasion interpreted these guidelines somewhat liberally in the years since Unna's death, making paths and building bridges in Glencoe and putting up visitor centres, both in Glencoe and on the flanks of Ben Lawers, and it has been criticised for doing so.

The arguments will surely continue, but there can be no doubt that without Percy Unna's farsightedness and generosity it would have been extremely difficult, if not impossible, for these magnificent mountain areas to have been acquired and safeguarded for the benefit of the nation.

touring but informal races were soon introduced, using a mass start system which became known as 'the geschmozzle' because of the frequent collisions and mix-ups which occurred on the way down the hill. A hut was erected in 1932 on the flanks of Beinn Ghlas above Loch Tay at a height of 2,300 ft and there, two years later, the SSC organised its first slalom race.

After the war, demand for uplift facilities grew steadily. The hut on Beinn Ghlas was renovated and expanded and by 1953 there were rope-tows running there and at Cairnwell. The Killin skiers also had the use of a 'weasel', a tracked vehicle which took them uphill for the ski down. But the focus was shifting away from Killin to three other areas where energetic people were preparing the ground for the commercial skiing which we know today – although they could not have foreseen either the huge commercial growth which occurred nor the environmental problems which have resulted. By the beginning of the 1960s there were tows in Glencoe, Glenshee (Cairnwell and Carn an Tuirc) and on Cairngorm; the last named was the result of many years of work behind the scenes by local interest groups leading to the formation of the Cairngorm Winter Sports Development Board. At this time the ski clubs were still the prime movers, but things were beginning to change as the numbers wanting to ski grew and the sport changed from being the province of enthusiasts to becoming a commercial winter sports operation. Companies were set up and an important development was the creation of the Highlands and Islands Development Board (HIDB) in 1965. The HIDB was able to grant-aid skiing developments and became even more closely involved when it took over the ownership of ground at Cairngorm from the Forestry Commission in the early 1970s.

The effort put in by those who wanted to develop skiing in Scotland was truly heroic and the obstacles they had to overcome were formidable. In the early days, however, little or no attention was paid to environmental considerations. The environmental movement

Paragliding and hang gliding attract people to accessible hills.

in Scotland was small and the overriding drive was for the provision of facilities for skiers. This was also seen at the Hillend artificial ski-slope in the Pentland Hills just outside Edinburgh. When it was opened in 1966, in the years since then it was the longest artificial ski slope in Europe; it has provided tremendous enjoyment and excellent training for thousands of youngsters, but close examination of the area reveals a serious lack of attention to good housekeeping in the environmental sense.

The same applied at Cairngorm and Glenshee in particular (the other developments at Glencoe, and later at the Lecht, are smaller in scale and have had less impact). By the end of the 1970s there was growing concern over erosion and scarring of the landscape, the spread of mechanical facilities and buildings and the increased ease of access provided by ski-roads and chairlifts into sensitive natural heritage areas. Matters came to a head with the application for a very large-scale development into the northern corries of Cairngorm in 1981. Uplift facilities were proposed for Coire an t'Sneachda, Coire an Lochain and Lurcher's Gully, with either a road or chairlifts across the mouths of these superb corries. For almost the first time the environmental movement in Scotland united in opposition. The case went to a public inquiry at which the developers were surprised to find the conservationists so well organised. The inquiry Reporter came down firmly on the side of conservation and, in

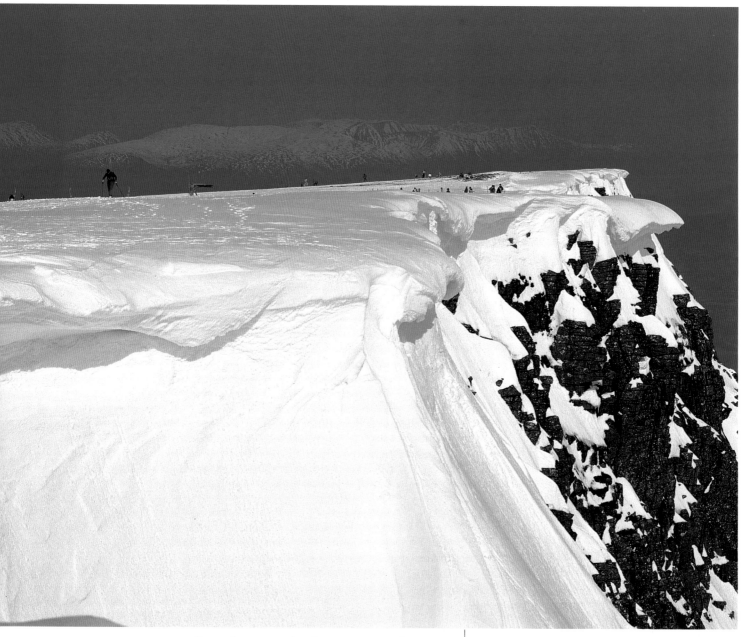

Skiers on Aonach Mor plateau, Ben Nevis range near Fort William.

December 1982, the then Secretary of State for Scotland, George Younger, confirmed the Reporter's decision: the development proposals were rejected.

The last year of the decade saw two significant developments. A new ski centre opened on Aonach Mor, near Fort William; for the first time environmental considerations were fully taken into account and it is generally agreed that the developers, Nevis Range, have done all they could to minimise the

environmental impact of the scheme. Cables and power lines have all been buried, and during construction everything was taken up by helicopter, no vehicles being allowed on the hill. The car park is low down in a forest setting and access to the main slopes and the restaurant is by gondola, another first for Scotland. The Aonach Mor development has set a standard to be followed by other ski centres in Scotland.

At the end of 1989 there was a fresh proposal for skiing development and road access into Lurcher's Gully. Once again the environmental movement came together in force; the 'Save the Cairngorms Campaign' was set up and both government agencies, the Nature Conservancy Council and the Countryside Commission for Scotland, objected to the development. In June 1990 the then Secretary of State for Scotland, Malcolm Rifkind, turned the project down. A further controversial plan, for a funicular railway on Cairngorm, is also facing major opposition from conservation bodies at present.

In many ways these proposals highlight the dilemma which faces skiing in Scotland today. The sport has enjoyed rapid growth and has brought considerable benefits into rural areas – Strathspey in particular. However, skiing faces two major problems: it is always going to seek development opportunities in environmentally sensitive areas, and it relies on an unreliable snowfall. In recent winters, snowfall has been erratic and regular periods of thaw in the midst of the normal pattern of winter weather has prevented the build-up of the snowpack. Some ski centres have only been able to operate at anything like full capacity for six weeks, which is not enough to ensure commercial survival. It could be said, with some truth, that people ski in Scotland despite the climate, not because of it.

It is essential that skiing organisations and environmental bodies unite in their efforts to work out acceptable solutions. Both sides may have to compromise, but it would be worth it if only to see an end to the bitterness and entrenched positions of the last decade.

OTHER RECREATIONS IN THE HILLS

Hill-running has grown in Scotland from very small beginnings to a sport with a full calendar and a wide variety of races – over seventy a year; these range from Black Meldon (just one mile long and won in eight minutes) to the West Highland Way Race (from Milngavie to Fort William), a distance of 95 miles, for which the winning record stands at fifteen hours.

An offshoot of hill-running is 'mountain marathoning', which developed out of

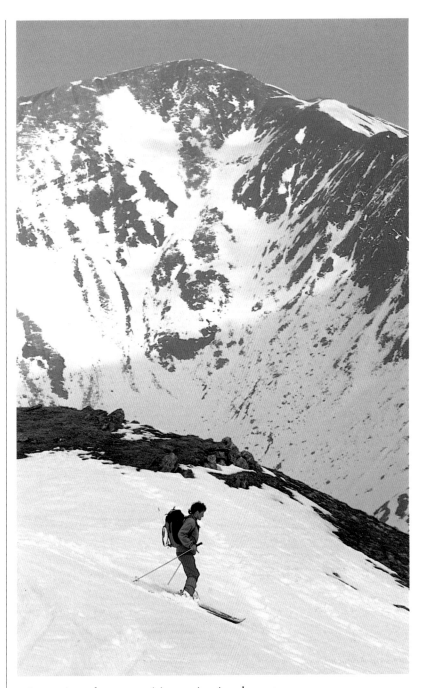

orienteering, the competitive navigational sport which started in Scandinavia between the wars. The first attempts to develop the sport in Scotland were in the 1960s, led by the universities and athletic clubs. There is now a full calendar of events at every level from club to championship every year.

There are many charity walks and climbs in Scotland each year. The question of mass

Ski mountaineering on Mamore mountains, Glen Nevis.

237

participation events arouses mixed feelings, for while the charitable aim is admirable, the effects of large numbers of people crossing sensitive ground within a concentrated period of time can be serious. The National Trust for Scotland now has a policy of discouraging such events on land owned by the Trust because of the path erosion which may result.

There seems to be no end to the ingenuity which people have shown in their determined pursuit of recreation. Paragliding, where a parachute is used to rise up over the hills, is a relative newcomer to the scene, as is hang gliding, where a fixed wing sail is used to ride the wind thermals. One of the big centres for hang gliding is at the Cairnwell near Braemar, where the chairlift for skiers is much appreciated by the gliders.

WHEEL AND HOOF POWER

Two-wheeled recreation is now making great inroads into the hills, and causing considerable concern. There is a long tradition of 'rough stuff' cycling in Scotland, using routes such as the Lairig Ghru through the Cairngorms; this pass rises to 2700 ft and gets pretty rough in places. The Scottish Rights of Way Society signs at either end of the pass proclaim that it is 'unsuitable for cycles', but that doesn't deter the real rough-stuff enthusiasts for one minute. They are a hardy fellowship of riders who go into the hills alone or in small groups; they enjoy and respect the solitude and wildness of the hills and expect no favours or facilities.

The same cannot be said of the mountain-bike fraternity. This new sport is posing problems for the countryside, for landowners and for the conservation agencies. When these bikes are used on good tracks or forest roads (as most do) they present few difficulties; but when they are used on the paths and grassy slopes of the open hill, especially in numbers, then there is a genuine cause for concern over the erosion damage they can cause. There are also issues related to disturbance of stock, to estate work and to other countryside users.

One mountain-biking guide includes a ride through Glen Nevis, which is certainly neither the place nor the environment where mountain bikes should be allowed in any numbers. The stretch between the road end and Steall through the gorge is a narrow and well-used footpath which is totally unsuitable for bikes of any kind; the guide itself describes the route as 'rocky, steep and almost totally unrideable'. So why encourage its use?

There is a warning for us from the USA, where mountain bikes are a matter of controversy. In California, routes have been closed and radar guns have been brought in to try to curb reckless riding and to protect walkers and horse riders. There have been calls to ban these bikes from some parts of the American countryside altogether.

Many parts of Scotland are ideally suited to horse-riding, and pony-trekking has become well established as a leisure pursuit. Using bridleways, old drove roads and other long-established tracks, horses and riders can cover good distances in a day, building on a very old tradition of travel on horseback. In the Borders, the annual celebrations known as the Common Ridings attract hundreds of participants.

BIG BUSINESS IN THE PLAYGROUND

Tourism is big business in Scotland; according to the Scottish Tourist Board (STB) it is now Scotland's largest industry, sustaining up to 200,000 jobs and generating £2.4 billion in the economy. A 1996 survey showed that hillwalking and mountaineering brought in £160 million a year to the Highlands alone. But is that all good news? Is the visitor expansion something we can afford to sustain indefinitely? How much more can, or should, Scotland take?

There are more large developments being planned in the Scottish countryside than ever before. Most have at least some recreational aspect built into them; golf, in particular, is experiencing a boom. A survey by the Association for the Protection of Rural Scotland revealed the startling total of ninety-one new golf courses in various stages of planning or development.

Mountain bikers climb into a steep, pathless area of mountainside.

All these proposals use substantial amounts of land. In some cases the land was lying fallow, waiting to be used. In many cases, however, the proposed developments would take out land currently zoned for agriculture, and in some cases there has been considerable local opposition to them.

Many of these developments have an element of housing attached, usually highly priced, and most are aimed at the top end of the market. Does that matter? It need not do so, provided that quality is maintained and the developments provide facilities which are genuinely needed and which fit into the local economy. Sadly, too many of them fail to meet these standards. Developments are out of scale with their surroundings – sometimes grossly so – or are so highly priced as to be out of reach of local people. Several have been found to rest on flimsy financial support which disappeared when objections were raised.

Such objections come from well-organised local pressure groups, from established environmental bodies and from local councils, but less commonly from the Scottish Tourist Board, whose role in all this presents curious anomalies. The Board's remit is to promote and encourage tourism in Scotland, which it has done so successfully that it can proclaim tourism as 'Scotland's largest industry'.

But should the STB not have an equal role in helping to conserve the scenery, landscape, wildlife and history which is the very basis of the industry that it promotes? Tourism is important to Scotland, but Scotland is far more important to tourism. Untrammelled development is biting into the very resource which tourism needs most. We must have better central planning, and a broader environmental stance. Fortunately, there are signs that this is beginning to happen. A project called 'Tourism and the Environment' is taking a careful look at

239

Sailing off the Ross of Mull in the Western Isles.

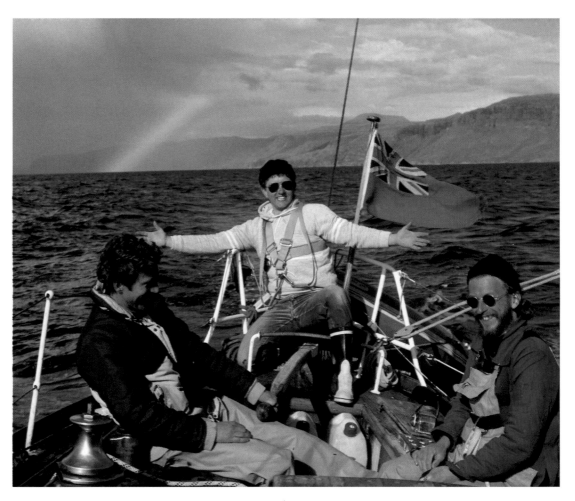

the whole issue, and it appears that, in future, a more balanced view is likely to be taken.

CONCLUSION

No one can predict what will happen to recreation in Scotland over the next twenty-five years, but we should certainly be thinking about it and deciding what we want the future to hold for our children and grandchildren. Do we want them to know the joy of walking the wild places without another soul in sight? Do we want them to be able to fish for trout and salmon in clear, unpolluted lochs, enjoying the view of hills which are unmarked by bulldozed tracks, ski-tows or any other intrusive developments? Or will we leave to them only a regimented countryside, formalised into 'recreation areas' where they may have to apply for a permit to climb, walk, ski or fish? It would be foolish to

think that this could not happen in Scotland; it has already started to happen in other places.

In the wilderness areas of the American National Parks, permits for wild camping and even for 'off-trail' walking have been required for years. In England and in a number of other European countries there have been cases where beautiful places with magnificent wildlife have been sacrificed to development. This has not yet happened in Scotland, although some would argue that the losses sustained from afforestation in the Flow Country come close to it (see Chapter 5). The vital lesson is that it need not happen here. We must learn from our own mistakes and those of other countries, and we must plan the future of our own land using the wisest minds we have. We must not let vast areas of Scotland be closed off for months of the year for the 'sporting pursuits' of a selfish and mostly wealthy few. We must not let the

Salmon fisherman on the river Spey, Grantown on Spey.

lure of short-term profit and the blandishments of 'planning gain' blind us to the long-term consequences of inappropriate development, whether it be in a city green belt or in the heart of the Cairngorms.

We must develop more effective ways of planning on a national as well as on a local scale. Our present complex system of countryside designations and protected areas is misunderstood and mistrusted. A consultation paper on natural heritage designations, published by The Scottish Office early in 1997, did not hold out much hope for radical change; it still laid considerable emphasis on the 'voluntary principle' – a method which has repeatedly failed the landscape and wildlife of Scotland in recent years. We are one of the very few countries which do not yet have National Parks.

There is no doubt that interesting times lie ahead. Scottish Natural Heritage (SNH), established in 1992, combines the roles of the

241

Canoeing on the West coast of Scotland.

former Nature Conservancy Council for Scotland and the Countryside Commission for Scotland – a difficult task in which, inevitably, it does not always succeed. But SNH is only one player on a stage where there are already rather too many agencies taking bit-parts and confusing the plot. The number of agencies and organisations which have influence on what goes on in the countryside is alarming (see Chapter 16). There are development agencies, enterprise companies, tourist boards, agricultural bodies, local authorities, conservation groups, recreational bodies, fisheries boards, forestry organisations, water authorities, parks, councils for this and that and dozens more. There is a real need for them all to work together towards the common good, and partnerships are becoming more common; but the tensions still remain.

The solution must lie in partnership and co-operation rather than separatism and conflict: a balanced approach, not rampant development or rigid sterilisation or the slapping of designations on every green area in the land. The countryside belongs to us all and we must work together to ensure its healthy future – not just for the richness of wildlife but also for the people who live and work in the countryside and for those who wish to take peaceful recreation there. In Scotland we have a majestic country of which we should all be proud; it deserves the highest standards of wise conservation and long-term planning we can give it.

Above all, we must all become less selfish. Whether our chosen recreation is walking, climbing, skiing, sailing, paragliding, shooting, fishing or dog-sledging, we cannot expect exclusive use of any part of the Scottish countryside. We must all be prepared to give up a little in order to gain a lot. We all need recreation in the best sense of the word, be we the humblest in the land or the highest born. The Prince of Wales clearly has the same feel for the land as did his great-great-grandmother, Queen Victoria: speaking of tourism in Scotland, he said recently:

> We need to spend a bit more time thinking about the long term and about what our grandchildren will feel about what we do. You see so many results of rapid development, taking the cheapest option, which turn out to be disastrous or leave behind an appalling legacy which we have to clear up. In the future, we should be thinking many years ahead.

For the sake of Scotland's countryside and all those who wish to take recreation there, that thinking about the future must start now.

Bibliography
Books for further reading

Baines, Chris, *The Wild Side of Town*, 1986.

Baker, Ernest, *The Forbidden Land*, 1942.

Bass, Rick, *Oil Notes*, London, Fontana, 1989.

Baxter, Colin and Goodier, Rawdon, *The Cairngorms*, Lanark, Colin Baxter Photography, 1990.

Blamey, Marjorie and Grey-Wilson, Christopher, *The Illustrated Flora of Britain and Northern Europe*, London, Hodder and Stoughton, 1989.

Boyd, J. Morton, *The Hebrides: a natural history*, London, Collins, 1990.

Burnett, John H., *The Vegetation of Scotland*, Edinburgh, Oliver and Boyd, 1964.

Cameron, A. D., *Go listen to the crofters*, Stornoway, Acair, 1986.

Carson, Rachel, *Silent Spring*, 1962.

Clapperton, C. M. (ed), *Scotland: A New Study*, Newton Abbot, David and Charles, 1983.

Coppock, J. T., *An Agricultural Atlas of Scotland*, Edinburgh, John Donald, 1976.

Corbet, G. B. and Harris, S. (eds), *The Handbook of British Mammals*, 3rd edn, Oxford, Blackwell, 1990.

Craig, G. Y. (ed), *The Geology of Scotland*, 3rd edn, Edinburgh, Scottish Academic Press, 1990.

Cramp, S. (ed), *Handbook of the Birds of Europe, the Middle East and North Africa, the Birds of the Western Palearctic*, Oxford University Press, 1988.

Crawford, B. E., *Scandinavian Scotland*, Leicester University Press, 1987.

Donaldson, Gordon, *Scotland: the making of the kingdom*, In: Duncan, A. A. M. (ed), *The Edinburgh History of Scotland, Vol 1*, Edinburgh, Mercat Press, 1978.

Emery, Malcolm, *Promoting Nature in Cities and Towns*, London, Croom Helm, 1986.

Emmet, A., Maitland and Heath, John (eds), *The Moths and Butterflies of Great Britain and Ireland*, vol 7, part 1 – The Butterflies, Colchester, Harley Books, 1987.

Fenton, A., *Scottish Country Life*, Edinburgh, John Donald, 1989.

Fraser Darling, F. and Boyd, J. Morton, *Natural History in the Highlands and Islands*, London, Collins, 1964.

Gordon, George and Dicks, Brian (eds), *Scottish Urban History*, Aberdeen, Aberdeen University Press, 1983.

Grant, J. S., *The Part-time holding – an island experience*, Coulnakyle, Nethy Bridge, Inverness-shire, The Arkleton Trust, 1983.

Grigor, I. F., *Mightier than a lord*, Stonoway, Acair, 1979.

Haldane, A. R. B., *New Ways Through the Glen*, Edinburgh, Nelson, 1962.

Halliday, Fred (ed), *Wildlife of Scotland*, London, Macmillan/SWT, 1979.

Halliday, Geoffrey and Malloch, Andrew (eds), *Wild Flowers and their Habitats in Britain and Northern Europe*, London, Peter Lowe, 1981.

Hawthorn, J., Reid, J. M. and Wyllie, G. A. P., *Scotland's Energy Future*, Royal Society of Edinburgh, 1987.

Hetherington, Alastair, *Highlands and Islands: a Generation of Progress*, Aberdeen, Aberdeen University Press, 1990.

Hume, John R., *The Industrial Archaeology of Scotland*, vols 1 and 2, London, B. T. Batsford, 1976 and 1977.

Aldo, Leopold, *A Sand Country Almanac*, Oxford, Oxford University Press.

Lindsay, Jean, *The Canals of Scotland*,

Newton Abbot, David and Charles, 1968.

Lister-Kaye, John, *The Seeing Eye: Notes of a Highland Naturalist*, London, Allen Lane, 1980.

Lusby, Phil and Wright, Jenny, *Scottish Wild Plants*, HMSO.

Lythe, S. G. E. and Butt, J., *An Economic History*, 1100–1939, London, 1975.

MacLean, M. and Carrell, C. (eds), *As an fhearann (From the Land): Clearance, Conflict and Crofting*, Stornoway, An Lanntair/Third Eye, 1986.

MacPhail, I. M. M., *The Crofters' Wars, Stornoway*, Acair, 1989.

Maitland, Peter S., *The Ecology of Scotland's Largest Lochs: Lomond, Awe, Ness, Morar and Shiel*, The Hague, Junk, 1981.

Morrison, Ian, *Landscape with Lake Dwellings*, Edinburgh University Press, 1985.

Muir, John, *The Wilderness Journeys*, Edinburgh, Canongate Classics, 1997.

Murray, W. H., *Scotland's Mountains*, Glasgow, Scottish Mountaineering Trust, 1987.

Nature Conservancy Council, *The Endless Village*, 1978.

Nature Conservancy Council, *Nature Conservation in Great Britain*, Northminster House, Peterborough, 1984.

Nature Conservancy Council, *Nature Conservation and Afforestation in Britain*, Northminster House, Peterborough, 1986.

Nature Conservancy Council, *Planning for Wildlife in Metropolitan Areas*.

Nethersole-Thompson, D. and Watson, A., *The Cairngorms: Their Natural History and Scenery*, Perth, Melven Press, 1981.

Payne, Madge, *Gardening for Butterflies*, Loughborough, British Butterfly Conservation Society, 1987.

Piggott, S., *Scotland Before History*, Edinburgh, Polygon, 1990.

Ratcliffe, Derek, *The Peregrine Falcon*, Calton, Poyser, 1980.

Ratcliffe, Derek, *Highland Flora*, Inverness, Highlands and Islands Development Board, 1977.

Raven, John and Walters, Max, (*New Naturalist* series), *Mountain Flowers*, 2nd edn, London, Collins.

Ritchie, G. and A., *Scotland: Archaeology and Early History*, Edinburgh University Press, 1991.

Scott, Michael *Collins Guide to Scottish Wildflowers*, Collins, 19xx.

Scottish Wildlife Trust, *The State of Scottish Greenspace* 1997.

Scroggie, Sydney, *The Cairngorms Scene and Unseen*, Glasgow, Scottish Mountaineering Trust, 1989.

Simpson, Myrtle, *Skisters: The Story of Scottish Skiing*, Carrbridge, Landmark Press, 1982.

Sissons, J. B., *The Evolution of Scotland's Scenery*, Edinburgh, Oliver and Boyd, 1967.

Stephen, David, *Living with Wildlife*, Edinburgh, Canongate Publishing, 1989.

Steven, Campbell, *The Story of Scotland's Hills*, London, Robert Hale, 1975.

Steven, H. M. and Carlisle, A., *The Native Pinewoods of Scotland*, Edinburgh, Oliver and Boyd, 1959.

Sutcliffe, A. J., *On the Track of Ice Age Mammals*, London, British Museum (Natural History), 1985.

Thom, V. M., *Birds in Scotland*, Calton, Poyser, 1986.

Thomas, Jeremy A., *The Hamlyn Guide to Butterflies of the British Isles*, London, Hamlyn Publishing Group Ltd, 1986.

Thomson, George, *The Butterflies of Scotland*, London, Croom Helm Ltd, 1980.

Timperley, L. R., *Directory of Landownership in Scotland c.1700*, Edinburgh, Scottish Record Society, 1976.

Turner, Frederick, *John Muir: From Scotland to the Sierra*, Edinburgh, Canongate 1997.

Twidell, J. W., *et al, Energy for Rural and Island Communities*, a series of Proceedings in four volumes, Oxford, Pergammon Press, 1981, 1983, 1985, 1987 and In: *Journal of Wind and Solar Technology*, January, Oxford, Pergammon Press, 1990.

White, Graham (ed), *The Scottish Environmental Handbook*, Edinburgh, Environment Centre, 1990.

Whitten, D. G. A. and Brooks, J. R. V., *The Penguin Dictionary of Geology*, Harmondsworth, Penguin, 1972.

Wightman, Andy, *Who Owns Scotland*, Canongate 1996.

Index